COWS, KIN, AND GLOBALIZATION

GLOBALIZATION AND THE ENVIRONMENT

This AltaMira series publishes new books about the global spread of environmental problems. Key themes addressed are the effects of cultural and economic globalization on the environment; the global institutions that regulate and change human relations with the environment; and the global nature of environmental governance, movements, and activism. The series will include detailed case studies, innovative multi-sited research, and theoretical questioning of the concepts of globalization and the environment. At the center of the series is an exploration of the multiple linkages that connect people, problems, and solutions at scales beyond the local and regional. The editors welcome works that cross boundaries of disciplines, methods, and locales, and which span scholarly and practical approaches.

SERIES EDITORS

Richard Wilk, Department of Anthropology, 130 Student Building, Indiana University, Bloomington IN 47405 USA or wilkr@indiana.edu

Josiah Heyman, Department of Sociology & Anthropology, Old Main Building #109, University of Texas at El Paso, 500 West University Avenue, El Paso, TX 79968 USA or jmheyman@utep.edu

BOOKS IN THE SERIES

1. *Power of the Machine: Global Inequalities of Economy, Technology, and Environment*, by Alf Hornborg (2001)
2. *Confronting Environments: Local Environmental Understanding in a Globalizing World*, edited by James Carrier (2004)
3. *Communities and Conservation: Histories and Politics of Community-Based Natural Resource Management*, edited by J. Peter Brosius, Anna Lowenhaupt Tsing, and Charles Zerner (2005)

COWS, KIN, AND GLOBALIZATION

An Ethnography of Sustainability

Susan A. Crate

ALTAMIRA
PRESS

A Division of
ROWMAN AND LITTLEFIELD PUBLISHERS, INC.
Lanham • New York • Toronto • Plymouth, UK

AltaMira Press
A Division of Rowman & Littlefield Publishers, Inc.
A wholly owned subsidiary of The Rowman & Littlefield Publishing Group, Inc.
4501 Forbes Boulevard, Suite 200
Lanham, MD 20706
www.altamirapress.com

Estover Road, Plymouth PL6 7P4, United Kingdom

British Library Cataloguing in Publication Information Available

Library of Congress Cataloging-in-Publication Data

Crate, Susan A.
    Cows, kin, and globalization : an ethnography of sustainability /
Susan A. Crate.
        p.   cm.
    Includes bibliographical references and index.
    ISBN-13: 978-0-7591-0739-7 (cloth : alk. paper)
    ISBN-10: 0-7591-0739-4 (cloth : alk. paper)
    ISBN-13: 978-0-7591-0740-3 (pbk. : alk. paper)
    ISBN-10: 0-7591-0740-8 (pbk. : alk. paper)
    1. Human ecology—Russia (Federation)—Siberia, Northeastern.   2. Sustainable
development—Russia (Federation)—Siberia, Northeastern.   3. Siberia, Northeastern
(Russia)—Social life and customs.   4. Siberia, Northeastern (Russia)—Economic
conditions.   5. Vilyui River Region (Russia)—Social life and customs.   6. Vilyui River
Region (Russia)—Economic conditions.   I. Title.
GF676.C73 2006
305.89'4332—dc22
                                                                          2006014199

Printed in the United States of America

⊗™ The paper used in this publication meets the minimum requirements of American
National Standard for Information Sciences—Permanence of Paper for Printed Library
Materials, ANSI/NISO Z39.48-1992.

Dedicated to my mother-in-law:
Matryona Naumovna Yegorova:
*Kyn Kihite!**

* Translates literally as "Sun Person," the highest compliment you can make to a Sakha person.

Contents

Illustrations

Preface

I first traveled to the Sakha Republic in 1991 to attend an international Jew's harp festival in the capital, Yakutsk. Since 1988, I had conducted ethnographic and environmental research in Ukraine, Tuva, Buriatia, and Mongolia, studying indigenous expressive forms, including songs, narrative, and ritual, and analyzing their connection to local landscapes and sacred worlds. Midway through the weeklong Jew's harp conference, attendees were sent out to various regions to participate in the *yhyakh* (Sakhas' annual summer *kymys* festival). The 1991 *yhyakh* was a turning point for me. This ritual was the first I had witnessed that had retained some semblance of the sacred despite the far-reaching influences of Sovietization. In the winter of 1992 I returned to the Viliui to research the contemporary *yhyakh* for a master's thesis in folklore. I found that the locus of Sakha ethnic identity within the celebration's contemporary form was the *ohuokai* (Sakhas' circle dance fueled by improvisatory master singing).[1] Concurrently, I was also learning more and more about the environmental devastation on the Viliui and, upon completing my thesis, returned to the Viliui to direct two two-year projects funded by the MacArthur Foundation, focusing on the environmental and sociocultural impacts of Soviet and post-Soviet diamond exploitation. I worked with regional and village specialists to document local ecological knowledge and research regional industrial development. With this material our research team wrote a Sakha language citizen's action guide to environmental issues on the Viliui, created a hands-on environmental education room and founded the Viliui regionwide environmental clearinghouse in the Elgeeii Nature Museum, and produced a video on the new diamond columns in Nyurba. In 1997 I began a doctorate in the ecology curriculum at the University of North Carolina (UNC), Chapel Hill, to research the human-ecological dimensions of post-Soviet Viliui Sakha adaptation. During 1999–2000, I conducted my dissertation research and came to the cows-and-kin strategy. My next questions were about Viliui Sakhas' future—the long-term viability of cows-and-kin and prospects for locally sustainable economies, the focus of my research to date.

That accounts for my academic trajectory since I have come to know Viliui Sakha. The personal story is also important. In 1995 I married a Sakha man, whom I had met during my master's research in 1992. We have one daughter. My relationship with him and with his parents, aunts, uncles, three brothers, six sisters, eleven nieces, fourteen nephews, and various other close and distant kin has brought me, in many ways, closer to Sakha culture and to a personal understanding of what it means to be Sakha in the contemporary world. I only hope that I do an accurate job of representing what I have come to know.

I owe thanks to many people for this book. I extend my sincerest gratitude to the people of Elgeeii and Kutana villages for opening their homes and extending their hospitality to me, especially those who worked as consultants on research and most gratefully to fifty-four elders I interviewed. I send similar thanks to the inhabitants of Kuukei, Khoro, Suntar, and all the other villages in the Suntar, Nyurba, Verkhnyviliuisk, Viliuisk, and Mirnyi regions of the Viliui that I have had the opportunity to work in since 1991. I was housed and taken care of during my first research trip to Elgeeii by Elvira Eremeeva—thank you, Elvira. During all subsequent visits I stayed with my kin—the various Yegorov families. I am grateful for that extended hospitality—thank you Yegorovs. Special thanks to local Suntar historian Arcadii Iakovlev, and Suntar regional archivist Ludmilla Petrova. In Yakutsk I extend thanks to all at the Institute of Humanitarian Research and especially to director Vasili Ivanov, and scientists Sardana Boyakova, Ekaterina Romanova, and Pyoter Sleptsov. Also in Yakutsk, thank-you to Ivan Alekseev, Mikhail Alekseev, Vasili Alekseev, Andre Borisov, Anatoli Chomchyev, Afanasee Fyodorov, Anatoli Gogolev, Elvira Myaryakova, Nadezhda Tolbonova, and Lubov Yegorova. Special thanks also to Lidia Fillipova at the Institute for Humanitarian Research archives, Natalia Komkova at the Yakutsk National Archives, and Vera Gavrileva at the Yakutsk Former Party Archives. Also in Yakutsk, I thank Edward Alekseev for inviting me to the 1991 International Jew's Harp Festival. I also extend a heartfelt thanks to Nadia Dasheiva, ethnologist at the Culture Institute in Ulan Ude, for her collaborations with me on research in Tuva, Mongolia, and Buriatia and her enthusiastic support of my work in Sakha.

I have many to thank for their support and constructive insights during my master's and doctoral work at UNC, Chapel Hill: thank-you to my master's committee: Glenn Hinson, David Griffith, and Donald Raleigh; and to my doctoral committee: Bruce Winterhalder, Richard (Pete) Andrews, Bruce Grant, Seth Reice, and Steve Whalen. I also add a special added thanks to Jack Weiss and Jack Kruse for their statistical expertise.

For their consultation and guidance with areas of the book addressing other world contexts of mining and indigenous peoples, I thank Ellen Bielawski, David Hyndman, Barbara Johnston, Stuart Kirsch, Kevin O'Reilly, and Pat Townsend.

I am grateful to a group of colleagues, many of whom have read parts of the manuscript in earlier forms or have helped by way of advice and example: Fikret Berkes, Craig Campbell, Mimi and Terry Chapin, Roz Galtz, Andre Golovnev, Anne Henshaw, Adelheid Herrmann, Janet Johnson, Flora Lu Holt, Henry Huntington, Anna Kertulla, Kathleen Kuehnast, Jack Kruse, Joan Larson, Barney Masuzumi, Katherine Metzo, Sue Mitchell, Carol Nechemias, Mark Nuttall, Gail Osherenko, Charlie Stevens, Niobe Thompson, Bram Tucker, Frank Sejerson, Kate Watters, Cynthia Werner, Gene Willeke, Emma Wilson, and Oran Young.

I have received much financial support for my work and research on the Viliui: this material is based in part on work supported by the National Science Foundation under Grant No. 0532993, a three-year National Science Foundation, Office of Polar

Programs, Arctic Social Science Program Grant; a Social Science Research Council Dissertation Write-up Award; a UNC Latane Interdisciplinary Summer Research Grant; American Association of University Women Dissertation Write-up Grant; UNC Smith Graduate Research Fund Grant; National Science Foundation Dissertation Improvement Award; Fulbright-Hays Doctoral Research Abroad Award; Social Science Research Council International Dissertation Field Research Fellowship; International Research & Exchange Board Individual Advanced Research Award; John D. & Catherine T. MacArthur Foundation (1994–1997); and an International Research and Exchange Board (IREX) On-Site Language Training Grant. Any opinions, findings, and conclusions or recommendations expressed in this material are those of the author and do not necessarily reflect the views of the above funding agencies.

I would like to add another expression of thanks to Bruce Winterhalder, who continues to be my mentor and friend as I navigate my way through academia and who gave me much useful feedback on early and late drafts of this manuscript. Additional readers for the manuscript were Mark Nuttall and Eric Lassiter—many thanks for your feedback! I also want to thank my editors, Joe Heyman and Rick Wilk, and AltaMira senior editor Rosalie Robertson for their support through this process.

I thank my parents, Cynthia Schoble Crate and James Harvey Crate, who have always supported my dreams even when it meant repeated traversings to the other side of the globe. You did a good job after all! And, at the core of my life and my days on earth, I thank my family—my husband, Prokopiy Mitrofanovich Yegorov, and our daughter, Kathryn Tuyaara Yegorov-Crate, for their loving support and belief in me.

S.A.C

Note

1. For more on this see Crate 2006a.

Prologue

We woke in darkness to the popping of the fire. Marusa switched on the light, revealing a patchwork of frost fans on the window by my head. At 7 a.m. the sun wouldn't be rising for three more hours but there was much work to do before then.

I rolled out of bed and caught Tania's sleepy eye. We stood and put on layers of clothes to protect ourselves from the −45° C cold. Four-year-old Maxime waited nearby to see the magic when we opened the heavy door to let in a gush of frozen air in a steamy wave that would sweep across the floor and disappear under beds and tables.

Outside it was still and cold. The frozen air hit my face, the only exposed part of me, stinging my eyes and nostrils with its bite and taking away any drowsiness that remained. The sky was dark to all horizons, offset by the twinkling of a dense array of stars. Our felt boots crunched along the shoveled path to the *khoton* (cow barn). Marusa heaved the *khoton* door open, releasing another wave of steamy cold air to spread across the barn floor. The cows looked up wide-eyed while the wave enveloped their legs. They took cautious steps away from me, the stranger in their midst, and Marusa calmed them to my presence with her vocal patter.

The *khoton*, home to five cows and their almost yearling calves, was unevenly lit by three bare bulbs hanging from ceiling wires. *Khotons* are purposely low to minimize heat loss. That morning, while Marusa slathered cows' utters with cream to soften them, I found myself looking up. I noticed that the entire ceiling was strewn with moist cobwebs. In among them I located two small chimney vents, each approximately four inches square. Then something strange caught my eye—what looked like a tiny clothesline—or several of them. With longer inspection, I saw they were strings of animal hair adorned with pieces of cloth and small shapes, strung between two of the middle roof rafters. I examined them as best I could in their shadowy position.

Then the milking began. I replaced full buckets with empty ones, while Marusa and Tania milked. When Tania finished milking, we went outside to the corral and made piles of hay, spacing them out evenly across the area, to fodder each cow. We led the cows outside then cleaned and skidded manure to an area just beyond the cow pen. The final morning cow task was to lead the cows to Marusa's *oibon* (a water hole cut in lake or river ice). We would wait until the sun lighted and warmed the air. In the meantime, we returned to the house for tea.

Over our cups of steaming tea I asked Marusa about what I saw hanging from the *khoton* rafters. She explained that it was *salama* (a sacrificial gift to honor the sky deity-protectors and that serves as their pathway from the sky into the *khoton*). It is necessary to hang a new one every year when the cows are close to calving to ensure their protection, fertility, and good health. The horse hair string symbolizes power and strength. The miniature birch bark bucket tied to one end is to place *aladye* (R., pancakes) in, to keep the gods satiated.

We returned to our tea drinking and I thought of how amazing it was that this sacred practice continued after the blatant oppression of ethnic rituals during the Soviet period. Next my mind flooded with all I knew about the other issues of historical change, survival, and adaptation that Sakha have persevered.

—Journal entry, January 9, 2000, Tumul, Russia

Figure x.1. Marusa's salama

That morning Marusa's *salama* became for me a vital symbol of and testimony to the adaptive resilience that has brought Sakha through to this day (figure x.1).

This book is an ethnography of Sakha, an indigenous[1] people of subarctic Russia. Theirs is a history founded both on adaptation—to an extreme physical environment, to colonial and Soviet impacts, to issues of contemporary post-Soviet processes—and on resilience—of culture, belief, and life ways that have persisted through a diversity of challenges. Contemporary daily life, described in journal entries, provides many windows into that legacy of adaptation and resilience.

This is also an ethnography of globalization and modernity, forces similarly prevalent in contemporary Sakha life. Journal entries frequently describe a daily life framed by uncertainty and change; perhaps most poignant are those entries about the alienation of Sakha youth from village life and local heritage:

> Today when I left an elder's house after a two-hour interview and entered the street, for a few moments I had the sense that time stood still. Local inhabitants worked stacking manure and tending cows, skidding

containers of drinking water from the river on small sleds, and splitting and stacking firewood. Their activities were congruous with the pre-Soviet subsistence practices my elder consultant described, albeit in the present-day context of a compact Soviet-style village settlement. In the next moment I was catapulted into a different present, when a group of teenage girls strolled by with orange, blue, and purple hair, wearing six-inch platform heels, bell-bottoms, and skimpy shirts revealing pierced navels. Time both stood still and raced forward. Later I had a chance to talk to several graduating seniors of the village school. Their main interest was to leave their home villages and "make something of themselves" in the outside world. Clearly the schism between youth and the older generation is not just a visual breaking away from the past by youth assuming western clothing and attitudes. On a deeper level young people are also disinterested in and unknowledgeable about their local history.

—Journal entry, March 19, 2000, Elgeeii, Russia

The post-Soviet opening of Russia to the outside world and the associated influx of western mass media and consumer goods increasingly draws Sakha, especially youth, away from their heritage and a livelihood founded on centuries-old survival skills. The opening has also brought market interests to the fore. On the Viliui this has meant intensified exploitation of the area's abundant diamond reserves and increased environmental and economic dislocation for local communities.

Lastly, I write this book as an ethnography of sustainability by exploring how communities balance adaptation and resilience in the crossfire of globalizing and modernizing forces. Local voices attest to how inhabitants are contemplating this balance:

Our Sakha ancestors lived from the land and we could now follow that on a village level. We need to make an ecological village and live in it as one community. If we did then each family would not need their own tractor. We could share a few tractors between all of us and use it as we need. If we can have strong community then there will be no one without work, no one with a drinking problem. Strong community could answer all the problems. The old Sakha lived that way and we need to also. If we did then all the ecology would be looked after. We wouldn't have people taking as much as they can but only what they need. We have land and we have water. Now we just need to take care of it and be stewards.

—Female focus group participant, 2003, Elgeeii, Russia

We need to lead ourselves. I think we need to build our own food processing plant to make our own butter and products and turn these things around ourselves. We have a lot of animals and so if we could build a mini-factory and process all these products we produce, that could be our first source of jobs and local wealth build-ing. From the money made with that minifactory, we could create our monetary base and begin other com-munity projects. For that we need to use our youths' strength. The old (Sakha) idea was that we use the strength of our youth to build the future. The youth now don't think about the future. There are many ways to develop our youth but we don't do them and so we don't get close to the youth—they are not with us. If someone's son brings in a few pieces of firewood, their parents will say, "Oh, look, our boy helps us!" So now all think that a strong, healthy, twenty-four-year-old boy who brings in one armful of wood is a huge helper! We don't teach our youth to work and we don't use their strength. We need to work with our youth and children to teach them our lifestyle and our mindset.

—Male focus group participant, 2003, Elgeeii, Russia

But how can Sakha reach a balance by putting these ideas into action? How does their environmental, historical, sociocultural, and political contact shape the choices they have? I explore these questions through this ethnographic inquiry by tracking the local history of events and examining the interplay of forces from the local to the global. In this ethnography I use multi-sited analysis to expand the context from a "committed localism" and explore the complex interactions of the larger world system that shape the local (Marcus 1998:83). I also employ a multi-sited analysis to fully understand how local actors and societies adapt to the multiplicity of natural and human forces:

> Adaptive strategy is a defined mode of cultural adaptation embraced by a human community in response to specific ecological and/or social conditions—conditions that are themselves changing as a result of multifaceted ecological processes, contact with other cultures, technological development, and population growth. Only on the basis of a wide range of sources can we peer more deeply into the past than with field ethnography alone and glimpse new relationships and interactions that previously were obscured from view. This makes it possible to trace these two interconnected but relatively independent dynamic phenomena of ecological and social processes.(Krupnik 1993:27)

The book also represents an experimental approach to ethnography by drawing on a combination of observational, applied, and participatory approaches to intentionally tease out the implications for sustainability.

The ethnography of Sakha is relevant to a broad audience interested in the globally shared issues and concerns of indigenous peoples whose lives and environments interface world-oriented, capital intensive extractive mining of diamonds and other commodities. Additionally, I write this ethnography for a diverse audience within and without academia. Accordingly, I don't begin with pages of theoretical groundings but by first immersing readers in the on-the-ground realities, an approach that mirrors my own inductive way of knowing about Sakha.[2]

Central Themes: Local Cultures/Global Forces

I frame the ethnography with three central themes that are woven throughout the chapters and to which I return in the final chapter discussion. Here I am including only brief definitions of how I will be using these themes.

1) Adaptation and Resilience: Human adaptation involves the implementing of strategies to increase chances of survival and reproduction (Redman 1999:43). Adaptation is a culture's capacity to abate negative factors when faced with rapid change. Resilience, or the cumulative effect of processes that maintain an ecosystem in the face of rapid change, is one measure of a system's ability to adapt (Berkes, et al. 2003:13).

2) Globalization and Modernity: Globalization is "the processes of economic, cultural, political and environmental change which are leading to the increased connectedness of different parts of the world" (Elliot 2002:190). Modernization alters the reality of a culture by aligning it with a homogeneous industrial-capital model and thereby disembedding a culture from its local orientation across both time and space (Giddens 1990:21).

3) Sustainability: Efforts to define sustainability have been ongoing since the concept gained status as a global priority in 1987 (WCED 1987). Research on socioecological systems defines sustainability in direct relation to resilience. "A resilient social-ecological system, which can buffer a great deal of change or disturbance, is synonymous with ecological, economic, and social sustainability"(Berkes, et al. 2003:15). Maintaining sustainability means working within the resilience "limits" of a system to enhance diversity and variability and to facilitate the system's capability for self-organization and capacity for learning and adaptation (Gunderson and Holling 2002).[3]

On the Use of "Indigenous"

This ethnography presents one in-depth case study and two comparative cases of indigenous peoples. Researchers, policy makers, NGOs (nongovernmental organizations) and governments often use the term "indigenous" differently (Beteille 1998; Kuper 2003).

I use the term as defined in Article 1 of the International Labor Organization's "Convention Concerning Indigenous and Tribal Peoples in Independent Countries" (ILO No. 169):

> People who are regarded as indigenous on account of their descent from the populations which inhabited the country, or a geographical region to which the country belongs, at the time of conquest or colonization or the establishment of present State boundaries and who, irrespective of their legal status, retain some or all of their own social, economic, cultural and political institutions.

Similarly, I use the terms "indigenous," "aboriginal," and "native" interchangeably (Brown 2003: xiii).

Throughout the book I refer to indigenous peoples and their ability to adapt to change. Much of the change they have faced and are facing is due to increasing pressure on local resources and ecosystems for the west's expanding global system of production (Watson 1997:389). This dynamic is real. However, my intent is not to create a polar contrast between indigenous peoples on the one hand and western peoples on the other. On the contrary, my aim is to show the complex and multi-sited ways that indigenous peoples are shaped by being within the world system in order to highlight both the tenacity and the susceptibility of their cultural survival—which itself depends on an intimate knowledge of and connection to the natural world—the very relationship that substantiates their utility for adaptation and resilience.

A Note on the Transliteration

Foreign words in this text are Sakha and Russian, with a majority being Sakha. Both use the Cyrillic alphabet and are transliterated here using the Library of Congress system. I define each word the first time it appears in the text, sometimes in parentheses and sometimes not, depending on the flow of the prose. For easy reference, I include a glossary at the end. Russian words are identified with an "R."; otherwise, the word is Sakha. If a word is used extensively in western sources with a different spelling than that of the Library of Congress, I use the popular spelling. For example, I use *Yakutsk* rather than *Iakutsk*. Additionally, the Sakha language has seven more letters than Russian. Here is the transliteration of those additional letters:

Ҕ = gh Дь = j Ҥ = ng Нь = n' Ө = o h = h Ү = y

Map-Out of the Chapters

I have arranged the chapters to guide my readers' inductive discovery of the three central themes. In chapter 1, I describe the Siberian subarctic environment and the successful adaptations of the flora, fauna, and humans who call it home.

I explore Viliui Sakha ethnohistory in chapter 2—the migration of Sakhas' Turkic ancestors to the subarctic and their adaptive responses to both an extreme physical environment and a changing political landscape. My exploration of ethnohistory also locates the roots of globalization and modernity, beginning with seventeenth-century Russian colonization and spanning through Sovietization to the post-Soviet context of today.

In chapter 3, I immerse the reader in the present. I first describe life in twenty-first-century Viliui Sakha villages, then I focus on the local responses to the collapse of the Soviet era. The Viliui Sakha responded by developing cows-and-kin, a food production system based on household-level cow keeping and interdepending with kin to pool resources, labor, and land. The most salient issue of post-Soviet era cows-and-kin survival is land tenure, both having and knowing the land.

In chapter 4, I discuss Viliui Sakha land issues by exploring local experiences of accessing and remembering. The legacy of Soviet and post-Soviet industrialization, specifically the impacts of ongoing environmental degradation of their watershed by regional diamond mining, also challenges contemporary Viliui Sakha livelihoods.

In chapter 5, I document the environmental history of the Viliui regions based on information made available in the late Soviet and post-Soviet periods. I then trace the beginning, evolution, and co-option of the Viliui Committee, a regional citizen-based NGO that disseminated information, educated local inhabitants, and lobbied policy makers to better protect the Viliui environment.

In chapter 6 I compare Viliui Sakhas' plight with the Canadian case of diamond mining and indigenous peoples. I next analyze what made for the success of indigenous stakeholders in Canada, and return to the Viliui Sakha case to explore local capacity for alternative futures.

In chapter 7 I engage inhabitants' voices to hear firsthand how locals understand and contemplate their future. I analyze community-based research to define sustainability in terms of community goals.

I next expand the Sakha comparison within the global context of mining and indigenous peoples in chapter 8.

In conclusion I revisit the threads of themes through the chapters to contemplate once more the balancing act of Viliui Sakha and other indigenous peoples and to more fully analyze the concept and practice of sustainability.

Notes

1. See p. xxiii on the clarification for my use of the term "indigenous." Another important point of clarification for our discussion is the classification of indigenous people in Russia versus in the world. The 1925 Soviet classification of "small-numbered peoples" included 26 peoples (now numbering 42) who practiced hunting, gathering and reindeer herding and whose populations did not exceed 50,000 (Slezkine 1994:2). This category did not include the "numerically large" peoples including Komi, Yakut (Sakha) and Buriat (Shnirelman 1999: 119). However, these same large-numbered peoples are classified as indigenous in global terms.

2. I thank the late Robert Netting for this writing approach that he used so effectively in *Smallholders, Householders* (1993).

3. The emerging field of "sustainability science" focuses on the complexity of human-environment interactions. It is a problem-driven science with both its end goals of creating knowledge for sustainable development decision-making and emphasizing the co-production of knowledge to ensure its utility and longevity to local users (Clark and Dickson 2003:8059).

1

At Home in Siberia

To be "at home in Siberia" presents most of us with an oxymoron. The word "Siberia" calls up images of a bleak, frozen wasteland—an empty, barren space—the *Gulag*,[1] a prison without walls. These images have persisted for centuries. But in the last decade there has been a growing awareness that Siberia and all of the arctic are much more than these stereotypes suggest. We can thank the advance of northern scholarship and the global sharing of information for more accurate visions (Coates 1995).

What are the historical roots of those long-standing stereotypes? Siberia has been many times reimagined over the course of Russian history and especially during the diversification and fragmentation of cultural and political thought in the last half millennium. The first image was as an imperial resource colony to extract "soft gold" or sable pelts, the major source of income for medieval Russia. By the 1800s when most fur resources were exhausted, Siberia took on the image of a place of exile and punishment, a wasteland and the epitome of backwardness. The Decembrists next reimagined Siberia as Russia's new world analogous to America's then newly found freedom. This third image cast Siberia as a symbol of hope, inspiration, freedom, and intellectual pursuit. The fourth image extolled Siberia as a nationalistic symbol, representing all the values that could free Russia from European assimilation (Bassin 1991). During the Soviet period the original mercantile-colonial image predominated, with Siberia the home to intensive resource extracting industries. We also see glimpses of the other images at that time. The 1970s compositions of Alexander Solzhenitsyn recall the fourth image by describing Siberia as "the hope and reservoir" for Russia's national revitalization via the development of its vast natural resources

(Solzhenitsyn 1974:29). Since the 1991 fall of the Soviet Union and its opening to the global community, stereotypes are gradually being replaced with (an often bittersweet) reality. We now can know the many divergent sides of Siberia—its rich geographic, cultural, biological, and ethnic diversity; its unique political and economic history; and its myriad of contemporary twenty-first-century challenges.

On a global scale, the predominant contemporary image of Siberia, and many other arctic regions, is as resource colonies for petroleum, natural gas, coal, and metallic and mineral ores. There is a second, less-known image, held by northern inhabitants and the researchers working there. This is the image of the north as a homeland to a diverse patchwork of resilient peoples, animals, and plants. The plants and animals that make their home in northern areas have done so through behavioral and physiological adaptations. Neanderthals lived in glacial times with some adaptation to the cold. However, they lacked the technology (needles, sewn clothes, warm houses, etc.) essential to survival in the coldest of climates. It was only after the invention of thread some forty thousand years ago, that humans could sufficiently clothe themselves and make a home in the north. Those with proper technology expanded into Siberia some twenty thousand years ago. On a global scale, humans inhabited northeastern Siberia later than other parts of the world and, once there, crossed the then existing Bering land bridge, the essential link to migrations to the Americas (Hoffecker et al. 1993).

Human inhabitants of the north consistently utilized large animals, either terrestrial caribou, reindeer, and musk ox, or maritime seals, walruses, and whales, supplemented with small game hunting, fishing, and foraging. Northern groups adhere to this subsistence pattern across the contemporary pan-Arctic with one exception—the horse- and cattle-breeding Sakha. The only other group that kept cows in the subarctic have long vanished (McGovern 1980).[2] Why would a people maintain a subsistence strategy that proves highly labor- and energy-intensive in a new environment? The answer, in part, is culture. Sakhas' Turkic ancestors migrated from Central Asia to southern Siberia circa

AD 900. Genghis Khan's armies ousted them from the area, and from the 1300s, Sakha followed the Lena River northward, bringing their horse and cattle culture with them. Today they are the highest latitude agropastoralists in the world. To provide a context for how Sakha adapted their southern subsistence to the north, I will describe the geography, climate, hydrology, and the life histories of native plants and animals.

Biogeography of the Viliui

The Sakha Republic of northeastern Siberia, Russia, is home to the majority of Sakha, a non-Russian Turkic-speaking indigenous people, at present numbering approximately 360,000. The territory covers over three million square kilometers, comparable to twice the area of Alaska (figure 1.1). Although it occupies one-fifth of Russia's total land area, the Republic is home to only one million inhabitants, or 1 percent of Russia's total population. The majority reside in the lowland areas and urban centers. Contemporary rural inhabitants rely on subsistence-centered mixed cash economies. Sakha predominantly practice horse and cattle husbandry and Evenk, Even, Yukagir, and Dolgan practice reindeer herding, hunting, fishing, and foraging.

Sakha living in the Viliui River watershed of western Sakha are called Viliui Sakha. Their Turkic ancestors made a direct migration via the Chona River system to the Viliui from the south (Ksenofontov 1992 [1937]:12). The major ecosystem of the Viliui watershed is *taiga*, or boreal forest, predominantly larch, spruce, fir, pine, and birch. Other important micro-ecosystems of the watershed include *alaas* (a round field bordered by woods, usually with a lake in the center), meadow and forest steppe, sandy desert, swampland, and tundra.

But northern Eurasia has not always been characterized by taiga and tundra. In geologic time, it recently was home to temperate ecosystems with specially adapted flora and fauna. It is fascinating to ponder how climatic change transformed this area from the tropics to a predominantly frozen land. Overviewing

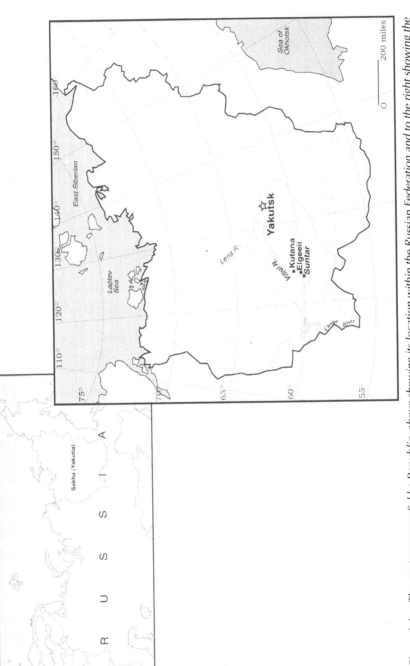

Figure 1.1.   The contemporary Sakha Republic, above showing its location within the Russian Federation and to the right showing the location of the capital city, Yakutsk, the Viliui River, the Suntar regional center, and main research villages, Elgeeii and Kutana. Also shown is the Chona River, one of the waterways that Viliui Sakhas' Turkic ancestors followed from the south.

the archaeological record of that change also helps to break down our long-held beliefs of the static nature of the north.

The Pre-glacial and Glacial Periods in the Sakha Republic

In the early Tertiary period, 50 million years BP, Eurasia's climate was warm and it was home to a diverse flora and fauna (Okladnikov 1970:9). Southern Eurasia was moist and tropical with species like laurel, palm, eucalyptus, fig, sequoia, and a broad range of evergreen tropical plants. Fossilized remains, found in the tundra of northern Sakha, of beech, hornbeam, alder, birch, elm, maple, oak, and walnut, show the former deciduous forests.

In the late Tertiary/early Quaternary, the climate grew markedly colder and more humid across the earth. The northern fossil record shows a shift from deciduous forest to cold-thriving species. This climatic change was partly due to tectonic transformations that produced extensive mountain landscapes and the submersion of the Bering land bridge (Okladnikov 1970:12–16; Suslov 1961:187–189). Increased precipitation brought heavy accumulations of ice and snow in formerly temperate areas, destroying rich flora and fauna. Many parts of Eurasia were covered with ice, which reached 2 kilometers (1.24 miles) in some places.

Siberia was the exception. With its protection from oceanic humidity and precipitation by high mountains to the east and south and by the cold Arctic Ocean to the north, glaciation of northeastern and central Siberia during the last ice age lagged behind Europe. Most of eastern Siberia remained free from aboveground ice shields and provided refuge for many plant and animal species that were "iced out" elsewhere. Siberia was affected by underground ice or permafrost. Mammoth, wooly rhinoceros, wild horse, and musk ox remains date the permafrost formation to that time (Suslov 1961:145). The eastern Siberian permafrost is a relic of the last ice age—a surrogate of the massive ice covers that were characteristic of adjacent high latitude areas.[3]

The earliest faunal inhabitants of Eurasia were the ancient pachyderms, the mammoth and rhinoceros, which are both now long extinct. Contemporary scientists speculate that overkill by human immigrants to Eurasia in consort with climate change resulted in the Pleistocene extinction of Eurasia's wooly mammoth and rhinoceros (Stuart 1991; Barnosky et al. 2004; Diamond 1999). Of the two, the mammoth was the keystone species for Paleolithic humans across Eurasia. Humans used mammoth as a main source of food and its bones and tusks for most of their utilitarian needs. Imagining upper Paleolithic humans without mammoths is like imagining steppe nomads without their horses or Inuit without seals and walrus. Researchers are still finding entire mammoth carcasses with soft tissues, hairy covering, and internal organs intact in the permafrost of eastern Siberia. It was only in the late seventeenth and early eighteenth centuries that we fully understood mammoth anatomy and way of life. Earlier travelers to Siberia called the mammoth "a gigantic earth rat," which they believed lived and roamed underground, because it would die a tragic death if it surfaced, and lifted the earth over it as it wandered (Okladnikov 1970).

Both the rhinoceros and wooly mammoth had dense, thick coats and layers of insulating fat to protect them from the severe climate, extreme cold, and piercing winds of the glacial epoch. Both foraged for fodder under the deep snow using specialized scrapers. The mammoth had spirally curved tusks, which provided ample lateral surfaces to scrape away snow to find fodder (Garutt 1946:139). Siberian rhinoceroses had exaggerated frontal horns to clear snow and procure food. Among the other fauna found among the carcasses of rhinoceroses and mammoths are reindeer, horses, wild cattle, musk oxen, foxes, and tigers. The most abundant of these are horse carcasses, suggesting that the area was then rich in high quality pasturelands.

During the most recent ice age, the area of the present-day Sakha Republic served as a haven in the north for many species that were unable to survive in adjacent ice-covered regions. At the very height of the glacial era, many subarctic and arctic plants and animals found refuge in this sheltered corner of Siberia, witnessed by the area's pronounced continental climate and broad spaces occupied by steppe flora, mountain forests, and tundra.

Geology of Sakha and the Viliui

The Sakha Republic is abundantly rich in mineral wealth. Within its borders you can find every element in Mendeleyev's chart. Sakha explain it this way:

> When the gods flew over the earth giving out the precious minerals and resources, it was so bitterly cold over the Sakha Republic that they froze and all the contents of their boxes spilled out.

> —Sakha legend

Western scientists explain the wealth based on eastern Siberia's geologic foundation of folded pre-Cambrian rocks, likened only to the distant East European Plain and Canadian Shield areas. All these sites are characterized by an abundance of Paleozoic and Triassic period outcrops of granites and trap rocks in association with rich metallic and nonmetallic mineral deposits.

The geology and unique landscape characteristics of the Viliui also explain the abundance of flat open expanses of pasture and taiga forests found throughout the watershed. These areas are located in the vast depressions of the Viliui River basin, formed where a folded foundation dropped below the mantle of horizontal or slightly dislocated Paleozoic and Mesozoic rocks (Suslov 1961).

Climate and Hydrology on the Viliui

Viliui Sakha adapted a temperate-region horse and cattle subsistence to the subarctic. To fully gauge that adaptation I need to describe both the limitations of climate and the way that water moves through the subarctic ecosystem. The Viliui watershed climate is extreme continental. The annual temperature range spans 100°C (180°F), from summer highs of +40°C (+104°F) to −60°C (−76°F) in winter. The Sakha Republic is home to the coldest human inhabited places on the earth. Such extremes are a result of the area's northern geographic position, its distance and protection from moderating water bodies, the character of its physical relief, and the direction, speed, and nature of air currents. Another factor making the climate more severe than adjacent 60th-parallel areas is exposure to a winter anticyclone[4] that begins in September and causes air temperatures to drop sharply through November.[5] From December through February the anticyclone reaches maximum development, producing temperature inversions, persistent fog, and calms (windlessness). The lack of wind, which lasts through March, helps all inhabitants to conserve heat at seemingly unbearably low temperatures (Suslov 1961:130).[6] Annual day-length change is also extreme, with the shortest winter day at four hours and the longest summer day at twenty.

After the long, windless, subarctic winter, the change to summer is sudden and tumultuous. Spring is windy, and blizzards are common with the sudden arrival of cold arctic fronts. Daily average air temperatures rise quickly in spring[7] and thawing is rapid. The quick warming collapses the anticyclone by April, ushering in a low-pressure system for the summer. Snow and ice are gone by June, and temperatures soon reach the the mid-20s C (70s to 80s F). Summer is typically dry with sudden bouts of torrential rain when the warming earth currents mix with incoming arctic air. Daily summer temperatures range between daytime highs of 35°C and nighttime lows of 5°C (95°F and 41°F respectively). The permafrost quickly cools the summer night once the sun is gone. Summer is short-lived. The first snows fall in September and a thick snow cover is in place by early October.[8]

Hydrology on the Viliui

The presence of a continuous permafrost layer is the main factor determining the hydrological characteristics of the Viliui regions. In summer, the top layer of soil thaws from 0.4 to 3.5 meters (1.3 to 11.48 feet) deep. The ground below remains frozen. The vertical movement of water in the soil is limited to the unfrozen top layer. The soil immediately above the permafrost is in a continuous state of supersaturation. Upper soil layers are moistened by the capillary action of water rising from the saturated layer and providing necessary moisture during low precipitation. These soil features also explain the swampy character of the landscape.

Permafrost is highly dynamic. It continually interacts with groundwater by absorbing the water's heat to convert groundwater to ice and to thaw itself. Groundwater performs different actions depending on whether it is above-frost, below-frost, or inter-frost groundwater. *Above-frost* groundwater comes from precipitation, surface water, or condensed vapor and lies on permafrost in either a liquid or solid state. It is oxygen-saturated and cold, maintaining temperatures around 0°C (32°F). *Below-frost* groundwater, held below the permafrost, is high in carbon dioxide (CO_2) and never freezes. It thaws adjacent permafrost, creating large openings. The *inter-frost* groundwater connects above- and below-frost waters, transiting between them to fill permafrost channels. Both the scarcity and high mineral content of groundwater explain why Viliui inhabitants depend on surface sources—the natural lakes, rivers, and streams—for drinking water. The area's climate and dynamic permafrost determine the morphology and properties of surface waters, both running and stable sources.

Lakes: The Eyes of the Earth

I'll always remember the first trip I took to the Sakha Republic fifteen years ago. I flew from Ulan Ude, the capital of Buriatia near Lake Baikal. As the plane flew north I remember my dismay as the landscape changed from the dramatic mountains that grace southern Siberia to the flatness that characterizes most of the Sakha Republic. I also wondered why there were so many lakes across the flat expanse. I soon discovered many more reasons to continue to travel, live, and work in Sakha.

But my first impression was correct—the Sakha Republic and the Viliui regions are flat with only minimal relief.[9] Most of the landscape is a patchwork of taiga (boreal forest) and *alaas*, "flat depressions caused by thermal processes in permafrost areas, usually with a lake in the middle."[10] Sakha call the thousands of *alaas* lakes in the Viliui regions "the eyes of the earth," because they are as numerous as the stars in the sky (figure 1.2). *Alaas* are

Figure 1.2. "The Eyes of the Earth"

highly productive ecosystems. The agricultural bounty of the Viliui *alaas* meadows supports the most northern region of horse and cattle husbandry on earth. The Viliui regions' *alaas* system pasturelands are rich in species including wild oats (*Bromus inermis* and *B. ciliatus*), barley (*Hordeum prateuse* and *H. jubatum*), rye (*Elymus dasystachys* and *E. excelsus*), couch grass (*Triticum repens*), oats (*Festuca elatior*), wormwood (*artemisia sr. r.*), various ranunculus (*Ranunculus achillea, R. millefolium, R. borealis, R. repens*), and over eighteen species of legumes (Seroshevski 1993:63–64).

   Most Viliui *alaas* formed from imperfections in the permafrost that either inhibited the invasion of predominant boreal forest cover, or exposed the soil surface to thawing temperatures. As upper permafrost thawing proceeded, a water-filled hollow formed with a flat, weakly concave bottom and jagged shore. Technically called a thermokarst, the lake continues to expand energetically as the ice underlying the banks thaws, settles, and moves to the lake bottom (Hutchinson 1957:100). Sometimes the lake dries or fills with sediments to form a hay meadow complete with hillocks and mounds formed by push-ups of underground ice. The *alaas* process can take decades and consists of four stages, each with characteristic vegetation: lake, swamp, meadow (watery), and steppe.

Anthropogenic factors have taken their toll on the *alaas* systems on the Viliui. Ever since Sakha have lived on the Viliui, their forest clearing and lake draining practices have altered the *alaas* formation cycle. Early Russian settlers (circa 1670) tried to grow wheat on the open treeless areas, but their early attempts were thwarted by the limited growing season. Other factors that continue to alter the natural *alaas* process and have rendered vast areas susceptible to thawing include forest fires; the cutting of forests for agriculture, road building, and heating fuel; and twentieth-century mining and logging. This is worrisome because the animal, plant, and human communities that make their home in Siberia are successful in their environment based on adaptations to a permafrost ecosystem.

Rivers: Ebe (Grandmother) of the Earth

Sakha call the Viliui River *ebe* (grandmother), a term of endearment used for all forms in nature that are larger than average—lakes, hay fields, rivers. This is done both out of respect for the greatness of that resource, which Sakha depend on for their subsistence survival, and as a customary way to protect the resource from harm (Pekarski 1958:215). Viliui Sakha call the river *ebe* and ask its protection because they know and appreciate their main source of water and life that even in the deepest cold of winter, still flows. Viliui Sakha living near the river or any of its many tributaries depend on it for drinking, fishing, and transport to land areas for haying, berrying, and hunting.

The Viliui regions are defined by the Viliui watershed system (figure 1.1). The river runs a winding course over 1,643 miles from its headwaters in the western neighboring Krasnoyarsk Krai to where it joins the Lena River just north of the Republic's capital city, Yakutsk. This rich running-water system is fed mostly by the intensive spring thaws and torrential summer rains. River temperatures range from slightly above freezing in winter to 12.8°C (55°F) in July-August.

The river has a life of its own. From October to May it is ice covered to an average thickness of 1.8 meters (6 feet). In spring the ice begins to pit and fissure from melt waters that increasingly invade from the banks. This causes the river to swell from beneath the ice, which eventually breaks the continuous ice cover into pieces that are carried by the current to clear the river from ice. Fall freezing starts in late September, when air temperatures drop quickly below water temperatures, causing the warm water to lose heat to the colder air and in-flowing cold water from tributaries. Although surface waters are limited compared to temperate watershed systems, the regions stay saturated due to the climate's low evaporation rates, short summers, and long periods of continuous ice cover on water bodies.

The Boreal Ecosystem: Floral and Faunal Adaptations

The main ecosystem of the Viliui regions is taiga or boreal forest,[11] part of a world bioregion that occupies 11 percent of the earth's surface, is circumpolar in extent,[12] and is characteristically low in species diversity.[13] The world's boreal forests are considered the second "lungs of the earth," after the earth's tropical forest systems, due to their ability to absorb CO_2 and produce oxygen, ecosystem services necessary to maintain global environmental balance (Shugart, Leemans, and Bonan 1992). Twenty-first century deforestation continues to result in diminishing areas of both Amazonian rainforest and large sections of taiga.

Boreal forest types are diverse due to the variation in temperature lows, precipitation, day length, and soil composition.[14] Climatic conditions range from extremely cold, dry continental regimes, like found in interior Alaska, Canada, and Siberia, to the warmer, moister, oceanic climes of coastal Alaska, eastern Canada, and Scandinavia (Bryson and Hare 1974). Fire is a natural part of all boreal ecosystems, and coniferous tree species commonly suffer from insect outbreaks.

Eurasian taiga is the northernmost forest zone of Russia, covering 9,000,000 square kilometers (3,474,000 square miles), and constituting two-thirds of the world's boreal forests (Larsen

1980:3).[15] The taiga is bounded to the south by temperate forests and grasslands and to the north by tundra. The extreme continental climate of eastern Siberia supports a relatively sparse-leafed "light taiga" forest that stands in sharp contrast to the shady, lush "dark taiga" of the west. There is no parallel for the eastern Siberia forest in North America (Heinrich 1979:235). Because of the extreme conditions of elevated relief, arid climate, and continuous permafrost, Dahurian larch (*Larix gmelinii* (Rupr.) syn *Larix dahurica*) replaces Siberian *Larix sibirica* as the dominant tree species. Eastern Siberia taiga also has fewer dark conifers, steppe plants, and animals than in the west. The adaptations of the Dahurian larch tell us a lot about what it takes to survive in this extreme "home."

Dahurian larch (*Larix gmelinii* (Rupr.) syn *Larix dahurica*) is a coniferous, deciduous tree, the most permafrost-tolerant of boreal species. It survives on top of solid frozen ground by sending its roots out laterally through the thin layer of moss covering the forest floor. The tree reaches a maximum height of 20–40 meters (65.6–131 feet) and can live from 250 to 400 years. *L. gmelinii* is very tolerant of low-nutrient, high-stress environments and a range of soil conditions, but it is very intolerant of shade, with a reputation as the most light-demanding tree of boreal Eurasia (Nikolaev and Helmisaari 1992). This has not been a problem since *L. gmelinii* lacks competition during colonization in the severe climate. It is usually found in pure, even-aged stands (Dylis 1961). It favors fire-prone, dry climates with large amounts of litter, and its thick bark makes it fire-tolerant. Low-intensity fires are beneficial to temporarily eliminate the thick litter layer, allowing for tree seed regeneration. *L. gmelinii* is also tolerant of the seasonal flooding that is characteristic of many parts of the Yakut (Sakha) taiga biome.[16]

Within the eastern Siberian taiga, the Viliui boreal forests are part of the "Yakut (Sakha) taiga," which covers more than 1,500,000 square kilometers (5,790,000 square miles) and includes the coldest inhabited area of the world, Verkhoiansk[17](Tsepliaev 1965). The mature Yakut (Sakha) taiga is a spruce-fir-larch forest predominated by Dahurian larch.[18] Plant diversity in the Yakut taiga is low because of the special adaptation needed to survive.

The Viliui regions are home to only those floral species that can survive some of the coldest, lowest-nutrient, and most stressful conditions on earth.[19] There is little water available during the spring growing period, when warming temperatures stimulate above-ground plant growth. Plant roots, still frozen in the permafrost, cannot provide needed moisture. Melting permafrost is a source of plant moisture during the dry summer months. Permafrost also acts as an inhibitor to plant growth and to microbial processes in the active soil layer. Nutrient levels are low, and decomposition is retarded, resulting in the slow build-up of humus.

Lichens cover most of the taiga floor. The understory is made up of several heath (*Ericaceae*) and thick-leaved herbaceous plants including *Pinus pumila, Alnus fruticosa, Sorbus sibirica, Juniperus sibirica, Spirea media, Rhododendron dauricum, Lonicera altaica, Betula middendorffii,* and *Rosa acicularis.* The swamplands support mostly heath species and scrubby birch, *Betula fruticosa* (Pall.) (Sokolov 1977). The first plants to invade open areas are aspen and birch. The lake and water edges are home to willow, and a dozen kinds of edible berries are found throughout the taiga and open pastureland ecosystems.

Fauna

Like the flora of the Yakut taiga, the fauna have unique adaptation to survive in extreme conditions. They avoid activity in the extreme cold either by migrating, hibernating, or limiting their exposure. Even during this time of inactivity, boreal fauna are engaged in a complex pattern of energy flow that possesses strength and stability. After the nine-month winter, spring brings a sudden increase of animals across the landscape. Seasonal migrations bring clouds of waterfowl that either breed in the Viliui regions or travel on to northern breeding grounds. Mammals' newborn young begin their first months of activity and strengthening before winter. Mosquitoes and black flies hatch out in great numbers, creating thick clouds that pose a nuisance to mammals and humans alike. Bears (*Ursus ardtos* L.) emerge from their dens after hibernation and gorge on an omnivorous fare, consuming leaves, berries, nuts, seeds, insects, and small animals.

In the Sakha Republic overall there are twenty-eight species of mammals,[20] close to three hundred species of birds, forty-three fish species, and approximately four thousand species of insects.[21] The wolf is the main predator. Wild reindeer (caribou) migrate through with the seasons. Moose and bear are year-round inhabitants.

Winter-active mammals limit their exposure to the cold. Hares (*Lepus timidus* L.) spend most of their time traveling in a network of tunnels beneath the snow and only run sparingly above ground. Some animals, like the Kamchatka suslik (black-headed marmot), hibernate in burrows in the permafrost, where the temperature may be as low as −29.4° C (−21° F) (Suslov 1961:140). Foxes and wolves come out of their dens only long enough to hunt their winter fare of mice, voles, and shrews. Other winter-active mammals include moose, reindeer, lynx, muskrat, mink, squirrel, and weasel.

The moose (*Alces alces* L.) consumes 25 kilograms (55.1 pounds) of buds, stems, bark, and deciduous leaves daily (Lomanov 1996). When winter turns to summer, they feed increasingly on aquatic plants. Moose densities can reach as high as ten animals per square mile. They tend to forage independently in the summer and move in small groups during the winter months.

Reindeer (*Rangifer tarandus* L.) feed on lichens and other plants. They have two specialized adaptations that enable them to make their home in range of terrestrial and aquatic taiga habitats. First, their hair is hollow, giving them extra insulating warmth. Secondly, they have very broad hooves that make travel across snow and marshy areas easy, an ideal adaptation in the boreal habitat with its sedge and peat bogs, upland wooded areas, birch/willow thickets, and lichen beds. Their range overlaps with moose but also extends farther north across the tundra.

Only about 10 percent of the bird species found in the Viliui regions remain year-round. Those that do overwinter, the partridge, grouse, and guinea hen, limit their exposure by making only a few flights a day into trees to gorge on birch catkins and willow buds. The rest of the time they remain buried in snow up to their necks. Owls hunt through the winter for mice, voles, hares, and squirrels. Fish survive winter by feeding intensely during spring and summer to save enough reserves to survive the scarce winter. River fish either hibernate or are marginally active in the river's depth. Lake fish "sleep."

Human Adaptations to Extreme Northern Environments

Like the roots of the Dahurian larch, humans spread out across the sparse taiga ecosystem to survive. The core adaptive principle for northern peoples is an extensive and flexible use of the environment. In lieu of an ability to hibernate (although I have heard many Sakha lament their inability to do so), humans have developed ways to survive in the subarctic ecosystem similarly to how the flora and fauna do: by limiting their activity in winter and spending the short summer in intense preparation for winter survival.

Historically, human habitation of the Old World taiga regions, adjacent waterways, and coastal areas, with their limited capacity for land cultivation and domestic animal breeding, has been by reindeer-herding and foraging cultures. Tungus (Even and Evenk) and Tumat inhabited the Viliui regions before Sakha settlement and subsisted on a mixture of reindeer herding, and foraging (hunting, gathering, and fishing). Some depended solely on reindeer for their food, clothing, and transportation needs, others only on foraging, and still others on both. There was no land ownership or permanent dwellings, since survival required continual movement in concert with the natural cycles, moving with their animals and after forage resources with the seasons. Some research shows that these two subsistence modes were practiced interchangeably as one or the other became more favorable according to climatic fluctuations (Krupnik 1993).

Sakha Subsistence Adaptations to the Subarctic

Sakha were the first inhabitants of the subarctic ecosystem to successfully introduce horse and cattle husbandry. Their success was due to both environmental and cultural factors: 1) the wealth of natural hay fields throughout the Viliui and Lena regions, 2) their ability to harvest sufficient hay to overwinter their herds for an average of 220 days of foddering, and 3) the adaptive resilience of their horse and cattle husbandry culture. Keeping horses and cattle in the subarctic meant a higher energy requirement than in more temperate climates. They needed more energy physically (kilocalories to harvest fodder, tend the animals, and generate body heat), temporally (additional time to perform these extra tasks), and spatially (more extensive land and resource use required).[22] The times when pasture was available and harvest of fodder was possible were limited. Cattle were kept indoors nine months of the year, necessitating a lengthened period of direct, intensive animal maintenance including daily feeding and care. Sakha settlements were organized according to *agha uuha* (patrilineal clan) groupings, scattered extensively across the subarctic landscape (Iakovlev 1999).[23] Clan settlements utilized summer and winter areas (figure 1.3).

Sakha controlled access to subsistence resources and land via a highly stratified social structure, a technique seen in other pastoralist societies (Ruttan and Borgerhoff Mulder 1999:636). Wealthy Sakha *toions* (elite clan heads) maintained the largest herds and used extensive pasturelands, hay fields, and labor to do so. They exercised the right to use land, to keep others off that land, to pass that land on to their kin, and to reap "rents" from smaller herd owners who used parcels in return for a percentage of hay or animal produce. They often were provider-protectors for the needy members of the population and shared food in exchange for labor (Pakhomov 1999). The rest of the population depended on a mixed subsistence mirroring the indigenous Tungus strategies of hunting, fishing, and foraging. Poorer Sakha households, who could not afford cattle and had no *toion* to work for, relied solely on fish. This was so common that the word *baliksit* (fisher) was used synonymously for "poor person" (Tokarev and Gurvich 1956:250).

Protection from the Elements: Shelter, Clothing

Sakha adapted the pastoral nomadism of their Turkic ancestors to the subarctic by moving only twice a year between a summer and a winter dwelling. Sakha built their winter homes at high

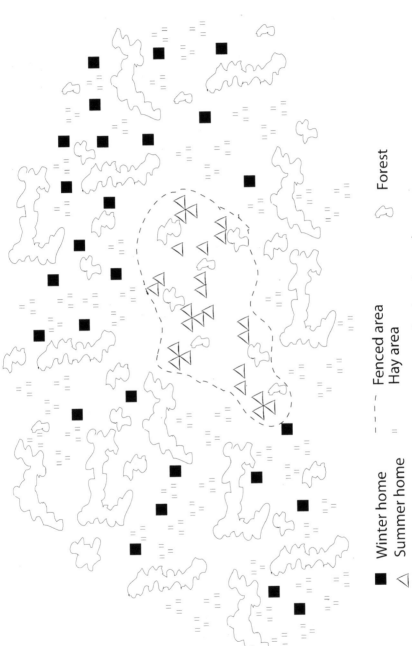

■ Winter home   - - - Fenced area   ⌒ Forest
△ Summer home   = Hay area

Figure 1.3.   *A clan settlement area, showing winter and summer areas*

elevations, to shelter from aggressive spring floods, and in wooded areas, to preserve pasturelands and for easy access to firewood. The *balaghan* (winter house)[24], was of simple construction and used a variety of timber sizes. It was built to conserve heat by being small in area and by having the cow barn attached (see figure 1.4 a, b, c). In vertical cross-section the structure was trapezoidal with vertical timbers placed at slight angles against a pole frame. Each autumn, household members sealed the structure with a mixture of cow dung and clay, applied in three layers each to a specific thickness to produce an insulative and impermeable layer. When the first snow fell, Sakha piled it high up around the *balaghan* for insulation. Sakha homestead yards were open with a variety of *ampaar* (outbuildings) to store tools, equipment, and food reserves, and several *dal* (corral) for the herds. Every homestead had a *sergei* (horse-hitching post) to secure a riding horse, usually with a horse head or other totem carved on the top.

Sakha covered the *balaghan* windows in the fall and spring with woven horsehair to keep out insects and, in winter with either thick ice, cow stomach, or afterbirth, stretched tightly over a frame to let in light (Kulakovski 1979:88). They cut and installed ice windows at about a 20-centimeter (7.8-inch) thickness and replaced them when they had thinned to several centimeters. This averaged three or four changes per winter season. The *balaghan* door faced east, so that the morning sun could warm the house. The structure had two halves; to the left of the main house entry was the side for people and to the right for the herd. *Balaghan* floors were earthen, except in richer Sakha homes that had wooden floors. Beds for household members ran along the walls of the main room, in order of the hierarchy within the household group. The main source of heat came from a *komuluok* (an open fire pit in the center of the room) supplemented only by the body heat of the herds. Sakha made the *komuluok*'s chimney from larch limbs and sealed it over with a mixture of clay and dung on the outside and pure clay on the inside. They stood firewood vertically in the pit to burn. With no flue, the *komuluok* burned constantly to keep the dwelling warm and to purify the air, which got quite thick from the herds. Elders today remember how the *komuluok* daily

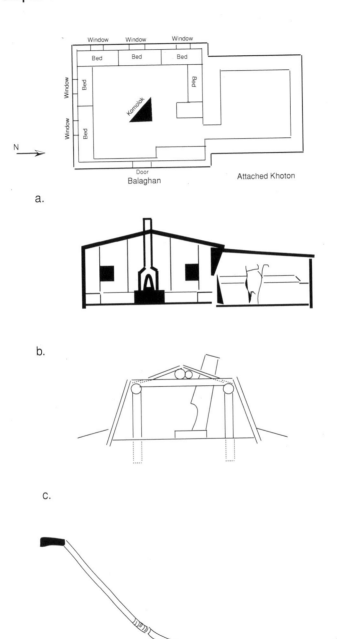

Figure 1.4.   Balaghan details and the Sakha scythe

burned an entire sledge load in winter, something they learned repeatedly since it was their job as youth to gather sticks and wood
from the forest floor to keep it fed.[25] The *komuluok* also gave Sakha
their sole source of light during the long dark winters.

After the floods of spring had subsided and the sun's warming
rays had brought new grasses, Sakha would move to the summer
dwelling. They located these in the woods on the edge of hay lands
so their herds could roam freely and graze in between the milking and food processing that went on throughout the temperate
months. Equally important, Sakha located their summer home
adjacent to forage areas for berries, plants, and fish and to the
nearby fields that they cut for winter fodder. Lastly, the summer
home had to be far enough from the *balaghan* to preserve its nearby
pasture for winter horse-grazing.[26] Most Sakha households sum-
mered in an *uraha* (an open, airy, birch bark teepee, resembling the
year-round dwelling of local Tungus). This protected them from
the sweltering summer heat. *Uraha* beds followed the *balaghan*
pattern, aligned along the walls in order of the household hierarchy. In the center was an open fire pit made in a clay-lined wooden
box. Smoke escaped via a hole at the *uraha*'s peak. Sakha had several pieces of simple furniture: short stools, chairs, and a table.
Clothing and belongings were kept in boxes. Every household
had a meat chopping block. On the floor to the right of the entry
door Sakha kept their tools for milking and containing milk. To
the left, they stored their tools for haying and working, including
all sizes of pitchforks, rakes, scythes, and shovels.[27]

Although it was typical for a household to have both a summer and winter dwelling, there was variance according to a
household's socioeconomic status. Wealthy households often had
several dwellings, and the poor, without herds, usually lived year-
round in the *balaghan*. The contrast in resources between households was great. Wealthy households had spotless homes, ate only
the finest cuts of their meat stores, used silver and china, wore
Russian clothes of fine cloth, and had several servants attending
them day and night. Most also had an "icon corner" (place for
prayer with Orthodox icons) in every dwelling. The poor lived
in filth with many children who ran naked even into their early
teens. A poor household of eight often had only one cow for all

their needs. Poor households had only a small number of wooden and birch utensils and at least one iron cook pot and often an iron skillet.

Sakha were skilled craftspeople. Early explorers to Siberia considered Sakha the most gifted of all the Siberian peoples (Maak 1994:371). Not only were they proficient carpenters and stone workers, but they were masters of wood and bone carving. They made beautiful knives, which they considered the most important tool for living. Sakha used a full array of tools and instruments to work leather, to build with wood, and to make wooden and birch bark containers and eating utensils. They made storage containers for milk and milk products from birch bark sewn with horse's hair and braced with either larch or pine roots. The exact shape, size, and name of each container depended on the kind of milk food it would be used for. Sakha fashioned intricately carved *chorons* (wooden chalices) in various shapes and sizes for daily and ritual drinking of *kymys* (fermented mare's milk). When there was an excessive amount of *kymys*, butter, and yogurt, they stored it in leather bags.

Sakha manufactured their shirts, pants, and dresses from calf-skin sewn with horsehair.[28] They used the insulating furs of taiga mammals to make coats, boots, hats, leggings, muffs, and gloves. They also fashioned some unique garments to protect themselves from invading cold. One was the wrist quilt, a small insulated button-on pad worn to cover the gap between the sleeve's end and the glove's beginning. Hats were commonly fashioned with an extended back panel to protect the nape of the neck from the bitter cold and were tight fitting around the face to prevent cold air from entering and freezing the temples. Other accessories included the *mooytoruk* (a hoop of several dozen squirrel tails looped several times around the neck) and *baachchy* (fur-lined vests and pants, both with removable linings).[29]

Animal Husbandry

Horses and cows have always been the central subsistence domesticates of Sakha. Historically and today Sakha depend on their meat, milk, and organs as their main food sources and use their hides, hair, and bones as materials for clothing, utensils, tools, decorative arts, and utilitarian purposes. Like other subsistence peoples relying on one or two main animals for survival, Sakha have a practical knowledge base pertaining to daily and cyclical care of the animals and a belief system that orients their use of the animals within the spiritual realm.

Horses: Sakha believe that the horse was the first creation of *Urung Ayii Toion* (Great Lord Master) the highest god of Sakhas' sky pantheon. "In the beginning, god made the horse and from it came the half-man half-horse and from there humans were born" (Seroshevski 1993:253). Sakha cultural practices make clear their high regard for the horse. Stories, songs, and the *Olonkho* (the Sakhas' epic poem), depict the horse as humans' main counselor, friend, and supporter who lends wisdom, keen insight, nobility, and modesty. Often the horse serves as its masters' advocate before the gods (Seroshevski 1993:253).

Up until the nineteenth century Sakha kept more horses than cattle (Seroshevski 1993:250; Maak 1994:332). The horse was Sakhas' most prized domestic animal and their major source of transportation, food, and clothing materials. Sakha intricately decorated their riding horses far beyond any utilitarian need, out of their spiritual respect for the animal. The horse accompanied them on all their tasks involving subsistence and was their closest friend. Sakha fulfilled many rituals and traditions to honor their horses. Undoubtedly, these beliefs and traditions were based in Sakhas' Tatar-Mongol origins, the source of all their horse culture.[30] At least two theories explain how Sakha horses came to the subarctic: 1) that they were a Mongolic race, brought when Sakhas' Turkic ancestors came north, and 2) that they were northern residents from long before, based on twentieth-century archaeological remains of wild horses dating back to the wooly mammoth era (Nikolaev 1970). Sakha had many unique horse husbandry techniques. In late winter, when they gave their horses supplemental hay, they mixed snow into the fodder to maintain the horses' strong teeth, since the snow made the hay easier on the teeth (Seroshevski 1993:161).

Sakha consider the horse to be clean, pure, and good. They will not leave the skull or skeleton of a horse on the ground but will hang it from a nearby tree. *Sergei* are sacred and left to stand until they fall down on their own. Even when rich Sakha with ornate decorated *sergei* would move, they left the post since it was considered that disturbing it would bring bad luck (Seroshevski 1993:252). Horses are considered the spirit residents of the upper world, whereas cows are the spirit inhabitants of the earth (middle world). A horse is the only sacrifice for the upper gods, and only a second-class spirit is given a cow in sacrifice. The base of *chorons*, the legs of tables and the other ornamentation on furniture are always in the form of horse legs, hooves, and heads—never a cow's. It is considered the highest compliment to compare a young girl with a mare and a boy with a stallion—and the lowest insult to compare either to cow forms (Seroshevski 1993:253). The ropes and bunches of hair used in rituals are always from the horse—either horse mane or tail. Bunches of horse hair adorn marriage and other ritual chorons. The *yhyakh*, Sakhas' main ethnic celebration is foremost a tribute to the horse. In the *ohuokhai*, Sakhas' circle dance, they sing about the horse and colt but never about the cow (Seroshevski 1993:252).

Cows: Up until the 1930s Sakha used a local cattle, the *Bos taurus* Sakha (Yakut) breed. It could live outside to temperatures of −50°C, finding the majority of its fodder under the snow, and it grazed opportunistically, like a modern goat, utilizing a variety of grasses and other plant materials. It was known to graze in surrounding forestlands and swamps, and to swim across water to reach pasture. The Polish ethnographer Seroshevski, writing in 1896 about Sakha culture and environment, referred several times to the adaptive qualities of Sakha cattle, "Sakha cattle can stand bad weather, hunger, cold, eat everything (twigs of birch, aspen, willow, cane, and fodder under the snow), eat very little, fatten quickly, and survive for a long time off their own fat reserves" (Seroshevski 1993:144–149). Sakha also used bulls extensively for transportation, work animals, and in hunting (Maak 1994:331).

In comparison to the European breeds that the Soviet government brought in to the collective and state farms across the Soviet Union, Sakha cattle possessed many redeeming adaptations for the northern climes. Although on average they gave less milk than their European counterparts, the milk was higher in fat content and provided needed calories in the subarctic climate. They were also more efficient in "milk manufacture," using only 65 percent of the feed that European breeds needed to produce an equal amount of milk. Sakha cattle had an increased growth rate in the short summers, and calves could gain up to 765 grams (24.5 ounces) per day as compared to the 580 grams (18.6 ounces) gained by European breeds. Sakha cattle could continue to produce high quality milk and meat on relatively low-quality fodder, and were resistant to various diseases that wiped out European herds including tuberculosis, brucellosis, and leukosis. Their coat was three times longer and four times thicker than European cattle, and it increased in density sixfold in winter.

Sakha cows could survive the subarctic climate year round, but most Sakha kept them in one half of their *balaghan* throughout the long winter as a heat source and for convenient milking. In deep winter Sakha took their herd to water once daily. Sakha began letting their cattle out to pasture beginning in early May with nightly returns until early June, when they were left to graze all night and day. By early September, Sakha began feeding supplemental hay to make up for the decline in grass as winter began. To replenish meat stores and take advantage of the nine-month subzero temperatures, Sakha annually slaughtered in November and stored animal products in either a protected outbuilding or in a *buluus* (a deep hole nearing the permafrost where foodstuffs remained frozen year-round). Having a storage capacity was an advantage compared to more southerly cow cultures, who only consumed meat for special feasts, and relied daily on milk and blood.[31]

In summer, milk was in bounty. Sakha kept milk reserves in a *taar ampaar* (a specialized building for milk products). Milk sat in *chabychakh* (shallow, wide, birch containers, that Sakha could skim cream off of daily). Sakha put excess milk reserves into *taar* (a fermented milk mash). This they prepared by first boiling and culturing milk into yogurt then adding excess milk as it was available over the summer. *Taar* stores were continuously supplemented with table scraps, including berries, herbs, and the bones from duck, fish, and game. In the fall the *taar* froze and Sakha cut it off in slabs for winter use, either eating it as a runny yogurt by whipping a small amount of water into it and adding wild grasses, herbs, and pine or larch pulp, or as a thick gruel with the addition of pine tree flour and/or ground grains. Sakha also used milk reserves for *khaiakh* (made in the same manner as butter but with added soured cream). Another favorite milk food was *kurchuk* (whipped cream sometimes with berries added for flavor).

Sakha spent summer harvesting hay to fodder their cattle. Hay was cut only after July 21, when the grasses had reached their full maturity and were at their prime ripeness and peak biomass.[32] Up until the 1890s, Sakha used a handled blade to cut hay, swung overhead in a circular manner (figure 1.4 d). Men and boys cut the hay initially, then all the household and extended family members raked, gathered, and stacked the hay. Haystacks were large to conserve the fodder quality since the less surface area exposed meant the less vitamin-depleting effects of sun and moisture. Sakha hayed adjacent to their winter dwelling for convenience during winter use. Summer work also included the maintenance of pasture for the year-round use of Sakhas' horses. Sakha practiced the controlled burning of trees and shrubs encroaching on fields. For the first years following a burn, they used the fertile areas for hay harvesting, then transitioned it to pastureland (Nikolaev 1970).

Often, finding enough hay nearby was a problem. If Sakha were unable to cut sufficient hay grasses, they would supplement the harvest with less palatable plants, including straw, lake reed, tussocks, larch branches, and assorted shrubs. Sakha would drain hay fields that were too wet or divert water to fields that were too dry for optimal hay growth. Sakha also made new hay areas to meet high fodder needs. The most common way was the draining of *alaas* lakes, an activity that required a local specialist to determine how to build proper canals. Lake draining was labor-intensive because canals often went through old larch forests that needed uprooting with axes, picks, and shovels. Canal digging was done either while the lake water was free to flow or when it was held back to be released later. The latter was easier digging but more accident-prone. Ethnographic accounts tell that in 1835 when Sakha were digging canals, when they let the water through, it came in such abundance that it took several workers with it (Nikolaev 1970). Sakha understood such accidents as being caused by an angered lake's spirit-keeper. For this reason Sakha would habitually fulfill a special ritual of animal sacrifice to appease the spirit. The larger the water body, the more powerful the spirit-keeper, and the greater the sacrificial offering needed. Sakha summoned a shaman to make the offering and to ask forgiveness for the poor herders who brought such unrest to the grandmother lake but who found it necessary to drain for their survival (Nikolaev 1970). Sometimes they opted to empty the lake only partially at first to expose the lake perimeter, which served as a fertile hay area for a few years while they could continue to exploit the lake fish.

Water and Wild Forage

For water, Sakha utilized the surface waters of adjacent rivers, streams, and lakes. In winter they harvested and melted ice (figure 1.5) or made *tammakh* (literally "water drop"), a forked branch packed solid with snow and hung by the *komuluok* with the melt water dripping into a birch-bark pan below. In winter, animals drank directly from an *oibon*. Sakha covered the *oibon* with several layers of animal hides or other insulating material, to protect them from freezing.

Sakha supplemented their diet with forage, game, and fish to the extent that they relied on domestic food production. Wealthy Sakha households, with their sizable herds, relied on a diet high in meat and milk and few wild sources. Within the Viliui regions, domestic horse and cow products were only the dominant foods in the more wealthy households of the Suntar and Markha (Nyurba) *uluse*s (regions), areas where there were ample hay fields to fodder herds and households had the land and labor resources to tend herds, harvest hay, and oversee their estate.[33] The middle and lower-class households of Suntar and Markha and other Viliui regions relied mainly on forage sources and considered meat second to their main food source of fish. Of all foraging resources, fishing was the more important supplement to domestic food sources, especially in middle to poor households.

Figure 1.5.   Contemporary Sakha continue to harvest ice for drinking water

Sakha depended more on lake fish than river species, even though the Viliui teemed with valuable fish including salmon, sturgeon, and trout. They preferred the lake fish, *sobo* (*Carassius carassius*) and caught it by one of three methods, either *kuyuur,* *mungkha,* or *ilim. Kuyuur* took advantage of early spring conditions when *sobo* floated in torpor (semisleep) near the under-side of the lake ice. Sakha would cut a 2-foot wide hole in the lake ice and swirl a *kuyuur* (a long wooden pole with a basket shape catch at the end) to gather the fish. In early winter, Sakha fished with a *mungkha* (large sweep net), which they placed under the ice at one end of the lake, pulled it across the lake water via a se-ries of holes, and brought it up at the far end, effectively netting the majority of fish in the lake. In the temperate months when lakes were ice-free Sakha used *ilim* (standing nets) which they harvested from daily. Since fishing nets were made of horsehair, only those households with herds owned nets and organized fish-ing parties within the settlements. Poor households, who lacked nets, relied on *mundushky* (*Cyprinus perenurus*), a small, bitter fish which was extremely time consuming to catch and clean. Fish were eaten fried or boiled and also stored for winter use by dry-ing or freezing in a *buluus*.

Sakha households also hunted water and wood fowl, bear, moose, squirrel, and hare to supplement domestic meat sources. They used bow and arrow, spears, and traps, most commonly the *samostrel* (R., self-firing crossbow). They even used a bull for cam-ouflage to approach prey, jumping up to shoot when they were in close range (Tokarev 1958:460).[34] Sakha hunted moose and bear, in parties. Unlike local Tungus, who hunted bear "head-on" with spear and bow, Sakha hunted when the bear was in its den and used spears and rifles in a hunting party of twenty or so. Sakha caught waterfowl with snares and traps during the two annual migrations in fall and spring. They used dogs extensively to hunt duck and geese during the molting period. A good hunting dog was routinely able to earn more than its keep.

Sakha harvested roots, leaves, and fruits from over thirty dif-ferent wild plants. The most common wild plants they used were sorrel (*Rumex acetosa*), horseradish (*Cochlearia sisymbroides*), wild onion and garlic (*Allium schoenoprasum* and *Allium lineare*), and sardana (*Lilium spectabile*) (Seroshevski 1993:306–307). They made various tonics and dishes from plants, ground indigenous grain to make a gruel called *salamaat*,[35] and made *kasha* or gruel from many plants of the plantago family (Seroshevski 1993:63–64).[36] Sakha also harvested a variety of wild berries that grew in the nearby woods and fields. This was mostly for fresh use since they had no access to sugar for preserving the fruit. They did not eat wild mushrooms prior to Russian colonization even though the woods were full of them in four or five varieties (Seroshevski 1993:308).

For flour, most Sakha used sap wood, either pine or larch.[37] To harvest sapwood, Sakha cut a tree in June or July, removed the bark, stripped long pieces out of the sapwood, and dried it first by a fire to prevent spoilage, then in the sun. They next stored the strips in bunches and hung them in a dry place. When they needed flour, they pulverized the strips in a *kelii* (a hand mill made from a vertically hollowed-out log in which materials are pounded with a club). Sakha mixed this sapwood flour into boiling *taar* with fresh milk and dried herbs for taste. Some harvested and ground the wild local grains. However, this did not produce the quantities needed for a household. In the 1700s Russians introduced domestic grains. However, it was only the better-off Sakha households who had the labor force to plant, harvest, grind, and save enough seed for planting the following season.[38] The majority went without this luxury and used sapwood for flour until the next century.

The Annual Production Calendar

Sakha used a thirteen-month lunar calendar up until the last century. Most months were named after the main subsistence activity of that time. The Sakha celebrated the New Year in late May. The first month, *Bes yia*, or "pine month," was the time to harvest pine sapwood. Table 1.1 charts the months and their meanings. October through February were named after the number they held in the thirteen-month lunar cycle, since there was little subsistence activity at those times.

Sakha Gender, Kinship, and Marriage

Sakha maintained clearly delineated gender roles to run their households and produce food in the harsh Siberian climate.

Table 1.1. Sakha Months and their Meanings

Sakha Month	English Month	Sakha Meaning
Bes Yia	June	"Pine" month, marking the month to harvest pine
Ot Yia	July	"Hay" month, marking the beginning of the haying season
Atyrjakh Yia	August	"Pitchfork" month, marking the time to make the stacks of hay
Balaghan Yia	September	"Winter home" month, the time to move to the winter home
Altynny Yia	October	"Sixth" month
Setinni Yia	November	"Seventh" month
Aksynny Yia	December	"Eighth" month
Toksunnu Yia	January	"Ninth" month
Olunnu Yia	February	"Tenth" month
Kulun Tutar	March	"Holding the Colts" month, marking the time to hold the colts from their mothers so households can consume some horse milk
Muus Ustar	April	"Ice Going" month, time to remove the ice *balaghan* windows.
Yam Yia	May	"Spawning" month, marking the month the fish spawn

Women were responsible for all inside activities. Their work included maintaining the living area and hearth; preparing and preserving food; making and repairing the family clothing; making containers and utensils of hides, hair, birch bark, and clay; caring for children; and tending the herds in barns throughout the long nine-month winter. Men were responsible for the outside tasks. The list was equally long, and entailed harvesting the hay to overwinter the herds, tending to all the daily outside work for the herds, hunting and fishing, the daily gathering of firewood,[39] procuring drinking water, building all the living and other structures on the homestead, managing the fences for the hay fields, slaughtering animals, woodworking, and blacksmithing. In the brief months of summer, both sexes worked and toiled in the warmth of the long subarctic days. Men cut the hay while women raked it into small piles. Men hunted and fished while the women foraged for berries, roots, and herbs.

Sakha kept strict kinship and marriage protocols. Households were made up of intergenerational extended kin. Sakha observed the principles of lineal exogamy. As the late nineteenth-century explorer Seroshevski noted, "Sakha always take wives originating from foreign clans and from as far away as possible" (Seroshevski 1993:308). Sakha considered nine generations as blood kin whom they could not marry. Any relations beyond the ninth generation were allowable. Some research show early Sakha counting fourteen levels out of their blood kin before they could consider marriage (Sleptsov 1989:11).[40]

Until their exposure to Christianity in the late eighteenth and early nineteenth century, Sakha practiced polygamy, most commonly among *toions*, the local clan heads and members of the wealthy class. Ides and Brandt, explorers of the late seventeenth century, noted that about one-third of all Sakha men had more than one wife. They concluded, "Sakha take as many wives as they can feed"(1967:288). In 1789, F. I. Langas listed the reasons that Sakha took many wives:

1. Sakha marry off their children at an early age and so when the men grow up they fall out of love and take a second wife;
2. They also take a second and a third wife, if the initial marriage(s) do not produce children;
3. They then can increase their herds by having each wife tend cows based at different homesteads;
4. They replace wives who prove to be poor herd keepers; and
5. By having a child-bearing wife at every homestead, they maximize the chances of having many children who can work and carry on their herds. (Sleptsov 1989:11–12)

The main reason to have many wives was for care of the herds. The wealthier a Sakha man, the greater his herds and hay land areas, and the more wives he needed. The wealthiest *toions* had from seven to nine wives, with the first acting as female household head. She and her children held first rights over all other wives and their children. The number of polygamous households sharply declined in the late eighteenth and early nineteenth century due to conversion to Christianity. After polygamy waned, women continued as the main keepers of the household herds.

Sakha followed several marriage customs. Commonly, parents promised children from a young age by a groom's parents paying a token of bride price.[41] Sakha betrothed their children in the first years of their lives but only gave the bride after exchange of the dowry and full *kurum* (bride price). The gifts and payment were done mutually. The bride's father gave a dowry of herds, allotting ten or more of horses and of cows, for a total of twenty to thirty head. He then demanded *kurum*, a bride price payment from the groom's side. This was paid in several head of horses or cattle each year for a total of fifteen to twenty head in a ten-year period. The groom also was expected to pay money, first in silver and the rest in credit notes. Finally, the groom would give "the sleeping gift," of three or four sides of horsemeat, which allowed him to sleep with his new wife. The woman made residence in the man's house. There she brought all the instruments and utensils that were needed to work in the domestic sphere. Sakha made inheritance only to sons. In the event of her husband's death, a widower was entitled to nothing, but was expected to rely on her sons to care for her with the inheritance they are given.

Another common tradition that facilitated the strict rules of lineal exogamy was *Agasin Ungyogun Tunnerii*, literally, "Return to the Sister's Bones." This involved a husband giving his sister to marry the brother of his wife, or "sister exchange," a simple and easy form of marital exchange (Fox 1983:180). Sakha also took up marriage to the wife of their deceased older brother on the occasion of the latter's death. Similarly, they would marry the younger sister(s) of their wife if the latter was infertile (Sleptsov 1989:15).

Sakha were socialized to be very inward and hold their emotions and feelings to themselves even in their most intimate relations within the household. Sakha women played the role of subordinate, as they were not only responsible for all the domestic chores but also for the care of the herds and children. Women were never idle, always busy with preparing the household meals and stores, working leather, making the family clothes, and raising and training the children. They never took time for personal care, even to stop for childbirth, a challenge they facilitated along with the many others through negotiations with the spirit world.

Negotiating with the Spirit World: Metaphysical Adaptation to the Extreme

The original Sakha belief is animistic and ascribes all animate and inanimate things with spirit (Maak 1994:280–297; Seroshevski 1993:593–655; Jochelson 1933:103–106; Gogolev 1994). To Sakha, the world is divided into three realms: the *khallaan* (upper), *orto* (middle), and *allaraa* (lower).[42] *Khallaan*, or upper world, is home to the *aiyy* (gods), organized in a nine-tiered pantheon, each level a home to one or more deity protectors. *Urung Aiyy Toion*, creator of all the universe, inhabits the highest tier. The deities below are manifestations of that essential power. The next most highly regarded are *Juhugey*, who sends horses to people of the middle world (Pekarski 1959 (1899):854), and *Aan Alakhchyn*, the deity of spring and fertility.

Orto Doidu, the middle world is home to earthly beings and *ichchi* (spirit keepers of nature). Sakha believe that all things animate and inanimate, including trees, rocks, and even words, have *ichchi*. They pay regular respect to the fire, forest, and earth *ichchi* and of them, it is *wot ichchite* (the fire spirit), to whom they give the highest regard. Personifying this spirit as a gray-haired elder man, Sakha regularly "feed" *wot ichchite* food and drink to solicit his continued protection of the home hearth. Sakha also use fire as a conduit to transfer gifts to the upper world *aiyy*. The earth *ichchi*, *Jaajay Baraan Khotun*, is personified as an old woman, an image carried over "from the times when women held a central role in society" (Ergis 1974:117). The spirits of plants, in the form of tiny children, assist her by cleaning and dusting the leaves and grasses. Sakha make offering to *Jaajay Baraan Khotun* when foraging, haying, and moving to their summer home. During hunting, Sakha pay tribute to *Baianai* (the spirit keeper of the taiga, forest, and all wild animals). Sakha imagine him as a jolly red-or black-haired elder wearing a coat of reindeer skin and either riding a reindeer or running through the forest.

Allaraa Doidu, the lower world, is an impassable swamp, inhabited by steel plants and *abaahy* (evil spirits), who represent the source of all existing and potential evil. *Abaahy* are in constant pursuit of middle world inhabitants. Sakha rely on the *ichchi* and *aiyy* for protection from the *abaahy*, by performing daily and annual rituals. When Sakha make the annual move in late May or early June from the *balaghan* to the *saylyyk* (summer home), the family perform the ritual *salama yiaahyna*, or hanging of the *salama*, a rope of twisted black and white horse's hair adorned with pieces of colored fabric, animal figures made from birch bark, duck beaks, and fish bones. Family members first light a fire and feed their best foods to *wot ichchite* while singing *algys* (a ritual song prayer):

> You, sacred fire, elder, gift giver,
> Protector of our place and our elder
> Who gives us strength and spirit
> And pardons, we will always bow before you
> Let joyful be, let joyful be. (Ignataev 1992)

Then the ritual moves to the lake adjacent to the *saylyyk*, where the family hangs the *salama* as a gift to the lake *ichchi*.[43] Once again, the *ichchi* are "fed" gifts to the intoning of *algys*:

> You, gift giver of the lake
> Who gives us food, and life and pleasure
> And existence and being,
> And pardons, we will always bow before you
> Let joyful be, let joyful be. (Ignataev 1992)

Following the rituals, seasonal work begins. Throughout the temperate months Sakha pasture and tend to their herds. They hunt duck and other wild game and gather herbs, plants, pine sapwood, and berries for winter use. They take birch bark from the trees and make a variety of containers and utensils. In July they begin the cutting, gathering, and stacking of sufficient hay for winter fodder. The hay-cutting season also begins with a ritual ceremony in honor of the earth spirits and sky deities:

> The rich time of summer has come
> All the heat of the sun has brought the strong green grass
> Give us the best grass
> So that in the winter our herds aren't hungry
> And so there will be more herds
> Help us to make the most grass
> We are joyful and we give you, through the fire,
> The sweets and fat meat and the richest cows milk
> And the strongest *kymys* to you
> We praise you with that. (Ignataev 1992)

Through the short summer, Sakha store away milk by making *taar*; gathering and storing berries and plants; and salting, drying, fermenting, and freezing fish for winter use. They return to the *balaghan* in early September, a move also marked by a ritual ceremony.

Sakha perform rituals for the births of people, cows, and horses, each recognizing the appropriate sky deities and earth spirit protectors. Sakha women face the challenge of childbirth with the assistance of *Aiyyhyt*, the Goddess of Childbirth, a female deity carried over from the Sakhas' matrilineal clan structure of the Paleolithic period (Okladnikov 1970:35–37). *Aiyyhyt* arrives seven days before the onset of labor to ease the process and stays for three days following childbirth to assist the woman. On the third day, *Aiyyhyt* leaves the mother, and Sakha women perform a special ceremony in her dedication. They smear their faces with warm fat and laugh hysterically, the more strongly they laugh, the more pleased *Aiyyhyt* is and the greater the insurance is for the life-long happiness of the new child (Kulakovski 1979).

The Sakhas' human mediator of the spirit world is the *oiuun* (shaman), a person born with or indoctrinated into possessing supernatural powers. Sakha have both *urung* (white) and *khara* (black) *oiuun*. The *urung oiuun*'s main role is the benevolent priest who mediates the sky world deities during the *yhyakh* festival.[44] The *khara oiuun* can travel throughout the three worlds and utilize the powers of good and evil. They combat illness and bad fate for humans. The *khara oiuun* knows which *abaahy* are the troubling source and his/her soul travels between the three worlds to fight it by their "spirit horse." The *khara oiuun* personifies the horse's rhythmic canter by a *dungur* (shaman drum) and by speaking and singing prayers (Alekseev 1975:162). Reaching the lower world, the *oiuun* chases the particular *abaahy* away, healing the ailing person. In the past the *khara oiuun* annually conducted a fall blood sacrifice of horse or cattle to the *abaahy*, a ritual event no longer practiced (Troshanski 1902:130).

The Sakha belief system, with its annual rituals and daily practices, works to mediate survival in an extreme climate. It also instills an essential environmental ethic by positing humans as part of, not conquerors of, the natural world. Sakha consider themselves guests of the middle world and their main duty is to placate the earth and sky spirits who in turn would provide for them. In the last century many Sakha moved away from this belief system because of the oppression of religious and sacred belief and the atheistic propaganda of the Soviet period. Sakha are working to revive the belief. Contemporary elders frequently comment about how modern Sakha treat nature. They remember doing only what they needed to do in order to subsist and when they did find it necessary to alter the natural world in some way, (burning to clear, draining to create pastures) they did it with minimal impact, accompanied with rituals and offerings to the spirits. The change in the accessing of hay lands is one of the starkest examples of the loss of a Sakha environmental ethic. Elders explain that early Sakha traveled to hay fields along trails in the adjacent woods to preserve the hay lands they considered sacred. Today hay lands are accessed recklessly and left scored with ruts from the multiple routes of heavy trucks and tractors. Unimpacted hay lands are few. In the subarctic ecosystem, these impacted areas take a long time to rejuvenate and their unique hydrological abilities to access melt water during summer droughts are impeded. Another stark example of the lack of a contemporary environmental ethic is the profusion of garbage in the woods surrounding contemporary villages. Similarly, hunting is now more of a grab-all-you-can-get activity, which contemporary elders claim is a grave insult to *Baianai*, the spirit of the hunt.

Although much is changing in how Sakha use and regard their environment, Sakha exemplify a stellar case of human adaptation and resilience. The subarctic ecosystem continually challenges all who call it their home, be they plants, animals, or humans. Those who inhabit this extreme habitat have done so through various ways of adapting. Indigenous flora are successful because they have a tolerance for the stressors of the subarctic environment. Native fauna survive by protecting themselves from the extreme cold either through hibernation or adaptive burrowing and insulation techniques. Viliui Sakha survive by sheltering their herds through the long winters and providing fodder for this period from an intensive summer hay harvest, adaptations that make them the only modern horse and cattle herders in the subarctic. Viliui Sakhas' successful adaptation is also based on a resilient belief system. By exploring the Sakhas' sacred world we see that successful agropastoralist adaptation in the subarctic is contingent on maintaining the proper relationships with the spirit world. But Sakha also have and continue to face many other challenges to their survival beyond adaptation to an extreme climate. In the last half millennium other peoples have come to make a home in Sakhas' area of Siberia. Sakha have also needed to negotiate the political changes over time and the growing forces of globalization and modernity—the focus of the next chapter.

Notes

1. *Gulag* is the Russian acronym that translates in English to "Chief Administration of Labor Camps."

2. Norse settlers arrived on Greenland between about AD 800 and 1000 with an economy based on domestic cattle. However, due to the 1250–1300 climate change and the Norses' inability to adapt alternative subsistence strategies, their settlement vanished within several centuries.

3. This protection also explains why Siberian permafrost extends farther south—in some cases to the same latitudes as Kiev, Paris, and Vienna—than permafrost in other parts of the contemporary world (Jochelson 1933).

4. The highest barometric pressure world area, which from October through March lies above Central Asia.

5. In Verkhoiansk (NE Sakha) the temperatures drop as much as 39°C (102°F) in one month.

6. In a calm at −45°C (−50°F), heat loss is comparable to the loss of heat at −19°C (−3°F) with moderate wind, or the loss of heat at 0°C (32°F) in a gale.

7. In Verkhoiansk rising an average of 1.08°F a day—the fastest in the world.

8. There are 116 frost-free days in the Viliui regions from May 27 through September 20 (Maak 1994, 413).

9. There are substantial mountains in Sakha but in the central and Viliui areas the landscape is mostly flat.

10. Technically described as "a negative form of 'mesorelief,'" usually with a lake, occupied by marsh, meadow, and steppe vegetation, which appears as a result of the degradation of the ice complex [permafrost] of Quaternary deposit and, in connection with that, the settling of the mixing sediment (Notes from the Yaroslavski Museum in Yakutsk with information credited to P. A. Solovyev).

11. "Boreal" is from the Greek, meaning "north." Boreal forests are found only in the Northern Hemisphere.

12. Occupying a belt in places 1,000 kilometers (621 miles) wide, in a band between 50 to 65° N latitude.

13. If compared to tropical ecosystems, where one hectare can contain more than three hundred species; in boreal forests one hectare can contain about thirty species.

14. Extreme lows in colder boreal forests reach −70°C (−94°F) and in warmer, only to −23°C (−9.4°F). Annual precipitation ranges from 10–20 centimeters (3.94–7.87 inches) in colder boreal forests and 50–90 centimeters (19.7–35.4 inches) in the warmer. Maximum day-length ranges from sixteen hours in southern boreal ecosystems to twenty-four hours in northern. A variety of soils determines water and nutrient availability.

15. The remainder in Europe and North America.

16. *Picea obovata* (Norway spruce) is also well adapted—tolerant to aridity, shade, and climate extremes and found across the boreal biome.

17. Due to the adjacent Verkhoiansk range that blocks influx of moderating air masses from the Pacific.

18. In 1965 the predominant Viliui trees were: 80 percent larch, 13 percent pine, 5 percent birch, and 2 percent spruce. Other main tree species include *Picea obovata* Ledeb. Syn. *Picea abies* var. *obovata*

(Norway Spruce), *Pinus sylvestris* L. (Scotch Pine), *Pinus sibirica* (Siberian Pine), *Populus tremula* L. (Quaking Aspen), and a variety of birch: *Betula alba, Betula pubescens* (Ehrh.), *Betula pendula* (Roth.), and *Betula exilis* (Sukacz).

19. The Viliui watershed is home to 882 floral species including 622 vascular plants, 189 mosses, and 64 lichens.

20. There are eight fur-bearing species including sable, arctic fox, common fox, muskrat, squirrel, ermine (weasel), kolinsky, and hare. In addition to those major hunting species, other commonly hunted species include weasel, wolverine, lynx, wolf, chipmunk, and water rat.

21. Of the mammal species the Altai mole, river otter, lynx, and roe deer are endangered and registered in the Red Book of Sakha, a registry of rare and endangered flora and fauna. Thirty-four bird species have protected status on the Republic, Russia, and worldwide levels.

22. Some Sakha adapted by relying more on the indigenous Tungus strategies of hunting, fishing, and foraging.

23. *Agha uuha* and *Iye uuha*, are the lineage of kin nine generations on the father's (*agha*) or mother's (*iye*) side. *Nasleg* (R., district or county) were headed by the highest, richest, and most intelligent clan head referred to as *kniaz* (R., prince) (Maak 1994:197).

24. "Balaghan is from a Persian word introduced by Russians." (Seroshevski 1993:338).

25. *Komuluok* fires burned quickly, did not hold heat, and gave only radiant heat. Modern, flued, multichambered woodstoves used by Sakha burn relatively little wood and give off convective heat for hours after burning.

26. Hay is not prepared for horses because they live outside year round and dig under the snow to graze.

27. Sakha used another conical structure, the *ityan*, for large-game seasonal hunting in the deep taiga, made of limbs placed vertically to a common center.

28. With the exception of wealthy Sakha who traded with southern Asian cultures for silk and other woven fabrics.

29. Along with the post-Soviet revival of Sakha fashion, there is renewed interest in how early Sakha clothing was designed to protect the body and keep it healthy against the cold.

30. Reindeer played a minimal role in the Sakha homestead but for Tungus households they represented a household's entire wealth by providing all transportation and hauling, all food and necessary materials.

31. For example, some of the bovine-centered cultures of temperate Africa: Nuer (Evans-Pritchard 1940) and Turkana (Little and Leslie 1999).

32. Except for the rich who began earlier in order to cut all their land.

33. In 1864 the highest cattle population was within the Suntar *ulus* but the highest ratio of cattle to people was in the Nurba *ulus* with 3.6 head per person, followed by Suntar with 2.7 head per person.

34. This is a unique technique found in no other culture and may have evolved from the Tungus way of hunting from behind a reindeer, or the steppe tradition of baiting an animal from horseback (Tokarev 1958:460).

35. These could have included any of the wild grains available, including wild oats (*Bromus inermis* and *B. ciliatus*), barley (*Hordeum prateuse* and *H. jubatum*), and rye (*Elymus dasystachys* and *E. excelsus*).

36. Including *Plantago major*, *P. paludosa*, *P. asiatic*, *P. canescens*, and *P. media*.

37. The use of pinesap wood for flour was least common in the Suntar *ulus*, where grain growing had the most success and where households were generally wealthier. Native Americans had two ways of using White Pine (*Pinus strobus*). They boiled the firm male cones in spring to eat and they used the inner bark as flour.

38. See chapter 3 section on domestic production about the introduction of grains, potatoes, and vegetables.

39. In pre-Soviet times Sakha did not harvest firewood annually but gathered it daily from the adjacent woods.

40. This sounds impossible considering the low density of the society at the time.

41. Commonly, the father of a toddler boy gave a *surekh* (heart necklace) to the same-class father of a toddler girl to ensure their joining when they came of age.

42. I change here to the present tense since many Sakha still embrace their traditional belief system.

43. *Salama* symbolizes the sky deities' "road" down to the earth and is an invitation for them to visit the middle world and be present during ritual.

44. For Sakha, the *urung oiuun* fulfills the function of a priest at the Sakhas' annual *yhyakh* festival, first noted in the eighteenth century (ILLA, 1). Later researchers describe *urung oiuun* as holy priests who

play a benevolent role without shamanic costume and who are not related to the more powerful "black shamans" (Romanova 1987, 15). In contrast to *khara oiuun*, *urung oiuun* use no drum and do not travel to the lower spirit world, but perpetuate goodness and fertility. Their main role remains praying and making offerings at the *yhyakh*.

2

Viliui Historical Ecology

To understand Sakhas' adaptation to the historical changes since they have made a home on the Viliui, we now turn our attention to the history of human settlement of the area. The peopling, by various cultures, of the Viliui regions over the last millennium has resulted in a diverse and dynamic cultural and physical landscape. Early human settlement was founded on extensive foraging and reindeer-herding. Sakha next introduced horse and cattle agropastoralism, which in the last century was transformed into centralized agro-industrial production. Sakha have played a central role in these changes, first as subduers then as subservient colonies to Russian and Soviet forces. The first part of this historical exploration is the story of how Sakha came to the subarctic initially.

Southern Origins

Sakha understand their Turkic ancestors' move to the north in the story of Omogoi and Ellai:

> At the foot of the mountains lived a man named Khonyos-Khaippar. He had four sons. One day he went hunting. With his arrow he shot a bird with beautiful multi-colored plumage. While plucking the bird he cut off the two wings and the tail. He gave two of his sons each a wing and another the tail. The last son was offended and angry and said crying, "He gave to his favorite sons but he didn't give me anything." From that time he held a grudge against his parents and held it in his mind to run away from them to a distant land. Khonyos-Khaippar was a Tatar.[1] He had a friend named Khogkhor-Saara. One day

43

he told his friend, "to the northeast of us, in all likelihood, is a beautiful country where those same beautifully plumed birds spend summer and get very fat." The fourth son hearing this and without saying a word to his parents, disappeared with his wife. He was called Omogoi and was about 70 years old. He found the headwaters of the Lena and, sitting on a floating tree, came downstream.

One day Khonyos-Khaippar was again with his friend and crying, told about how his son had disappeared, "When I told that day about the northeast country, the son listened with special interest. More than likely he ran to that empty place where there are no people and no herds. Because of that there is no news of him." When Khogkhor-Saara got to his home he told about the escape of his friend's son to his family. He also had a few sons of which one was named Ellai, whom his parents didn't love. Ellai, hearing his parents' telling of the escape of Omogoi to the mysterious northeast edge, also decided to run there. He reached the Lena headwaters and discovered foam from a fallen larch and the traces of a fire, and guessed that another person had recently been there. All along his journey down river he found the same traces of fallen trees and fires. Finally he reached the Lena valley (present day Yakutsk) and met with Omogoi there who already had horses and horned herds and a few children. Ellai asked, "How did you start herds without bringing them with you?" to which Omogoi answered, "I found them here. Being here without herds made me very sad and I cried. I prayed to my gods to give me horses and horned herds so that I had something to eat and exist from. And one day, walking about the place behind *Ytyk Khaya* (sacred mountain), I found a pair of colts, one male and one female. They grew and multiplied and I had mares. Then at the north of *Ytyk Khaya* I found a pair of calves, also one male and one female. That is how I got herds." Omogoi had two sons and a daughter. Ellai liked Omogoi very much and stayed to live and work with him (Ksenofontov 1975:55).[2]

Not long after Ellai begins to work for Omogoi the two begin to disagree and fight. When Omogoi learns that Ellai has married his only daughter, his anger explodes. To spite the newlyweds, Omogoi gives only a hunch-backed piebald horse and a one-horned cow as a dowry. Ellai and his wife decide to build their home like the houses of the indigenous Tungus and far away from Omogoi. They create the first Sakha *uraha*. Ellai next burns the first *tupte* (horse dung burnt to ward off insects). Omogoi's herds gather at Ellai's *tupte* and he and his wife steal the mare's milk in the night and make a great amount of *kymys*. Next Ellai takes the birch bark from the trees, brings it to his wife who makes first the great *saar-yagas* (a huge ceremonial birch bark container) and many smaller birch bark containers. Ellai fashions the first horse hair ropes to tie the newborn colts, and carves the first *choron*, the wooden chalices made from birch wood. After all these preparations, he organizes the first *yhyakh* in these new northern lands. To this day, Sakha recognize Ellai as the founding father of Sakha culture in the north. The Ellai and Omogoi legends emically explain Sakhas' southern ancestry and their horse and cattle agropastoralism in the subarctic. (Alekseev 1995)

Legends, expedition records, linguistic and folkloric materials, hypotheses and theories all verify the strong southern Turkic traits of Sakha culture. Scholars postulate that Sakhas' Turkic ancestors migrated northward between the thirteenth and fifteenth centuries to flee from southern aggressors (Maak 1994; Seroshevski 1993; Gogolev 1986; Okladnikov 1955:227–365; Okladnikov 1970; Constantinov 1975:106–173; Zikov 1978). Participants in Sibiriakov's 1894–1896 Russian Geography Association Expedition were first to propose scientific theories of Sakha origins (Gogolev 1986).[3] One member, N. Veselovskii noted:

Uprooted from their Asian motherland and the main center of all Turkic peoples to their new home in the distant Siberian Far East ... Sakha have preserved many characteristics of the earliest Turkic cultures. ... the study of Sakha explains the similar presence in lifestyle, belief, and world view of other (Turkic) groups related to Sakha, of whom these early (Turkic) ways have not preserved as well. ("Expedition News" 1895:35)

Another expedition member, Edward Karlovich Pekarski, a Polish linguist, wrote a three-volume dictionary of Sakha language while in exile in Sakha.[4] This great life work assisted contemporary researchers in describing the Sakha language as

Turkic in origin with 25 percent Mongol, 4 percent Tungo-Mazhurian, and 10 percent unidentified (Gogolev 1993:3). Another expedition member, ethnographer Waldemar Jochelson, showed the cultural kinship of Sakha with that of the steppe cultures in central Asia (Jochelson 1933:164).

Nineteenth- and twentieth-century research, combining archaeological, ethnographic, and mythic representations, substantiated these earlier theories of Sakha Turkic origins. (Maak 1994; Seroshevski 1993; Gogolev 1986; Okladnikov 1955:227–365; Okladnikov 1970). Despite some unresolved debates over Sakhas' exact ethnic origin (Constantinov 1975:106–173; Zikov 1978),[5] there is agreement that Sakha culture possesses many elements of medieval central Asian and southern Siberian cultures. The most accepted contemporary theory attests that Sakhas' Turkic ancestors migrated between the sixth and seventh centuries from Central Asia to the Lake Baikal regions of southern Siberia, then fled north in the thirteenth and fourteenth centuries to the middle Lena after their defeat by Ghenghis Khan. Archaeological remains of an entire thirteenth-century cattle- and horse-raising settlement in the central regions of Sakha bolster that theory (Constantinov 1975:183–184; Gogolev 1993:3; Okladnikov 1955, 1970).[6]

Sakha share a common belief and ritual system with the ancient Scythian-Siberian cultures of the Eurasian steppe, who once spanned the western region from the Black Sea to the Don River, the Predkavkas steppe and Povolzhe (lower Volga) and to the east from the southern Priural steppe, Kazakhstan, southern Siberia, and central Asia (figure 2.1). These cultures believed that all things animate and inanimate were kept by spirit-protectors that required regular prayers, gifts, and homage.[7] These cultures all considered the horse and its spirit-protector deity as the most powerful and swift, and as the medium of travel for all earthly humans and sky deities.[8] Scythian-Siberian cultures tied colored ribbons on the mane of a sanctified horse and considered it sacred: *yzykh* by the Khakas, *ydyk* by the Tuvans, and *ytyk* (sacred) by the Altaics and Sakha. Waldemar Jochelson recorded a cycle of Sakha legends that portray the horse as a godly being of sky-sun origin, the "fastest god–fastest animal," and linked its deification to the Scythian-Siberian herders. Twenty-first century Sakha

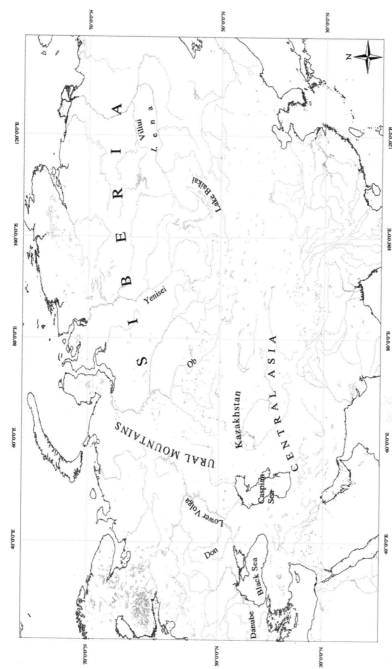

Figure 2.1. Detail of areas inhabited by ancient Scythian-Siberian cultures of the Eurasian steppe in Russian context

researchers are reviving their ancient horse deity cult though careful reconstruction of folkloric, ethnographic, linguistic, and historical materials (Vinokurova 2002).

Sakha and their southern Turkic counterparts also share a belief in both white and black shamans. The former they consider the "priests of the tribe cult *aiyy*" who performed *algyshi* sung during rituals to honor *eezi* (in Sakha, *ichchi*), the spirit-protectors of mountains, rivers, forests, and fields. Like Sakha believed, these tribes also considered the white shaman's major role to be the master of ceremony at *yhyakh*. Sakha folklore credits the first subarctic *yhyakh* to Ellai. Of all the *kymys* festivals still being celebrated, the fullest elements of that ancient practice are represented in contemporary Sakha culture (Okladnikov 1976:231). The festival's roots trace back to a more ancient *kymys* festival, widely found among the Central Asian nomadic peoples.

> From time immemorial the herding people of Siberia and Central Asia celebrated a holiday similar to the Sakha *yhyakh*. Even the Gunni (Huns), long before the new era celebrated the 5th Moon at the beginning of summer for sacrificial offering to the sky, earth, spirits and ancestors. Ceremonies of common drinking up of *kymys* of the Turkic peoples began in the 6th century of our era.... The ancient ritual of serving the fire with drink from the first poured cup was preserved by the Altaic shamans.... (Okladnikov 1976:229)

Early Scythian nomadic cultures held a summer ritual reifying their allegiance to the sun and horse deities by offering them *kymys* in a sacred chalice, then serving the hierarchy of presiding patrilineal clans.[9] To this day Sakha celebrate the *yhyakh* in mid-June, during *uluu tunakh saghana* (time of summer milk abundance). Like the tradition of other Scythian cultures, the *urung oiuun* offers prayer and the chalice of *kymys*, first to the sacred sky deities then to honored participants.

Viliui Sakha Origins and Local History

Viliui Sakha inhabit the Viliui River regions of western Sakha. Like all Sakha, their ethnic origins, horse and cattle breeding subsistence practices, native cosmology, and worldview are linked to southern Turks. Within the Sakha ethnicity they are considered a distinct group based on ancestry and folkloric traditions. Twentieth-century research suggests that Viliui Sakha are descendant of three waves of northern migrations, the Uraankhai, Kurykan, and Ugursky (Ksenofontov 1992:331–442).[10] The abundance of rich natural hayfields found in the Viliui made it an attractive settlement area for northerly migrating agropastoralist tribes (Ergis 1960).[11]

Legends also tell us about the diverse origins of Viliui Sakha. The Nurbakaan legend suggests that Viliui Sakha also descended from both central region Sakha and indigenous Tungus:

> Long ago, all around Nyurba, before Sakha came, were ten *uraha* of Tungus who lived off fishing with willow nets. One day Tumat (another ethnic tribe) came and massacred them, all except one girl named Nurbachaan, who escaped in a birch bark canoe. Traveling down the Viliui then up the Lena, she made it to Saisara (present day Yakutsk). Tigin's father, Sata, took her as one of his wives and she stayed and watched his herds. She had three sons by him: Tyuk Bulgudakh, Boskhon Belgetii (who was born deaf-mute), and the youngest Suuruk Birkinaa, and also one daughter. After Sata died, the three boys, girl, and mother worked as the cattle watchers for Tigin.[12] The three sons were all good hunters who always hit their marks. Tigin's other sons were proud and powerful. They saw how strong the Nurbachaan sons were and said, "We see your Nurbachaan ways (Tungus, hunting . . .) and you will not rule in these parts—you must always kneel down to us." Soon after Tigin himself was angry because the three Nurbachaan boys could not keep his herds well. Tigin came with a spear to fight with Tyuk Bulgudakh, who grabbed the spear out of Tigin's hands and hit him with the dull side of the blade. Then the mother advised her sons, "Tigin and his sons are coming to wage a war and if we don't escape we will die. Quickly, let's go to my birth land." The sons, by their mother's request, first gathered ten horses, one stallion and four mares so they would have milk to drink on their way. Tigin arrived with an army of forty soldiers on horses. They fought and fought and soon Tigin could see that Nurbachaan's sons were very strong indeed. Tigin's army was growing weaker against them so he stopped the fighting and

said, "Boys, you are doing the correct thing to flee—so go! It is true, we cannot live together! You go and fight the Tumat and if you win, come to me and I will give you cows and cattle for your own." So the sons and the mother went with the mother guiding them along the way. They came to Nurba and found forty Tumat *uraha*. The brothers fought and killed them all. They took all their riches and reindeer herds for their own and began to live there. The youngest son, Birkanaa, later had three sons. He named them Torbyokh, Tarkaai, and Omoldoon. These three sons each founded an early *nasleg*: Torbyokh *nasleg* in Suntar *ulus*, and the Tarkaai and Omoldoon *naslegs* in Nyurba. Having accomplished what Tigin had said, the three traveled to him and returned to the Viliui with twenty head of cattle. (Petrov 1991)

The foraging-reindeer herding Tungus tribes who made their home in the Viliui River watershed were gradually overtaken by newcomers over the last five hundred years. The Tungus' demise began with the arrival of agropastoralist Sakha in the mid-sixteenth century. Although the historical record is lacking for that period, legends and oral narratives tell how Sakha, a substantially larger and more aggressive group, took over available lands and either killed, assimilated, or ran off Tungus. Sakha were reputed as sly and clever traders who deceived and exploited the local inhabitants, stealing their wives and their hunting caches (Seroshevski 1993:215). Furthermore, Sakhas' agropastoralist practices, including controlled burning and the creating of new hay pasturelands, destroyed lichen groundcover and wild animal habitat, both crucial resource bases for foraging, reindeer-herding Tungus. This prompted some Tungus to move to remote mountainous areas unsuitable for Sakha subsistence. In the centuries that followed local Tungus lost many of their reindeer to disease and trade. Herd numbers fell precipitously during an 1830s disease epidemic. Similarly, with the mid-1800s opening of the Olekminsk gold mining trade came a high demand for reindeer to use as pack animals in the mines. Many Tungus sold their deer for lucrative prices but were left without animals to continue subsistence. They either took up full-time hunting or horse and cattle breeding with neighboring Sakha.[13]

Within a few short centuries after Sakha began settling on the Viliui, the ethnic make-up of the area had changed dramatically. By the late nineteenth century, Sakha had displaced most of the foraging-herding Tungus settlements and made up the majority on the Viliui (Maak 1994:22–24).[14] There were Russian inhabitants but their numbers were few and they lived in either Viliuisk city or the town of Nyurba. But what were the local realities of Viliui Sakha ethnic enclaves, and how did power struggles accrue and resolve within them?

Local History: The Elgeeii Area

"Elgeeii" is a Tungus word meaning "a long thin lake that lies along a river." The Elgeeii area has many such lakes. They are geo-morphologically similar to oxbows and form from an earlier path of a river. There are forty-four of these lakes in the Tretiy Bordong area alone. The early Sakha called Elgeeii *Toydaakh Alaas* (clayey field), named after the poor, clay-filled soils of the area. These conditions also explain why early Sakha settlement in Elgeeii proper was sparse.

Viliui Sakha organized their settlements according to extended *agha uuha* groupings (refer to figure 1.3). The male head of the wealthiest household within a given clan controlled the clan's land and owned most of its herds. The wealthy household's role was as provider-protector for the remaining members, sharing food resources in exchange for labor (Pakhomov 1999). Elgeeii and areas adjacent fell into the jurisdiction of Bordong, a wealthy clan leader:

> Bordong's father, Chemilis, lived as Tigin's neighbor [in the present day area of Yakutsk on the Lena River] and it is believed that they were distant relatives. When war broke out with the Russians, Perviy Bordong [literally "First Bordong"], then all his *agha uuha*, fled to the Suntar *ulus*. First they came to Sette Sinay, a land place near where the Viliui meets the Lena. They stayed there a while with their herds and then came further. Bordong had five sons and each established a *nasleg*. Oduny, Orokh [Perviy Bordong], Chukaar, Bordong [Tretiy Bordong,

literally 'Third Bordong'], and Khatirik. From Bordong came many children of which little is known except for Beken Kniaz. There are many legends about him and especially about his son, Chokhoroon. (Petrov 1991:138)

The five *naslegs* of the greater Bordong area were based on five patrilineal clan groups and it was in Tretiy Bordong where populations and herds flourished. The area's abundant crop yields and lush pastures were a result of the engineering work of seventeenth-century clan leader Chokhoroon, who cleared the land and created an intricate system of irrigation. To this day, Sakha, of Chokhoroon's lineage, praise his doings and herald him as a prime example of the "wealthy Sakha clan provider," who shared freely what he had with those in need. They tell of how during his ruling he met regularly with locals to decide collectively how to hunt, to keep cows, and to pay the taxes.[15] Chokhoroon also had power in the neighboring Khangalass *nasleg*, in the contemporary Kutana area, where he created the productive hay lands of Ariilaakh.[16] The following is an account of Chokhoroon's doings as told by his fifth-generation descendant Nikolai:

In Tretiy Bordong there was a *kniaz'* [R., meaning "prince" but in this context designating the local clan head]. Chokhoroon's father was called Beken Kniaz and he lived at the headwaters of the Oruktaakh stream [refer to figure 4.2]. There didn't used to be any productive land there. There were very dry or very wet years and never any hay at all. It rained every day and was cold and the hay wouldn't grow at all, and they fed the animals *talaakh* [willow] and spruce trees. It was the way they had to live when there was no hay. So Chokhoroon, when he became the *kniaz'*, said to his father that if they made more land then they would get rich. So he burned all the shrubs and small trees around the lake and cleared a huge area. Then he rechanneled part of the Multyur stream and then made a canal through there and many small lakes here and there across that wide land. He named them all according to what they looked like in his mind. After that the land really produced, and the wood that he used to build that canal is still standing there to this day. They say the land then made him (and many others there) rich. He went to

Ekaterina II in Moscow and bought names for all his people—
Antonov, Nogovinsov, Ivanov—for his relatives and people in
his *nasleg*. (April 28, 2000)

Chokhoroon's engineering feat marked the beginning of a
productive period for the Tretiy Bordong area. The series of lakes
with their interconnecting waterways were functional until the
late Soviet period, when the area was abandoned because it was
considered too distant from the centralized production efforts of
that time.

Although Chokoroon is a local folk hero to many in the Elgeeii
area, he is not praised by all. Other oral history accounts portray
a very different side of Chokhoroon:[17]

In Chokhoroon's day, all the men cut his hay and the women
gathered it. He lived with all prepared for him. And in the fall,
when the cow slaughter came, he would leave his slaughtered
cows in his yard with no guard. He took the greenest hay and
made a trail with it into his yard. When someone's horse or
cow came into his yard to eat that hay, he slaughtered it for his
own. When the neighbor's dogs came into the yard, following
the scent of the slaughtered meat, and begin eating the meat, he
would demand that the dog's owner repay him with a cow or
horse. This is how he grew his wealth. He had many ugly habits.
If unknown guests came to visit he would fix food for them in
such quantity that they could not possibly finish it. When they
reached their limit and explained they couldn't finish, he would
flail them and send them out of his house. He was a harsh person
with a fiery temper, thus his name is the same word for a sharp
axe. (Alekseev 1995:123–133)

Nikolai traced Chokhoroon's lineage to the present and identified many contemporary Elgeeii residents. He commented how
interesting it was that every one of them is well employed and
had some level of power in the present-day village's political
hierarchy.

The present Elgeeii head of administration is a Chokhoroon
descendent. From hand to hand it goes. All the original powerful ones, starting with Chokhoroon, continue to be in power.

They are all kin associated, all the contemporary *toion*s. The communal services *toion* is a Chokhoroon descendent. You see, the power is still according to the *agha uuha*. All Chokhoroon's descendants are in power now. That person's child and that person's child, and when present head goes they will get the next Chokhoroon descendant. The Suntar *ulus* head is also a Chokhoroon descendant. They are all talented people. And so the local Mafia develops here as in many other countries, all in the family. Before the present head a man, another descendant, was Elgeeii village head. He is now in Yakutsk. Before him was the father of the man who now controls the Tretiy Bordong area. They are all Chokhoroon people. From hand to hand it goes. If they vote here then the Chokhoroon person will win as most are from there (Tretiy Bordong). Our administration is all the grandchildren and great grandchildren of them, and if any other person outside of Chokhoroon's people come and try, they couldn't work here. They choose all their own people. (Nikolai, field interview, May 2000)

If the choice for putting locals into places of power is clan-based, this brings an interesting twist to the contemporary importance of "kin," a theme I will explore more fully in the next chapter on post-Soviet Viliui Sakha adaptive strategies. In the context of local village power structures, kin relations are central to the political positioning needed to claim some part of scarce resources, especially employment. Chokhoroon's legacy and its contemporary relevance suggest that kin relations may have been revived in post-Soviet context, but have also been operative all along, even during the political oppression of the Soviet period. On the one hand kin is positively associated with adding resiliency to household-level subsistence strategies and on the other hand it represents a negative force by favoring certain individuals and their households.

What does this tell us about Viliui Sakha resilience and adaptation? First, that the success of Sakha settlement in the Viliui regions was not only a matter of adapting horse and cattle agropastoralism to a subarctic climate but also of the displacement, assimilation, and partial ethnocide of the preceding foraging-herding inhabitants. Second, that much of the success of Sakha agropastoralism in founded in a hierarchical *agha uuha* organization, which worked and continues to operate as a means of Viliui Sakha subsistence survival, for better or worse. With a better idea of how Viliui Sakha accrued power within their ethnic enclaves, we next turn our attention to a much larger movement that had already been in the making for some time—and one that would be long-lasting and this time render Viliui Sakha the subdued—the Russian colonization of Siberia.

Invasion from the West

When Czar Ivan the Terrible's armies captured the Kazan khanate in southwestern Siberia in the sixteenth century, the gates were opened for Russian imperial expansion across Eurasia.[18] Russia's colonization of Siberia began in the early 1600s,[19] in lands just east of the Ural Mountains, and Cossack troops continued eastward, building a network of fortresses across the vast area (Forsyth 1992).[20] The goal of Russian colonization in Siberia was twofold— to increase imperial territory and to exploit the valuable "soft gold" (precious furs) for Russia's economic benefit. To accomplish the latter, the government imposed a system of taxation called *iasak* (R., fur tribute) on all the Siberian inhabitants. This meant the reallocation of time and energy to track and hunt sable and other precious pelts—time that was already at a premium given the challenging subsistence survival of the Siberian natives (Slezkine 1994; Raeff 1956). Additionally, Russian colonizers brought with them a host of new diseases that led to epidemics of smallpox, syphilis, typhus, dysentery, and scarlet fever, often wiping out indigenous populations (Slezkine 1994:268; Raeff 1956).

In 1822, the Russian imperial government decided that what was needed to better control the Eurasian hinterlands was "administrative Russification." Imperial state-builders achieved this noble goal by implementing Speranskii's "Statute of Alien Administration in Siberia." Accordingly, native populations were classified as either "settled," "nomadic," or "wandering." They granted the greatest autonomy to natives who most resembled Russians, involved in land use, governance, and religion (Suny

1993:25). The government further classified Siberian native peoples as *inorodtsy* (R., "people of another stock"), based on their barbaric ways, animistic religions and inferior forms of social life. The government made the same effort to convert *inorodtsy* to the Orthodox faith (Slezkine, 1994) as they made to "Europeanize" the upper stratum of Russian society (Seton-Watson 1986:18). The government offered strong incentives to *inorodtsy* to profess faith—by being baptized and assuming a European name, converters were relieved from most of their fur tribute. Later in that same century Alexander II (1881–1894) introduced new *russification* policies that strengthened military presence, orthodox conversion, and the imposition of superior Russian culture in Siberia. The years that followed were fraught with conflict between official Russian and non-Russian nationalism.

This broad-stroked overview provides a framework for the history of Russian colonization in Siberia and the general affects those processes had on its many indigenous inhabitants. However, it fails to capture the diversity of ways in which local actors responded to the taxes, policies, diseases, conversions, and multitude of other reverberations of Russian colonization. Every local context had differing results based on environmental, cultural, and socioeconomic particularities. How did Viliui Sakha respond to these forces?

Local Impacts of Russian Colonization in Viliui Sakha Settlements

Understanding how Russian colonial policies affected Viliui Sakha settlements shows both local nuances and broader parallels to general impacts of state policies for Siberian native peoples (Slezkine 1994; Raeff 1956; Suny 1993; Seton-Watson 1986; Smith 1990; Basharin 1956; Grant 1995; Viola 2000; Fitzpatrick 1999; Hindus 1931). Sakha population numbers declined sharply following several years of bloody feuds with Cossack armies during the early stages of Russian colonization (Borisov 1996). Russian colonizers had achieved the collection of *iasak* from all Viliui inhabitants by 1630 (Basharin 1956). The government grouped *naslegs* into *volost'i* (R., districts) to collect *iasak* based on Sakha *agha uuha* groupings. This reorganization changed "liquid" clan boundaries, that previously had moved according to interclan warfare, to permanent geographic borders. In 1630 there were forty *volost'i* in the contemporary Sakha Republic territory (Iakovlev 1999).

Russian colonization and imposition of the fur tax set up a series of dependencies among Sakha, Tungus, and Russians. Sakha, who relied on horse and cattle husbandry, enlisted resident Tungus to hunt pelts for *iasak* payment in exchange for meat and dairy products (Basharin 1956:38). Russian colonizers, who depended on local Sakha for meat, milk, and the resources for growing grain, granted local Sakha *toions* the right to occupy lands and maintain ownership of their herds in exchange for those services (Basharin 1956:30). The first Iasak Commission of 1760, organized to reform the collection and delivery of *iasak*,[21] granted local *toions* the legal power to collect *iasak* within their area. Russian colonizers designated Sakha clan leaders *kniaz* within their *nasleg* empowering them to collect taxes and to act as military leaders and carry out imperial government policies (Maak 1994:197). Sakha *kniaz* were ceded the most valuable lands within their jurisdictions and could assume ownership of locals' herds in the name of their new administrative power (Maak 1994:39). They decided *iasak* fees based on each individual's holdings and parceled land according to *iasak* payments.[22] *Toions* routinely took the prime land for their own and their kin's usage (Basharin 1956:120). These developments further magnified the already socially stratified Sakha clan systems (Borisov 1996). A local example of a *toion* area is Perviy Bordong.[23] The Perviy Bordong *nasleg*, inclusive of Elgeeii and Tretiy Bordong territories, was ruled by the *toion* Ivan of the Krivoshapkin clan. Ivan the *toion* allotted himself five times the normal amount of land, located in the center of the settlement and gave his kin all the prime lands adjacent to his.[24]

The first Russians settled in Elgeeii in 1761. The Russian nobleman Aleksey Danilov and ten Cossacks built the first house in Elgeeii. Two years later they abandoned the settlement after several unsuccessful attempts at growing barley, rye, and wheat, and relocated to the less forbidding climate of Olekminsk. The early frosts and general poor climate of the Viliui regions for growing grains continued to deter permanent Russian settlement for decades (Kharitinov 1996). The next century, Russians returned to settle on the Viliui, this time in the quest to spread Christianity. In 1875 Elgeeii became the home to the first of eight Orthodox churches in the Suntar *ulus*, the *Elgeeiiski Predtechiskoy Tserkvi* of the Yakutsk *Dukhovnoi Konsistorii* (R., The Elgeeii Orthodox Church of the Yakutsk Religious Filial).[25] True conversions were rare among Sakha. Like their indigenous counterparts across Siberia, Sakha were attracted to baptism and the taking of European names because it relieved the heavy burden of *iasak*. The Church organized the first school in 1875 using teachers from the central regions of Sakha and offering church Slavic, Russian language, and arithmetic. Contemporary elders recall their parents' praise of these early efforts to teach reading and writing.[26]

The *Tetricheskiie knigi* (R., church records) of the Elgeeii church recount births, marriages, and deaths with their likely causes.[27] The gamut of diseases listed verifies the harsh conditions at the time. A sampling of entries includes: TB, headache, old age, "inner," colds, swelling of lungs, parasites, allergies, scarlet fever, giving birth, water on brain, dysentery, uterine tumor, small pox, diabetes, freezing, puerperal fever, dropsy, scrofula, kidney stones, infancy (shortly after birth—direct reason unknown), stabbing, heart problems, stomach problems, spinal problems, measles, hernia, diarrhea, catarrh of the stomach, whooping cough, weakening (Central State Archive [CSA]: 2). The age-sex pyramid, derived from the 1897 census results in the Sakha Republic, shows relatively high birth and mortality rates, especially for children and young females (Fedorova 1998:71–72). It was common at the time for women to have ten to fifteen children so that three or four would survive to adulthood.

Travel between the center, Yakutsk, and the Viliui regions was difficult. Only in the early twentieth century did the Yakutsk government establish a permanent route to transport clergy and other government officials traveling to Suntar. They named it the "Akaray" road, after the highest priest of that time. Today you can still see the horizontal posts, that made up the road's bed, in the woods just across the Viliui River from Elgeeii village (CSA: 3). Groups traveled from Yakutsk on horseback, making many stopovers, especially in the depths of winter when day-length and temperatures were prohibitive. Perviy Bordong was a major stopping place. Travelers found places to sleep, eat, and rest their horses, and used the local *bania* (R., bathhouse) and church. One high priest, while traveling through Elgeeii to the church in Suntar, recorded in his diary his amazement at the variety of vegetables grown by local Sakha (Iakovlev 1999).

Table 2.1 shows early-twentieth-century Suntar *ulus* demography.[28] *Ulus* population numbers in 1998 were 26,630 compared

Table 2.1. Demographics of the Suntar *Ulus*, 1901–1902

Category	1901	1902
Kniaz (Prince)	1	1
Kniazhna (Princess)	1	1
Church Workers:		
Male	14	15
Female	16	17
Russian Wheat Growers:		
Male	5	4
Female	7	7
Locals:		
Male	2	—
Female	2	—
Sakha:		
Male	7266	7437
Female	7699	7843
Tungus:		
Male	5	5
Female	5	6
Revolutionary Prisoners:		
Male	39	47
Female	6	6
All Horses	5374	5851
Mares and Stallions	3404	3871
Yearlings	1970	1980
All Cows	12866	12883
Milkers, Bulls, and Workers	8598	8323
Yearlings	4268	4560
Human Births	525	561
Human Deaths	244	246

to 15,068 and 15,389 for 1901 and 1902 respectively (GosKom-Stat:1).

Elgeeii was the center of the *ulus* from 1822. In 1898 a fire destroyed the *inorodnoia glava* (R., administrative center) in Elgeeii (Perviy Bordong), and the *ulus* center was relocated to Kutana. In 1921 the *ulus* center moved again, this time from Kutana to Sheia for protection during the ongoing civil war.

Some of the impacts of Russian colonization on local Viliui settlements challenged Sakha subsistence survival—the imposition of *iasak*, the devastation of new diseases, and the attempts to realign native belief systems with Orthodoxy. We can also argue that Russian presence on the Viliui brought positive change with the establishment of schools and the introduction of transportation infrastructure. In the midst of these positive and negative developments, Viliui Sakha households continued with horse and cattle agropastoral food production scattered across the taiga landscape in clan groupings, much as they did before the Russian presence. At the same time, with Russian colonization, the world on the Viliui, like in other parts of Siberia at the time, opened to the beginnings of globalization. The most profound changes for Viliui Sakha, and their Siberian counterparts, have come about in the last one hundred years of the Soviet and now post-Soviet periods.

The Soviet Period: From Lenin's Socialism to Stalin's Legacy

During his brief rule, Lenin began to create the largest state possible, based on the *sblizhenie* (R., rapprochement) and eventual *sliianie* (R., merging) of nations. He aimed to accomplish this not by coercion but by the will of the workers. He proposed full regional and national autonomy in the new state. During this brief ten-year hiatus, native peoples were given relative freedom to determine aspects of their native life, including a native system of administration. His major policy to bring this about was *korenizatsiia* (R., nativization), aimed toward consolidation of nationality via the support of native languages, the creation of national *intelligentsia* (R., intellectuals) and a political elite, and the formal institutionalizing of ethnicity into the state apparatus (Suny 1993:102). *Narkomnat* (R., People's Commissariat of Nationalities), later known as The Committee of the North, was the new state organ to negotiate this policy to ensure an independent cultural life for native non-Russians (Grant 1995:69,74,77). The organization's members remained divided, however, on how to achieve a backward people's passage to socialism through an active proletariat, with one camp advocating reservations and the other assimilation.

Lenin's life ended before he had time to bring his socialist principles and policies to full fruition. Any progress the committee achieved during his rule was soon undone after Stalin came to power. Under Stalin's policies of collectivization, Lenin's native village leadership was replaced with administration by those who were literate in the great Russian culture of the elite, chosen more for their technical abilities and loyalty to the Party line than for their ethnic and class background (Suny 1993:108).[29] Stalin is best known for waging a "war against the past," by implementing policies to erase the ethnic and class differences of the diverse populations across the USSR. One of his main protocols was *dekulakization* (R., the liquidation of wealthy land/resource holders). Collectivization was a "revolution from above," to result in the "socialization of the countryside" by upgrading agricultural production and integrating agriculture into the system of central planning (Pitassio and Zaslavsky 1985:9).

These goals were never fully realized. Instead collectivization efforts resulted in massive slaughters of livestock, devastating famines, and a drastic decline in overall productivity (Pitassio and Zaslavsky 1985:10). Collectivization transformed what had been an independent peasantry overseen by traditionally patriarchal village leaderships into subjects answering to state officials (Suny 1993:107). Collectivization had poignant realities for many. In Ukraine there were widespread famines due to the imposed target for grain collections, which far exceeded the peasantry's production capability (Conquest 1986:225–259). In other parts of the vast Soviet Union, the state forced nomadic peoples into settlements. Some responded by destroying their herds, exemplified in the case of Kazakhs who destroyed 80 percent of their herds with millions more dying from violence and starvation (Suny 1993:107; Conquest 1986:189–198). Peoples practicing native economies including herding and hunting, fishing and foraging, were forced to integrate into larger cooperative units of specialized "brigades," devoted to one type of economic pursuit (Slezkine 1994:204). Traditional techniques and practices were deemed "backwards" and replaced by more sophisticated methods (Slezkine 1994:205). Rapid, forced industrialization resulted in social and geographical dislocation that further disrupted traditional patterns of authority and cultural practices.

In concert with these sweeping changes, the mandate of the Committee of the North also changed from reifying native ways to "cultural construction," the remaking of cultures based on streamlined Soviet ways. This new mandate was in strict opposition to the committee's original protocol. Native language and culture were now considered inferior to Soviet culture and the Great Russian language, and could only be supported if they worked to promote socialism. The state transformed ethnographic practice. Ethnographers working with native peoples had a clear political agenda. Based on the deterministic model from the new school of Marxist ethnography, the backwardness of the natives was a direct result of their extreme natural environment. The only path to socialism would be a revolutionary change of the natives' environment, through the introduction of Soviet technology, economy, and ideology (Slezkine 1991).

The World War II period was a time for building solidarity among the "Soviet" people. Inhabitants of the USSR were called, despite their nationality, to take part in defending their fatherland. This fight against fascism refocused attention to the collective cause and away from the losses of the purges. Siberian natives, who to that point had maintained a minimal involvement with the socialist cause, were forced to participate. Men were sent to defend the war front and the remaining women, children, and elders worked in the men's place. In the postwar period the economy boomed, and living standards for native inhabitants began to rival those of Russians.

The Soviet Period for Viliui Sakha

How did the changes of the Soviet period play out on the Viliui? The Soviet period ushered in modernity to Viliui Sakha via increased agricultural efficiency, formal literacy programs, health care and sanitation efforts, and involvement in the industrial economy with the advent of regional diamond mining. However, these advances came at a high cost, including the loss of indigenous ecological knowledge, the massive resettlements of native communities, the influx of migrant workers, and unabated environmental degradation. By chronicling these changes we can better understand how local actors adapted their livelihoods accordingly and also how modernity and globalization affected their lives.

Literacy for All

The first effect of the new Soviet state on local Viliui Sakha life was Lenin's push for "literacy for all." This effort included a policy to unite the over one hundred nationalities of the USSR through the use of a single Cyrillic alphabet. Up to that time Sakha, like many of their non-Russian counterparts, used the Latin alphabet for their relatively recently developed written culture. In 1917, the academic Novgorodov published the first Sakha language *bykvar'* (R., language primer) in Cyrillic, intentionally leaving out capitalization and punctuation to speed the learning process.

The literacy for all campaign on the Viliui began with *Lik-Bez* (R., liquidation of illiteracy) programs, administered locally in *Aaghar Balaghan* (reading houses). The first two Suntar *ulus Aaghar Balaghan* opened in Elgeeii in 1920. They were run by church-schooled community members who taught adults to read and write, who read *dokladi* (R., papers), and showed plays.[30] Sakhas' local form of Lenin's universal *Korenizatsiia* policy to bring native language into the schools was called *Yakutizatsiia* and mandated that all school teaching be done in the native Sakha language. Up to that time all instruction had been in Russian. The first propaganda to enforce *Yakutizatsiia*[31] was printed in 1931 to canvas populations and enlist all who had not yet taken the required seven-month literacy course (CSA: 8).

In the early 1920s the Sakha *intelligentsia* coordinated efforts to begin publishing in the Sakha language.[32] Two Yakutsk-based groups, *Sakha Omuk* (Sakha People) and *Yraas Olokh* (Clean Life), were active in disseminating published Sakha language materials. They also worked to improve health and hygiene in Sakha settlements, most notably by enforcing a new policy to separate the *khoton* from the *balaghan*.

During that same period the Sakha government organized *Kholbos*, a distribution and exchange center, to supply the villages with previously unavailable goods and supplies. The 1922 store inventory shows the variety of goods available and goods taken in exchange including: assorted porcelain tableware including dishes, bowls, tea sets, cups, and saucers; flatware; sewing material including linens, silks, and cottons; a variety of tools; tea; sugar; assorted meat and fish pâtés; tobacco; garden seeds; samovars; calendars; and mustard; in exchange for ermine, arctic, black, gray, and red fox, rabbit, wolf, lynx, squirrel, sable, and chipmunk pelts; mammoth tusk; duck feathers; duck down; swan skin; horse tails and manes; reindeer forelegs; and calf skin (CSA: 5).

In 1929, after Lenin passed and Stalin came to power, state policies changed drastically. All languages, including Sakha, went back to the Latin alphabet. We can see the disruption this caused on a local level. The tax records for the Perviy Bordong *KX* (R., abbreviation of *kollektivni khazaistvo*, or collective farm) workers are recorded in half-Latin and half-Cyrillic (CSA: 7). Local schools began teaching in the Latin script and contemporary elders recall the confusion of studying Sakha in Cyrillic one year and then having to learn the Latin alphabet the next.[33] Samsonov, a former *toion*, opened the first school in Kuukei village, about 35 kilometers (22 miles) from Elgeeii. He published Sakha primers using the Latin script. The primer's text was filled with propaganda about Soviet-period modernity and political norms. Every sample composition in the primer glorified collective and socialist ways:

> Our life before the Revolution was difficult and a constant struggle. We had only a tiny bit of land and the rest was owned by the rich exploiters. If we took our cows and calves out of our yards, the local *toions* would fine us to be on their lands and we could get help from no where. Now the land belongs to the KX and the KX makes a lot of profits. Our life is good and we are joyous. The wrongs of the past have been righted and our bellies are full. No one takes the pay of another's work. Those who work will eat, those who don't work will go hungry. This is the socialist principle that has come with each working KX.

Another composition, teaching the use of the letter "q" (pronounced as "kh"), focused on the Sakhas' new use of their small cow barns (figure 2.2):

il

i Я

Artьal qoton tuttar. Qotonnoro ulaqan, ytyө. Mannьk ulaqan qoton urut suoq ete. Urut ьal aqsьn kьra-kьra qoton вaara. Urut ьnaq kьra вuolara, yyte, arььta mөltөq ete.

Anь qolquos qotonun ykse ulaqan, ytyө, sьlaas, qolku. ьnaq kөnnө. Yyte, arььta ykseete.

Qoton araqsььta ulaqan suoltalaaq suol.

ii	it	i-lii	i-lin
iis	i-ti	si-lii	i-lik
tiis	i-tii	i-liim	si-lik
tiit			
tiir	si-tii	i-lim	si-lis
tiil	si-tim	si-lim	Si-lip
ti-rii	sir	i-ni	i-ti-rik
ti-вii	siir	ki-ni	ti-ti-rik
ti-tiik	kir	ki-niit	ti-ti-riir
ti-mir	kiir	ki-hi	

ι ....
ι ....
ιι ιιs tiis tiit tiir tiil it iti itii.
sitii sitim. ilii silii iliim ilim.
silim ilin iliк siliк silis tirii sir
tiвii titiiк timir sir кir кiir...
ini кini кihi ....

40
41

Figure 2.2.   *Excerpt from Samsonov primer*

The *artel'* (R., collective work brigade) builds the *khoton*s. The new *khoton*s are huge and pleasant. Before we didn't have these great *khoton*s. Before every household had their own small *khoton*. Our cows were small then and they had poor meat and little milk. Now the *khoton*s are big and pleasant, bright and warm. The cows are healthy and there is a lot of milk and butter.

And each primer included many passages praising Stalin:

For us a bright future has come. We are now all equal and of good principles. For all this we owe thanks to comrade Stalin—Thank you for the correct and decent life you have given us, Joseph Vissariyonovich Stalin!!!!

Collectivization on the Viliui

Beginning in the late 1920s and culminating in the late 1950s, Soviet-era collectivization transformed Sakha land use practices from extensive to centralized. In the early years of collectivization, inhabitants across the Soviet Union were either overtly or covertly forced to turn over their land rights and privately owned resources to the collective farm. This dealt particular challenges to the Sakha and other non-Russian nonagriculturist peoples who depended on the extensive use of lands and resources for their subsistence.[34] With the final consolidation efforts of the 1950s, which resulted in the establishment of state farms, all collective resources, including land, were made the property of the state.

Until the early 1930s, Sakha lived in *agha uuha* clusters of single-family *balaghan*s in four main areas around Elgeeii—Elgeeii, Toloon, Ugut Kuol, and Khaar Elgeen. With the majority of the population poor, many were eager to join the collective when news of the first agricultural reforms came to the area. Locals formed the first collective, *Bastaki Sardanga* or First Ray, in 1929. Its forty members acted as the main agitators to bring the rest of the local inhabitants into the *KX*. Their protocol read:

All upper, lower and middle class! The Perviy Bordong *nasleg* of Suntar region invites you to join in the agricultural collective in order to work in common and provide for our households.

> By joining the work collective you will be fighting the forces of
> the *kulak* (R., of the wealthy class), who are the exploiters and
> the enemy of the people. (CSA: 6)

By 1930 several more *KX* were operating with many to soon
follow. Table 2.2 shows when the collectives formed and consolidated over the decades that culminated in the 1957 Elgeeii
State Farm. Stalin stepped up collectivization efforts through terror tactics aimed at wiping out remaining kulaks.[35] Local stories
abound of how those who refused to give over their herds and
land holdings were shot.

The early collectives allowed each household five private milk
cows or a total herd of ten to twelve. The remainder had to be
given over to the collective. In protest of this "taking," many
households chose to slaughter their herds over the quota to use
for immediate household meat stores. These actions resulted in
a sharp decrease in cattle numbers in the early 1930s. To further
deter private cow holding, Stalin introduced substantially high
taxes on household herds, which put many in bankruptcy.[36] Elders today recount the many ways their parents struggled to keep
their private herds after these taxes came into effect.

The state's efforts to deter private cow keeping were aimed
to increase the time and energy devoted to collective production.
Farm administrators calculated an individual's labor according
to *kuluhun kune* (literally "sweat day" and referring to a day of
work), a measure of work hours based on a *norma* (R., quota) of
standardized times for all work tasks.

Table 2.3 details how many *kuluhun kune* a worker could
expect for cutting and harvesting hay, depending on the field
conditions and whether they had the assistance of a horse or
not.

KX members were paid once a year, on New Year's Eve,
according to their year-long accumulation of *kuluhun kune*. Pay
was in the form of farm "profits," what remained of the butter,
meat, and wheat after the farm had paid its taxes to the government. Viliui collectives sometimes went years without making
any substantial profits, and household survival largely depended
on home food production.

Table 2.2. **Schema of the Formation of Collectives and Consolidation to the Elgeeii State Farm**

	Elgeeii	Toloon	Ugut Kuol	Tretiy Bordong
1929	Molotov			
1930		First Rays	Telman Sanga Olokh	Sierpe
1931	Kalandarashivili	Kihil Toloon	Telman	
1932	Sirjit			Vorosholov Stalin
1933		Ulgutta Tyuk		
1934				
1935		Komintern	Litvinov	Soviet
1936				Stalin
1939	Molotov	Komintern		
1940		Molotov	Telman	
1950				Kommunism
1952		Molotov		
1957	Molotov joins Kubishev, Kalinin, Lenin, and Kommunism Suola to form the Elgeeii State Farm			

Table 2.3. *Kuluhun kune* Amounts for Hay Work Done

Entry #	Work Description	Land Conditions	# of Workers	Area (Hectare)	# Kuluhun Kune	Ruble Value
35	Hand cutting hay	Flat	1	1	.7	1.50
36	Hand cutting hay	Hussocks	1	1	.5	1.50
37	Hand raking hay	Flat	1	1	.9	1.25
38	Hand raking hay	Hussocks	1	1	.6	1.25
39	Raking with a horse	Flat	1	1	5.00	1.50

The collective process brought many unforeseen changes. Work on the farms grew increasingly specialized and, in the process, Viliui Sakha stopped using much of their mixed subsistence herding, hunting, fishing, and foraging knowledge. Fishing and hunting was the business of specialized brigades and engaged only a small sector of the total village populations. Similarly, the gradual intensification of farming practices transformed the surrounding landscape. In the early collective period, the first agricultural growing fields were made on the Viliui. Their areas grew and widened, especially after the first tractors came in the late 1940s. In the early 1930s the department of agriculture brought eight "Semantal" (European breed) bull-inseminators from Archangelsk and began a breeding program that systematically replaced the hardy local Sakha cattle. By 1960 this Sakha-Semantal mix was considered one of the highest quality and quantity milk and meat producers across the USSR (Nikolaev 1970). Post-WWII agricultural innovations included the use of superphosphates and other highly concentrated chemical fertilizers that replaced the age-old use of natural fertilizers rendered from the burning of fields and the application of animal manures.

The early KXs grew a variety of crops including barley, rye, oats, wheat, potatoes, cabbage, and carrots. They fed their herds with hay harvested within their KX territories. In 1944 all the Viliui area KX began growing tobacco. They were raising a variety of animals, many that were previously foreign to the subarctic climate, including pigs, chickens, sheep, and goats. Two of the area farms, the Stalin *KX* (Tretiy Bordong) and the Telman *KX* (Ugut Kuol) had reindeer up until 1944, when they were discontinued only to reappear after state farm establishment in the late fifties.

World War II brought many setbacks to the collective process. Adult males left the farms for the front, leaving only women, children, and elders to run the nascent collectives (Suntar Regional Archive [SRA]: 2). Nineteen-forty-two, the *achchyk jyl* (starvation year), was the year of a devastating drought. The nearby salt-rich Kempandai settlement had operated as a penal colony for more than a century by the time World War II began. The government needed an increased amount of salt to preserve food for the front, and many *KX* workers were sent there to work as civilians, as one elder remembers, "The Kempandai colony supplied the entire Suntar *ulus*—all the members worked—cutting wood and mining salt—It was great there because although you worked very hard, they fed you 3x's a day—it was in 1942 and there was starving everywhere—I was an orphan and had nothing—no home—so I was better off there."

After the war, Stalin introduced policies to further consolidate the collectives. At the 1950 meeting of the Kommunar, Bolshevik, and May 1st *KX*s, members voted unanimously (98.9 percent overall) to consolidate (SRA: 3). Table 2.4 shows the demographic results of that combination.

Similarly, in 1950 the Stalin and Vorosholov *KX*s were brought together to form the Kommunism *KX* in Tretiy Bordong. Concomitantly, former *naslegs* were assigned formal administrative centers. Perviy Bordong and Tretiy Bordong's new administrative center became Elgeeii and Kutana the amalgamation of Khangalass and Mochinski *naslegs* (SRA: 4).

As a result of these consolidation efforts, by 1952 the number of Suntar region *KX*s dropped from one hundred to twenty-five (SRA: 5). The consolidations meant the liquidation of *KX* administrative offices that were brought under the organization of the more centrally located *KX*. In the Suntar region three such liquidations occurred. The Tretiy Bordong process shows how

Table 2.4. Demographics of the Three *KX*s Separately and Combined

	Kommunar KX	Bolshevik KX	May 1st KX	Combined
# of Households	77	51	28	156
Total Population	245	191	97	533
Working Males	45	34	14	93
Working Females	59	47	22	128
Total Workforce	104	81	36	221
12–16-year-olds	30	12	20	62
Total Cattle	424	390	213	1027
Milk Cows	142	116	68	326
Work Bulls	37	18	16	71
Total Horses	313	175	73	561
Mares	91	44	30	165
Work Horses	69	39	16	124
Hay Fields (hectare)	561	811	333	1705
Growing Fields	222	147	84	453
Pasture	223	328	92	643
Total Land	996	1286	509	2791

populations were resettled to work at the center, taking huge areas of productive lands out of use.

At a regional farm meeting on February 24, 1951, *KX* members voted in favor of joining the Kommunism *KX* (Tretiy Bordong) with the *KX*s of the Perviy Bordong *nasleg*. On December 10 of the same year, all *KX* members present voted for the Molotov, Telman, Komintern, and Kommunism *KX*s of the Perviy Bordong *nasleg* to be joined together as one Molotov *KX*. Following this consolidation Molotov *KX* had 261 households, and 833 people of whom 358 were *KX* workers. The *KX* had 1348 horses, 1614 cattle, 83 sheep, and 105 reindeer. The *KX*'s new land area was 25,000 hectares. Archival map reproductions show how the new boundaries were drawn.

After the liquidation of the Tretiy Bordong *nasleg*, Kommunism *KX* became part of Molotov *KX*, and the new border encompassed all the territory of the two *KX*s combined. In connection with this, the center of the Molotov *KX*, pictured on the map as slightly above the Elgeeii village center, was relocated to Elgeeii village proper. The school, the medical facilities, the store, and private homes were to be relocated from Tretiy Bordong to El-geeii to provide incentive for residents to relocate to the center and to accommodate the needs of the growing population of El-geeii (SRA: 6).

Consolidation was also ongoing on a regional scale beginning in the 1930s (refer to figure 5.2).[37] Most of these "moving administrative borders" were made to accommodate agricultural production and later to designate diamond-rich areas "industrial." After 1947 Sadinski region was gone—Chona and Sadin joined the Suntar region. Botuobuya (where present-day Mirnyi and the first diamond pipe are) joined the Lenski region. In 1955 the government formed the Mirnyi village and then the Mirnyi city proper in 1959 (no longer within a region but, like Yakutsk, independent) (Iakovlev 1999).[38]

The Politics Behind the Elgeeii State Farm

During his brief leadership from 1957 to 1961, Nikita Khrushchev made the final push to maximize the economic and administrative efficiency of Soviet agricultural production by implementing policies that consolidated collectives into agro-industrial state farms.[39] The Elgeeii State Farm was one of the first to consolidate. In response to the All Union Soviet Ministers' decree, "For the organization of new and expanded land and resource use to form new State Farms," on April 8, 1957, the Sakha Republic decreed the formation of three such massive farm operations, in the Lensk, the Nyurba, and the Suntar regions (SRA: 7). Each new farm was formed through the amalgamation of the surrounding collectives. With this new status, the three farms were given full material and moral support from the central government. Materially this included unlimited fuel supplies; imported (mostly Russian and Ukrainian) specialists including agronomists, veterinarians, economists, animal breeders, inseminators, medical doctors, and farm directors; and dozens of tractors and other necessary machinery to increase overall production. Village inhabitants, for the first time, had access to a bounty of consumer products. In Elgeeii the consolidation of nearby collective farms was already well underway. It culminated with the establishment of the Elgeeii State Farm, an agro-industrial enterprise encompassing 150,000 hectares, an area the size of Indiana (refer to figure 4.2). The Elgeeii village population increased severalfold as adjacent collective farm centers were closed down and entire villages moved to work from the center. Evidence of the resettlements remains to this day. Houses moved from the Vorosholov KX, one of two KX in Tretiy Bordong, make up the Vorosholov street in contemporary Elgeeii.

The swiftness of the Elgeeii and other Viliui region state farm consolidations was directly associated with another important moment—when diamonds "got a life" on the Viliui. With the 1950s push to industrialize, geological expeditions discovered diamonds in the Viliui regions. The government redrew regional boundaries to designate the diamond-laden areas as industrial, and mandated that the outlying agricultural regions, organized into agro-industrial state farm operations, produce food for the nascent diamond industry. As stated in the annual accounts of the state farm from 1957, "The Elgeeii State Farm was organized with the objective to produce to satisfy the meat and milk demands of the workers of the newly established diamond industry" (SRA: 8). A more prosaic directive comes from the Russian farm director's opening story in the 1967 publication, "Elgeeii State Farm," a compilation of memoirs by farm officials to commemorate the farm's winning of the prestigious Lenin Medal:

> Before I came to work here as the director, I worked on the geological expeditions searching for diamonds. After we found the diamond wealth, we then had a new path to travel to lead us to our future wealth and prosperity. It is part of this great responsibility for the local indigenous inhabitants to produce meat and butter, potatoes and vegetables to feed the working settlements. This responsibility is the Elgeeii State Farm's foremost objective. (Zhuravlev 1967:3)

From this moment until the late 1980s, diamonds for Viliui Sakha were a symbol of regional pride and their local contribution to state wealth that would build the Soviet society, mainly through defense and armaments (Argunova-Low 2004:259). Town square monuments, like the one in Verkhniviliuisk, combined pan-Soviet

Figure 2.3. "Mat' Viliui" (The Mother of the Viliui)

icons with images of local resource wealth to create powerful daily reminders to village inhabitants (figure 2.3). Although most rural Viliui Sakha had never held a diamond in their life, they knew that all work efforts on the state farm were in their name.

The discovery of diamonds on the Viliui transformed local livelihoods. In the change from collective to state farm, Viliui Sakha went from being part owners of collective operations to being members of the working class in a vast state-farm system. Viliui Sakha had a serf-like relationship with the diamond industry. Instead of earning *kuluhun kune* for a percent of their cooperative's annual profit in meat and milk, workers punched the clock for biweekly wages. The move to a working class changed the indigenous diet. The government rationed meat to one kilogram (2.2 pounds) a month for state farm workers' household consumption in order to increase the supply of foodstuffs to the mining areas. Households could consume more meat if they kept their own cows. However, most did not have the time or energy for private cows since work on the state farm kept most busy for ten to twelve hours a day. At this point most people had more money than time and so the tendency was for the natural Sakha diet to be replaced by imported store-bought foods. Dairy products, especially milk and cream, were also scarce consumer products. Inhabitants recollect the sound of the daily helicopter that came to Elgeeii to pick up a ton of crème fraîche for delivery to the diamond workers.

With the state farm consolidations, work was further specialized. In 1957 the Elgeeii *SX* (R., abbrev, of *Sovkhos* or State Farm) kept a total of 8878 cattle—one-third of the total cattle in Suntar *ulus*. To support these numbers and to continue to increase production, workers had limited tasks to perform with large numbers of animals. A milker—who formerly tended their cows' new calves; hauled water, hay, and supplemental feed; cleaned stalls; and hauled manure—now only milked. The other duties were assigned to new specialties: the calf watcher, the barn manure cleaner and hauler, and the feed and water carrier.

Salaries were based on a norm for the work performed. Work norms were measured in kilos of milk produced, number of successful birthings and weanings, and weight gain of new calves (SRA: 9). Salary could also be increased if a worker went above the expected productive capacity. The farm administration held frequent socialist competitions at every farm sector between all who worked in meat and milk production to stimulate higher levels (SRA: 10). The "socialist" competitions were an effective means not only to increase production but also to maintain the work ethic and morale. Contests included which milker could get the most milk out of their cows, who could hand-cut hay the fastest and most proficiently, and who could produce the most meat out of their herd. Winners got a monetary bonus and their name posted on the *pochyetnaya doska* (R., respected worker board). Perhaps more valued than the monetary compensation for overfulfilling the plan, those in milk and meat production were presented *gramota* (R., certificates of achievement), medals, and titles of honor that established their names solidly in state-farm history (SRA: 11).[40]

A few years into his directorship, Zhuravlev initiated a strategic production plan entitled, "Activities Necessary to Make the Farm Work Better," based on protocols to become "a powerful and unique example of unprecedented production done in the most modern and technologically advanced ways" (SRA: 10). The plan included an increase in production areas by either draining, irrigating, disking, de-hussocking, and/or clearing. It included the introduction of new domesticates, successful only through the extensive use of incubators. The initiative also increased production with the introduction of centralized electricity.[41] It increased animal production through new techniques including separating calves from their mothers, using bottles instead of udders, feeding milk cows concentrated feeds in their own separate area, and pasturing milk cows in alternating pastures to make full use of pasture before moving into the next. Lastly, the plan entailed replacing the old *balaghan*-style barns of slanted vertical poles with hewn upright horizontal constructions.

On paper the success of the state farm was undeniable. Even after the first eight months the farm was touted as producing three times the meat and twice the milk of the former collectives (SRA: 11:6–7).[42] The socialist incentive programs were clearly effective.[43] The major difference was that in the collective farm period all farm products (after taxes) went to the workers as pay for their *kuluhun kune*. By 1966 most went to the diamond settlements (SRA: 11: 6–7).

The award-winning success of Elgeeii State Farm production is credited to the former geologist turned farm director, Zhuravlev. It was under his directorship that the farm won the *Ordena Lenina* (R., Lenin Medal), an honor given to only a handful of farms across the vast USSR for unprecedented growth in production. Locally, Zhuravlev is remembered for bringing decent housing, medical facilities, preschool and boarding school facilities, and improved farm buildings and working conditions. The Elgeeii State farm boasted its 229 workers who had received medals and high acclaim across the USSR for their milking and meat raising abilities. An additional 26 workers received the highest honors as workers within the Sakha Republic (Korotov 1967).

Zhuravlev left the Elgeeii SX in 1971 at the age of sixty-three to retire in southern Russia (Pavlov 1999:77–78). He left during the Brezhnev period, known as the time of stagnation across the USSR. Elgeeii State Farm production, like that of SX across the country, began a gradual slow-down. Although the new director completed Zhuravlev's plan for "full electrification of the state farm,"[44] this achievement only partially masked the decline in farm production. The state farm workforce suffered a gradual decline in morale, and the work level fell drastically. With guaranteed paychecks and ready access to plentiful cheap vodka, alcoholism became a rampant problem (SRA: 13).[45]

Many inhabitants associate this decline in morale with the historical loss of ownership and self-worth, forfeited when the state farm became a huge agro-industrial complex in the 1950s. Some refer to the dehumanizing effect of increased specialization that depersonalized the production process and led to complacency. Still others blame the demanding work regime and personal limitations imposed by the state-farm system. Households were allowed only one cow in the SX period and could only pick berries on one specified day for each berry season. As one elder remembers,

> You had to work all the time and if you went off and did something by yourself it was against the common way—so they made one time for all to go berrying together. It was in the 1970s—when there was a law about how many cows you could have—you could only have one or two cows and the rest you had to give to the SX. Later there was no such law but because you could only get 20 percent of the hay you cut, this put a great limitation on the cows you could keep.

The abandonment of cutting-edge projects signaled the failure of the administrative infrastructure. In 1968 the administration initiated a plan to "gasify" the Viliui regions, to take advantage of the "seemingly endless" reserves of natural gas under the watershed area. The line was to begin at the source near the city of Viliuisk, then run to Verkhny-Viliuisk, Nurba, Suntar, Mirnyi, and Lensk. The administration clearly stated the need to build this gas line: "Every year the Suntar region uses 262 thousand cubic meters of wood for household heating. If we can realize the gas line, then we will cut our need for wood by 50%, or 131 thousand cubic meters ... "(SRA:14). The project was dropped due to budget constraints.[46]

Coming Out of Stagnation: The End of the Elgeeii State Farm

A short three decades after implementing the 1950s state farm consolidation protocols the Soviet government restructured its economy to accommodate global markets. In 1987 Gorbachev initiated two radical reform policies, *perestroika* (R., restructuring) and *glasnost* (R., opening). The government granted agricultural and industrial endeavors their economic independence and freedom to engage in wholesale trade and international business (Wegren 1998:63). Local and regional economies, already in decline, plummeted still further. Although Gorbachev's policies encouraged the individual acquisition of land for independent farming, those who began private farming encountered major obstacles. Mainstream policies continued to advantage state and collective farm production.[47] Even so, the collective and state farms could not survive the momentum of reform that was taking place. Production continued to decline, and workers' wages dropped drastically in 1990 as compared to other sectors of the national economy. Many of the early subsidies for the state farms in Siberia came from sales of oil, gas, diamonds, and other natural resources. In 1985 the price of oil plummeted, and Gorbachev banned the sale of alcohol when he introduced *glasnost* and *perestroika*. The Soviet economy collapsed. To save face with the populace, Gorbachev continued to subsidize farming, but the system went gradually down and down. During this period, the diamond industry of the Viliui found cheaper sources of meat and milk from temperate regions of southern Siberia, most commonly Novosibirsk. This put an end to their patronage of the Elgeeii and other regional state farms.

In 1991 the Soviet Union disbanded and marked the end of centralized government and the beginning of decentralized regional control. Soon after the Sakha government took up the responsibility for the Republic's internal economic affairs (Tichotsky 2000), Yeltsin passed legislation privatizing collectives and farmland (Wegren 1998). The Sakha government transformed the Republic's 178 state farms into 4569 agricultural endeavors, including approximately 100 GUP (*Gosudarstvennye Unitarnye*

Predpriiatiye, R., state-subsidized agricultural enterprises), 150 collectives, 8 agro-farms, 4 horse farms, 2 poultry farms, 5 agro-manufacturing plants, and 4116 *BKh* (*Bahanai Khazaitsvo*, peasant farming cooperatives). The state conferred the responsibility of deciding the exact forms of these new operations and of seeing through the downsizing to the local state farm directors and village heads.

In June 1992 Elgeeii State Farm officials voted to disband the farm and to divide its assets among members.[48] Each sector of the massive state farm was free to decide just how to divvy up their farm assets. All sectors except one continued some level of cooperative work by transferring members' farm assets into two cooperatives called Elgeeiiski and Khorinski (SRA:16). Each was run by a small group of village farm managers and operated independently of state support. In 1993, the coop's managers liquidated "Elgeeiiskii" and reorganized themselves into village-level enterprises or *TOO, Tovarishchestvo s ogranichennoi otvetstvennost'iu*, (R., "Limited Liability Company"), one in each of the seven former state farm branches.[49] The members of three of these, Daban (in Elgeeii), Kuukei, and Kutana, decided to liquidate their work cooperatives at the end of six more months (SRA: 17). The resulting assets of each cooperative were to be turned over to their members, who would work in small groups know as *BKh*.

Although given the choice to remain a collective, each administrative body of the Elgeeii State Farm's seven branches chose to disband and liquidate farm assets. The process was rapid and corrupt. Local actors transferred state-farm resources, including machinery, animals, land allotments, and other capital reserves, first to themselves and their cronies, then to those in upper-level farm positions, ostensibly to form *BKh*. They then divided the remainder among village households. The result was an uneven allocation of resources and land among inhabitants that left many without sufficient resources to generate household-level subsistence.

Locals and administrators still ponder why such a model state farm plummeted into decline. Elders associate the demise of the Elgeeii State farm with the many years of material and moral decline when people worked poorly, beginning in the 1970s:

> They no longer had the drive toward the wonderful future like we had in the early years. This was partly because the state began cutting budgets across the board and where there used to be plenty to run the farm, suddenly it was run on a shoestring. So this made the administrators do corrupt things like a lot of fuddling of their numbers on the accounts so they could get more resources. (Fyodorov 2000)

Others explain the downfall of the farm in economic terms. The state subsidies that so generously funded the farm's first decades, gradually lessened and by the late 1970s and early 1980s, "real" economics became the rule. One kilo of meat cost 2 rubles ($1.32 USD) at the market but cost 5–6 rubles ($3.30–3.96 USD) to produce.[50] Butter cost 3.60 rubles ($2.38 USD) per kilo at the market but cost 8–9 rubles ($5.28–5.94) to produce.[51]

A former director of the Elgeeii State Farm during the final Soviet years described the times in this way,

> It was a very busy time. We still received some state subsidies, we had lots of equipment and got paid on time. However, people worked very poorly then and still were getting paid no matter how well or poorly they worked. They got it all for free, their health, education, and all was taken care of for free. People worked very poorly. The only good workers were the elders who still had a strong work ethic. I remember in the morning over thirty of us, all who worked in some faction of the *SX* administration would gather at the *khontyora* (main offices). It was a big waste of time. No one did anything they were supposed to and there was no order. I spent the rest of my day going about trying to get people to work. I did this just like all the other brigadiers and administrators of the *SX*. The root of the problem was that people didn't own the land or anything for that matter, and so they didn't care about it and they knew that they would get paid whether they worked well or not. We spent all our time checking up on the workers to see if they showed up for work and to get them to work better. The brigadier's main job was to agitate the workers to work harder. He spent

all summer going from field to field to agitate the workers to cut hay. He would talk about how they needed to cut hay.

The former director went on to give a local depiction of the signs of decline and how the original prosperity and abundance of consumer products for all had changed dramatically by the 1980s:

> In 1985 there were two jeeps for the entire SX. People had no furniture, no color TVs, and no cars. Everyone had motorcycles. Most were happy to have bread, butter, and the quilted coats they wore. Then only the highest up's wives wore fur hats. It was against the law for any others to have fur because all the fur was to go to the SX and sent to Irkutsk to the *Pushnaia Baza* (R., fur stores). It was also against the law to sell any fur for your own profit.

He also accounted the measures that were taken by local authorities to both accommodate for the gap in labor and to try and keep the Soviet reward system for production a vital incentive,

> It was sad how they cut the spruce and ravaged the forest to make extra feed for the cows. They took the trees and put them through the chopper and mixed this with the hay to make a sour mix when they weren't able to cut the amount of hay they needed to overwinter the herds. At the end of grade school, all students worked for two years on the farm. Girls worked as milkers, and boys did various work. They also spent a lot of time going about and waking them up to work in the summer. They also met with the milkers on Fridays to check on their production. If they had fulfilled the pan, they gave the ten or twenty rubles as a prize.[52]

The rise and fall of the Elgeeii State Farm represents a microcosm of events occurring simultaneously across the country at that time. The Soviet policies of collectivization and industrialization transformed the landscapes and cultural orientations of the vast nation. Despite these pervasive forces and due to a resilient adaptive capacity, Viliui Sakha maintained much of their cultural ways and subsistence skills that served to sustain their communities in the turmoil of the USSR fall.

The history of the ever-changing political landscape on the Viliui, especially in the Soviet period, is central to understanding Viliui Sakha cultural resilience and adaptation:[53]

> We need to search out the causes of the present in the past. Only in this way could we come to comprehend the forces that impel societies and cultures here and now. We seem to have forgotten that human populations construct their cultures in interaction with one another and not in isolation. The insights of anthropology have to be rethought in the light of a new historically oriented political economy. (Wolf 1982:ix–xi)

In historical context Sakha have been both the subduers and the subdued. Viliui Sakha represent a population of Sakha who have inhabited the Viliui regions of western Sakha Republic since at least the sixteenth century and, according to some sources, long before. Like Sakha, their ethnic origin, horse and cattle breeding subsistence practices, native cosmology, and worldview are linked to southern roots, most notably to Turkic peoples of Central Asia. Their hierarchical *agha uuha* clan system is a foundational aspect of their culture and subsistence since the earliest records indicate. Remnants of this early clan system are evident in contemporary times and witnessed in Elgeeii's local hierarchy.

Contemporary Viliui Sakha adaptation is directly tied to the local history of Russian colonization and, most notably, Soviet period collectivization and subsequent decollectivization. Prior to the seventeenth century, Sakha practiced subsistence horse and cattle husbandry in relative isolation from the outside world. The centuries that followed saw increasing infringement by Russian colonists on Sakhas' lands and resource wealth and the introduction of products foreign to native cultures. With the twentieth century Soviet collectivization process, Sakha were forced to give up their traditional subsistence lifestyle, including their private holdings, and live in compact villages to work in some facet of the Soviet agro-industrial farming system.

Soviet collectivization brought more pervasive changes in the agropastoralist subsistence of Viliui Sakha. The Soviet push to industrialize meant collectivization and consolidation of lands and herds along with exploration and exploitation of the natural resources of the ancestral homelands across the former USSR. In the Viliui regions the natural resource wealth was diamonds. The discovery of diamonds in the late 1950s, and consequent rapid development of the diamond mining industry to extract them, created an influx of industrial workers. This disproportionately raised the demand for meat and milk products. As a direct result, Viliui Sakha were further consolidated to live in compact villages to work in some facet of the new agro-industrial food production system. Through the 1950s, 1960s, and 1970s, the Elgeeii State Farm flourished along with the diamond industry. Beginning in the mid-1980s, on the heels of *glasnost* and *perestroika*, the direct flows of needed farm products in exchange for farm subsidies began to wane, as the diamond industry grew more transnational. In the late 1980s the state farm lost much of its direct subsidy, and the diamond company turned to the south, most notably to Novosibirsk and Irkutsk, from where they could import the same products at far reduced prices. This exploration of how the processes of Sovietization, specifically of forced collectivization and industrialization, affected Viliui Sakha survival adaptations, sets the stage to explore what happens when those collective and industrial infrastructures "pull out." The early 1990s demise of Soviet power and the concomitant loss of those encompassing agrarian infrastructures present Sakha with a variety of problems related to adopting new subsistence strategies in the post-socialist context.

Notes

Historical ecology is "the important work of environmental historians, anthropologists, geographers, and others who seek to combine evidence of the human past with evidence about the environment . . . " (Crumley, 1994: p. xiii).

1. Tatars, or Tartars, are members of any of the various tribes or hordes, mostly Turkic, inhabiting parts of Russia and of central and western Siberia, loosely, any Siberian Mongoloid.

2. An earlier variant describes Omogoi as a Tartar descended from Tartar *Saat* from the family *Sakhi*. These stories represent a legend

cycle that bolsters theories about Sakhas' southern origins (Ksenofontov 1992).

3. Namely, F. Stralenberg, G. Miller, E. Fisher, Y. Lindenay (Gogolev 1983).

4. Pekarski himself lived in Sakha for twenty years from 1881 to 1899 and wrote his Sakha dictionary for fifty years.

5. A. I. Gogolev argues that Sakha are a new ethnicity founded on southern and northern cultural minglings (Gogolev 1993).

6. A. P. Okladnikov theorized Sakhas' recent southern ancestors to be Kurykan Turks of Baikal who created petroglyphs in the Lensk area of southern Sakha, and dates their northern migration from the tenth to the mid-sixteenth century. Based on a common practice of human burial with a horse, I. V. Constantinov theorized four periods in the formation of Sakha ethnicity: 1) Pre-Kurykan (Gunni or Huns), from the end of the first to fourth centuries, 2) Kurykan from the sixth to tenth centuries, 3) Mongolic from the eleventh to thirteenth centuries, and 4) Yakut (Sakha) from the fifteenth to sixteenth centuries. He explains northern Sakha elements as a result of mingling with Tungus (Constantinov 1975:183–184).

7. Tuvans prayed to the deity *Yotuken* that Pekarski and Ksenofontov show also exists among Sakha.

8. The name of the Sakhas' upper gods is "aiyy," which comes from the verb "to create." Ubriatova declared this ancient verb to have vanished from all Turkic languages except from Sakha and the Turkic noun "aygir," which means "stallion" (Dugarov 1991:267).

9. The Gunni (Huns) main holiday was during the fifth moon of the Chinese calendar, or late May, early June. This was the time when milk was in abundance after spring foaling. "At the 5th moon all sit in a great gathering where they bring ancestral sacrifice to the sky, earth, spirits of people and sky spirits" (Gogolev 1986). The original Gunni (Huns) common prayer to the sky was an appeal to the sun and the fertility deities.

10. Ksenofontov defined three periods of northward migrations—1) when hunter-gatherer reindeer people "Uraankhai," descendants of Tungus with Mongol blood, arrived on the Viliui from the Angara regions of southern Siberia during the fall of the northern Gunni, 100 BP; 2) when horse and cattle herding Kurykan arrived, via the Priangara through Nuyu, Olekma, and Suntar, beginning in the seventh and eighth centuries; and 3) the Ugursky who came from PriBaikal to the middle Lena from the ninth to twelfth centuries (Ksenofontov 1992: 331–442).

11. Called *Buluu*, in Sakha, and long referred to as *Sya Buluu* or "Fat/Abundant *Buluu*" and *Butei Buluu*, meaning a haven of wealth and abundance, referring to the area's rich pasturelands.

12. Tigin was a wealthy leader ruling the Khangalass area of present-day Yakutsk.

13. In 1859, among all Viliui regions there was a total of 2748 reindeer, of which most had been bought from or traded with Tungus for use in the gold mines. The numbers of northern reindeer among Viliui Tungus in the late 1800s, compared with earlier years, was insignificant (Maak 1994:339).

14. Maak described the Viliui reindeer-herders as nomadic herders, hunters, and fishers, "Tungus of the Viliui regions have a wandering life and are reindeer-herders, hunters and fishers. They usually live along the river and lakeshores to fish and hunt waterfowl. They go several thousand *versts* [a Russian unit of measure approximately equaling two-thirds of a mile] from their continuous dwelling place to practice their subsistence lifestyle." He described their range in the late 1800s as limited to the Lower Tunguski and by the Chona River (Maak 1994:22–24). In these remote areas they not only succeeded in resisting assimilation, but many agropastoralist Sakha who settled near these remote areas took up the Tungus lifestyle of hunting, fishing, and reindeer herding. However, assimilation of Tungus to agropastoralist Sakha culture was of greater magnitude than of Sakha to Tungus. In the late nineteenth century P. Klark noted that there were many local Tungus but their lifestyle, disposition, clothes, and language was no different from the agropastoralist Sakha, a fact that also gained them the same social status as the Sakha.

15. The *balaghan* where they held meetings stood until World War II, when it was dismantled for firewood. Only the *sergei* was left standing and stood until it fell over in 1999.

16. Oral history accounts tell how Chokhoroon engineered this huge area also:

During Chokhoroon's time there was a 80-hectare lake in the place called "Aringnakh Ariilaakha." Chokhoroon drained the lake and used it as his own. In ten years a new head came to the Khangalass and confronted Chokhoroon about the inhabitant's dispute, "How is it that one man can have 100 desiatina for his own hay use, especially someone from Tretiy Bordong, on the other side of the river." He picked up a sharp stake at which point Chokhoroon fell to his knees and begged mercy. The lands returned to the Khangalass people. Later, when he once more ordered the people to cut the hay, it being a very dry season, his fields, then overtaken with brush and shrub, burnt up. After that, his lands in Tretiy Bordong were left open and bountiful with hay. It was then called the "Chokhoroon" field. He built a water system and named the largest lake there "Kunday Chokhoroon" (Alekseev et al. 1995:130–132; Ivanov 1995:8–9).

17. Such conflicting impressions are due to the pervasive propaganda of the Soviet period:

> The wealthy were depicted as criminals and enemies of the people only after the October Revolution as part of the propaganda of those times. Now there are no records left of it and no one who lived then is alive now to tell their view. But the local Suntar historical record strongly suggests that the rich were exploiters of the local poor and that was how they got rich.(Iakovlev 1999)

18. Ivan became tyrannical in the latter years of his reign, confiscating land and privileges from peasants and aristocrats. He also killed his eldest son and heir in a fit of rage and murdered some of his seven wives.

19. In 1581 the Stroganov family hired the Cossack Yermak and his band to protect their lands at the foot of the Ural Mountains from local Siberian tribes. Yermak conquered Sibir, the capital of the Tartar khanate, and gave the land to the czar. Although the area was lost and reconquered several times and Yermak himself killed in the following years, the Russian army eventually secured the region in 1586. The word "Siberia" was coined for the Tartar capital.

20. Pushing east to the Sea of Okhotsk, where they were stopped by a Chinese northern army.

21. Since the beginning of *iasak* tribute they had trouble with theft and the losses of taxes reported collected.

22. The 1776 "Bulletin of Dividing Lands in the Viliui District According to Sable and Fox Tax Rates," announced the first land decree and listed land allocations for each district of the Viliui regions. According to the decree each household was allowed to cut a set amount of hay, regardless of the number of members in the household (Borisov 1996). In 1900 a new system was introduced. Each household was then allowed hay based on household size, two *sirgha* (a wooden trailer, holding approximately 2 tons) per adult household member (Iak-Epar 1900). As a result of set boundaries for *iasak* payment, by the end of the nineteenth century the *agha uuha* areas were no longer based on more fluid kin associations but on rigid district boundaries.

23. Since 1771—all through the czarist time, present-day Elgeeii, Tretiy Bordong, inclusive of outlying regions, was called Perviy

Bordong. The entire area was 80 kilometers (50 miles) long and 20 kilometers (12.5 miles) wide, extending halfway to present-day Kutana.

24. There were eighty-five households paying sable and sixty-six paying fox (CSA: 1). According to the 1895 five-year census, Perviy Bordong was sparsely settled compared to contemporary times (now it is home to seven hundred households and more than three thousand people), with only 306 yurts (households), made up of six *agha uuha*, with 819 males and 718 females, 123 land names for hay and pasture areas, 1 church, 1 watch tower, 1 school, 720 hay stacks, and 9 wheat storage places (Iakovlev 1999:35).

25. After 1917, the church stopped functioning and the building was used as a Culture House, to show films and have concerts and lectures. The building burned down in 1954.

26. In Elgeeii one teacher, a Sakha, Dmitri Dmitrievich Tsivzev, from Khangalass, taught for twenty-seven years.

27. These records today can be found in the Yakutsk central archives for ten of thirty-one years from 1877 to 1908.

28. Some prices and salaries at the time: Prices, in *kopeika* (R., kopek, a Russian money form, 100 kopek equals one ruble, which had an exchange rate of 28 rubles to the U.S. dollar in 1999) and per 1 *funt* (R., a weight measure, one *funt* equals 1 pound sterling), were: sugar: 50; tobacco leaves (unworked): 50; hay: 18 per *pud* (R., one *pud* 16 kilograms, 35 pounds), butter: 18.50 rubles per *pud;* and meat: 3.60 per *pud*. Fieldworkers got paid 7 rubles to work one *desiatina* (R. a unit of area approximately equal to 2 3/4 acres) and 4.50 rubles for haying the same area. A list of hay in reserve on January 1, 1901: In I Bordong *nasleg* hay was kept in 25 places at a total of 15,424 *pud*. In 1902, also in 25 places, there was a total of 23,025 *pud* (CSA: 4).

29. The 1929 Bordong I KX tax records include an area to mark if a member was suspected of practicing shamanism. Since at that time local cadres were still local clan members, no one is recorded as practicing. Only later in the mid-1930s, when non-Sakha arrived to run the KXs were shamans forced to stop or were sent to prison to die (CSA: 7).

30. By the mid-1930s, the state had opened *Lik-Bez* in every Viliui KX. The course lasted one year.

31. The mandatory training in reading and writing of all state workers.

32. This group included Oyunski, Ammosov, and Kunday. In the 1930s they were all repressed.

33. In 1932 a committee was formed to Latinize native scripts, the majority of which had been cyrillicized, to break with the imperialist past. The teachers of this new script were the local leaders of existing Soviet infrastructure—from Party members to the young *Komsomols* (R., the youth party affiliate of the Communist Party) and the Soldiers of Culture. Instruction included teaching Soviet values and served well the new protocol of "(Soviet) Cultural Construction."

34. See the case studies of Grant 1995, Humphrey 1998, Anderson 2000, Fondahl 1998, Golovnev and Osherenko 1999, and Ziker 2001.

35. The local record of Stalin's late-1930s purges went largely undocumented. The first Soviet census was in 1927. The results of the next census in 1937 were never released since the population had barely increased in that ten-year period and this would give Stalin's socialism a bad name. The results were destroyed. However, a record did survive of the preliminary count, or the *Predvarytelniie itogi perepisi 1937* (R.) made between January 7 and January 25. The count showed a precipitous drop in numbers across the former Soviet Union, which they account for by Stalin's purge tactics (Iakovlev 1999).

36. New taxes of 4 kilograms (9 pounds) of rendered butter per cow annually deterred many from meeting even the five-cow limit.

37. In 1930 Suntar and Khocho regions came together to form one Suntar *ulus*. In 1930 there were three *naslegs* that formed the Sadinski regions and at first this was an Evenk "National Region" and comprised Botuobuya (Taas Yurekh), Chona (Toy Khaia), and Sadin (Suldukur).

38. "Contemporary Elgeeii was called Perviy Bordong until 1934 when Elgeeii was formed out of Perviy Bordong, Tretiy Bordong and Khoro. From 1919 to 1934 Toloon was called Elgeeii then it joined Bordong I and was called that. In 1934 when the new borders were drawn, that Oruktaakh area was given to Tretiy Bordong—to Stalin *KX* and the other to the other side of the river—to the various Kuukei *KXs*" (Iakovlev 1999).

39. The over one thousand *KXs* in the Sakha Republic before WWII were collapsed into seventy state farms by late 1960.

40. Results of the April 1960 competition declared two first-place milkers, one man and one woman, who each milked an average of 320 kilos of milk per cow each month, and received a 300-ruble bonus. The two second-place winners, both women, milking an average of 235 kilos per cow per month, received a 200-ruble bonus. The three third-place female milkers, averaging 225 kilos per cow per month, received a 100-ruble bonus.

41. Nineteen-fifty-seven marked the beginning of electricity in the village, with the opening of the first diesel electric station. It was

not until 1973 that Elgeeii and other villages in the area were given centralized electricity from the high voltage lines coming from the Viliui hydroelectric company.

42. In 1956 each milk cow produced 783 kilograms (1723 pounds) of milk annually, in 1966 each cow produced 1643 kilograms (3615 pounds). Zhuravlev described it in his memoirs:

In 1956 the 892 hectares of the former collective produced 3.1 tons of grain, 8.4 tons of potatoes and 2.5 tons of garden produce. From the same land in 1966 the state farm produced over 300 tons of potatoes, 276 tons of meat and 1596 tons of milk. In the collective period and as late as 1956 it cost 26 *kuluhun kune* to produce 100 kilos of meat. In 1966 it cost 8.9 workdays to produce the same amount. Additionally, it cost 7 *kuluhun kune* to produce 100 kilos of milk whereas now it costs 2.23 work days. (SRA: 11: 6–7)

43. The annual records from 1959 through 1961 (SRA: 12) show the state farm's planned and actual growth and decline from one year to the next (see table 2.5). There may or may not have been some fudging going on of the numbers recorded.

44. Referring to the 1973 completion of high voltage lines from the Viliui hydrostation. The downside was that while building the hydrodam, all the farms within the regions downriver suffered severe droughts in spring when the ice flows normally brought waters to flood the hay fields and pastures throughout the watershed. As a result, the farms experienced huge losses (see SRA: 13).

Table 2.5.   Elgeeii State Farm's Planned and Actual Growth, 1959–1961

	1959		1960		1961	
	Plan	Results	Plan	Results	Plan	Results
All Cows	9200	9353	10876	11549	11550	11712
Milk Cows	3300	3322	3975	4116	4100	4187
All Horses	4630	4630	5538	5631	6300	9192
Mares	1400	1457	1950	2106	2200	2056
All Pigs	455	181	673	694	640	499
Sows	41	32	45	83	25	93
All Reindeer	320	321	365	368	500	344
Cows	110	140	149	131	160	110
All Fox	200	199	271	284	290	280
Dogs	150	149	211	219	225	225
All Chickens	—	—	1379	3008	2000	2914
Lay Hens	—	—	1240	1684	1800	1268

45. Canvassing materials included information about alcohol abuse and instructions for how to deal with alcoholics, by using public disgrace and embarrassment or pay decreases (SRA: 13).

46. The plan did surface in January 1992. However, it again went under a short five months later with the folding of the state farm. The Elgeeii State Farm director at that time, Ivanov, responded to a Republic-wide decree entitled "For the Development of Gasification of the Villages," by appointing one of the farm's senior engineers as the head of a gasification plan for the villages within the state farm territory (SRA: 15). In the post-Soviet period, plans to sell the gas for hard currency to China have permanently altered this locally sustainable forestry and energy conservation plan.

47. Gorbachev's Fundamentals of Land Legislation (Feb 1990), indicated that USSR citizens could lease land for peasant farming (no ownership). After December 1990, Russian legislation allowed members of state and collective farms (and their families) to leave the farm and use a land plot from the parent farm free of charge. Gorbachev held out against private property and to maintain the state and collective farm structure (Wegren 1998: 46).

48. Following the proposal put forth by the April 29 conference of Elgeeii State Farm employees, the Supreme Soviet of the USSR administered a decree in June 1992, "About the Decentralization and Reformation of the Ordena Lenina State Farm Elgeeii into the Ordena Lenina Collective Enterprise 'Elgeeiiski.'"

49. Detailed in SRA: 1.

50. Prior to *perestroika* the exchange rate was at a constant level of 1 dollar to .66 rubles (Prokhorov 1980: 1598).

51. It takes 100 kilograms (220 pounds) of milk to make 3.5 kilograms (7.7 pounds) of butter.

52. I asked if he was a communist and he said he was:

I couldn't have been a director without being a communist. I would have never advanced higher than being an engineer if I weren't in the Party. Being a communist made you above everyone else. There was a moral code to be in the Party which included rules like no drinking but everyone did anyway and absolute loyalty to your spouse but no one paid that any heed either. The Party officials didn't solicit intelligentsia into the party—they wanted only the working class. There was an annual plan for all administrative center regarding the number of communists they were to bring into the party—the percent milkers, tractorists, teachers, doctors and other workers. But again, the percent of intelligentsia was very low because they were intelligent and would shout and stand up for their opinions—Party officials didn't want that so they focused on the working class.

53. History didn't get the attention of early cultural ecologists. Roy Rappaport especially downplayed the importance of history by assuming his consultants had had these traditions 'forever' (Rappaport 1967). Robert Netting didn't do much history in his study of the Kofyar (Netting 1968) but later he used history extensively in his study of an Alpine village (Netting, 1981).

3

Cows-and-Kin: The Cultural Ecology of Post-Soviet Viliui Sakha Survival

Viliui Sakha Villages on the Eve of the Twenty-First Century

In Viliui Sakha villages, cows are everywhere—they freely roam the streets, exercising their right of way over a milieu of motorcycles with sidecars, pedestrians, occasional cars, and bicycles. Where there is not a cow, there are cow signs—the ever-growing piles of dung that line the snow-covered streets in winter, the *khotons* with their corrals that consume half of each cow-keeping household's yard, the cow paths that wind through the scraggly spruce, fir, larch, and birch lining the village lanes and the river's banks.

Cow rhythms and cow signs change with the seasons. From late spring through early fall, when there are green fields on the village outskirts to graze, cows follow a daily pasture regime—in the first few hours of morning light they flow in a constant train out of the village to graze for the day and, in a similar processional, return home in the last several hours of evening light. During the subarctic winter they are confined to barns. Their manure piles grow steadily then vanish with spring cleaning. Households incorporate some into their garden plot, but most they haul away to the village dung dump or to the forest at the edge of town. Cow paths also change seasonally—from the muddy, wet paths of spring to the dusty dry of summer to the well-trodden, ice-crusted snow paths of winter.

Figure 3.1. A classic cow yard

The presence or lack of cows is obvious upon entering a household yard. If a household keeps cows, their yard is dominated by cow space—the *khoton* and adjoining corral (figure 3.1). Cow-keeping yards also are storage areas for cow fodder, holding at least one and up to five haystacks, positioned by seniority from the *khoton*. All yards, cow-keeping or not, are fenced. Fences act not only to keep dogs and drunks out, but also to keep young newborn calves in and "roaming to pasture" cows out of households' tasty green garden produce and flowers.

You will also see many signs of cows inside a cow-keeping house. The first room of most households is an uninsulated entry room. Besides serving as an all-purpose mudroom, this room is where household cow keeper(s) hang their clothes before entering the house. The room also is used as a meat locker from November to April, when outside temperatures are consistently below freezing. It is not uncommon to find several entire cow sides propped against the entry-room walls. In November, freshly slaughtered cow meat, in whole carcass or meal-size portions, is stored here, positioned to move, piece by piece into the household for winter consumption or to be stored for spring and summer use in the household's or nearby kin's *buluus*. In lieu of access to a *buluus*, households store their meat and other animal products in a wooden chest in the entry room or an outside building under padlock, in either case, consuming the stores or moving them to an electric freezer before the spring thaw. You may also see various internal organs and blood sausage, all Sakha delicacies, stored in the entry room until eaten over the winter holidays. In the warmer months, the entry room is storage for dry goods, including sacks of flour, sugar, rice, buckwheat groats, boxes of macaroni, and cases of canned foods (figure 3.2).

The entry room is also a center of milk-processing activities. In the winter months, household members pour excess milk into shallow round pans to freeze for future use or to send to kin in need of milk. Frozen discs of milk can travel to a needy next-door neighbor or as far as students in the capital city, Yakutsk. Sakha also make *bohuuke* (ice cream) in the entry room by dropping tablespoons of whipped crème fraîche sweetened with berry preserves or sugar, onto a flat surface, where it freezes in minutes.

Figure 3.2.   The uninsulated entry room, used to store a wide range of things

Households who still make *taar* keep the barrel in the entry room for easy access when they need to chop off a section for winter use. In the summer, households often use the entry room for milk separating, butter making, and the manufacture of *kymys* or, since few households hold horses, *bipak* (fermented cow's milk).

Inasmuch as cows and their signs are ubiquitous in rural Viliui Sakha life, kin are also everywhere, albeit their signs are more subtle. The presence of kin in a given household's daily life, like that of cows, determines how well a household lives in the post-Soviet context. A thirty-five-year-old mother of five said it succinctly, "Aimakh—naadalaakh shtuuka" (Relatives are a most necessary item). Kin relations are so regular and vital to contemporary rural life that you could represent the village just by tracing the flows between households of kin-based exchange and interaction. Sakha have always shared money, meat, wood, time, hearth, labor, and other resources with kin. What is compelling in the contemporary context is how kin interdependencies have arisen anew in the post-Soviet context of product scarcity and economic decline after a long period of relative economic stability and political oppression.

I show in this chapter how Viliui Sakha have adapted to the sudden loss of Soviet infrastructure, employment, and consumer products by developing household-level food production based on cow-keeping and interdepending with kin. This "cows-and-kin" system is Viliui Sakhas' adaptive response to a rapidly changing political context. In the process of discovering the cows-and-kin adaptation, I was also able to explain a phenomenon that had piqued my curiosity for years—namely, how household tables are laden with food within five minutes of a guest's arrival, when local store shelves are well-stocked only with alcohol, cigarettes, and candy but are glaringly empty of nutritional foods.

In contrast to the Soviet period, when households had the funds for and the access to a variety of food products in local stores, today a household only eats well if they or a kin household keeps cows. In the pages that follow I will guide you to discover this for yourself by taking you on the ethnographic trail through two Viliui Sakha villages, Elgeeii and Kutana, that I followed from July 1999 through July 2000. My main questions at the time were, "How are Viliui Sakha adapting their household food production strategies in the post-Soviet era, and, how are those adaptations affected by kinship patterns, land tenure systems, resource rights and access, and issues of regional mineral exploitation and environmental justice?" I begin by explaining the workings of contemporary village life and household subsistence strategies.

Moving through the Seasons: Village and Household Life

It is a challenge to live and extract a subsistence within the ecological constraints of the subarctic, with its brief growing season and long winter period. Every Sakha waits in great anticipation for summer, when the weather is finally warm enough to don just a shirt and shorts. Summers are warm, and household doors stay open with screen valances to keep out abundant mosquitoes, midges, and black flies. The days are long, highlighted by a month around the summer solstice when the sun only fleetingly sets, creating an ethereal nocturnal world.

Sakha contend that summer is both the best and the worst time of year. I've often heard them comment, "We never see the summer," in reference to the endless work of the brief season. Rural Viliui Sakha have no time to enjoy because they must hurry through summer, harvesting enough hay and crops; gathering and preparing forage and firewood; building and repairing houses, cow barns, and other structures; and fulfilling the many other necessary activities in preparation for winter. Summer work is winter survival, or as Sakha say, "A day in summer is worth a week of winter."

Sakha personify winter, the most challenging season for them, in the form of the *Jyl Oghuha* (Bull of Winter), a white bull with blue spots, huge horns, and frosty breath. In early December the *Jyl Oghuha* arrives from the Arctic Ocean to hold temperatures at their coldest ($-60°$ to $-65°$ C; $-76°$ to $-85°$F) for December and January.[1] By January's end, winter has reached its peak. On the last day of January, a mighty eagle arrives from the south. Child of the warm sky, he scoops up snow in his nest and lets out a loud cry. From the eagle's cry, the bull of winter retreats and his horns, one by one, fall off. Later, as spring approaches, his head rolls off. During the ice flows, the trunk of the bull of winter swims at the bottom of the Lena to the Arctic Ocean, and the ice flow takes away the spirits of dead people and herds (Ergis 1974:123–124).[2] Popular oral accounts that I have heard don't mention an eagle. They instead relate that in early February the bull loses one of his horns, and temperatures soften. By early March the other horn falls and, as the bull has no horns to defend himself and prove his strength, spring begins.

Sakha count on a regular series of spring heralds. The first is the late March appearance of *tammakhtar* (droplets), from melting icicles that begin their dripping when the sun's angle is great enough to melt ice despite freezing ambient temperatures. In early May migrating ducks arrive to nest or fly on to the Arctic. Around this same time the first *n'urguhunnar* (snow drops) push up through the frozen, still snow-covered earth. Mid-May is when you first hear the *keghe's* (cuckoo) songs echoing through the villages and forests. By late May the *kuoregei* (meadowlarks) begin their courtship dancing, hovering for several minutes in the sky singing a frantic buzz-call and then plummeting to the earth like a rock (Andreev 1974:166, 134). These heralds bring life and activity to Sakha villagers, who become busy with spring cleaning and preparations for the long-anticipated arrival of summer.

Village surrounds also come to life. From mid-May, forests and pastures transform quickly from dead browns and grays to fresh bright greens. The springtime growth of new larch needles appears as a slowly intensifying green haze across the woodland. True summer has arrived when the new bright green birch leaves are the size of *sobo* tongues. June can often still be chilly and damp, but July is consistently hot and dry. Villages become ghost towns, with most inhabitants off haying and foraging, preparing for the winter to come. Then suddenly summer is over and the time has come to gather tools and bring in the last harvests before the snow falls in September. The Viliui Sakha household and its web of interdependent kin households is the core of economic activity in the village. The descriptions and analyses that follow give a close-up of how household and inter-household dynamics worked within the 1999–2000 village contexts of Elgeeii and Kutana.

Households average from three to five members but can range from one to eleven. Over half of all households are nuclear in make-up, with a husband, wife, and their dependent children, and often function intergenerationally with kin households in their village. One-fourth of all households are intergenerational, including three or more generations under one roof. The remaining households are either headed by a single, widowed or divorced member or multiheaded by a mix of relatives.

When the 2000 village population is represented in an age-sex pyramid, two age groups are underrepresented, sixteen- to thirty-year-olds and fifty- to sixty-year olds. The former are absent because high school graduates tend to leave the village either to get a higher education; find employment in the regional center, Suntar, or capital city, Yakutsk; or marry and move to the spouse's village. The rest remain in the village to help parents.

The low numbers in the elder age group reflect the effects of World War II, when there was both a low reproduction rate with men gone from the household to fight the war, and a high infant mortality rate from starvation. Elders are also absent because many have moved to the regional center or Yakutsk for better living conditions.

In general, employment and opportunity are largely found outside rural Viliui Sakha villages. This creates a pull to these places for both high school graduates and those who desire work by their professional training. The village is a place for young families (parents aged thirty to forty) who are raising children in the context of their kin. The elder peaks above sixty are pensioners, most of whom live in intergenerational households, who often supply childcare and a majority of the cash for the household's mixed cash economy from their monthly pension.

Origins, Ancestry, and Mobility

Contemporary Viliui Sakha have strong ancestral ties to their homelands. Most Elgeeii and Kutana household heads were either born in their present village or in an adjacent one, all of which were part of the massive Elgeeii State Farm system. Many were resettled, willingly or forcibly, to the farm centers when the state liquidated smaller villages during state farm consolidation. A handful of residents in both Elgeeii and Kutana are Soviet period "newcomers" who arrived from different parts of the USSR on a state order to work as a technical expert for the farm. Most were brought to Elgeeii, the state farm center at the time. Similarly, many inhabitants of smaller villages moved to Elgeeii in the Soviet period for their children's schooling, since it was the only settlement in the state farm territory that had a school beyond the fourth grade. Elgeeii, overall, is home to a more transient, less kin-involved population than Kutana.

Most Sakha today only know their ancestral lineage to their grand- or great-grandparents. Sakha historically knew their ancestry through the ninth generation to facilitate exogamy when they lived in extended clan settlements. This practice was broken by the spatial changes in settlement patterns of Soviet period collectivization and state farm consolidation. Kin networks were further disrupted covertly by replacing local solidarities and native power structures with Soviet representation espousing obedience to the state. Now, in the context of post-Soviet ethnic revival, many Viliui Sakha are reconstructing their kin lineages and reestablishing contact with their extended relatives.

Despite the high unemployment, delayed salaries, shortages, and primitive living conditions including lack of running water, toilets, paved roads, and central heating, most village inhabitants wouldn't move even if they had the opportunity to do so. The few that leave go for their children's education or more job opportunities. The parents and relatives of high-school graduated youth encourage them to leave the village for the regional or capital centers, where they can get a degree and find employment. Most youth who do leave plan to return to their birth village despite the allure of a brighter future in the more cosmopolitan areas. They leave with the intent to get a higher education and return to their home village to work and raise a family. They often cannot return for years due to the lack of village jobs.

Household Income

In the post-Soviet context Viliui Sakha households depend on a mixed cash economy,[3] a combination of traditional subsistence production and cash inputs. Household cash is from state transfer payments in the form of salaries, pensions, and subsidies, and to a lesser extent from unofficial transactions.[4] Most households depend on one or more pension incomes, either from elder kin living in-house or within the immediate village.[5] The majority of salaried jobs are state-subsidized white-collar positions in administration, health care, and education. The remainder are blue-collar and highly seasonal, including shoveling coal for one of the many village furnaces or haying for a village cooperative. Half of all households depend on "freelance" or self-employed income, including odd jobs,[6] home crafts,[7] the sale of plant and animal products, and income from hauling hay, wood, or ice by tractor and truck.

For rural Viliui Sakha it was not the women who disproportionately suffered from lost employment, as was the case in most of the Former Soviet Union (FSU). The disbanding of Viliui regional state farms generated unemployment mainly among men, leaving women slightly more employed as wage earners than their male counterparts. In 2000 women brought home 56 percent of household income. Women also continued to perform the majority of work in the home, juggling child rearing, food preparation and production, and cattle husbandry, bearing the "double burden" of wage and domestic work established in the Soviet period (Buckley 1989).[8] On top of that, many women were single mothers and household heads, factors that make their work load even heavier.

Household economic characteristics from 2000 show that unemployment, lack of products, and decreased purchasing power has replaced the full employment, product availability, and fluid purchasing power of the Soviet period. While the majority of surveyed households had one or two state-salaried workers, some had none (table 3.1). Similarly, a majority had one or two pension incomes but one-third had none. There is crossover in this data resulting in some households having both salary and pension incomes, while others have neither. Therefore, the village household income data reflects a new trend of income disparity between households, a break from the Soviet period, when household incomes were relatively the same due to state subsidized employment, subsidies, and pensions.

Table 3.1.   Percentage of Surveyed Households
with Incomes from a Salary and/or a Pension

Number of Incomes	Percentage of Households
Salary Incomes	
0	24
1	42
2	29
3+	5
Pension Incomes	
0	33
1	40
2	24
3+	3

In households with both a salary and pension income, state salary makes up about half of a given household's monetary resources, with the remainder from pensions, child subsidies, and money made through informal means. The 2000 total average household income of surveyed households was 2431 rubles ($87 USD) per month. The official poverty-line indicator set by the state in 2000 of monthly income per household member was 1400 rubles ($50 USD). Just to reach this minimum, a household of four would need to make 5600 rubles ($200 USD) per month, or over two times the average income of surveyed households. Residents and administrators question how relevant the state's minimum income level is, since the amount of cash a given household needs depends more on that household's capacity to produce its own food.

Most households are involved in home food production, which ameliorates a lack of monetary resources. Over half of all households keep cows and other domestic animals to produce meat, milk, and eggs. Seventy percent grow a substantial portion of their own food and 65 percent forage, hunt, and fish to supplement domestic food production (figures 3.3 and 3.4). In the post-Soviet context of high unemployment, Sakha, like their counterparts across Russia, have increased their dependence on both pre-Soviet and contemporary household-level modes of

Figure 3.3. Mungkha *fishing for* sobo (Carassius carassius) *on Ulgutta Lake*

food production to supplement the gap left by a shift from dependence on the socialist infrastructure for employment and consumer goods to the unemployment, poor distribution, and other economic hardships of post-Soviet times.

Tapping the Energetic Pathways

For centuries, Sakha have successfully tapped the flow of energy from natural plants to their livestock, horses, and cows. Contemporary rural Viliui Sakha, like their ancestors before them, supplement their cows-and-kin subsistence by accessing a wide range of "energetic pathways,"[9] both domestic and wild. Domestic meat and milk are Sakhas' dietary staples, and are supplemented by a variety of energetic pathways to buffer risk. The contemporary Sakha production calendar shows the "menu" of energetic pathways. Below are two production calendars. The first is an historical schema from a local Sakha specialist (table 3.2).[10] The second is a contemporary production calendar that I created based on time allocation observations from July 1999 through July 2000 (table 3.3).[11]

Figure 3.4. An elder has successfully taught her granddaughter how to snare ptarmigan.

If these chronological activities are charted according to activity categories, the following schema results (figure 3.5).[12]

This chart shows that Viliui Sakha spend most of their energy tapping pathways in the summer through the late fall period. Charting observations of activities related to the tapping

Table 3.2.   The Historical Sakha Calendar

Date	Activity
May 28	Sakha New Year
End of May	Planting of cold hardy garden crops
Early June	Prep and planting of greenhouses
June 21–28	Yhyakh—in old tradition, nine days of festival
July 12–October 5	**Hay Harvest**
July 12–Aug 1	Bastaki khotuur, the first cutting of hay
Aug 2–25	Ot ulete ugene, culmination of harvesting—make big stacks, secure in household yard or in field with fences
	Hay Harvest (after frost):
Aug 25–Sept 10	Khadang ot, harvesting the remains (no vitamins)
Sept 25–Oct 5	Muus otono, cutting around lake edges when water frozen
July 15–Aug 25	Berry foraging (in order of appearance): khaptaghas (red currants), jejen (strawberry), malina (R., red raspberry), sugun (blueberry), monyoghon (black currant), oton (cowberry)
Aug 20–25	Fall duck hunting season begins and lasts until around October 5, if mild, or earlier, when water bodies frozen and ducks can not survive.
Aug 25–Nov 1	Household return from saylykh (summer home)
Sept 5	Potato, cabbage, and all root crops harvested, stored in root cellar, or canned Prep for winter—all outside work done before snow covers
Sept 12	Supplement cows with hay portions as hay in pastures already freezing
Oct 10–12	Time of first snows—cows stop going to pasture—now feed cut hay
Oct 15–Nov 10	Mungkha fishing
Oct 15–January	Game hunting: several weeks/months for moose, reindeer, bear, squirrels
Oct 28–Nov 10	Main time for ice harvest for drinking water
Nov 7–14	Cow slaughtering time—done in household's yard
Nov 18–25	Horse slaughtering time—done in pastures where horses stay
January	Begin supplementing horses with hay
Late March–Early April	Kuyuur fishing
March	Spring begins
April	Snow begins to go down, horses can't walk—feed extra
April	Cows out of khoton and eat in open air
Late April–Mid-May	Sahaan—firewood cutting and prep
May 10–17	Spring duck hunting season
May 15–June 15	Households move to Saylykh
May 25	Cows first to pasture

Table 3.3.   A Contemporary Sakha Calendar based on 1999–2000 Time
Allocation Observations

Date	Activity
March 23–April 16	*Kuyuur* fishing
April 10–October 12	Period when households live at *saylykh*
April 16–May 31	*Sahaan*—firewood cutting and prep
April 29–August 18	Prep, planting, and maintenance of greenhouses
May 12–May 24	Duck hunting, spring
May 24–September 25	Prep, planting, and maintenance of open gardens
May 31–July 24	River fishing
June 5–December 1	Housebuilding
June 11	Hay prep—securing fences
July 19–August 17	Summer hay cutting
July 22–Sept 25	Berry, mushroom, rosehip foraging
July 24–August 12	Outbuilding repair and construction
August 6–18	Duck hunting, fall
August 6	*Ilim* fishing
August 6–August 18	Harvesting potatoes, open crops
August 6–November 24	Firewood hauling
August 18–October 30	Seal *khotons*
August 18–November 6	Game hunting
October 12–November 16	*Mungkha* fishing
October 19–31	Cow slaughtering time—done in household's yard;
November 6–April 10	Horse tending in outlying pastures
November 24–January 7	*Sylyhar* fishing
November 24–January 7	Winter hay hauling

of pathways adds the perspective of local household involvement. The top graph of figure 3.6 shows how many households, out of twenty I observed per day in time allocation research, were involved in some form of food foraging activity.

Again, the chart shows that most of these activities are highly seasonal except for fishing, which in its various forms can be done throughout the year.

The bottom graph of figure 3.6 uses the same type of data to show annual activities related to tapping the domestic sources of energetic pathways. This graph emphasizes the central reality of Sakha life—that cow-care is a year-round, constant, and paramount activity.

Seasonal Activity Schedule

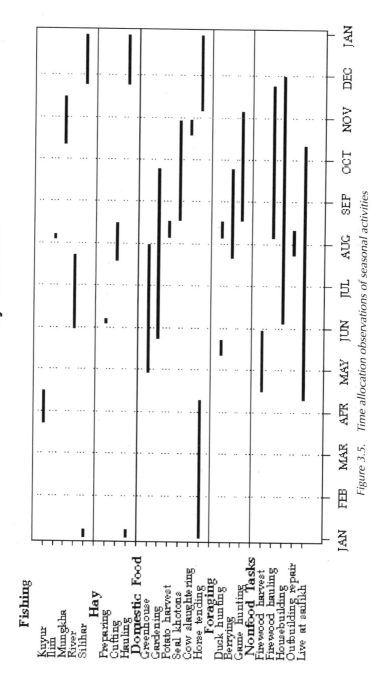

Figure 3.5.   Time allocation observations of seasonal activities

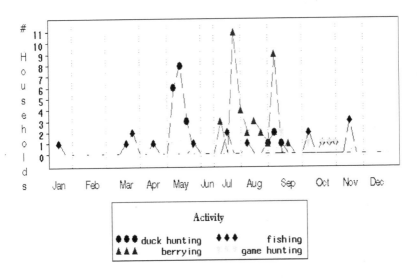

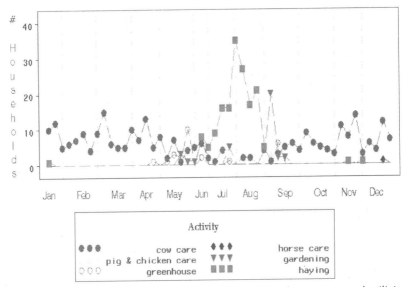

Figure 3.6. Tapping the energetic pathways: Harvesting from nature and utilizing domestic pathways

Successful Viliui Sakha households depend on cows and a variety of "energetic pathways" to supplement home food production. Of them, horse and cattle husbandry, hunting, fishing, and foraging are subsistence practices from before Russian colonization (Seroshevski 1993; Maak 1994). Russian Cossacks and clergy introduced the practice of domestic gardening and agricultural production when they settled on the Viliui and cultivated grain for bread and grew potatoes and other vegetables. Grain agriculture, first documented on the Viliui in 1760, was a fairly common practice on a household level among both Russian and Sakha homesteads by 1864 (Basharin 1989:206). Likewise, by 1842 many Sakha households were cultivating potatoes, and a majority grew grains and potatoes by the early twentieth century (Basharin 1989:275). Some inhabitants cultivated vegetables, including cabbages, turnips, carrots, and cucumbers, beginning in 1794 in the Suntar regions (Basharin 1990:38). Greenhouse production and small animal husbandry are household-level adoptions of strategies introduced by Soviet culture workers. In the Soviet period, local state farm workers were trained in modern agricultural techniques including greenhouse production of tomatoes and cucumbers, field production of cabbage and other cold weather crops, and diversified domestic animal production including chicken, pig, duck, goose, and rabbit husbandry. With the end of state farm production, households lost their access to local vegetables and meats. The only way for households to have fresh products is to raise them themselves.

To Tap or Not to Tap

Contemporary Viliui Sakha households have a variety of energetic pathways for the tapping and most make an effort to tap them. Most households with young children make a great effort to tap pathways in order to provide a variety of foods, a vitamin-rich and well-balanced diet, and in some cases household income. But just because these energetic pathways are available does not mean that all households can or do take advantage of them. There are inputs required to tap the energetic pathways and not every household has those inputs to "spend," or chooses to "spend" them in these ways. Some households fail to tap the available pathways even when children are present. Several of the households I worked with had six and more children but kept only one or two milk cows and failed to participate in any foraging, hunting, or fishing. Even though they depended only on an elder pension, they bought all their food and remained in a constant state of debt. Reasons for this are varied and include poverty, alcoholism, disinterest, neglect, lack of kin support, and lack of production knowledge.

There are also forces beyond the local that deter households from tapping the available energetic pathways. The use of local resources has become a political tool for financial gain. Since these once isolated villages of provincial Russia have been a part of the global phenomenon of transnationalization, the government began to value and quantify the use of local resources by introducing taxes, fees, and licenses to exploit them. Locals are getting a mixed message. On the one hand, the Sakha government has been a strong advocate of home food production and has introduced supportive policies and subsidies in recent years. At the same time, with the combination of increased pressures on limited resources and continued economic decline, the state sees it fit to charge inhabitants to utilize what were once "free" products.

Despite the nuances of tapping the various energetic pathways for contemporary Viliui Sakha village subsistence, the core household-level survival strategy in the post-Soviet context is cows-and-kin. I take the rest of this chapter to explore the history, mechanics, and many modes of this adaptive strategy.

Having What It Takes: The Demands of Keeping Cows in the Subarctic

Cows are not only *everywhere*, but they are *everything* to survival in Viliui Sakha villages. If you keep cows, meat is in constant supply for daily soup and main dishes. Similarly, you have milk for tea, considered the only way to drink tea. With a supply of milk, you are able to produce all the Sakha milk foods.[13] You also have a ready supply of milk for any young children in your, in neighboring, or in kin households. The Sakha proverb, still used today, "Bys da sya, bas da aryy," (Cut the fat and spoon the butter), means that if you have fat meat and butter by the spoonful then you are wealthy (Sleptsov 1972:354).[14] In contemporary Viliui Sakha villages, a cow herd continues to signify wealth and is the basis of survival.

Viliui Sakha are a cow-centered people, an attribute that links them with other of the world's bovine-centric cultures like the Nuer of East Africa (Evans-Pritchard 1940) and herders of the American Midwest. Sakha share many of the same characteristics and habits of world cow cultures, including a primary dependence on cows not only for food but also for clothing and construction materials, for draft animals, and for spiritual grounding. *Eiekhsit*, the cow deity, plays a major role in the Sakhas' ancestral belief system among the pantheon of sky gods.[15] Even after the oppression of spiritual practices in the Soviet period, many households have an ancestrally based spiritual relationship with their herd.[16] Sakhas' annual calendar of subsistence activities is essentially a cow calendar, dominated by cow-care and cow activities. We can think of Sakha as "The Nuer of the North."

Contemporary Sakha villages are built for cows, in the same way that cities are often designed for cars. Each household's allotted yard has ample room for a *khoton*, for open-air corrals for cows, and for the storage of cow fodder and cow-related equipment. Similarly, each household is allotted an area within the village territory for hay harvesting to overwinter their herd.

Cows provide Sakha with their main subsistence source, but at a high cost. Having cows is labor- and time-intensive. If we plot the annual cycle of all (seasonal and year-round, not including haying activities) cow-care activities, we see peaks of activity during spring calving and fall slaughtering, and a decrease in activity in the summer, when cows spend most of their waking hours at and traveling to and from pasture.

A time allocation analysis of cow labor shows that it is age- and sex-defined (table 3.4). Elders are the primary cow-caregivers in intergenerational cow-keeping households. Such a labor division makes sense in a society where adult household members

Table 3.4. Time Allocation for Cow-Care by Age/Sex

Age/Sex of Members and Household Cow Status	% of Annual Time in Daily Cow-Care	% of Annual Time in Hay Production
Cow-keeping Households		
Male Elders (age 56+)	20	6
Female Elders	17	3
Male Adults (19–55 yrs)	10	8
Female Adults	10	1
Male Youth (12–18 yrs)	1	5
Female Youth	3	1
Male Children (4–11 yrs)	—	2
Female Children	1	1
Average across age/sex of cow-keeping households	**10**	**4**
Non-cow-keeping Households		
Male Elders	—	3
Female Elders	0.3	—
Male Adults	—	3
Female Adults	0.2	—
Male Youths	—	—
Female Youths	—	—
Male Children	—	—
Female Children	—	—
Average across age/sex of non-cow-keeping households	**0.5**	**1.5**

are regularly employed. But in most Viliui Sakha households one or both adult heads are unemployed. Elders explain their continued role as the main cow-caregivers in terms of habit—they have done it all their lives, it gives them purpose, and they are most knowledgeable at it. Daily cow-care labor also comes from the adult and elder females of non-cow-keeping households to reciprocate for a supply of cow products from cow-keeping kin households. Cow care involves a slate of activities year-round and others that have high seasonal variance.

Year-Round Activities

Year-round cow-care duties revolve around tending the household herd and require from two to six hours a day depending on the season. Although summer is the bottleneck period for haying activity, it is least labor intensive for daily cow-keeping chores. In the temperate months from the end of May through early September, cows go to pasture each morning after milking, to return only in the late evening for a second milking. After the morning milking, the cow-tender heads the herd out of town to pasture.[17] Once the cow-tender has watered and fed the calves, which stay in the household yard, they are free of cow duties until the herd returns late at night. On average summer cow-care takes from two to four hours daily, depending on if cow-tenders are young or elderly. Half of that time spent in the straining, separating, and overall transformation of milk into various Sakha milk foods. Another important summer cow-tending duty is making *tupte*, a mixture of dry manure and other cow corral debris that smolders in a heap to ward off mosquitoes and biting flies, near the cow corral or street where the herd gathers (figure 3.7).

Cow-tending duties increase substantially once winter comes and cows are not making a daily journey to pasture. Winter cow-care is spent tending the herd in the *khoton* for an hour or more three times a day, in the morning, at noonday, and in the evening.

Figure 3.7. Cows gathering by tupte *to ward off biting insects*

Morning duties include feeding and watering the cows, milking, and cleaning manure out of the barn and hauling it to make *bal-baakh*, (see "Seasonal Cow-Care" section below). At midday, cows are fed and taken to water at a nearby river or lake. In the evening cows are watered, fed, and milked, and the barn is cleaned of manure again. In the deep winter, when temperatures remain below −30C (−22°F), cows are kept in the *khoton* around the clock.[18] This daily regime that lasts from early September to late May can take household cow-tenders anywhere from three to seven hours.

From January through May cows are calving.[19] If cows calve when the herd is not yet going to pasture, new calf care duties are added to the already high-labor duties of winter cow-care. New calves also mean increased milk production (cows are not milked at all for about six weeks before they are expected to calve), adding the additional tasks of separating and transforming the milk products into various foods for the household larder.

Beginning in March, when the sun climbs higher and higher in the sky each day, warming the daytime air and bringing the first *tammakhtar*, cows start coming out of their *khotons* to feed in their corrals and to go to water. They also begin roaming the village and can be seen standing along the streets in the sun's warming rays, like solar collectors, with no movement except the rhythmical chewing of their cuds interspersed with exhales of steam. I imagine they are delighted to finally get out of their dark barn and feel the warm sun on their fur. Come the end of May, cows begin their summer routine and cow-tenders get a break.

Seasonal Cow-Care Activities

Seasonal cow-care activities peak beginning when cows are *khoton*-bound and manure needs to be managed. Higher peaks also occur during the November time of annual slaughter. Midsummer (June, July) is a period of low activity.

Manure Management

Balbaakh making, or manure management, is a twice-daily cow-tending duty from early October through mid-May. Cow-tenders

Figure 3.8. Balbaakh *patties set to freeze*

typically form *balbaakh* into symmetrical shapes, which freeze and are easy to transport, either in single blocks or large columns. Single blocks are approximately 0.6 meters long × 0.3 meters wide × 15.24 centimeters deep (2 feet × 1 foot × 6 inches), molded in either a homemade metal form, shaped from an old beat-up pan or thrown-away container, or formed to this approximate size with a manure shovel, once the manure sled is emptied outside the cow corral (figure 3.8). Large columns are mounded on the base of a metal sheet or a set of rails, to slide the column over the snow in early spring to the *balbaakh* dump. Fresh manure is packed on top of the base to form a 1.2 meter long × 1.2 meter wide × 1.8 meter deep (4 foot × 4 foot × 6 foot) column. A wire loop is usually added about one-third of the way up for easy pulling to the dump.

Although the column method is less time consuming in making *balbaakh*, the end product, a solid mass of manure, is not as easily or quickly transformed into a composted material. Small patties break down readily and are popular for sharing *balbaakh* with non-cow-tending households who want fertilizer for their gardens. *Balbaakh* patties are stood up in household gardens, half in and half out of the snow at two foot spacings, when seen from afar, resembling small cemetery plots. *Balbaakh* piles grow through the winter. In late March households either haul it away themselves or arrange to have a tractor take it to the local *balbaakh* dump.[20] Some households haul fresh manure directly to their garden plot or another area of their household yard for soil building purposes. Fresh manure is also essential for the annual early fall activity of sealing the *khoton*.

Feeding and Watering

Cow-tenders need to feed and water their herd several times a day when cows are *khoton*-bound. The day begins with the morning parceling of hay, placed in separate piles in the cow corral for each cow. Hay is cut from the stack like a slice from a loaf, using a special stack cutter, then pulled off with a hay hook and divvied up into cow-size portions (figure 3.9).[21] If ambient temperatures

Figure 3.9. Hay is cut from the stack like a loaf of bread.

are below −30°C (−22°F), portions are brought into the khoton for feeding.

Most household yards can't hold all the stacks needed to over-winter the herd. These extra stacks are left in the hay fields to be skidded in when needed over the winter. Households use a *stogovoz* (R., a large skid for a haystack), built out of mature full-length tree logs and pulled by a tractor or bull. Stacks also need to change place in the yard when old stacks run out and new ones come into use.

Except for the deepest cold of winter, cow-tenders lead their herd to a nearby water source, either a lake or river, for water once or twice a day (figure 3.10). Each household has a set location and either maintain their own or share an *oibon* with several house-holds. Often they will pay a local person to clean the manure and keep the *oibon* free of ice.

Khoton Maintenance

Cows living in the subarctic need good housing. *Khoton* construc-tion is a simple horizontal pole construction with each house-hold designing their barn to suit their particular needs. *Khoton* are built with a certain cow number in mind to maximize body heat, the sole source of warmth through the winter. Some inhab-itants remarked that they housed their cows at a kin household where their additional cows made the barn's internal tempera-ture suitable for all. A sure-fit *khoton* for three milkers, for a total of six to seven cows, is 4.5 meters × 4.5 meters (15 feet × 15 feet) and requires ninety 25.5-centimeter (10-inch) diameter, 1.8-meter (6-foot) poles. Sakha build a *khoton* in about two days with two men working (figure 3.11). The cow corral adjoining the *khoton* is usually at least twice the size of *khoton* area, so in this case there needs to be at least a 6.5 meter × 6.5 meter (21 foot × 21 foot) corral area.

When a household's cow herd grows or diminishes, it is of ut-most importance to resize the *khoton* to maintain proper warmth and to avoid trampling of newborn calves. Sakha build and re-size khotons in the temperate months, usually toward summer's end, when winter preparation is more imminent and exact herd

Figure 3.10.   Cows at an oibon *on the Viliui River*

numbers are known. All khotons require insulation to retain cow heat in the barn throughout the winter. Most commonly, Sakha annually apply a sealing of fresh manure in the early fall.[22] The sealing is done in stages over a period of two weeks and requires at least three layers, beginning with a 5-centimeter (2-inch) thick

Figure 3.11. An almost-finished khoton

"primer" followed by a 2.5-centimeter (1-inch) second coat and a 1-centimeter (0.5-inch final coat.[23]

The Fall Cow Slaughter

I learned about the how and when of slaughtering through direct experience, the same way I came to know most other details of Viliui Sakha cattle husbandry. In late October of 2000, with ambient temperatures below freezing, I started seeing clouds of steam billowing up from behind household fences while on my village data collection wanderings. I quickly learned that this came from the rapid escape of body heat when a cow was opened during slaughter. Other telltale signs included the crowd of village dogs that gathered in anticipation of receiving a scrap or two and the blood-stained skin hanging on the household's fence.

Male adults perform most of the slaughter. The process begins with a man delivering a hefty blow on the animal's forehead with the back of an ax head to knock the animal out.[24] The body is then bled, utilizing the heart's power to pump the blood out into several buckets for use in blood sausage. The animal is then killed, its hide peeled back and the body cut lengthwise to remove internal organs and parcel the body meat with an ax. At this point, women, children, and elders help to divvy up body parts and arrange them for freezing and storing. No part of the animal is wasted. The large intestine casings are emptied of their contents and filled with blood for blood sausage. Small intestines, the tongue, and liver are set aside for slicing and eating raw, frozen, or fried. The stomach is cleaned of its bristly lining and put aside for stomach soup, a Sakha delicacy. Hooves and forelegs are set aside to make *dyrahaangka* (aspic). The head is stored away to make soup and sausage in late spring when other meat stores have run out. Horns are dried and hollowed to make various tools. Sakha most often choose to slaughter two-year and older castrated males. However they will also choose cows that are not calving, that have cantankerous characters, or that have been crippled during the pasture season.

Other Cow Duties

Calving occurs from February to May and adds extra time and energy to the normal cow routine. Cow-tenders depend on having an intimate knowledge of their herd. Six weeks before expected gestation, milking needs to stop. As birthing time approaches, cow-tenders look for signs, "the cow moans a lot and moves about—also her teats are swollen and very white milk comes." During birthing, cows need assistance, and new calves need allotted space in the *khoton* so they don't get accidentally crushed. Cows and their calves require medical attention. Most households use local vet services several times a year for insemination and shots. Cows average one calf a year if they interact with a bull or are inseminated. Keeping a bull for this purpose is costly since they consume an additional 50 percent more hay than a regular cow, an investment that produces relatively low returns for the bull's owner but high returns for their neighbors. Both the seasonal and year-round cow-care duties reach their low point in the summer. This is a good thing since summer is the period of highest intensity for hay laboring.

Haying: Foraging for the Quintessential Crop

The short subarctic summer is a labor intensive period for Sakha because of the need to harvest sufficient hay to overwinter household herds. If we plot annual haying activities, we see a sharp peak throughout much of the summer, and two more spurts of activity during the winter hauling from November through January and the working of household hay when the spring thaw arrives in March.

Households need two tons of hay for each cow with a new calf to fodder them over the nine-month period. For this the household needs the land, the tools, the labor, and the machinery to harvest and transport the hay. Adult and elder males spend the most time haying,[25] but all household members are called to help preparing and stacking, across the age/sex groups. In short, a successful hay harvest for Sakha involves the pooling of labor, resources, equipment, and land, all of which I explore more fully in the next chapter.

Getting to Cows-and-Kin

I came to understand the Viliui Sakhas' cows-and-kin adaptation while I was conducting field research to understand how households were coping in the post-Soviet context. Before I went into the field, I assumed that I would be able to place households on a continuum of home food production ranging from "neo-traditional" to "market-oriented." Exactly where a household would fall on that continuum would be related to its status in the Soviet period. From what I had observed up to that time, I knew that when the Soviet Union broke up and local state farm operations disbanded, that farm resources had been unequally distributed. Local Soviet elite had allocated the majority of those resources to themselves, their kin, and their constituents. By default, household resource wealth would be one important variable determining a household's place in the Soviet hierarchy, or Soviet standing.

In terms of the continuum, households closer to the "neo-traditional" pole would be relying on indigenous Sakha life ways, including household-level food production based on strong interdependent kinship relations and local ecological knowledge, and a desire for private land ownership. The indigenous knowledge intrinsic to these life ways had been passed down from ancestors who were successful agropastoralists in pre-Soviet times, but who had lost their private holdings with the advent of Soviet power.[26] The generations to follow maintained a central reliance on the ancestral life ways with minimal participation in the local Soviet infrastructure. On the other hand, those tending toward the market-oriented pole would be depending minimally on home food production since they were in a position to buy their food products and, still being part of the employed sector of the village, would have little time for home food production. In the contemporary context they would live in relative independence of their kin networks and ancestral life ways. Historically their ancestors would have been less successful in pre-Soviet times and therefore had everything to gain from the Sovietization process.

My field research showed that households with members who were formerly part of the local Soviet elite did in fact have more wealth and resources. However, this usually meant that they were equally and often more involved in home food production for subsistence and for market, because their wealth was in exactly the resources needed for food production: access to adjacent and plentiful land, farming equipment, and/or *BKh* status.[27] Similarly, households closer to the neo-traditional pole were not consistently depending on home food production, with some households involved in all facets of home production and others not involved at all. In the process of contemplating such household diversity, I did see a clear pattern—that the common denominator of high food production was *cows*, and that cowless households accessed cow products via their *kin* networks.

Inter-Household Cows-and-Kin Dependencies

Households implement a diversity of modes to acquire what they need, either in labor and resources, in the case of cow-keeping households, or in cow products, in the case of non-cow-keepers. Households can be classified as having "reciprocal," "one-way," or "non-kin" dependence.[28] *Reciprocal dependence* means either having cows and providing meat and milk products in exchange for labor in the haying season or supplying labor in the haying season in exchange for year-round products. If a household is not reciprocal dependent, they can have a *one-way dependence*, meaning that they either receive cow products from kin with no direct exchange of labor in return or give products to kin expecting no labor in return. If a household is neither reciprocal nor one-way dependent, it either has cows and is internally independent by having both cow-tenders and hay laborers "in house," or had no cows and either went without or purchased all the products they needed from non-kin sources.

Kin-based distribution via these types of inter-household dependencies indirectly increases the overall household-level food production for the villages by evening out the distribution of cow products among households. Two-thirds (63 percent) of all households are supplied with milk and meat products from their own cows yet if household supply includes both household production and inter-household distribution, 90 percent of all households are supplied.

When type of reciprocal dependencies is broken down (table 3.5), 29 percent of all households depend on receiving kin labor in exchange for products, 20 percent depend on receiving kin's cow products in exchange for labor, and 4 percent both have

Table 3.5. Breakdown of Cows-and-Kin Dependencies

Dependency Type	% all Households	Variations within Type	% all Households
Reciprocal	53	Products for Labor	29
		Labor for Products	20
		Both	4
One-way Dependent	15	Gives Products	4
		Receives Products	8
		Gives and Receives	3
Non-kin Dependent	32	Internally Independent	22
		Goes without	2
		Buys/Barters with Non-kin	8

cows and depend on kin for labor and products. On average, in both villages 15 percent of all households surveyed had one-way dependence, with half of those on the receiving end, one-fourth on the giving end, and the remainder both receiving and giving with no expected reciprocation. Households with no reciprocal or one-way dependence are either internally independent or have no inter-household interaction, the latter case due to having no kin in the immediate village or to being on nonsociable terms with the kin they have. Across the two villages, of the households with no reciprocal or one-way dependencies, 2 percent go without meat and milk products, and 8 percent purchase and barter. Twenty-two percent of all households in both villages are "independent," meaning they are self-sufficient in producing meat and milk by having an ample labor force in-house for haying and cow-tending. Besides these village-level inter-household relations, there are also many households who routinely send products out of the village, most often to cowless kin either in the regional center, Suntar, or the capital, Yakutsk. One-fourth of all households surveyed send products.

The Centrality of Kin

For the majority of contemporary Viliui Sakha household, kin, like cows, play a major role in subsistence survival. Close to all of the households surveyed said they had close kin (parents, grandparents, siblings, cousins, aunts, and uncles) in their immediate village (table 3.6). Over half of these are sibling or parental relationships. When asked how it would be to live without their kin, well over half (57 percent) of all households surveyed said their lives would be difficult or significantly changed without their kin (see total percentages of first four responses in table 3.6). The remainder were either independent and not needing any outside help or they relied on friends or monetary resources.

The centrality of kin is not a new development. Traditional Sakha proverbs, still standard fare in contemporary conversation, emphasize the long-standing reliance on kin. When discussing kin, many Sakha refer to one of two proverbs, either *Aimaakhtaakh siljar ere kihi buoluo* (Only the person who has kin can call

Table 3.6. Attitudes toward Kin Relations: Responses to a Survey Question[a]

How Would It Be to Live without Kin?	Elgeeii #	Elgeeii %	Kutana #	Kutana %	Both #	Both %
Couldn't survive w/o their help	38	18	26	33	64	23
It would be very difficult w/o them	20	10	9	11	29	10
Could—but with kin better—only kin help	34	16	11	14	45	16
Can't live w/o helping and getting help	21	10	3	4	24	8
Could manage—could pay for all kin do	5	2	0	0	5	2
Could—don't depend on kin at all now	63	30	23	29	86	31
Could—don't depend, and have friends	19	9	7	9	26	9
Could—we only give to them, we are fine	2	5	0	0	2	1

[a]# = number of responses; % = percentage of village households surveyed (in Elgeeii, n = 211; in Kutana n = 79); Both = Elgeeii and Kutana combined.

him- or herself a person), or *Oiuurdaakh kuobakh oiuurtaan tuspet* (The rabbit in the woods is not shot down), meaning that with kin all around you, you will survive. Such references to kin are common in other pastoralist cultures. A colleague conducting research in Outer Mongolia quoted a Mongolian saying she first heard from her grandmother, *Hun nembel huns nemne*, or, "As your people increase, your food increases" (personal communication, Manduhai Buyandelgeriyn).

Kin serving as a major source of household labor and exchange of goods is nothing new to Sakha or other cultures across the world (Chayanov [1986 (1925)]; Netting 1993; Humphrey 1998; Wilk 1999; Schweitzer 2000). Kin are the main operative ideology of intracultural relationship for most world cultures (Morgan [2000 (1870)]; Engels [1985 (1902)]; Schneider 1984; Needham 1971; Collier and Yanagiasko 1987; Faubion 1996; Goody 1990). What is interesting and compelling about Viliui Sakha kin relations is understanding the extent to which kin networks have had a central function over time and the extent to which kin networks are being utilized anew after a long period of political oppression of such social relations, economic abundance, and relative stability.[29]

Despite the apparent utility of kin in the contemporary Viliui Sakha context, kin is not valued by all. Since the fall of the USSR kin relations are often strained, largely a result of the growing gap between "haves" (those with resources for high home food production) and "have-nots" (those without any of the aforementioned) and the unprecedented rise of alcoholism and crime. Of the households surveyed, the "haves" complain that they are seeing too much of their "have not" kin. "Have nots" complain that their "haves" kin are cutting them off. Many inhabitants referenced a kin proverb expressing antagonism, *Uu chugaha, uuru yraakh*, translating literally, "Keep water close and kin/in-laws far." I heard several interpretations of this saying. The most popular was, that water is essential for life and it will not deceive you or be offended—so it is safe and important to live near. Kin, however, are deceptive and offensive, so it is best to keep them at a distance. Clearly, antagonism toward kin is nothing spurred by the post-Soviet times but, similar to the congenial post-Soviet kin relations, has also been revived in the last decade. For the most part these antagonistic relationships exist between "haves" and "have-nots" outside the context of exchange within the cows-and-kin system.

It is interesting to explore how inhabitants themselves perceive the reemergence of kin relations since the Soviet break-up. Half of all surveyed consultants said there has been no change—that they interact with kin to the same degree they did in the Soviet past. One-third said there was more kin interaction now due to the need to help each other in order to survive, especially as the division of "haves" and "have-nots" grows. The remaining few said there was more kin interaction in the Soviet period when everything was inexpensive and all could afford to house and feed each other.

Despite the differing opinions, antagonistic attitudes, proverbs, and cultural orientations, kin dependence remains an essential element of daily survival for most. One strong testimony to this fact is the frequency of inter-household kin sharing (table 3.7).

Table 3.7. Number and Percentage of Households that Reported They Share[a] (Based on Household Survey Data)

Product Category	Elgeeii # hshlds	Elgeeii % Share	Kutana # hshlds	Kutana % Share	Both # hshlds	Both % Share
Cow products	124	65	63	92	187	79
Horse products	42	69	26	88	68	79
Pigs and/or chicken products	42	26	21	33	63	30
Garden produce from gardens	147	53	62	56	209	55
Berries from foraging	137	81	58	86	195	84
Ducks from hunting	126	58	60	66	186	62
Sobo from fishing	109	75	61	85	170	80

[a] # = number of village households who reported that they share; % = percentage of village households who reported that they share (in Elgeeii, n = 211; in Kutana n = 79); Both = Elgeeii and Kutana combined.

One-third of households keeping pigs and chickens share these products with their kin. Of those with gardens, a little over half share their garden produce with kin. Eighty-five percent of households who forage for berries share their berry crop with kin. Similarly, over half of all duck-hunting households share a substantial portion of their ducks with non-hunting kin households. Over three-fourths of sobo-fishing households share their catch with kin.

Sharing among kin households is not limited to food production resources. Monetary resources are also shared, most often in the form of elder pensions redistributed to young kin households. Money is in short supply in the villages, with paychecks and other subsidies arriving several months late. Elder pensions, so far, are received on time and are regularly reallocated among most cows-and-kin networks.

Cows-and-Kin in Case Studies

On a case by case basis, the cows-and-kin adaptation takes many forms depending on a household's make-up, access to resources, and network of kin relations. I identified six main patterns: 1) Household type A is a young to middle-aged family, with one or both sets of individual parents also resident in the immediate village. The parents perform the daily tasks of cow keeping, supply the children's household with meat and milk in exchange for all or part of the labor required to cut, stack, and haul the hay to overwinter the cows. 2) Household type B is a young to middle-aged family whose parents may be present in the village but are too old or unable for health reasons to tend cows. The children keep cows and provide the parents with all their meat and milk. 3) Household type C is a young to middle-aged family with one elder parent living with them who performs all or most of the cow-care on a daily basis, and the children perform all the heavy work of haying. 4) Household type D is a group of siblings who never married and whose parents are deceased. Their oldest female siblings, who were taught cow-care and were responsible for taking over the cow-care in the household they all were brought up in, live in the village with their own families and tend cows. The sibling households get all their meat and milk from the cow-keeping households in exchange for performing most of the heavy labor involved in haying. 5) Household type E is a young to middle-aged couple who both work and whose parents live in nearby villages where they were brought up. They get all their meat and milk from these parents and spend the summers commuting to their homelands to cut all the hay for their parents. 6) Household type F is a young couple with cows and a parental household(s) in the village also with cows. Despite their ability to produce independently (having their own cows and labor "in-house") they interact with the elderly households to supply labor in the summer and to receive extra resources to make ends meet.

To give a sense of how these interdependencies function, I will next discuss two cases, one that shows Household type A and exemplifies the most common cows-and-kin pattern and another that shows nascent entrepreneurial activities within the Household type F cows-and-kin framework.

Household Type A: Yelli's Household

The first cows-and-kin pattern is a young household dependent on a parental household for cow products in exchange for labor

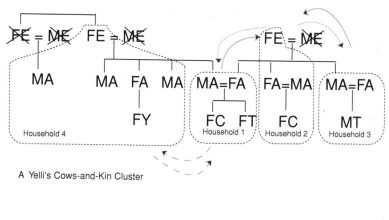

A Yelli's Cows-and-Kin Cluster

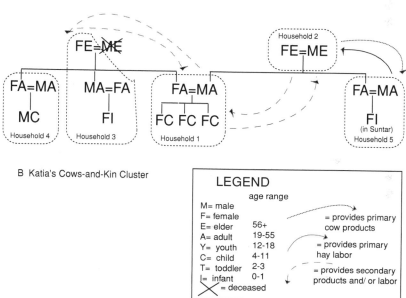

B Katia's Cows-and-Kin Cluster

LEGEND

age range

M= male
F= female
E= elder   56+
A= adult   19-55
Y= youth   12-18
C= child   4-11
T= toddler   2-3
I= infant   0-1
✕ = deceased

⟶ = provides primary cow products

⟶ = provides primary hay labor

⤑ = provides secondary products and/ or labor

Figure 3.12.   Yelli's and Katia's cows-and-kin clusters

during the haying season. In this example Yelli (age twenty-eight) lives with her husband Sasha (age thirty-one) and two young daughters, aged four and seven, in a new house on the village perimeter (figure 3.12: A: Household 1). She and her husband both have full-time jobs, she is a dance choreographer at the village culture center and he is a local fireman. One of Yelli and Sasha's children attends preschool, the other elementary school. Both Yelli and Sasha's mothers live in the village center, convenient to day care, school, and work places. Yelli and her family spend most of their time when not at work or school, at Yelli's or Sasha's mother's house. Yelli and Sasha's mothers not only supply the young family with all the meat and milk products they need, but also provide childcare and regular meals.

Yelli's mother, Rozalia (age sixty-two) (Household 2), is the main supplier of cow products to Yelli's household, with a majority of those products given in the form of daily meals. Rozalia keeps five milk cows or a total herd of twelve cattle. One is her own, three belong to each of her three children, and the last one is owned by her late husband's brother, whose cow-tender and wife died several years ago. This brother-in-law provides the tractor needed to care for all the cows, in exchange for Rozalia's daily tending of his cow. Yelli's cow, not unlike the cows belonging to her sister and brother, was a gift from Rozalia upon marriage. The mother continues to give her children the gift of daily care and tending for the cows. Each child's cow produces a calf annually, which, when slaughtered after two to three years growth, provides a year's worth of meat for a family of four. With the meat from an average cow slaughter at 160 kilograms (353 pounds), this represents 526,400 kilocalories (kcals). For Yelli's household, this is one-fifth of their annual total kcal requirement. But Rozalia also gives daily meals to Yelli's family of four, which supplies a majority of the rest of Yelli's household's total kcal needs. Rozalia lives with Yelli's sister, husband, and two small children. Yelli's brother also has his own household (Household 3) in Elgeeii but, like Yelli, depends on the mother for all his meat, milk, and daily meals.

Rozalia spends from late May until the end of August at her *saylykh*, located seven kilometers from the village. Rozalia purchased the summer house in 1994 for 1000R ($40 USD), which, she said, "was a lot of money back then but I can't live in the village in the summer—at the *saylykh* the air is fresh and my kids come there daily—they can't live without me and the *urung as* (white or milk foods)." She not only maintains the cow herd and chickens throughout the summer, but also grows all the potatoes and greenhouse vegetables for her and her children's households. In exchange, Yelli and her family, along with her sister's and brother's family, cut all the hay that Rozalia needs to overwinter the family cow herd.

The balance of Yelli's household's annual kcal needs comes from Sasha's mother's household (Household 4) consisting of his mother (age sixty-eight), three of her five children including two sons (ages thirty-five and forty-two) and a daughter (age forty), and an orphaned nephew (Household 4). The household keeps five cows and, because the mother is feeble, relies on one daughter to perform the daily cow-care. The two sons have a membership in a village *BKh*, and supply all the household's tractor needs and access to ample hay land for fodder. The five cows produce meat and milk mostly for the consumption of their immediate household and for another daughter's household in the village. Yelli's family mostly relies on this household for childcare and occasional meals. They participate marginally in the hay season, since the two brothers readily supply all the hay needs to the household through their *BKh* cooperative.

Yelli's cows-and-kin pattern shows how these households are able to negotiate among themselves to maximize the meeting of kin household needs with available labor and resources.

Household Type F: Katia's Household

The sixth cows-and-kin pattern is a young family with a parental household(s), all of whom keep cows. The elderly kin or parents' household(s) are dependent on the younger household(s) for labor help during hay cutting season. This pattern is the case for the two generations of Spiridonovs (figure 3.12: B).

Andre and Katia (aged thirty and thirty-two respectively) live with their three young girls, ages nine, six, and five (Household 1). They keep cows and chickens, grow a home garden, and forage, supplying most of their household's needs. They keep two milk cows, which supply them with ample meat and milk for their household, and for sharing and selling. Over the year they produce an average of 5000 liters (1323 gallons) of milk from which they make 200 liters (53 gallons) of *suugey* (crème fraîche),

100 liters (26.5 gallons) of *sorat* (yogurt), 200 kilograms (440 pounds) of *yejegei* (curds), and 200 liters (53 gallons) of *kymys* (fermented milk). They slaughter two cows annually, one for their own eating and sharing with kin or *kehii* (a house gift) and the other to sell, in part to finance Katia's two trips a year to Moscow for therapy for their invalid child.

Both Katia and Andre are avid gardeners and produce all the vegetables they need. They eat this produce all year, either fresh from the garden, preserved in the form of the annual forty or more gallon jars of pickles, marinated vegetables, dilled carrots, and canned tomatoes, or from the five bushels of root crops, including carrots, beets, and turnips that they store in sand in their cellar. The area of their back yard that is not taken up by cow pen and haystacks is a potato field, which produces an annual average of 350 kilograms (772 pounds), half of which they use within their household. The rest they either share with kin or sell.

To supplement home food production Katia and Andre hunt, fish, and forage. They use most of their berry forage within their household as an essential source of vitamins for their young children. Over the 2000 diary year they shared 25 percent of their hunting and fishing resources with kin households.

Although Andre and Katia are relatively independent in terms of their home food production, they do depend greatly on their parents (Household 2 and 3) for other needs, first and foremost, childcare. Andre and Katia both work full-time and both go away each year for six to eight weeks at a time. Since Katia's mother is fifteen years an elder to Andre's parents, they limit childcare requests from her to last-resort needs. Over the course of the diary year, Andre's parents provided ninety-two days of childcare, on some days caring for all three girls.

Katia's mother (age seventy-three) lives in Elgeeii with Katia's twin brother, his wife, and their infant (Household 3). They are relatively independent, keeping two milk cows, using the majority of the products within their immediate household, and performing the bulk of the annual hay cutting themselves. Interaction with Katia's household is on occasion mostly because the households are located at opposite ends of the village, inconvenient to daily foot travel to and from work and schools.

Andre's parents, Nikifor and Tania (aged sixty and fifty-eight respectively), are independent for home food production (Household 2). However, they depend more and more each year on Andre's help during the summer hay season. Andre's parents grow their own vegetables and raise all of their own meat. They have two milk cows and fifteen chickens. They slaughter two cows annually, of which they eat three legs and send one to their daughter, Maria, in Suntar (Household 5). The other cow they sell. Their two milkers produce approximately 5000 liters (1322 gallons) of milk a year. From this milk Tania and Nikifor make a wide variety of milk foods for their household and for commercial purposes.

Nikifor is an avid fisherman. He leads two village fishing brigades, one to trap *sylyhar* (burbot or *Lota lota*), a bottom-feeding anadromous river fish, and one to *mungkha*, or to sweep net the lakes in winter for *sobo*, or crucian carp (*Carassius carassius*) (figure 3.13).

In the temperate months from late May to early September Nikifor regularly checks his *ilim* for *sobo*. Table 3.8 shows the

Figure 3.13. Nikofor and his brigade sylyhar *fishing on the Viliui River*

Table 3.8. Nikifor's Annual Fishing Activity for 2000: Totals Harvested, Use Allocations, Time Spent, and Income

Category	Sylyhar	Sobo: Mungkha	Sobo: Ilim	Totals
Kg caught	67.5	396.0	300.0	763.5
Kg to kin	30.0	111.5	76.5	218.0
Kg sold	20.0	181.5	105.0	306.5
Kg to household	17.5	66.0	113.5	197.0
Kg to charity	—	33.0	—	33.0
Kg for barter	—	—	5.0	5.0
Total hours	50	150	116	316
Total income	**845 rubles ($30 USD)**	**2450 rubles ($88 USD)**	**2486 rubles ($89 USD)**	**5781 rubles ($207 USD)**

annual tally of Nikifor's 2000 fish harvest, how he allocated that harvest, the time he spent, and the income realized.

In addition to being active in foraging resources, Tania and Nikifor purposely produce excess animal and vegetable products to sell or barter. They sell about 30 percent of the milk, meat, fish, and garden products they produce. These transactions can as much double their income in a given year. Table 3.9 shows Tania and Nikifor's annual 2000 income broken down by source.

Table 3.9. Tania and Nikifor's Total 2000 Income Broken Down by Source

Income Source	Annual Amount	% of Total Income
Tania pension	17,820 rubles ($636 USD)	24
Nikifor pension	17,460 rubles ($624 USD)	23
Nikifor salary	8500 rubles ($304 USD)	11
Total salary/pension	**43,780 rubles ($1564 USD)**	**58**
Sales from home: meat	10,450 rubles ($373 USD)	14
Sales from home: fish	5781 rubles ($207 USD)	8
Sales from home: dairy and vegetables	3815 rubles ($136 USD)	5
Suntar sales	8420 rubles ($301 USD)	11
Special orders: berries	800 rubles ($29 USD)	1
Special orders: milk foods	2650 rubles ($95 USD)	3
Total sales	**31,916 rubles ($1140 USD)**	**42**
TOTAL INCOME	75,696 rubles ($2703 USD)	100

Commercial sales give Tania and Nikifor an income substantially higher than most Elgeeii households. They share their excess income with their children. Andre's sister Maria lives in the regional center of Suntar, where she took a job in 1998 with the regional statistics bureau. Recently her parents bought her a one-bedroom apartment for 55,000 rubles ($1965 USD) plus about ten days of the father's time in negotiation and apartment renovations. Tania and Nikifor consider this their expected duty to their daughter. They had done the same for Andre's family, by supplying all the materials and organizing all the labor to build their house and set them up with a cowherd and chickens. In Maria's case, she needed affordable housing in the regional center close to her work at the statistical department.

One of the main obstacles to most households when they consider producing to sell, like Tania and Nikifor do, is access to a market. Most village households fill their product needs in the cows-and-kin mode, leaving only a small local population in need. Even if there are households needing products, they usually don't have money to buy them with since salaries and subsidies are often months late. For these reasons, Nikifor travels to the regional center, Suntar, to tap the market there, going first to the regional administrative buildings to peddle his wares then to the local stores to sell the remainder.

In addition to giving most of their financial resources to their children, the elder Spiridonovs give their human resources. In addition to childcare, they secure raw materials for ongoing building projects; distribute food products from fishing, hunting, domestic animals, gardens, and foraging; and negotiate hay land rights for their kin networks.

These two cases exemplify the cows-and-kin dependence of Viliui Sakha post-Soviet adaptation. The extent to which resources flow between these two cows-and-kin cases is the norm for the majority of contemporary rural Viliui Sakha households.

The Theoretical Context of Cows-and-Kin

Subsistence survival in the twenty-first century for rural Viliui Sakha focuses on keeping cows and exchanging labor and products with kin (Crate 2003a). Theoretically, the cows-and-kin adaptation is congruent with Robert Netting's smallholder-householder theory (1993). Netting argues that in times of change, the household system is the most resilient unit for subsistence production, having both integrity and longevity through ethnic, political, and geographic changes due to its several inherent resilient features. First, the household is a repository of ecological knowledge with which its members are able to make the most effective use of resources, based on their intimate understanding of the specific microenvironments of their smallholding. Since the fall of the Soviet period the focus of Viliui Sakha survival has gone from dependence on the socialist infrastructure for employment and consumer goods to dependence on household-level cows-and-kin production. To accomplish this, Viliui Sakha depend on an ancestrally known landscape for their usufruct land holdings and on centuries-old knowledge pertaining to horse and cattle husbandry in their subarctic environment.

Second, Netting purports that the household is a joint enterprise based on implicit labor contracts. Netting describes parallels between the household and a corporate entity in that both maintain their own labor force, manage their own productive resources, and organize consumption for the household unit. The household generally also produces for subsistence and for the market, with at least one of its members involved in outside employment. The household has ownership or usufruct rights over its land base to maintain production. The Viliui Sakha case shows how households are analogous to corporate entities because they maintain their own labor forces, manage their own productive resources and organize consumption for their household units, both internally and with dependencies between kin households. Viliui Sakha households produce first and foremost for subsistence, with some involved in nascent entrepreneurial activities for the market. The majority of households have at least one member involved in outside employment. Viliui Sakha households have usufruct rights over their land base (hay meadows, garden sites) to maintain home food production. Most Viliui Sakha households are restricted to a ration of hay land as well as the limitations of their immediate household yard for growing produce. The households who raise animals and grow produce as a sole means of income are able to do so because of special allotments of land (*BKh*) given to certain individuals when the Soviet power fell. This makes a difference because if more households desire to move into market production, they will need access to more land, specifically to harvest more hay and to grow more gardens. Overall, in the post-Soviet context, Viliui Sakha have moved to household-level production with their household possessing many of the characteristics that Netting describes.

Third, Netting suggests that the bonds of kinship, family, and household enact a strong work ethic and a specialization of work by gender to dependably fulfill the labor load of daily chores and seasonally specific bottleneck demands. Similarly, he argues that the implicit contracts bind household members in an innate social security system, providing for children and elders. As the household continues to function and pass the title of its operation on to its inheritors, generations move through a cycle of either the cared for (children and elders) or the caretakers (youths and adults).

Another aspect of the household-as-joint-enterprise is the implicit contracts that bind the household members. Viliui Sakha households and their kin networks function efficiently on a daily basis, caring for their herds, engaging in food production tasks, seasonally harvesting hay and other consumption resources, foraging for wild foods, and slaughtering. Due to renewed kin interdependence, 35 percent of all households, those that have no cattle, are supplied with cow products. With exchange a total of 90 percent of all households are self-sufficient for their milk and meat needs. The remaining 10 percent make enough money to buy their cow products. This cows-and-kin adaptive pattern also is the key to survival in nearby Kutana village, a former sector of the Elgeeii State Farm.

On average, a household of four needs two milk cows or a herd of five or six head total to supply its daily needs of meat and milk. However, to keep a herd over the nine-month subarctic winter, each household must harvest an average of two tons of hay per cow and new calf. The majority of households depend on kin labor to realize this production.

To a large degree the efficiency of the household is credited to specialization by gender, a tendency best exemplified in Viliui Sakha labor specialization during the intensive summer period. During this time males spend their waking hours cutting and stacking hay while females are busy foraging for wild berries and plants, tending the home gardens and greenhouses, and keeping the herds when they return from daily pasture in the late night.

Netting states that households do not live in isolation from important external markets. This is also the case for a small group of Viliui Sakha, about 10 percent of all households generate substantial income through entrepreneurial efforts marketing garden and greenhouse produce, meat and dairy products, and traditional crafts, all with a grounding in the essential cows-and-kin knowledge. In one sense the contemporary trend of cows-and-kin survival strategies is a return to the pre-Soviet reliance on animal husbandry, haying, foraging, garden production, and inter-household clan dependence. On the other, it reflects a society's ability to adapt to modernity by appropriating seemingly "old-fashioned" life ways to respond to contemporary trends such as market forces and globalization.

The cows-and-kin system is based in implicit contracts among kin groupings within a home village, less frequently among adjacent villages. Most typically this involves a parental household, which performs the daily tasks of cow-care, and one or more children's households, who perform the intensive bottleneck labor of the summer hay harvest. In all cases task specialization is determined by gender and age. This is made clear by looking at time allocation data. Work is performed as it needs to be done by those most able or most available. Other household members perform the tasks that remain to the best of their ability. These cows-and-kin systems epitomize Netting's points regarding the social safety net provided by household systems. Typically elders perform cow-care, maintain household herds, and supply dependable income from pensions. As they age and can no longer perform these duties, the children assume cow-care tasks and supply their aging parents with products. The household wealth, in the form of the cow herds and land rights, are passed on to the adult children, who in turn assume care-taking responsibilities of the parents and whose children begin entering the labor force to participate in the hay harvest. Although in the Elgeeii village we see many single-parent and nuclear-family households, the households most involved in home food production are either internally multigenerational or function this way on an inter-household basis.

In Viliui Sakhas' case, the dependence on kin for necessary labor is integral to subsistence survival. The personal knowledge investment and the trust inherent to kin networks is key to the daily-negotiated labor demands of the food and resource activities that are crucial to Viliui Sakha survival. Households have neither the material resources to buy labor nor the time to train and manage outside laborers. It is during the summer bottleneck of labor, especially the high demands of hay production, that we see just how efficiently the kin networks function for Viliui Sakha. Characteristically kin groups coordinate their efforts to work their various hay plots through the initial cutting to the final stacking. Decisions are made on a day-to-day basis in accordance to the local conditions of the various hay fields and the daily weather. Additionally, these kin groups either pool their own or negotiate with others for the use of technology (i.e., tractors and their haying attachments) and necessary resources to realize their hay harvests. Kin are also essential as a means of pooling land resources in the resource-scarce subarctic environment.

Household production is a matter of balancing labor and need. In most of the cases where these are imbalanced (less labor and greater need or more labor and less need), kin often provide the compensating factor, supplying labor and resources or receiving surplus products. In several cases in which households are producing above and beyond their household needs, they sell the surplus for a profit. Even here the household member labor force is used to its maximum as well as the available kin labor force. The latter is compensated with products or labor in return.

Contemplating Cows-and-Kin

Having cows and the daily and seasonal care they require ties a household to their *khoton*. However, most Sakha do not consider this an inconvenience, since the household-level production of meat and milk is the only way in the post-Soviet context to access cow products. Both the number of cow-keeping households and each household's herd size have increased in the post-Soviet era. Whereas in 1992 10 percent of all surveyed households kept cows and of them only one milk cow, in 2000 55 percent of all households were keeping cows and the average among them was three milk cows. When asked why they keep cows most households said they did so in order to have fresh meat and milk products, which they could not afford to buy otherwise and which were no longer available for sale in village stores.

There exists local antagonism between cow-keeping and non-cow-keeping households. Cow-keeping households consider themselves the hard-working "real" Sakha and perceive non-cow-keeping households as lazy and transient. In contrast, many non-cow-keeping households explain that they presently don't keep cows precisely because they were not raised in a cow-keeping household and are used to a non-cow household regime and diet. Most of them drink black tea and depend on wild game meats, including duck, rabbit, squirrel, reindeer, bear, moose, and water and wood fowl for their protein source. Many of these non-cow-keeping households are however playing an active role in cow-keeping via their inter-dependency with a kin cow-keeping household. They supply much-needed labor during the summer hay-cutting bottleneck in exchange for a significant supply of bovine products from kin households.

In the broader context, contemporary Viliui Sakha cow-keeping is a mixed blessing. Cow keepers are locally revered as the true Sakha who are maintaining the traditions and are not fleeing the village for the "better life" in the regional center or capital. They maintain ties to the land to harvest hay and pasture their herds. The social status of being decidedly more Sakha is a positive attribute and a response to increased ethnic awareness in the post-Soviet setting. However, in the wake of the "new market economy" and overall economic restructuring, cow-keeping is considered by many a dead-end occupation with no future prospect, despite its overwhelming centrality to contemporary survival.

Since the demise of Soviet power in 1991 and the collapse of the encompassing agrarian infrastructure, Viliui Sakha are facing a variety of both challenges and opportunities related to defining new subsistence strategies. In concert with the decentralization of the post-Soviet period, subsistence production has shifted back to an emphasis on household and family/kin networks. To survive the transition from dependence on centralized socialist agriculture to decentralized household-level production, Viliui Sakha tap a variety of wild and domestic energetic pathways. Their main mode is the cows-and-kin system. Contemporary kin relations, for the most part beneficial but sometimes contentious, are paramount to the cows-and-kin system. Case studies illustrate the diversity of cows-and-kin relations and demonstrate the flexibility of Viliui Sakha adaptations in the face of unprecedented change. Cows-and-kin exemplifies the adaptation and resilience of contemporary Viliui Sakha.

Notes

This chapter is based on material previously published in *Human Ecology* (Crate 2003a) and in *Post-Soviet Women Encountering Transition* (Crate 2004). Both are included here with permission of the publishers.

1. The Bull of Winter: Creating the world, the Gods asked humans, "Do you want winter to be longer or summer?" The humans answered, "Ask our friends—the horse and bull." The horse wanted summer longer because in winter its legs and hooves felt very cold. But the bull wanted winter longer because in summer heat its nose got wet. Then the Gods made winter longer and summer shorter. Having got angry, the horse kicked the bull in the nose and knocked out its upper teeth. The bull butted the horse into its side and pierced through its bile. Since that time horse have not bile and horned cattle no upper teeth (Sivtsev 1996:131).

2. There are several explanations of how the bull arrives and leaves. For example, "*Jyl Oghuha* is the personification of winter in the form of a bull. Sakha believe that he comes every year from the Arctic Ocean and brings with himself cold, starvation, need, and etc. In spring, near Afanasee Day, he loses one horn, then near the second Afanasee day, he loses the other. Whether he dies in the spring or returns to the Arctic

Ocean—the Sakha either forgot or did not know" (Kulakovski 1979:45–46). Seroshevski provides more detail: The freeze is definitely a bull and he has two horns—the first falls of on the first Afanasee Day (March 5), the second on the second Afanasee Day (April 24) and on the third Afanasee (May 14) the whole body falls (Seroshevski 1993:27). These dates are according to the old calendar so in our calendar would be February 19, April 10, and April 30, respectively.

3. For more on this see www.spri.cam.ac.uk/research/social/projects/maher.html.

4. Based on the 2000 survey results, involving a random sample of 30 percent of all Elgeeii households (n = 210, N = 700), the average monthly breakdown of total household income was: from salary = 1200 rubles ($43 USD); from pensions = 880 rubles ($31 USD); from child subsidies = 140 rubles ($5 USD); and, from informal sales of products or services = 211 rubles ($8 USD) for a total average income of 2,431 rubles ($87 USD) per month.

5. Pensions are for elderly, invalids, single mothers, and so forth. Forty percent of households have at least one pensioner, 29 percent have two, and 4 percent have three or four.

6. Including anything from cow-care for another household; one-time house or barn building; tractor hauling services for hay, firewood, and ice; and so forth.

7. Including reindeer boot manufacture and repair, tailoring, fur hat and coat making, quilt making, and so forth.

8. Soviet policies worked toward gender equality to the extent that women were as likely to be employed as men on the collective and state farms. However, women still carried the double burden of domestic chores. The concept of "double burden" commonly cited in reference to Soviet women was first introduced by Mary Buckley (1989).

9. I use this term like the energy flow literature, to analyze pastoral subsistence (Coughenour 1985).

10. Reconstructed by a Sakha linguist and teacher who argues that Sakhas' New Year begins at the end of May, when all is green with renewed hope.

11. I was unable to record observations from June 7 through July 18 while traveling into and out of the field.

12. Based on my every-sixth-day time allocation observations (Borgerhoff Mulder and Caro 1985) using adapted standard activity codes (Johnson and Johnson 1988). For this chart, each observation is equal to a six-day span.

13. Sakha have thirty-five different milk foods, of which eight are most popular now: crème fraîche, butter, cream butter, whipped cream, kefir, *kymys*, curds, and ice cream.

14. The root of the word "capital" is cattle.

15. Also called *Inakhsit* and *Ihigai*.

16. At a cow slaughter, I learned that the female household head had taken the herd away while their cohort was killed. Later she said she had prayed to *Eiekhsit* the cow god and asked that this cow be able to come and join them in a safe haven in the sky world. Since that discussion I have seen this action repeatedly.

17. From Elgeeii cows walk anywhere from one to three hours to reach suitable pasture. Many of the pasturelands near the village have been fenced off to protect them for haying.

18. If cows go to water at this time, they wear quilted udder protectors to protect from freezing.

19. Cow-tenders know which cows are pregnant and when they will calve. If a bull doesn't bother a female then she is already pregnant. Each cow shows oncoming labor differently. One tender explained that her cows act "more touchy," or appear a bit removed from their usual cow self. It is important to assist cows when they are calving, because they have complications and calves need protection from being accidentally trampled in the barn. The cow-tender milks the mother to get the *wohakh* (first, colostrum-rich milk) flowing and get the calf suckling. After a calf is born the milking regime steps up to three times a day.

20. In the years past large eighteen-wheel trucks would come from Mirnyi to buy the *balbaakh* and use it for fertilizer on agricultural fields. They stopped this ten years ago, and the Elgeeii administration built the village *balbaakh* dump.

21. Some households supplement their herd's hay with grain, especially in spring when they need an extra boost to continue and increase milk production. A few make slop from grain and kitchen scraps to supplement.

22. I know three households who insulated their *khoton* and never had to seal. They had made a shell around the barn with slab wood to create a 6-inch air space, which they then filled with sawdust for insulation.

23. Some stored soft manure to do each layer simultaneously while others applied it each day as available.

24. It requires strength to move the carcass and also a certain mindset. Many males admitted they couldn't do it.

25. 8 percent and 6 percent respectively for cow-keeping households, 3 percent and 3 percent respectively for non-cow households.

26. I use the term "indigenous knowledge" because it includes knowledge that is not just "traditional," or Traditional Ecological Knowledge (TEK) (Wenzel 1999), but also includes contemporary knowledge (Stevenson 1996: 280).

27. Shortened from *Bahanai khozaistsvo*. See chapter 4.

28. I use the term "reciprocal" because only in this dependency category do households exchange either labor for products or vice versa. The term is not used to call up the reciprocity covered by Sahlins (1972:188–275).

29. The Soviet period was marked by a deliberate policy to break down "clan survivals" (*rodovyye perezhitki*) by separating kin households within and across villages (Humphrey 1998:283).

4

Having and Knowing Land

Pre-Soviet Viliui Sakha agropastoralist production was founded on having access to and knowledge of land. Soviet period policies reoriented Viliui Sakhas' relationship to the land by deeming all land the property of the state, distancing land by resettling inhabitants to compact villages, and undermining local ecological knowledge by replacing extensive family-clan subsistence with centralized intensive industrial-agricultural production. In the post-Soviet context, with the move to dependence on cows-and-kin production, access to and knowledge of the land is key to survival. In this chapter I analyze contemporary Viliui Sakha land issues by exploring past and present experiences of having and knowing land.

Having Land

Two moments come to mind when I reflect on post-Soviet Viliui Sakha land issues. The first was on April 13, 1993, when, at 9 a.m., while sitting down to tea with my host family, the Petrovs, the Elgeeii village land specialist knocked at the door. He came to speak with Kolya, the Petrov's eldest son, to solicit his help in dividing up the Kuol Elgeen fields, the last of the former state farm areas to be divvied up as *pai* (R., shares) for household use. The village head wanted Kolya to oversee the allotting because "everyone trusted him." We reached the Kuol Elgeen fields at 10 a.m. to find a gathering of inhabitants, standing ready to stake their claim. All worked diligently to measure and stake out the plots. What struck me was the inhabitants' desperation and vying for Kolya's attention to get the biggest, best plots.

The second moment was a few months later, when I was a fictive member of Kolya's extended family for summer haying. We were working in a distant field that took over an hour to reach by motorcycle. En route, we turned off the main road, passed through a first field, then into a wide, even plot with lush green grasses. "This field should have been ours. It was my great grandfather's but the administration claims it is going too far back to give it to us. We would have to make do with Kuchukanga (a remote plot, swampy with poor grasses)." Kolya continued, "These fields are used by other locals." I asked how it could be since his family clearly had ancestral linkages to that land. He explained, "The local *mafiosa* [R., mafia] just made the excuse about going too far back so they could take all the high quality land, close to the village." It seemed incongruous to me how the village authorities could in one moment enlist Kolya's services in dividing up lands adjacent to the village and, in the next, blatantly disregard his family's ancestral rights.

I have revisited these two moments often while contemplating post-Soviet Viliui Sakha land issues. Not unlike most rural inhabitants of the FSU who have come to rely on household-level production for daily subsistence, Viliui Sakha are challenged by land issues. The last decade has seen a groundswell of discussion on property relations among post-Soviet and post-socialist peoples (Fondahl et al. 2001; Fondahl 1998; Gray 2001; Hann 2001; Osherenko 2001; Verdery 2002; Ziker 2001). For aboriginal peoples,[1] who practice reindeer-herding, hunting, and gathering, post-Soviet land use either still follows the state farm brigade assignments of the Soviet era or has turned to some form of communal or kin-based land tenure system, reminiscent of pre-Soviet *obshchina* (R., communal kin-based grouping) (Fondahl et al. 2001). In other areas where groups practice agriculture and/or sheep, cattle, and horse husbandry, inhabitants have either formed independent collectives (Hann 1997; Humphrey 1998; Kovacs 1996) or divided the local state farm resources into shares for individual households. Most Siberian collectives and state farms chose to retain farm status to continue crucial social services in the post-Soviet context of massive unemployment, shrinking social services, and empty store shelves, and do not operate for profit but to provide a means of subsistence for their members (Buckley 1995).

Viliui Sakha are adapting to the very drastic post-privatization context not by depending on official land allocations but by pooling land with kin in immediate and adjacent villages. Like cows-and-kin, land access is based on both past and present kin relations and cultural norms. In pre-Soviet times Viliui Sakha based land use on a hierarchical social structure that privied the local *toions* to the largest land holdings for their herds. Soviet policies transformed Sakha land use from those extensive family-clan holdings to centralized state property. With the fall of the Soviet Union, Elgeeii State Farm officials chose to dissolve the central farm and divide farm shares among local stakeholders. How was the land allocated locally?

The Great Divide

When the Soviet Union ended in 1991, the central government conferred the responsibility of deciding whether to disband the state farms to local level authorities. If village administrators and farm directors decided to disband their state farm, they allocated farm resources, including the use of the farm's lands, to inhabitants according to state norms. Their first priority was to allot 10 hectares (25 acres) to each individual interested in forming *BKh*s to produce products for local sale to accommodate the lack in consumer products after state farm disbandment.[2] They next designated 10–15 percent of total village hay and pastureland for emergency reserve use. What remained they divided equally among private households for subsistence production.

When Elgeeii State Farm officials decided to disband the farm in 1992, they inequitably divvied the resources within the farm's seven branches over the course of several years of reorganizations (see chapter 2). It was at that time that they also determined access to and allocation of land Their land allocation deliberations resulted in three main modes of village-level food production, each with a correlating system of land access. Private household, based on a standard hay allotment (1.5–2 hectares; 3.75–5 acres); kin-based *BKh*, using an 8-hectare (20-acre) allotment per member;

and large *BKh*, accessing an 8-hectare allotment per member plus use of supplemental pastures and agricultural fields.

Private Households

Since the state farm consolidations of the late fifties, Viliui Sakha have lived in relatively dense village settlements (figure 4.1). Access to sufficient land means constant movement out to and back from outlying areas for haying, pasturing, and foraging resources. A village's size correlates to the amount of land available per household. The larger a village, the sparser and more distant its hay land is. Village size also correlates with employment opportunities: the higher the population, the more jobs.

Suntar, the regional administrative center of Elgeeii and Kutana, has a large, working-class population. Most village land is occupied by household yards. The 10 percent of households that keep cows do so by relying on kin's hay land in adjacent smaller villages. In Suntar, as in most large population villages or regional centers, households depend more on cash from salaries than on home food production to support their households.

The hay land allotments in mid-sized villages (approx. one thousand pop.) average 1.5 to 2 hectares (3.75 to 5 acres). With more land available per household and less salaried employment than large villages, midsize village households depend less on cash and more on home food production, barter, crafts, and reciprocity. In villages with populations of one thousand or less unemployment is high, plentiful land is available, and households depend mostly on home food production for survival. Household hay allotments in these villages average about 10 hectares (25 acres) per household.

In Elgeeii, with a population of thirty-five hundred, hay land is scarce. Although all households qualify for a hay land allotment of 1.5 hectares (3.75 acres), in 2000 only 70 percent had one. The rest were either told they were not native and so had to access land through their birth village, were uninterested in the land available since it was distant and across the river, or were told that there was no land left. Even if a household had an ample hay allocation, changes in climate often rendered it unusable. Almost half of all

Figure 4.1.   Aerial view of a Viliui Sakha village showing density and resource access

households with hay land allotments could not use them between 1998 and 2001 due to excessive rain. In this case, households can write a *zaiavleniye* (R., declaration) to access village reserve lands. However, none chose this option because reserve lands were too distant and most of them were also waterlogged. As a gesture to assist households, in 1998 village administrators allowed open haying on any land that still had harvestable hay after August 15. The administrators abruptly discontinued the program after local complaints of opportunists cutting in areas that were marked off-limits and of hay stealing.

Considering all the complications of accessing land, how *do* households harvest sufficient hay to overwinter their herds? Even if a household can harvest the hay from their village allotment, most need several times that amount for their herd. Many barter, or buy the hay they need. Some rent hay land in a smaller adjacent village. Only a few said they would resort to slaughtering some of their herd if they couldn't cut sufficient hay. Most inhabitants depend on pooling land with their kin in adjacent villages where hay lands are more plentiful. The Petrov family case illustrates how these kin interdependencies work.

The Petrov Family's Land Strategy: In 1999 the Petrov family included an elderly mother, Maria (her husband was deceased), ten children (six daughters and four sons), and twenty-three grandchildren. Maria lived in Elgeeii with her eldest son, Kolya. Next door lived her youngest son, Makar, with his wife and four children. On the other side of the village lived one of her daughters, Jana, with her husband, Nikolai, and their four children. Three of her daughters, Sardana, Toma, and Valya, and one son, Stepan, lived in Suntar with their families. Maria's youngest daughter, Lana, lived with her mother's sister in Tumul, outside Kutana. The remaining son, Alesha, a professional jeweler, and daughter, Natasha, a single, career woman, both resided in the capital city Yakutsk. Both children's households in Elgeeii kept cows and supplied the elderly mother with daily milk and meat.

The mother had a 2-hectare (5-acre) hay allotment in Toyon Uyatigar, one of the outlying hay land areas (figure 4.2). Kolya had a two-hectare allotment at Ugut Kuol for helping with the *sir tungetige* (division of land), described earlier and an 8-hectare

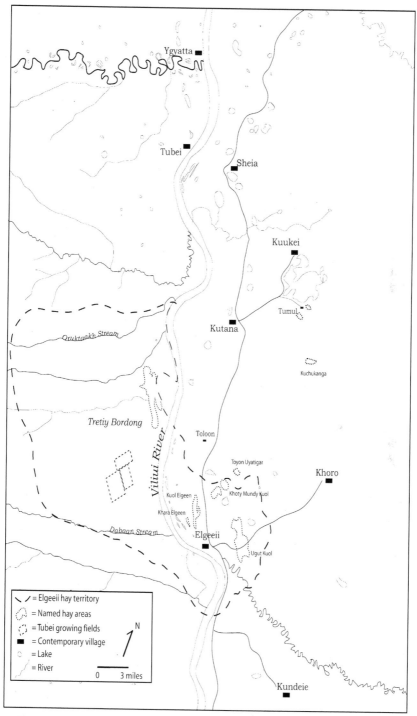

Figure 4.2. Former Elgeeii State Farm area with contemporary Elgeeii hay areas

(20-acre) plot in Kuchukanga, part of the Petrov's ancestral lands. They were offered more land but declined it since it was distant and of poor quality.

The two other Petrov households in Elgeeii had standard allotments, Makar's in Khoty Mundy Kuol, and Jana's in Ugut Kuol plus another 2 hectares (5 acres) in Kuol Elgeen that Jana had received as *pai* for work as a state farm nurse. In total, the three households pooled 17 hectares (42.5 acres), sufficient to keep all three households in meat and milk.

Only one of the four Petrov households in Suntar kept cows. Sardana had one milk cow and a standard 1.5-hectare (3.75-acre) hay allotment, which she had not used in five years due to water. She held on to the land, continuing to pay annual taxes, since she had no other options for land. She is a widow with no spousal kin to pool other hay lands or to help with the harvest. She buys hay from year to year.

Ejiiy Anya ("older sister" Anya), the sister of the elderly Petrov mother, never married. She raised two of her sister's thirteen children, Lana and Alesha (two died in infancy and one in adulthood).[3] Lana lives full time with *Ejiiy* Anya, helping with daily cow-care. Alesha and his family come every summer to harvest hay in exchange for a year's supply of cow products. *Ejiiy* Anya, who cared for hundreds of calves and helped the Elgeeii State Farm win the title of "Hero Farm," continues to keep a large herd, including six milk cows, six two-year-olds, and several others for a total of fifteen head. She needs 30 tons (15 large stacks) of hay annually and gets that much by using her standard 2-hectare (5-acre) allotment supplemented by renting land from Tumul *BKh*, paid by barter with either cow products or half of the hay she cuts. Figure 4.2 maps the Petrov's extended kin haying areas and table 4.1 charts household allotments and hay work schemas.

The Petrov's 1999 summer hay routine shows how the pooling of kin labor, land, and resources works. In early July, Kolya, Makar, and Nikolai began the cutting of the family hay plots around Elgeeii (figure 4.3). Soon after, Alesha and family came through Elgeeii en route to Tumul, where they began the

Table 4.1. Petrov Extended Family Hay Areas and Work Schemas

Household Name	Household Residence	Cows	Hay Land Allotment	Hay Work Schema[a]
Maria	Elgeeii	No	10.0 hectares[b]	—
Kolya	Elgeeii	No	2.0 hectares	TU, UK, KE, KK, TM
Jana/Nikolai	Elgeeii	Yes	3.5 hectares	TU, UK, KE, KK, TM
Sardana	Suntar	Yes	1.5 hectares	KK, TM
Stepan	Suntar	No	—	ST, KK, TM
Alesha	Yakutsk	No	—	TM
Toma	Suntar	No	—	—
Natasha	Yakutsk	No	—	—
Valya	Suntar	No	—	—
Makar	Elgeeii	Yes	1.5 hectares	TU, UK, KE, KK, TM
Lana/Anya	Tumul	Yes	2.0 hectares	TM

[a] Name places have the following codes: TU = Toyon Uyatigar, UK = Ugut Kuol, KE = Kuol Elgeen, KK = Kuchukanga, TM = Tumul, ST = Suntar.

[b] This includes the 8-hectare (20-acre) parcel for the family.

Figure 4.3.   Hay cutting

Figure 4.4. Hay stacking

cutting with Lana and *Ejiiy* Anya. Stepan arrived from Suntar, after helping his in-laws hay, to help with the cutting and stacking of hay (figure 4.4) in and around Elgeeii, and accompany the Elgeeii crew to cut in Kuchukanga.

During this time *Ejiiy* Anya, Lana, Alesha, and family were cutting and stacking *bugullar* (small waist-level high stacks) on the various plots in Tumul. Toward the end of August, the Elgeeii crew finished haying in Kuchukanga and headed to Tumul, where hay was cut, *bugulled*, and ready for final stacking. *Ejiiy* Anya contracted a Tumul tractor driver to help, and in two days, working from early morning to late at night, fifteen people made sixteen large stacks.

The Petrov family's pattern of harvesting hay by pooling hay land and labor with their kin, is how the majority of post-Soviet Viliui Sakha cow-keeping households get ample hay for overwintering their herds. The private household mode contrasts sharply with how both the large and the kin-based *BKhs* access land.

The BKh*s*

The government's purpose in mandating the formation of *BKhs* when the state farms disbanded was to produce meat and milk to accommodate local demand previously supplied through state farm production. To these ends *BKhs* received many perks including larger hay land allotments, access to machinery, government subsidies, and a five-year release from taxes. In 2000, there were twenty-four *BKhs* in Elgeeii. Since their formation ten years earlier, they continued to hold the majority of land yet only produced for their members' subsistence. Four *BKhs* sold their products under contract with state-subsidized village institutions—the hospital, preschools, geriatric home, and the *MMK* (R., *Molochnyi-Miasnoi Kombinat* or the Meat and Milk Complex). Although *BKhs* could access markets in the regional center, Suntar and beyond, the short shelf-life of products and the high cost and relative lack of transportation deterred most.

Considering the local deficit of hay land for private households, it is understandable that there would be animosities toward the large landholdings of the *BKhs*, especially since the majority of *BKhs* operate no differently from private households. A 2000 state policy renamed the smaller kin-based *BKhs* "malyi predpriiaimatel" (R., small proprietor), while the larger *BKhs*, having eight members and more, remained *BKhs*. Despite the name change, they all pay the same taxes and receive similar state subsidies.[4]

Elgeeii and Kutana each have one larger *BKh*, Tubei and Martinov, respectively. None of the members from either operation received a salary in 2000 but were instead compensated with a portion of the *BKh*'s profit in the form of meat and milk. Most members are not in a larger *BKh* for a salary. More importantly, these large *BKh* provide members with ample hay for their private household herds, tractor services, firewood, and fuel, in all saving member households valuable time and money that would normally go toward these subsistence necessities.

The Workings of the Tubei BKh: The only Elgeeii *BKh* that had not downsized to smaller kin-based *BKhs* in 2000 was Tubei *BKh*, with thirty-six members including twenty active workers and sixteen pensioners. In the Soviet period, all these members were employed at the state farm's Tretiy Bordong "Dabaan" horse farm (figure 4.2). Tubei *BKh* formed after the Dabaan TOO (Limited Liability Company) folded in 1994.[5] Members' collective *pai* included all the structures, animals, and land of the Dabaan farm, plus six tractors, two jeeps, one three-axle truck, and a sawmill.

Prior to November 1999 slaughter, the cooperative had 154 head of cattle, including 54 milkers, all held at members' village homes. The Tretiy Bordong farm was exclusively for Tubei's 275 horses including 150 productive mares (120 of which were foaling), 25 stallions, and 100 yearlings. They also kept a small herd of Sakha aboriginal cattle.

Viliui Sakha horse breeding is highly seasonal, with two periods of intensive work: summer haying and winter slaughtering. Horses "graze" year round in the open field, digging under snow for fodder (figure 4.5).

Unlike cows, there is no daily milking regime. Tubei employed five full-time *sylgyhyts* (horse watchers) to live at the

Figure 4.5. Sakha horses live outside year-round and feed during the harsh winter by foraging for fodder under the snow.

Tretiy Bordong farm year-round and monitor the horse herd. All Tubei members spent summers at Tretiy Bordong haying to fodder their private cows, since horses only need a minimal hay supplement in late winter. The other period of intensive work is the late November slaughter of yearlings. During the rest of the year Tubei members worked in various facets of *BKh* operation in Elgeeii, bringing hay in from Tretiy Bordong, harvesting and transporting firewood, and working at the Elgeeii *BKh* facilities.

The amount of annual compensation each member got was dependent on how much *pai* a member had to start with and the profits for that year. When the state farm broke up each member got between two to four mares as *pai*. Most took one yearling for their private household's use and gave one to the collective, which it then sold to Suntar markets. These monies were used to pay the *BKh*'s overhead including 9,171 rubles (approximately $327.54 USD in 2000) in rents for 403.3 hectares (1008 acres) and the taxes on the *BKh*'s allotted land. Although not a source of income, most Tubei members felt that the many other perks they receive via their affiliation with Elgeeii's remaining large *BKh*, including priority to get credit, first dibs on newly arriving equipment, excess fuel stores, and extensive agricultural land, make it worth the affiliation.

In an effort to generate more salaries, in the late 1990s Tubei took on two projects—raising aboriginal cattle and creating a protected preserve area. During the Soviet period Sakha aboriginal cattle populations plummeted from 494,000 in 1928 to 40 in 1989. This was due to their replacement by European cattle breeds that were favored for their high milk and meat production. While discounted in Soviet times, Sakha aboriginal cattle are now valued for being highly adapted to and resilient in subarctic conditions. Now, ten years later, after the first breeding program in Eveno-Bytantaiskii of Sakha, there are three farms in different microclimates of the republic. Cattle numbers in 2002 were reaching one thousand.

To give incentive for breeding programs the government offered compensation at a rate of 1500 rubles (approximately $54 USD in 2000) per head annually. The Suntar *ulus* began a Sakha aboriginal cattle-breeding program in Tretiy Bordong in 1999 under the direction of the Tubei *BKh*. Sakha cows were flown into the Suntar regional airport in mid-January and transported to Tretiy Bordong the next day.[6] Two Tubei members lived at Tretiy Bordong full time to watch the aboriginal cattle herd. By spring 2000 the operation was receiving 2000 rubles (approximately $71.50 USD) per Sakha cow or, a total of 40,000 rubles (approximately $1430 USD in 2000) annually, monies used to pay salaries and overhead. The operation also received supplemental monies from the Suntar *ulus*, the legal owners of the cattle.

The second project to diversify Tubei *BKh* was the 1998 re-designation of Tretiy Bordong to an *Osobaia Okhraniaemaia Territoriia* (R., Area of Special Preserve Status), enclosing a 56,000-hectare (140,000-acre) area between the Dabaan and the Oruktaakh streams. The land within this territory is largely cut off from other land areas with its border to the east by the Viliui River, and to the south and north by the Dabaan and Oruktaakh Streams respectively. The areas immediately to the west are sparsely populated. The two natural stream boundaries isolated the land parcel like a wildlife oasis, considered ideal for maintaining the genetic purity of the aboriginal cattle (figure 4.2).

Most locals interpreted the redesignation as a means for Tubei *BKh* members to exclusively exploit Tretiy Bordong hunting resources. After visiting Tubei *BKh* households and seeing the abundance of wild food resources available relative to other households, I tend to agree. Tubei *BKh* officials argue that they have legal licenses for all their hunting pursuits, including a *kultovoi* license (R., a license permitting taking of wild animals for immediate use when working in the woods and fields) and a bear license. They maintain an exclusive right to cut hay on the reserve lands, provided their tractors do not damage the earth. Locals insist that due to the *BKh*'s close ties to the regional government and the Republic-wide Ministry of Ecology, their own needs take precedence over the ethic of conservation and protection. It may be an ominous sign that the *BKh* hired one of their own members to enforce control of the area. On a more optimistic tone, it may be possible that the reserve could become a successful common property management system.

Although these two projects were intended to generate salaries for Tubei *BKh*, so far they have only advantaged the *BKh* directors, the workers who care for the cattle, and those who police the reserve lands. This leaves about thirty members continuing to live on lesser perks—hay, wood, and one yearling's worth of meat. When asked, all Tubei members confided that they received no monetary gains but continued their *BKh* affiliation in order to have hay for their household's and kin households' cows and a horse's worth of meat annually, which they used for household consumption and to barter for needed goods.

Most larger *BKhs* are fraught with similar issues, including uncertain employment and benefit status for members, internal struggles with labor resources (i.e., many members not pulling their weight), and a lack of profit. Most are also unable to fully utilize their extensive land allotments. There needs to be a more efficient and equitable land arrangement that will make private household land access more available and utilize the excess lands that larger *BKhs* cannot use.

Kin-Based BKhs: The Best of Both Worlds?

In 2000 in Elgeeii there were twenty-three *BKhs* with fewer than eight members, or "kin-based" *BKh*. They operated no differently from private households—depending on a mixed economy of salaries, subsidies, pensions, barter, and reciprocal exchanges. There was one difference—they held the clear advantage of access to significantly larger land allotments, a perk they enjoyed without the larger *BKh* demands of high membership. In contrast to private households, those with kin-based *BKh* status also qualify for a pension over the tenure of their peasant farm involvement.

The "Emis" Kin-Based BKh: Of the twenty-three kin-based *BKhs*, one relied on marketing produce, including vegetables, flowers, and animal products, for their sole source of household cash. Vara and Sergei kept six milk cows and two mares, annually slaughtering three cows and two yearlings to supply meat for their household, send a leg to each of their two children studying in Yakutsk, and have plenty left over to sell and use in barter and as gifts.

Sergei headed and was the sole member of *Emis BKh*, an association that provided access to all the land they needed for hay and commercial production. Vara and Sergei used 35 hectares (87.5 acres) of land: Sergei's *BKh* allotment of 25 hectares (62.5 acres) in Tretiy Bordong and Vara's *pai* of 10 hectares (25 acres) in Toloon (figure 4.2). Vara is a prize-winning gardener who raises bumper crops of tomatoes, cucumbers, and potatoes. In 1999 they harvested 140 sacks of potatoes and harvested 40 tons (20 stacks) of hay, giving 8 stacks to kin for labor, leaving them with 12 stacks, ample to overwinter their herd.

Both speak openly about their reasons for registering their *BKh* in the early 1990s. "We got into it for the land, lots of land—that is the only good of it." Now they find themselves reassessing the situation, "It had gotten to be so much paper work and taxes—so much bureaucracy—if they change the law so private farmers can qualify for pensions I am going to change to private. If they do this, we can still hold the land."

Like with private households, interdependence and reciprocity with kin is central to Vara and Sergei's success. Sergei is from a central region with no kin in the Elgeeii area. Vara's kin in the village are her two brothers and her aunt's household, the Nikolaevs, elderly cow-keepers who depend on Vara's household for hay land access, tractor help, and minimal hay labor, and on her two brothers for hay labor in exchange for an annual supply of meat and milk. The elders keep three milk cows and split all the products three ways between their household and the two nephews. This hay team works the elder's allotted fields, consisting of four hectares on the outskirts of the village, after which they join up with Sergei to help on his hay lands. Sergei does all their hauling with his tractor as well as shares some of the hay his larger hay allotment produces.

After finishing the harvesting of the elders' plots, Sergei and the brothers head to his 25 hectares (62.5 acres) of hay land in Tretiy Bordong for the final three-week period of cutting. In the last three years kin have also come from a distant village, Kempendai, since their allotted hay fields were flooded. Vara comes to help hay for a few days in between a heavy schedule of berry foraging. Table 4.2 below charts their 1999 hay work. In total they

Table 4.2. Vara's Household's 1999 Haying Activities

Date	Work Hrs	Location, for Whom, and Type of Work	# of Workers	Who Worked	Method of Compensation
7/17–7/22	250	Ugut Kuol, for kin Tractor cutting, raking, stacking	5	Male head, 2 brothers, and 2 elder kin	½Hay = 5 tons
7/23–7/28	300	Elgeen (not on map but located halfway between Elgeeii and Kundeie), for kin Tractor cutting, raking, stacking	5	Male head, 2 brothers, and 2 elder kin	None
8/2–8/22	600	Tretiy Bordong, for selves Tractor cutting, raking, stacking	3	Male head and 2 brothers	½Hay
8/7–8/9	120	Tretiy Bordong, for selves Tractor cutting, raking, stacking	4	Male and female head and 2 brothers	½Hay
8/10	40	Tretiy Bordong, for selves Tractor cutting, raking, stacking	4	Male head, 2 brothers, and 1 kin from other village	½Hay
8/16	50	Tretiy Bordong, for selves Raking, preparation for stacking	5	Male and female head, 2 brothers, and 1 kin from other village	½ Hay
8/22	40	Tretiy Bordong for selves Finished haying—return home	4	Male head, 2 brothers and 1 kin from other village	4 tons to kin who helped, 12 tons for selves
Total hrs	1175				

Table 4.3. Vara's Household's 1999 Winter Hay Hauling Activities

Date	# Hay Stacks	For Whose Household	By Sergei with Whose Help?	Compensation for that Help
12/17	1	Selves	1 experienced tractor driver	Fresh vegetables including 2 kg beets, 2 kg carrots, and 2 kg cabbage
12/21	2	Selves	1 experienced tractor driver	200 rubles and a full tank of gas
12/25	2	Kempendiai kin	1 experienced tractor driver	200 rubles
2/3, 2/4	4	Selves	1 experienced tractor driver	2 sacks of potatoes
2/12	3	Kempendiai kin	1 experienced tractor driver	300 rubles

cut 21 tons or 11 stacks of hay and invested 1175 work hours. This totals 107 work hours for each cow and new calf or 2 tons of hay harvested.

Although Sergei has a tractor and uses it freely in the summer months, they bring most of their hay in during the winter months, which requires much more experience and skill. For this they "hired" an experienced tractor driver, whom Sergei accompanied to haul hay from Tretiy Bordong. Table 4.3 details the trips and the compensation paid.

The working of Vara and Sergei's operations also brings to light the lack of community support found in contemporary villages. In late February Vara and Sergei hired a man to come and move their haystack 10 meters (11 yards) to better access their backyard. As pay the man wanted vodka, so Vara gave the man 40 rubles since she had no vodka on hand. She commented, "Now everyone wants vodka for everything they do, we could easily have helped each other—but he had to get vodka...so I do a lot of things myself that I would normally ask men to help me with—like haul the ice myself and the soil for the greenhouses." Despite the hardships, Vara and Sergei manage to generate an income that fully supports their family solely from household production. They could not do this if it weren't for their abundant access to land.

The Three Modes in Sum

Sakha land issues are in a state of flux. In Elgeeii in the last decade of the twentieth century, original *BKh*s downsized to resemble private household operations and many of those were considering going private. The remaining big *BKh* teetered on the brink of downsizing. If these local trends are generalizable, there is reason to argue that the time of the *BKh* is coming to an end. The original policy supporting *BKh* initiatives, which designated them as collective-type operations to produce a surplus for sale in local village markets, has not been (and never was) realized. This is not only due to the lack of demand for those products in villages, where households have moved toward their own production and operate largely outside of a cash economy, but also the universal lack of trust in working with others outside kin and former-colleague networks.

Of the three modes, household-level production is clearly the most efficient and sustainable mode, for reasons described succinctly by a former Elgeeii State Farm director:

> *Ketekh* [private] households cut small amounts of hay land and do a good and thorough job of using the land well. The *BKh*s have large land tracts and manage them poorly. For example, the Tubei *BKh* cut an area half the size of Ugut Kuol [approximately 350 hectares, or 865 acres] in one or two days and then it rained the next two days rendering the hay useless. Small is better. Now people have more time and concern about their hay and the use of their resources. I worked as *SX* director from 1986 to 1990 and all the time my main activity was agitating people to get up and work—and now I see that their apathy was due to the lack of ownership of their own production. The household-level focus is better. People have ownership over their own production and so they care, are productive, and use their resources efficiently.

However, in both Elgeeii and Kutana, private households overwhelmingly resent kin-based *BKh*s, because they operate in all ways like private households but enjoy a significantly larger land parcel.[7] And for good reason—private households keep seventy percent of all cattle and pigs, over half of all horses and reindeer, and produce over seventy percent of all meat, milk, potatoes, and vegetables in the republic yet they are designated only eighteen percent of available agricultural land. No private household is amply provided for by the prevalent land policy, designating each household 1.5 hectares (3.75 acres) for hay harvesting. This is little if considering that cow-keeping households keep an average of three animals. Secondly, there is no suitable back-up in years of a poor hay crop. As a result most private households are forced to seek hay land resources in adjacent villages and via their nearby kin networks.

The Question of Ancestral Right to Land

Most Elgeeii and Kutana inhabitants know the location of their ancestral lands, the areas that their forbearers used in pre-Soviet times. Several issues prevent the reallocation of those lands to their original users. Distance is a major problem. Most households now live 15 kilometers (9.3 miles) or more from their ancestral lands. Similarly, many of these parcels were abandoned during the early years of collectivization and would take substantial work to bring them back to productive hay fields. Lastly, many areas were allocated as *pai* to others. Attempting to find settlement with current owners would result in multiple disputes.

Returning to pre-Soviet home sites was a popular thought following the dissolution of the state farm, but many now realize they are not prepared for the reality of such a move. Only several households said they would return to their ancestral lands to live, if given the opportunity. One household in Elgeeii attempted such a move. They researched and located their ancestral home site, built a small cabin and moved there. They explained that they returned after one year because *abaahi* were living at the site and frequented their cabin over the winter months. They took this as a sign to return to the village. Skeptical villagers interpret this as an excuse, commenting that no one in contemporary times is prepared to live without the conveniences of electricity, refrigeration, television, and a community base. The reinstatement of ancestral rights to land, promoted by some as one answer to the land problem in rural Sakha villages, would not prove beneficial for the majority.

The Second Village Factor: An Argument to Return to Smaller Settlements?

Perhaps there are creative solutions to the land issue if we compare the contemporary trends in Elgeeii to Kutana. The most sustainable (in terms of households being able to produce enough to subsist) models of the cows-and-kin system are in the smaller settlements, where there is not only sufficient land available to support a herd that supplies household needs but also more intact kin networks that are essential in providing labor. According to 2000 research results, 20 percent more Kutana households keep cows than in Elgeeii, averaging one more cow per household. This difference is due to the fact that Kutana households, although subject to the same 1.5-hectare (3.75-acre) hay land quota, have closer and more abundant access to hay lands in even smaller adjacent settlements (figure 4.2). Additionally, Kutana family-clans are more local than in Elgeeii and so there is more interdependence among kin groups, which is essential to pooling hay land and other subsistence resources.

For these reasons many Elgeeii inhabitants consider Tretiy Bordong as a potential area for half of the Elgeeii village to relocate. It is the birthplace and homeland of many contemporary Elgeeii elders (see discussion later on knowing the land). From the early 1950s to its demise in the late 1970s it was a thriving farm complex with two village centers. Many contemporary elders recall both the vibrancy of the community there and the remorse felt by the majority of inhabitants when the protocol arrived to close the villages and relocate to Elgeeii proper. What are the impedances now? There would have to be some way to settle with Tubei *BKh*, which currently uses most of the Tretiy Bordong area, and there would have to be sufficient resources and subsidies to actually relocate and support a population in Tretiy Bordong until the settlement could hold its own.

Final Thoughts on Having Land

In lieu of the changes on the horizon for land access, in the post-privatization context, rural Viliui Sakha practice three modes of subsistence production, private household-level, kin-based *BKh*, and larger *BKh*. The majority are involved in private household-level food production and are challenged to find sufficient land to support their agropastoralist subsistence. As on that April 1993 morning when Kolya was called to divide land parcels, most inhabitants are pushed to desperation in search of land to support their families and kin. Currently larger *BKh*s are failing mostly due to their inability to generate sufficient income for their large memberships and the lack of work incentive that results. Kin-based *BKh*s are for the most part prospering but face strong opposition from private households due to their inflated land resources. Private households negotiate constantly to support their subsistence production by pooling their hay land, labor, and other necessary resources within their kin groups.

How can the land be allotted more equitably? A return to pre-Soviet lands, in the case of Kolya, regaining rights to his great grandfather's lush pastures, at first appears an equitable option. But settlement patterns are no longer extensive as in pre-Soviet times and reestablishing ancestral land rights would work only to favor those with ancestral tracts adjacent to their home village. Similarly, privatizing land would also work in favor of a few, those wealthy enough to purchase land. There needs to be a more equitable redistribution plan for land that ensures convenient access and equal lot sizes for all inhabitants. It does not appear that such an equitable allocation will evolve on the local level, given the dynamics of land access described in the cases above. One hope is that new laws could address the inequities in land allocation by resorting to a collective or common property regime system. However, even if such policies are introduced, the determining factor will be how local actors follow through with or disregard such nascent policies.

Knowing Land

Like having access to sufficient and productive land, possessing an intimate ecological understanding of the landscape and its resources is equally important to contemporary Viliui Sakha survival. The processes of Soviet-period collectivization, agricultural industrialization, and acculturation worked to spatially, temporally, and socially undermine Viliui Sakha local knowledge. Contemporary elders, who remember the local reality of collectivization, state farm consolidation, and the break-up, straddle between two worlds—a Soviet past and a post-Soviet present.

When interviewing Viliui Sakha elders to gauge both the local response to and effects of Sovietization and strategies of post-Soviet survival, I paid close attention to what they remembered about their childhood and how they interpreted the changes of the Soviet period. It never failed to amaze me how they could recall the details of a life that had undergone such quantum change in such little time. It also puzzled me that their children and grandchildren showed little interest in their remembered past. On the other hand, such disinterest did coincide with the general alienation of Sakha youth from both village life and their ancestral past.

The alienation of youth from village life and the infiltration of Western consumer culture are not phenomena unique to the experience of Viliui Sakha but are common trends in rural circumpolar societies in the twenty-first century. There are exceptions. Some Greenlandic Inuit communities boast an intergenerational continuity resilient to the impact of outside change, credited to a value system formed by names, kinship, sharing, and a feeling of community (Nuttall 1992:168). In Alaskan Native communities there have been efforts ongoing for several decades to document local cultural heritage and to educate youth via oral history projects. But no such efforts exist in Viliui Sakha communities, and local heritage is going unrecorded. In addition to the wealth of historical, genealogical, utilitarian, geographical, and cultural information that Viliui Sakha elders possess, they also know a great deal about pre-Soviet land use and subsistence practices.

The Elders and Their Life Stories

Countless broken-down and abandoned structures dot the open fields and forested landscapes between contemporary villages. In talking to elders it soon becomes obvious that these buildings, initially unheeded by the visitor's eye, are actually the remains of dwellings in which they had once lived (figure 4.6). Until relatively recently (1950s) the characteristic settlement pattern of the

Figure 4.6. An abandoned homestead with standing sergei *near Elgeeii*

Viliui regions was of scattered homesteads bordering *alaas*. One of the biggest effects of the Viliui Sakhas' "century of perestroikas" (Grant 1995), is the change in local settlement patterns and subsistence strategies, resulting from the replacement (both willing and forced) first of homesteading, and later of collective farming, with agro-industrial practices and settlement in compact state farm villages.

These changes are evident by locating the places where the elders I interviewed were born and spent their early lives (figure 4.7). A part of local history that might be forgotten is reawakened as the elders describe their lifetimes and refer to now-abandoned landscapes as home sites—places where they were born and spent their childhood, adolescence, and youth. These memories recast seemingly timeless villages as transient and impermanent settlements, "places people move through" (Povinelli 1993).

Fifty years ago these elders, who now all reside in a compact village, were settled across the landscape. The landscapes of their childhood memories, abandoned in the late 1930s and 1940s as forced collectivization was in full swing, most often fell prey to the encroaching forest succession of cedars, birch, spruce, larch, and pine. In some cases the homesteads, their foundations, and other identifiable artifacts remain. Elders born in these places follow the tenets of Sakha tradition and maintain a relationship with the spirit of their home place by making a pilgrimage to feed the ancestors annually or, if distance is prohibitive, every few years. Most, however, don't have that privilege. From the late 1950s and onward, many of these sacred homestead sites disappeared, turned under to become agricultural fields to fulfill the increased production goals of the state farm system.

In the last months of 1999 and into the first months of 2000, I collected and analyzed fifty-four Viliui Sakha elder oral histories in both Elgeeii and Kutana villages. "Oral history is a flexible tool that is particularly well suited for use in projects that involve understanding and reconstructing historical ecosystems" (Fogerty 2001:101). It is also a method that works well to reconstruct cultural landscapes of the recent past. Each elder I interviewed described their early life in a clan cluster of single-family homesteads, scattered across the landscape, and depending on subsistence-level household food production. They each remembered what followed—several moves into increasingly compacted settlements as collectives were consolidated. Their stories reveal how individuals, households, and communities

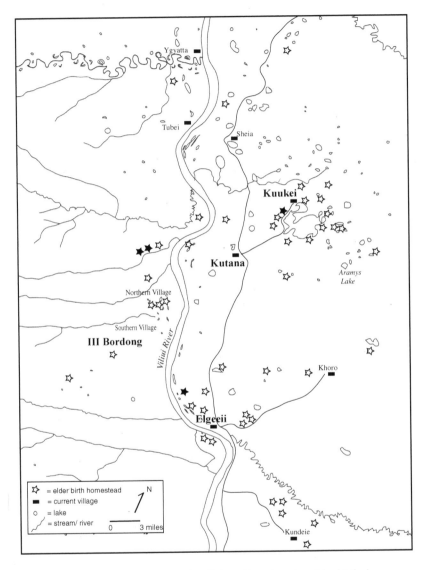

Figure 4.7.   Territory of former Elgeeïi State Farm locating elder birthplaces

adapted to these changes. The elders' witness to their personal experience of World War II and other hardships brings a local vividness to contemporary Viliui Sakha history. These recollections revitalize the mostly abandoned landscapes beyond the present-day village perimeters, infusing those landscapes with life and local history. The narratives reveal how much has changed in the course of these individuals' lifetimes. The experiences of the elders testify to the way in which the survival of pre-Soviet Viliui Sakha depended on household-level food production, extended kin networks, and indigenous knowledge.

The fifty-four elder life histories include accounts of the landscapes in all the villages that once made up the Elgeeii State Farm (figure 4.7). Here I focus on narratives about three main areas where over half the present-day Elgeeii village elders were born and raised: Tretiy Bordong, Perviy Bordong (the territory of present-day Elgeeii), and the Kuukei Island region. Over the elders' lifetimes the Tretiy Bordong and Kuukei areas were abandoned while the Elgeeii population increased severalfold to accommodate the new working class of the massive Elgeeii State Farm.

Tretiy Bordong

Over the course of the last century the settlement pattern of Tretiy Bordong has gone from (1) scattered clan-clusters of single-family homesteads to (2) a group of collective farms (1930s to 1950s), which became (3) a branch of the Elgeeii State Farm run by the inhabitants of two thriving villages (1950s to 1970s), and, as it is to this day, (4) the site of seasonal residence for temporary Tubei *BKh* farm crews. Most contemporary elders argue that if it were not for the forced consolidation policies of the 1950s and 1960s, Tretiy Bordong would still be a densely settled, highly productive village and a substantial asset in the post-Soviet context by providing subsistence and production resources to half of Elgeeii's contemporary population.

Ten of the Elgeeii elders interviewed were born and spent part of their youth in the Tretiy Bordong area (refer to figure 4.7). Images of life in Tretiy Bordong and memories of the local impact of larger historical events on the community are vivid in the minds of Elgeeii elders today. According to the historical record, the Tretiy Bordong area was a popular Viliui Sakha settlement from as early as the eighteenth century through the mid-twentieth century, to this day largely credited to the engineering work of a seventeenth century clan leader, Chokhoroon, whose engineering feats marked the beginning of a productive period for the Tretiy Bordong area (see chapter 2). The series of lakes he created with their interconnecting waterways were functional until the late Soviet period, when the area was abandoned.

Elder Nikolai of Elgeeii detailed his childhood memories of Tretiy Bordong and provided rich accounts of living close to nature and depending on pre-Soviet subsistence practices (refer to figure 4.7: left dark star):

> It was a wild land back then with nature all around us. The moose grazed with our cows and there was lots of good hunting. When we slaughtered the cow and put them into the *ampaar* bobcats and other wild animals would get in and eat the meat. There were so many wild animals there and we lived a lot off hunting. I remember sitting at tea and seeing grouse and ptarmigan on the trees outside the window. The fields were thick with rabbits and we ate lots of fish. There were 44 lakes in the Chokhoroon area and they all had fish. (May 25, 2000)

The abundance Nikolai describes contrasts with contemporary conditions. Up until the mid-twentieth century, hunting provided most families with a substantial supplemental food source. Due to the crowding of modern-day villages and the pressure on natural resources, hunting is now practiced by few and makes up only a small percentage of the resources obtained through subsistence activities.

Nikolai recommended that I interview one of his childhood neighbors from Tretiy Bordong, the elder Katrina: "Katrina lived close to us on Oruktaakh [a stream]. We could hear their sleigh bells ring and their cows mooing in the winter. Katrina's grandfather was a great hunter, fisher, gardener, and herder. They lived well" (April 28, 2000).

Katrina's Life Narrative: Katrina's telling lent an immediacy to the local manifestations of Soviet control. After locating herself in time and space, born in 1934 in Tretiy Bordong, in Maar

Khomustaakh (refer to figure 4.7: right dark star) She explained
how her father was taken from their household:

> In 1940 when I was six years old I remember the house being
> packed up. The KGB man came and took my father from our
> house. He said he was an "Enemy of the People." In 1940 there
> was a war with Finland and the KX had a meeting. They said
> that all should give or sell their herds to the KX and the state and
> in 1939 it had been a very dry year and people really suffered.
> My father, who was very opinionated and outspoken said, "That
> is crazy! Don't get rid of your herds. Soviet money is paper and
> you can't eat paper. This war with Finland is a small one and
> soon there will be real war with Hitler. All the strong workers
> will be sent to the front and the elders, women, and children
> will be left here. We need to keep our herds for our food and
> clothing." And after that the officials came and tried him and
> sent him to prison. That was the last time I saw him. They sent
> him to the salt factory where he died. (May 10, 2000)

This story personalizes the local reality of Soviet forced collectivization policies. After losing her father Katrina was raised
by her mother and grandparents. She drew a detailed map of the
homestead, although she only lived there until she was thirteen
and had not been back since (figure 4.8).

Her intricate memories of the physical terrain, as well as the
methods and practices of utilizing the land and resources, bring
particular attention to the importance of indigenous knowledge.
Similarly, the depiction of the homestead provides a useful por-
trayal of Sakha pre-Soviet agropastoralist subsistence life.

> Our homestead was five kilometers north of the Khotu village.
> The first land place was *Uraha turda*, which means "place where
> the *uraha* [teepee] stood." It was a small open area with a lake,
> and next was *Sylgylyyr yrgha*, which was a big open pasture
> where they gathered the mares to milk. Then after a *dargha*
> [an open area] came Ingerche, a Tungus name, with Ingerche
> *chagda*, a pine woods just above it; then came the Maar land
> place where our pasture and hay land was and our cows grazed
> there. It was six or so hectares. At that point the main road
> veered off to the right toward Norukteeii and Sheia. The first
> land place toward our house was Kungekhteekh named after

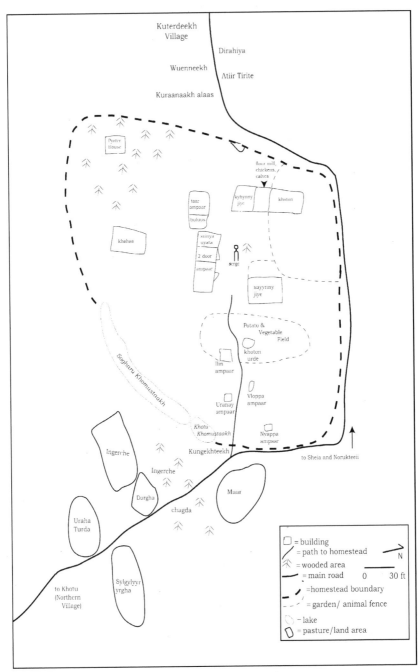

Figure 4.8. Katrina's homeplace

the small fish about as long as your finger and they filled the two lakes there: Khotu Khomustaakh and Soguru Khomustaakh. Inside our fence, first came several *ampaar*. First Nyappa *ampaar* named after my *ehe's* [grandfather's] cousin; then Vloppa *ampaar* [Vloppa was Nyappa's brother]; then Uranay *ampaar*, a very small *ampaar* where Nyappa stored his *ytyk* instruments, the sacred horse ropes and things. Nyappa had sacred horses and he held the *Ytyk Dabaty* [sacred ceremony in which a herd of horses is chased away]. He called an *oiuun* to work for several days and give horses to the sky gods. And inside the *ampaar* were lots of horse hair ropes which had alternate black and white hair braided. The sacred horses wore those ropes and bells and other decorations. There were no windows but we peered through the cracks between the logs. Nyappa was also gone long before me. Then came the Ilin *ampaar* that housed the *buluus*, it went several stories into the ground. You open one door and there is storage and then another door and go deeper and another and another. We would put ice in there and drink cold *kymys* [fermented mare's milk] in the summer, and store meat there to eat all summer. Across from there was a *khoton urde* [an old khoton of which only roof and corner posts are still standing] where people had lived before us; then the rest of the area within the fence was garden where my *ehe* grew potatoes, turnips, onions, and cabbage. He was my mother's father and he knew this land the best. He never lived in the village. Beyond there we had a two-doored *ampaar*, and our *sayynny jiye* [summer house]. It was a big *ampaar* house. It had no roof but was covered with bark at a slight angle covered with stove ashes; when heavy rain fell my *ehe* would go up and put more ash where it leaked. Between the summer house and the two-door *ampaar* was a *sergei* and a tree. Here was the *taar ampaar* with a basement area. It had no floor but bare ground and was full of *chabychakh* with milk. Across from [it] there was our *kyhynny jiye* [winter house] and the front room had all the beds and a table and the *komuluok*. Into the next room was the flour grinding area and the chicken place, then the calf place and the cow area. So, you went from the house to the wheat room to the calves then the *khoton*. On the back of the big two-door *ampaar* was the *sibiinne uiata* [pig house], then the *khahaa* [stable] where colts stayed. Then in the woods was Pyoter's House which my *ehe's ehe* built. (May 19, 2000)

Katrina describes a classic pre-Soviet Sakha subsistence homestead, where several kin households often worked together to be self-sufficient for their meat, milk, garden produce, and forage products. These homesteads passed from one generation to the next, a practice made evident by the abandoned outbuildings of former kin that remained on the property. Her memories of the *ytyk dabaty* also demonstrate the extent to which indigenous belief was integral both to the survival of subsistence practices and to their use.

Katrina also recounted one of her clearest memories, concerning the departure of local men left to serve in World War II.

> They were haying in the fields above our house when they were called to the front. They made sure to finish the haying since they knew there would only be women and children left after them. So they finished the haying very late at night. Above us was Kuraanakh Alaas, then Atyyr tiriite, Wyen-neekh, and Dirahiya [place names]. Then came Kuterdeekh village, which was the hay brigade center. Their haying territory was fifty to sixty kilometers above that village place. The brigadier lived there, Semyenov Nikolai Tataar, he would come and visit us a lot. He was a great man. When they were called to the front they came by our house on their way to the Khotu village Sel'sovet [figure 4.8] and had tea with us as a farewell. They came through the top fence gate; there were five or six of them and they tied their horses and came in and said farewell. (May 10, 2000)

Katrina left the homestead to begin school in 1942, staying with relatives in Khotu village and going home to help her grandparents on the weekends and for the summers. In 1947, to continue formal schooling past the fourth grade, she left her birth home place and has not once returned.

Kuukei: The Lake, the Island, and Its Surrounds

Sixteen, or close to one-third, of the village elders I interviewed grew up around the Kuukei Lake, the largest lake in the Viliui regions (figure 4.7). Up until the last half of the twentieth century, like the Tretiy Bordong area, the Kuukei Lake shores

supported clusters of homesteads. These Sakha, like Sakha today, lived by keeping cattle and horses, by growing gardens that
included wheat and potatoes, and by foraging for wild berries,
plants, game, fowl, and fish. Many elders told a similar version
of a legend about the way the Kuukei Lake was formed:

> Kuukei, one of the greatest hunters in his time, challenged an-
> other fierce hunter to see who could shoot from the farthest
> distance. Both stood on the Batamai mountain and each shot
> an arrow at ducks in the fields below. Kuukei, who was sure
> he had shot and killed a duck at a greater distance than his op-
> ponent, was unable to find his arrow and forfeited his victory.
> In his anger, he returned to the top of the mountain and shot a
> burning arrow into the fields below. This started a fire, which
> burned for three years to form the great Kuukei Lake. (Yegor
> Mikhailovich Nikolaev, April 14, 2000)

For centuries inhabitants depended on the lake and its surrounding shores for their water, fish, waterfowl, hay, and pasture
lands. To this day Viliui Sakha refer to the lake as *Ebe* (Grandmother).

Yanna's Life Narrative: Yanna was born and raised in
Kuukei. Her recollections are important for several reasons.
First, she intimately depicts the former community on the now-
abandoned Kuukei Island, and the way the community worked
together to adapt production techniques on the island landscape
and to survive the starvation of World War II. She also relays a
wealth of ecological knowledge pertaining to growing vegetables.
In the contemporary context, garden production is a major locus
of entrepreneurial activities, supplying 10 percent of the household income of local inhabitants (Crate 2001). Her narrative also
describes indigenous healing techniques, which are presently in
high demand due to the high cost and unavailability of the Western medicines commonly used during the Soviet period. Additionally, Yanna describes how the older generation used to teach
the youth respect for the land and stewardship of nature, an environmental ethic largely lost in the Soviet period.

Yanna stopped me in the street one day and, in a low whisper,
asked if I wanted to hear about her experiences on the island

where she grew up. She said that no one else had recorded them—that the director of the local history museum was not interested since Yanna came from outside the Elgeeii village limits. She was afraid her vivid recollections of the island community would go unrecorded.

At the interview several days later she began by explaining how she came to live on the island, "I was born in 1931 in the Muchuhun land place (see figure 4.7: dark star near Kuukei). My uncle had no children; he was my mother's younger brother. Then my folks died. They were ill and old. So I was raised on the island by my uncle and aunt" (March 14, 2000). Yanna drew a map of the island as she remembered it (figure 4.9). She said there were eight households there in the summer, of which only four remained year round. She explained that the island was really a peninsula, however, the spring thaw waters rose and cut it off

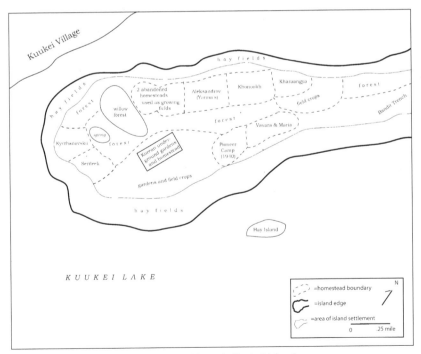

Figure 4.9. Yanna's Kuukei Island

from the mainland. They called the land bridge "Bandit Trench" because bandits once lay there and fought off their pursuers.

Along the north edge of the island were several homesteads. The first had been abandoned for as long as Yanna could remember. In the next lived a distant relation of Yanna's mother. He was a wise old Sakha healer, who never had formal schooling in medicine but learned from nature how to heal. He kept no cows but had extensive gardens. The collective farm workers came to him for healing. He would place his hands on their wrists, on their chest, and on their temples and heal. He taught her uncle to catch the crows and rats in spring and make a healing broth of them.

Yanna lived in the next homestead with her uncle and aunt. They had a large house toward the front of their lot, where they lived during the summer, and a smaller house for winter dwelling. A pig house stood next to the winter house. Behind that was the cow barn and yard and the area for storing hay. On the other side of the yard was the horse area, consisting of a corral with a plain roof where the horses could get protection during storms. Yanna's aunt's job on the collective farm during the war was to make the *kymys*. "The island workers would come by every day to get their portion, along with a piece of flat bread that she made from the ration of wheat. That was all they got to eat back then. Only if they had gardens and stores at home could they eat more. The war years were very hard times" (April 3, 2000).

Yanna remembered many instances of her uncle teaching her how to both survive in the natural world and to pay respect to the earth for its abundance. He taught her to show thanks to the island for its abundance by giving it sacrificial gifts, including feeding the lake special bread and foods at certain times. He taught her to respect the island and keep it tidy. They would gather the fallen branches and trees. He taught the children not to run and yell recklessly on the island but to walk in a deliberately mannered way. He showed them how to gather the dark hardened sap of willow and birch to use as a tea. He also knew how to heal. She remembers how in the spring they would catch crows and rats at the lake edge and make a broth and drink it as a spring tonic. She said that they believed it gave them strength and rejuvenation in a period of vitamin starvation.

Next to Yanna's house were two abandoned homesteads, and beyond them thick woods. Hay fields grew all around the edge of the island. Toward the tip of the island was a spring with very pure water, and two wealthy families who only came in the summers had big fancy homesteads there. Two elderly women, Vavara and Maria, lived in a homestead along the southern edge of the island and beyond them was a homestead belonging to three Koreans.

In the mid-1930s many Koreans fled their homeland to work in the Aldan gold mines, located in eastern Sakha (Tishkov 1994:203–205). When government officials discovered their illegal status they were exiled to work for the collective farm system as gardeners. Three of these, named Bahylai, Oloksoi, and Muksuun, had been brought to exile on the Kuukei island. Yanna said her earliest memory was of these three Korean men on the island, "They had no right to vote. I remember that they didn't go to vote and thinking it was odd. It was only later I understood. My first teacher explained that they had first gone to Aldan and stolen the gold and so were sent here to live like in a prison" (March 14, 2000). The Koreans were expert gardeners and directed the vegetable brigades for the collective farm on the island. They built an underground greenhouse on the island, heated by a stove and a huge glass skylight, where plants could be started as early as February. They used seed collected from one year to the next. They had a small cabin next to their underground gardens and they used every inch of earth around their place for fields and raised beds. They also grew vegetables in all the abandoned homestead yards on the island.

Yanna remembered how hard the work was:

> We grew lots and lots of plants: potatoes and cabbage, carrots, beets, cucumbers, radishes, tobacco, and poppies. In spring the Kuukei island thaws and warms earlier than the mainland. The island has many shrubs and trees; in amongst them we made fields and grew plants. We worked hard, from the morning early, as soon as the sun made it bright enough at 5 a.m. or so. We worked until 11 a.m. planting, cleaning the earth by hand, watering with water brought from the lake in birch containers or by bull. Then from 11 a.m. in the heat of the day we didn't work.

We rested until about 5 p.m., then from 5 to 2 a.m. we worked and worked in the cool. So we slept three hours by night and in the afternoon. They let us rest and take breaks. We worked hard and had great plants. (March 14, 2000)

Then World War II broke out and during the famines of 1943 and 1944, when mortality by starvation was rampant in the nearby villages, the island gardens fed the local inhabitants. The Kuukei area was unique in having had no fatalities at that time:

It was during the starvation years. In the fall we even gathered all the turnip and cabbage leaves and stored them under the snow in a big pile. All winter we ate them; we would cook them in water and mix in wheat to make gruel. We ate potatoes. There were lots of plants, the carrots and turnips. The Koreans understood and they had us gather everything in the fall and everyone ate everything and no one starved. Also, in the fall when the ice was forming on the lake, wood birds, fox, and rabbits were plenty on the island, and we hunted those animals and ate them. We ate lots off the island and for that we are grateful to the lake. (March 14, 2000)

Yanna's uncle died just after World War II when she was fifteen. With no adult male to perform the heavier tasks, the household disbanded. Yanna went to different area schools and earned her keep by washing, cooking, and cleaning. Once she completed the tenth grade, she took an opportunity to get training as a bookkeeper in the capital city, Yakutsk. She completed the course of study with advanced training and returned to Suntar to work for the *Raisovet* (R., the District Soviet) where she married a coworker. They soon returned to his homeland in Nam (central Sakha). When her husband passed away in 1970, Yanna returned to the Suntar area. By that time all the inhabitants of Kuukei Island and the vicinity had been relocated to the Kutana or the Elgeeii villages to work for the state farm system. Yanna went to Elgeeii to work. She described the Elgeeii farm as being huge, with thousands of cows, horses, pigs, chickens, geese, fox, and ducks. The village was abuzz with cars and motorcycles, and every house had a television and new furniture.

To this day Yanna visits the island every few years and takes the island and the lake special gifts of food, "I walk to all the places I knew as a child and feed the spirits there and say what I need to say in those places" (April 3, 2000). Yanna's recollections filled two visits and she said there was much more to tell.

Early Elgeeii

Like Tretiy Bordong and Kuukei, the village territory of present-day Elgeeii (formerly called Perviy Bordong) was inhabited by single-family households clustered in clan groups across the landscape. Unlike Tretiy Bordong and Kuukei, the Perviy Bordong lands were not abandoned. These lands are the allotted hay lands for contemporary Elgeeii village and are under increasing pressure from the Elgeeii population. Here I include excerpts from the life story of one elder born just outside of the present Elgeeii village in 1933 (refer to figure 4.7: dark star near Elgeeii).

Like Nikolai, Yanna, and Katrina, Isaac told of growing up on a relatively isolated, self-sufficient homestead and his personal experiences relating to collectivization and other hardships.

Isaac's Life Stories: Isaac's narrative is useful in several ways. First, he retold many of his grandfather's stories about pre-Soviet Sakha life. One in particular is important because it documents the practice of many Sakha who regularly traveled to more southern towns to trade surplus cow products,

> My *ehe* Ivan had a lot of cows and horses. He would slaughter cows and rig up the horse and cart and go to Olekma, Maacha, Bitiim, Botuobuya, and Mukhtuia, which was the old name for Lensk. He would go there and sell meat and butter and then bring back other items including clothing material, cooking containers, and work tools, axes, etc., and alcohol, wheat, tea, tobacco, and candy. (April 13, 2000)

Prior to Soviet rule many Viliui Sakha depended for their subsistence survival on such long-distance trading. Trips were annual events. Sakha stored their excess butter and other milk products over the summer when milk was plentiful then, after the fall slaughter, they took their surplus meat and milk products to trade for other necessities. Trading households tended to be the more prosperous herders who had a surplus beyond their basic needs, demonstrating the ability of some to successfully multiply their herds in the extreme subarctic climate. The Soviet period brought an end to this interregional trading and to the relative prosperity of individual households. In contemporary times many rural Sakha are developing new entrepreneurial endeavors based on household-level food production. The lack of markets for their goods is the major impedance to these nascent efforts.

Isaac spent his early childhood living with his grandmother and remembers helping her with the cows and storing the milk. He recalled a lot of valuable knowledge pertaining to indigenous foods.

> Before they didn't have separators so they poured the milk into a *chabychakh* and they put it in the *taar ampaar*. It had no floor so it was cool, and in a cool place the cream will go to the top of the milk and then you skimmed it off with a *khamyyakh* [shallow wooden spoon] then the remaining milk would be boiled and made into *sorat* and curds. Any leftover *sorat* they put into an *uhaat* [wooden barrel] for *taar* the *ampaar* was like a refrigerator and into the *uhaat* you threw all the leftover *sorat*, the fish and duck bones—all that was leftover you put in there and it stood all summer and then froze in the fall. When it froze you took the top off it and threw it away and then cut pieces of the frozen *taar* and brought it in to the house to make *taar kaahi* [fermented milk mash gruel]—full of vitamins, a little sour, and very good. We lost the tradition of making and using *taar* as a food during the Soviet period. (April 13, 2000)

Taar was the way that Sakha used every bit of the food products they produced through their domestic and foraging efforts. It still carries a reputation as being the ultimate source of vitamins and the reason pre-Soviet Sakha were able to maintain their health on a relatively vitamin-deprived diet. Indigenous foods like *taar* are important both from a cultural heritage standpoint and for their utilitarian value in the present-day.

Isaac also brought personal insight to the larger policies of his time. On one occasion he told about the impact of the Soviet Cultural Revolution:

Neither of my parents could read or write, but me and my six siblings all got a higher education and went on to work as teachers, doctors, and engineers. So the politics of my time was that all were to get an education; it was part of the Cultural Revolution. Another part was they separated the *khoton* from the house. They said to live with the cows was bad. From a sanitary standpoint, I guess. And so to live a clean life all had to disconnect from their *khotons*. The Cultural Revolution came, in '35 or so. I remember living with the *khoton* and also my *ebe* had many fewer cows after the Soviet time came—only three were left. She had ten or twenty before because the first *khoton* was very big then they moved the *khoton* to Elgeeii and three were fine. In the Soviet times you weren't allowed to have a lot of cows. So later she only had one cow. (April 13, 2000)

Isaac shared his mixed feeling about the changes. Most notably he was an eyewitness to the early changes in Elgeeii. He began attending school in Elgeeii in 1942 and drew a detailed map of the Elgeeii village at that time (figure 4.10).

It is in stark contrast to contemporary Elgeeii, now home to over three thousand people who make up seven hundred households:

All in front of the drugstore was a deep ravine. On the other side of that there was only the *MTC* [R., abbreviation for *Mashinno-Traktornaia Stantsiia* or "Machine and Tractor Station"], which was organized in 1939. The church with Aryngakh's grave, the former rich ruler, was also bordered by a deep ravine. There were a lot of graves around the church too. Next to the church was the old school. They used it as a dormitory for the boarding school after building the big new school that went through the seventh grade. Next to the boarding school was the TB hospital, the bakery, and the *Selpo* [R., abbreviation for "village distribution center"] with a big storage house beside it. On the bank above the ravine was the hospital. There were several wealthy merchants at the time. Their houses are: Tereshkin the

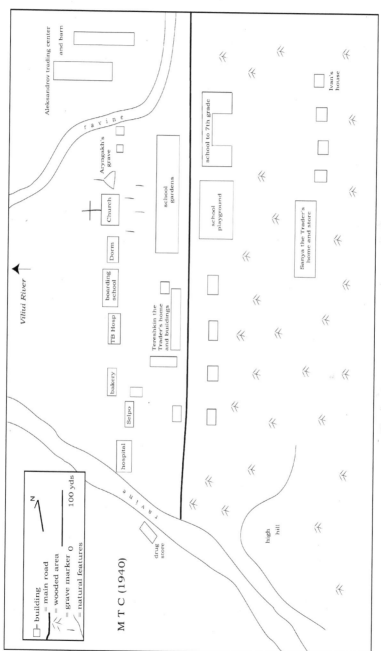

Figure 4.10.   Isaac's early Elgeeii village

Trader's house, Sania the Trader's house [a Russian man] and
Aleksandrov the Trader's house, who had a huge *khoton* for one
hundred cows. He was a rich man and sold many cows. The
big school was there when I came, and it had a playground and
a school garden where they planted different vegetables. The
small blank squares [on the map] are the few private houses.
We lived here [Ivan's House]. On this side was a big high hill.
We would play on it in spring. The snow would melt from it
first and so we played there; we fell down it. All around were
woods. There was only one street [in the town] and it had no
name. (April 13, 2000)

Up until the late 1950s the Elgeeii village was sparsely populated.
Other elders described the "wildness" of the village and explain
how they often saw moose on the village streets and would gather
oton (cowberries) in the forests between the village houses. In
contemporary Elgeeii inhabitants need to travel at least a thirty-
minute ride for berries, and moose are scarce even in the hunting
areas several hours from town. Such changes resulted from the
massive resettlements of the residents of the state farm that increased the village population manyfold. Isaac's family moved
into the village proper in 1954.

In the early 1950s they consolidated the five nearby collectives
into one Molotov *KX* and this brought lots of profits. Then in '57
they started the *SX* and named it Elgeeii *SX*. And they brought
in Kundeie, Khoro, Kutana, Tubei, Sheia, Ygytta [refer to figure 4.7]. They brought them all in and it was a huge *SX*. Across
Russia the consolidation politics came with Khrushchev's time.
I think it was a mistake. It was too big. The *SX* was too big, too
many animals and they all were sick with diseases because they
were crowded. Then people didn't work like they used to. They
stopped caring. (April 13, 2000)

Isaac's descriptions of Elgeeii in the early state farm era provides a clear sense of the massive changes that have brought Elgeeii from a small pre-Soviet outpost to the booming state farm
center it became. The challenge in contemporary times is to maintain a subsistence based on the extensive resource demands of the
cows-and-kin survival adaptation.

The three elders' recollections bring to life the local history of Elgeeii area Viliui Sakha. Broadly speaking, the testimonies demonstrate (1) how larger policies and practices of the time affected individuals' lives at the local level, (2) the intensity of the struggle for survival during the early years of collectivization and during the World War II period, and (3) the enormity of the massive relocations resulting from the consolidations of the Soviet period and the effect of such relocation on the landscape and on the practices of local people. The stories emphasize the reliance on kin and household-level subsistence. The elders' narratives also describe important details of early-twentieth-century life. Katrina's recalls her uncle's fulfillment of the *ytyk dabaty*—the indigenous sacred horse ceremony of the Sakha. Her recollection verifies the continuance of Sakhas' indigenous belief system, which had been largely (though not completely) erased during the Soviet period. Similarly, their experiences reveal a great deal concerning the indigenous knowledge on which daily life once depended. Yanna's narrative shows how lives were sustained by knowledgeable use of Kuukei Island's wild resources and how the careful stewardship of the land produced plentiful gardens. Finally, Isaac tells of inefficiency and poor conditions during the state farm period, and describes the ubiquitous diseases that plagued domestic animals at the time. These details are especially valuable since they are not included in the official records of the time, due to political censure of such information.

Elder Narratives and the Loss of Local History

The other elders interviewed in Elgeeii and Kutana villages shared similarly rich life histories, detailing how they grew up in remote areas and depended on kin networks and indigenous subsistence methods for survival. They described what they had to do to keep going during the historical changes that occurred during their lifetime. All described their birth homesteads as now abandoned. Fifteen elders told me outright that I was the first person to whom they had told these stories; I suspect this is true of most of the others. In short, the physical landscapes of those memories have been lost as settlement patterns shifted, leaving

lands abandoned or reshaped, and oral histories are being lost
now as these elders pass away.

What do the youth, the grandchildren and great grandchildren of these elders, know about their past? In Viliui Sakha villages youth are not taking an active role in learning and carrying
on the cultural history of their forebears. Witnessing this loss of indigenous knowledge brought to mind Henry Glassie's work, *All
Silver and No Brass* (1975), in which the author, through in-depth
interviews with elder Irish mummers, documented a tradition no
longer practiced. I now feel the same sense of urgency that Glassie
must have felt.

During the Soviet period the main focus was collecting folklore rather than oral history as such. As one elder recounted,

> The old time Sakha had no writing and so the storytellers and
> tellers of the *Olongkho* walked and told. Then the Party said that
> they needed to write down all the songs and such that these
> walking people sang. They went to the village and studied the
> dances and the singers, recorded them on the tape recorder and
> wrote it all down. The Sakha had no education. Folklore is the
> people's wisdom and so they ordered them to write it all down.
> The culture workers are interested in the folklore but no one is
> very active now. (Ivan Ivanov, personal communication 2000)

Soviet folklore research began in the mid-1940s and the goal
was to record all that was indigenous in order to transform it into
propaganda for the Soviet party (Miller 1990). In short, little about
practical life during the Soviet or pre-Soviet period was recorded.
Since the fall of the Soviet empire most, if not all, efforts to record
the local past have ceased due to budget cutbacks. As is the case
in Elgeeii, there are village museums but they function mainly to
collect artifacts, record genealogies, and reconstruct a "nostalgic"
past. Efforts to record the living history of local inhabitants are
nonexistent.

Another function of post-Soviet museums is to glorify and
often construct local ethnic "heroes." Since 1991, when I began
research in the Sakha Republic, I have been advised on the formal level to consult with those who are deemed experts on Sakha

culture, most often the local former communists and culture workers. They have taken me to recently rehabilitated gravesites, monuments, and museums, which honor their own local hero. This is no different from what Julie Cruikshank and Tatiana Argunova mean when they point out that any contemporary rural Sakha efforts to preserve the past are more geared toward establishing collective memory in order to substantiate claims for ethnic identity (2000:98). Although establishing such claims is an important task in the twenty-first century global setting, in which underrepresented peoples tend to lose ground in the name of progress and development, efforts to preserve ethnic identity often override the need to record individual accounts of the past. Elders and bearers of past knowledge continue to grow older, their memories continue to fade and be lost, and so also goes the local history.

For the past five hundred years Viliui Sakha have practiced horse and cattle herding in the extreme subarctic climate. Their success is founded in centuries-old and contemporary indigenous knowledge and ancestral use of land. The Soviet-period reorganization of production from clan-based subsistence to agro-industrial production changed Viliui Sakhas' relationship to the land and undermined the local ecological knowledge base. In the post-Soviet context, survival depends on a cows-and-kin strategy, a household-level production system reminiscent of pre-Soviet Viliui Sakha subsistence strategies. The success of the cows-and-kin system depends on access to sufficient land resources. In the post-privatization context, rural Viliui Sakha use three modes of subsistence production, private household-level, kin-based *BKh*, and larger *BKh*. The majority of Viliui Sakha are involved in private household-level food production and are challenged to find sufficient land to support their agropastoralist subsistence.

The successful use of the land for cows-and-kin household-level production is also dependent on local ecological knowledge. Although seventy years of Sovietization worked to make indigenous knowledge obsolete, contemporary elders know extensively about regional ecosystems and biological resources, the local impacts and changes due to the last century's events, the working of pre-Soviet clan settlements, and local manifestations of climate change. In the post-Soviet context, elder knowledge is an invaluable resource for survival, but there are no local, regional, or state efforts to document, interpret, and use that resource. Instead, knowledge is lost due to the lack of time and resources to document, interpret, and disseminate it and, more importantly, because of the lack of local valuation for its utility in modern life. The time is ripe for this kind of work, not only to preserve and pass on an invaluable cultural legacy and to educate local youth, but also to facilitate a contemporary rural survival strategy founded on knowing and accessing land.

Notes

This chapter is partly based on material published in *Europe-Asia Studies* (Crate 2003b) and *Arctic Anthropology* (Crate 2002) and is included here under permission by the publishers.

1. I use the term "aboriginal" to refer to the "numerically small peoples of the North," a legally distinct subset of indigenous peoples in Russia who qualify for communal use lands. Sakha are not numerically small but can also qualify for these lands in the Sakha Republic (Fondahl et al, 2001:552).

2. To include a 1-hectare (2.5-acre) agricultural field, a 5-hectare (12.5-acre) hay field and a 4-hectare (10-acre) pasture.

3. Sakha will give children to relatives who are unable to have their own to share the childcare and to fill labor gaps for childless households.

4. In 2000 the tax rate for land was 7.58 rubles (approximately $0.27 USD in 2000) per hectare. The tax triples to 22.74 rubles (approximately $0.81 USD in 2000) per hectare if a *BKh* rents land.

5. "Tubei" is the original Sakha name for the area and means "a thick primeval forest, usually by a river."

6. Inhabitants still recall how one cow escaped once off the airplane, only to be found the next day after being out all night in −50°C (−58°F). It was one of two pregnant cows and had a strong and healthy calf that spring.

7. They also resent absentee hay land holders, former village inhabitants who have resettled in a center, retain their Elgeeii hay lands and either rent it to locals or allow kin to use it. One man relocated to Yakutsk and exchanges hay land use for one leg of meat. His taxes equal $1 USD yet he receives the value of $100 USD.

5

An Environmental History of the Viliui

In the last four chapters we explored how Viliui Sakha have continued to make their home in Siberia by adapting to a variety of physical, historical, and political changes. Most recently, they have successfully adapted, in fundamental cultural ecological ways, to the uncertainty and unpredictability of the post-Soviet period—a transition from central state farm dependence to decentralized production—by developing the cows-and-kin system founded on retrieving production knowledge, reviving ecological knowledge and relying on kin—and not by adopting the forms of market capitalism that came recommended by the West. However, survival for contemporary Viliui Sakha involves more scales of negotiation for livelihoods than cultural ecological analysis alone can tease out. How can we contemplate the larger forces of globalization and modernity that are impacting these local strategies?

To start, we know that Viliui Sakha households depend on a mixed cash economy and that the majority of that cash comes from state government transfer payments of salaries, subsidies, and pensions. The state generates ninety percent of its revenues from diamond mining activity. In turn, the state supports diamond mining by giving companies tax breaks, incentives, and relaxed environmental laws. All diamond mining takes place in the Viliui regions. Since the first mining activity in the late 1950s to this day, mining has proceeded without environmental controls and has caused much damage to local ecosystems and human health. By tracing full circle this flow of monetary and production resources, we see that Viliui Sakha household-level survival is dependent on an industry that threatens the health of the ecosystem and its inhabitants supporting household-level subsistence. Viliui Sakhas' monetary dependence on the diamond economy today in some ways parallels their Soviet dependence on the subsidies the state provided to first consolidate their collectives into agro-industrial state farms, and then to run those operations with the main objective to provide meat and milk for the nascent diamond mining industries (Crate 2001; Crate 2003a; Tichotsky 2000). Although the state still owns, operates, and profits from the diamond industry, it no longer subsidizes the adjacent rural communities' farming production or general welfare (Crate 2003a).

A major divergence with that past is how the symbolism of diamonds has changed for Viliui Sakha. Since its post-Soviet opening to the global economy, the Russian diamond industry has been driven by the world demand for both gem and industrial stones. With that opening, diamonds were no longer symbols of collective economic pride that Viliui Sakha interpreted as their regional contribution to building the communist state. Instead they came to symbolize self-administration, economic freedom, and relative independence (Argunova-Low 2004:261). Another change further augmented the symbolism of diamonds on the Viliui. With the release of information about the multiple environmental offenses of the mining industry and the ecological devastation that had ensued, the Viliui regions went from being the pride of Sakha for its diamond wealth to the *'znak bedi'* (symbol of poverty) (Maksimov 1992). The press had frequent articles in the early 1990s that paralleled Sakhas' diamonds to Sakhas' tears (Nikolaev 1992). During this same period, the state made many attempts to rebuild Viliui Sakhas' positive image of diamonds. One foreboding symbol that was often used to promote the republic's mineral wealth and Sakha culture was that of a *choron* on its side, spilling over with diamonds. Local Sakha often have interpreted this more as a premonition, since a spilled *choron*, according to Sakha cultural norms, is a sign of poor fortune. Another symbol, less-known but equally ironic, was a photograph of Sakha dancing their traditional *ohuokhai* circle dance superimposed on a photo of a diamond mine (figure 5.1).

Figure 5.1. Ohuokhai *in a diamond pit*

The image was used to announce a 1993 celebratory meeting of company officials with Viliui Sakha who guided and hosted the early geological expeditions that led to the discovery of diamonds (Ushnitzkai 1993). According to several participants, such shallow gestures by the state do little to change the company's public image. A few years later, and after a heavy propaganda campaign by the government and elite company interests, the diamond had successfully worked itself into the realm of destiny for Sakha inhabitants—the symbol of their move into the modern, civilized world. Sakha artwork, depicting Sakhas' historically based cultural symbols; horses, *sergei*, *choron*, and so forth, began incorporating the symbols of diamond activity; the hydrodam, mounds of diamond granules, mining trucks, and the like.

Today the diamond industry continues to degrade the local environment while it prospers with little compensation or benefits to local Sakha beyond minimal state transfer payments. What possibilities do Viliui Sakha have out of their predicament? Are there other options for sustainable futures of these communities? To answer these questions we first need to understand the environmental history of the diamond industry, the changes that came about in response to *glasnost* and *perestroika*, and the growth and decline of citizen activism on the Viliui.

Glasnost on the Viliui

Glasnost entitled Soviet citizens to open access to information and the right to speak out. Armed with information about a multiplicity of abuses, environmental and otherwise, citizens protested across the FSU from the major cities to the isolated provinces. Some scholars refer to the movement as *eco-glasnost*, since it was citizens' outrage about the environment that effectively undid the Soviet Union.

Under the momentum of *glasnost*, Viliui Sakhas' protest focused on the gamut of local environmental damage from past and continued diamond mining. They succeeded in winning access to information on the pollution caused by mining and industrial experimentation. This period of access to information and open critique emerged rapidly, but it disappeared almost as suddenly in the late 1990s due to co-option by elite diamond interests. This story is a vital one to the ethnography's ultimate discussion of sustainability because it shows clearly how local actors across post-Soviet Russia, in this case, Viliui Sakha, lack the political engagement necessary to protect their environment and control their own future.

The Sakha Republic is unique within post-Soviet Russia as an emerging economic power with strong ethnic representation in its state apparatus. The region, twice the size of Alaska, is rich in mineral wealth and natural resources, a phenomenon explained emically in the Sakha legend quoted in chapter 1 on p. 7. Hence, they say that all the elements of Mendeleyev's chart can be found within the contemporary republic's borders. These resources, developed during the Soviet period, today provide the republic and the Russian Federation with sizable income (Tichotsky 2000). Diamonds alone make up 80 percent of the republic's revenues. Those same gems make up 99 percent of Russia's diamond production and represent 20 percent of the world market. Sakha diamonds are found only in the republic's western area, appropriately named "The Diamond Province" (figure 5.2).

Due to their republic's economic power and their sizable ethnic population, Sakha, unlike other post-Soviet non-Russian

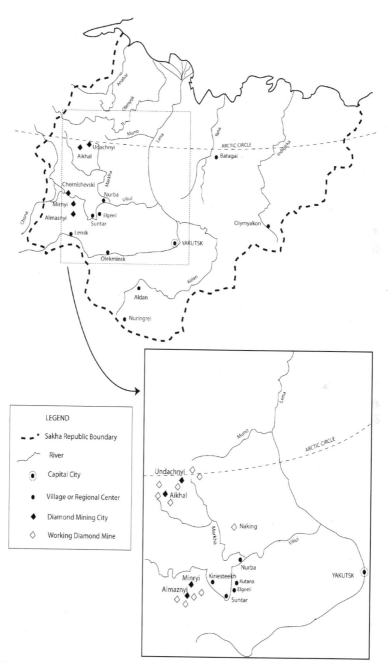

Figure 5.2.   The Sakha Republic with detail of the western "Diamond Province"

peoples, have emerged on equal, and in some cases superior, footing with their Russian counterparts, in controlling their republic government and social status (Balzer and Vinokurova 1996). The republic is also known for its unprecedented environmental record, thanks to former President Nikolaev's designation of 20 percent of the republic's area to protected status. From the West, from Moscow, and from the capital city, Yakutsk, the Sakha Republic appears to have overcome the hardships of the post-Soviet period with its robust economy and cutting-edge environmental policies.

However, there is a divergent side to this success story, one that accounts for the environmental and sociocultural impacts of the republic's diamond mining activities on local communities and ecosystems. Among Western coverage of the Sakha Republic's post-Soviet progress, research to date has only referred to two specific aspects of these impacts. One aspect is the colonization of native populations (Tichotsky 2000), and the other focuses on the health impacts of industrial development (Marples 1999; Espiritu 2002). My objective is to tell the story comprehensively through a historical and contemporary analysis of the discovery, exploitation, and effects of diamonds on the Viliui.

Soviet Industrialization

The effects of collectivization and state farm consolidation altered the natural environment on the Viliui. However, it was Soviet period industrialization that resulted in the most devastating effects. The foremost objective of the Soviet government following World War II was rapid industrialization (Forsyth 1989). Just before that time in 1941, geologist Victor Sobolev attested to the similarities of geologic structure in diamond regions of central and southern Africa, and that of the Viliui regions. Spurred by the postwar need for industrial diamonds to supply the growing military-industrial complex, the Soviet government immediately invested substantial resources to find the expected diamonds

(Duval et al. 1996). In 1949 the G. H. Fainshtein geological expedition first discovered diamond granules near the present-day town of Kiresteyekh in the Viliui River basin (Kharkiv et al 1997) (figure 5.2).

In the years to follow, expeditions came regularly to locate more natural pipes of kimberlite. On August 21, 1954, the young geologist Lorisa Popugaeva discovered the first kimberlite pipe *Zarnitza* (R., literally "lightning"). In 1955 the diamond industry began mining the *Mir* (R., literally "peace") and the *Udachnyi* (R., literally "successful") pipes. In addition to finding diamonds in kimberlite columns, geologists also found substantial kimberlite deposits in the Irelakh River, which ran adjacent to the *Mir* pipe. The government built a "drag" to extract these deposits, an enormous machine, similar in looks to a one block, five-story office building, to move up and down the river, dredging up the riverbed strata to sift and sort it for kimberlite.

Like all Soviet-period industrialization, the exploitation of diamonds did not need to abide by environmental laws and regulations. Such laws existed but were disregarded and themselves impotent, having been written by the industrial ministries and economic planners, whose priority was industrial development (Peterson 1993:175). With the advent of diamond mining in the Viliui regions, the main protocol of the recently established state farms was to produce meat and milk for the diamond industry, essentially colonizing Viliui Sakha as servants of the Soviet industrial complex.

From its beginnings, this new and extensive diamond mining industry required large amounts of electric energy. The government met this need by constructing the Viliui Hydroelectric Station (Viliui GES) in Chernoshevski, the first hydroelectric power plant built on permafrost. The government solicited local Viliui region inhabitants to supply most of the person power for dam construction (figure 5.3).

The nascent diamond industry also required substantial manpower, a problem it solved by the "importation" of workers from outside the area, mostly from the Ukraine, Byelorussia, and European Russia, a move that increased regional population and

Figure 5.3.   Viliui inhabitants helping to build the GES hydrodam, circa 1963

ethnic diversity. The Soviet period ushered in quantum change for Viliui Sakha. In the post-Soviet period local inhabitants need to reconcile with that past on at least two levels, in terms of their daily subsistence survival (covered in the previous chapters) and the myriad of environmental offenses to their homelands and health.

The Post-Soviet Period: Reconciling the Past

The Sakha Republic suffered severe environmental damage in Soviet times when it was plundered for its diamond, oil and gold reserves. Diamond mining, for example, has polluted the Viliui River with traces of thallium and other toxic chemicals. In the '70's and '80's the river basin also experienced 11 underground nuclear tests, seven of which had a yield greater than or equal to that of the bombs dropped on Hiroshima, according to Sakha officials. Dead forests now surround the explosion sites and the permafrost is radioactive.

—Open Media Research Institute (OMRI 1997)

News clips such as this, revealing the local reality of Soviet period environmental disregard, were common in the post-Soviet period. The Viliui regions were no exception. The area and its inhabitants were subjected to contamination from diamond mining, nuclear testing, and second-stage rocket debris. By the late 1980s, when the public was first privy to information about these activities, they had already been ongoing for thirty years. Even then, inhabitants were and continue to be left without full knowledge of the impacts, on their own and on their children's lives, that these Soviet legacies had.

Impacts of Industrialization on the Viliui

Physical Impacts of Viliui GES

The construction of the Viliui GES and its adjacent reservoir changed the river's natural ebb and flow, altered the local climate, and inundated native settlements and valuable land resources.

The hydrostation activity changes the natural regime of the watershed's streams and rivers (Shadrin 1984). Water is released in excess to the watershed ecosystem during the frigid winter when electric energy demands are high. Conversely, in spring and summer less than the natural flow of water is released, as electric energy demand is lower and water reserves are retained. Additionally, released water originates from the reservoir's cold bottom, decreasing average downstream water temperatures (Nogovitzin 1985). These disruptions further alter habitat for fish and animals, changes the species composition downstream and above the reservoir, and affects subsistence resources.

The only pre-hydrodam "picture" of the river's ecosystem is anecdotal evidence offered by contemporary Sakha elders, who speak freely of the change in the river below the dam since the reservoir was built.

> Before GES, the river was FULL of water—an absolute abundance of water—and in springtime, especially, the river would swell to the brim and more so. Spring is also memorable for the waterfowl migration—they came in such numbers that you couldn't see the blue sky through the mass of birds. Now the former clouds of birds that flew through have been reduced to a trickle here and there. It's not that they have disappeared but that they have changed their flight pattern. (Anonymous elder, 1994)

Similarly, Sakha elders describe the pre-hydrodam Viliui River as having crystal clear waters abundantly teeming with sturgeon, freshwater salmon, and other valuable fish species, now only seen rarely. The river otter (*Lutra lutra* L.) and black or hooded crane (*Grus monacha*), once common to the Viliui and its tributaries, are gone (Andreev, 1987). The presence of the hydrodam may also be responsible for a local climate change. Inhabitants' testimony and some research support the claim that there has been a moderation of local climate. However, the research community cannot substantiate these claims without comprehensive data and proper measuring instruments.[1]

In the process of creating the reservoir, 1440 square kilometers (356,000 acres) of prime fields and woodlands; haying, pasturing, and hunting areas; and economically valuable timberlands, were lost.[2] The reservoir also flooded indigenous settlements, home to approximately six hundred people, along the Chona River, an upper tributary of the Viliui flowing north along the republic's western border (figure 5.2). These communities made up one of the last two "outposts" of reindeer communities left on the Viliui at that time. The forced resettlement policies to promote industrialization in the Viliui regions delivered the final blow to these two groups, the Shologinskii (meaning "inhabitants of the upper river areas" (Tugolukov 1985:188), and the Sadinskii, whose ancestors had settled in these more mountainous areas several centuries prior (see chapter 2). The Sadinskii herders lived along the Chona River. This area underwent several changes in the Soviet period that resulted in the demise of the Sadinskii herders. First, the 1930s regionalization of northern and national territories of the Sakha (Yakut) Republic, reconfigured three western *naslegs*, the Chonskii, Bragatsko-Sadinskii, and Botobinskii, into one independent Sadinskii National Region, based on the common subsistence lifestyle of its reindeer-herding inhabitants.[3]

With Soviet efforts to improve overall efficiency through further collectivization and consolidation of farms, the Sadinskii National Region was increasingly seen as incongruous to notions of progress. Geographically the Chona/Sadinskii area was rugged with mountainous regions and free-flowing rivers and streams. There were few pasturelands, and the inhabitants mostly relied on reindeer herding, hunting, fishing, and foraging. The area was hard to access due to a lack of permanent roads. Based on the area's seeming lack of future perspective, the government abolished the Sadinskii National Region in 1947 and made it part of the adjacent Suntar region. The justification for this included: 1) that the hunting and reindeer-herding communities would never develop agriculture, considered their only hope for progress; 2) that the overall population was too small and dispersed to ever become independent collectives; and 3) that the population was too dispersed and distant from the Sadinskii regional center, which made their administrative guidance difficult.

The final blow to the Sadinskii herders came in the 1950s after the discovery of diamonds. The Soviet government determined the best use of the rugged Chona Valley area was to be flooded and function as the Viliui hydrostation reservoir, to provide electricity for the exploitation and processing of diamonds. To these ends, hundreds of thousands of acres of prime fields and woodlands containing haying, pasturing, and hunting areas and economically valuable timberlands were slated to be lost. Additionally, the reservoir would flood the indigenous settlements of about six hundred people who lived along the Chona River.

Chona inhabitants, most of whose ancestors had inhabited the Chona River areas for generations, protested when they heard that their homelands were to be flooded. But Soviet authorities gave them no say in the matter. Over a period of several years, state officials gradually subdued the local outrage with promises of a brighter future for them and their children through their relocation to areas near large towns and cities. Their children would go to better schools, they would have a higher standard of living and their farming operations would thrive. The state designated the main resettlement area as the "Novyi" (meaning "new") state farm adjacent to the Mirnyi industrial center. Novyi State Farm would operate as one of the main agro-industrial complexes to supply meat and milk for the new mining city, Mirnyi. Chonians were promised conditions far better than they had in the Chona Valley.

From the early 1960s Chonians began to relocate. Between that time and 1967 when the waters consumed the Chona Valley, all six hundred people relocated except for one elder man who refused to leave and drowned in his home. With this flooding of the Chona regions came the end of the Viliui reindeer-herding complex. In 1997, the year the Sakha Republic recognized the thirtieth anniversary of the Chona Valley flooding, surviving Chonians looked back at the move with remorse. One of them, presently a doctor at the Novyi State Farm, explained,

Many moved from Chona, from Toy Khaia (literally "Clay Mountain") when they built the Viliui Sea. Today we look back at this as a great loss but at the time our parents really had no choice. They were simple people with fourth grade educations and when the Soviets told them the relocation was the best for them, they had to go along with it. I came to Novyi State Farm as a girl, finished schooling and have worked as a doctor since—I see the medical results of this relocation. Two hundred seventy people moved (to the Novyi State Farm from Chona) and from them 207 have died, mostly from cancer and from the stress of the move and being torn from their (ancestral) land. The conditions were bad then and remain bad to this day. (Kondakova 1997)

In the post-Soviet context many of the evacuated Chona residents still do not have adequate housing, initially promised them by the Soviet authorities. A small percentage of Chonians relocated to live with relatives or found work in established Viliui settlements. All former Chonians I interviewed spoke about the Chona Valley with words similar to these:

It was such a lush and wild place. Moose and bear came up to our door. We lived off of hunting and reindeer-herding. Toy Khaia was the highest point for miles around and there, in spring, the first snowdrops bloomed. We would gather on the mountain's peak and dance the circle dance.

Many Chonians now reinterpret the renowned Sakha singer-improvisator Sergei Zverov's 1970 dedication song for the Viliui GES. Zverov fulfilled the required patronage to Lenin, the Party, and the progress at hand but also interspersed lines forewarning the imminent destruction this progress would bring to the local inhabitants. Throughout the song he referred to the reservoir as "Wot Kundulu Baikal," the same name used to describe the fiery underworld lake of the Sakhas' traditional epic poem, the Olongkho (Zverov 1995; Ukhkhan 1992).

The Shologinskii was an Evenk clan and they were also resettled for diamond mining purposes. They originally made a home and traveled with their herds on the upper Markha River. By the 1920s all Shologinskii had abandoned their native Tungus language for Sakha. Of the two settlements documented at that time, one was solely reindeer-herding and the other a mix of reindeer-herding and agropastoralism (Tugolukov 1985:189). In 1952 the Soviet government ousted the Sholonginskii from the Viliui area by relocating them to a far northern arctic region. Only in the post-Soviet context with full access to information about Soviet period industrialization efforts, have Shologinskii been able to verify that their people were relocated to open the area to diamond mining. In fact in 1954 and 1955, respectively, adjacent to the former Shologonskii homelands, the Soviet government first opened the Udachnyi and the Aikhal diamond mines.

Chemical Contamination

There are three main sources of surface water contamination on the Viliui: phenol, thallium, and highly mineralized brine water. The flooding of 2500 square kilometers (965 square miles) of uncleared taiga, pasture, and swamp, and the anaerobic decomposition of vegetation that resulted, released a surge of phenols and copper into the watershed system.[4]

The river is also contaminated with thallium from using liquid "Klerich," a highly toxic thallium-containing compound, to separate diamond granules from their natural substrate, kimberlite.[5] Klerich-rich wastewater was routinely emptied into surface water systems until the early 1990s, when the industry discontinued the use of klerich due to public outcry. In an effort to contain thallium contamination, in 1986 the diamond industry installed holding ponds to contain the wastewater. The thallium-containing water was then piped to these ponds, where it was decontaminated after passing through a series of specialized filters. Investigations since that time have shown the system was ineffective (IAE, 1993).[6]

The third source of surface water contamination is highly mineralized brine water, which seeps up from under the permafrost layer[7] to collect at the bottom of the diamond pipes (figure 5.4). Until 1986 the brine was dumped directly into the surface water system. This water is high in salts and metal elements such as copper, chromium, nickel, iron, zinc, and lead. The diamond company continues unsuccessfully to try various methods of containment of these waters (IAE 1993; Crate 1995a:11).

Nuclear Contamination

Between 1974 and 1987, the Soviet government performed a dozen secret underground nuclear tests in the Viliui regions. In

Figure 5.4. The Mirnyi Diamond Mine with the city of Mirnyi on the horizon

1987 an insubstantial newspaper article about the blasts generated persistent citizen inquiry. The state had to publicly acknowledge the tests and announce that two of the twelve, "Kristall" and
"Kraton-3" had had catastrophic above-ground nuclear fall-out
(Burtzev, 1993).

The lesser of the two, called "Kristall," occurred in 1974, just
2.5 kilometers (1.5 miles) from the industrial town of Udachnyi.
It was the first of eight explosions planned to free the subsoil
of permafrost to build a dam for one of several waste filtration
ponds of the Udachnyi diamond industry. To accomplish this,
the company's engineers located the detonation points an uncon-
ventionally shallow 99 meters (325 feet) underground. After the
catastrophic fall-out of the first explosion, the remaining seven
were canceled.

The second and more severe fall-out, "Kraton-3," occurred in
1978, a mere 183 meters (600 feet) from the shore of the Markha
River, a major tributary of the Viliui. The explosion was the same
power of the bomb dropped on Hiroshima in 1945 (Pavlov and
Afanaseeva 1997) at 19 kilotons (Burtzev and Kolodoznikova
1997). It is considered as "constituting one of the most serious

problems in the history of nuclear explosions" (Yablokov 1992). The river is a major source of drinking water for villages that border it. Today, plutonium-239 levels can be found that measure higher than those in Chernobyl. There was no recording of the levels in 1978 when the explosion occurred.

In 1990, state specialists and researchers from the Russian Academy of Sciences (RAS) investigated the situation and found Cesium-137, Strontium-90, and Plutonium-239 and -240 in the soil, rain, lichen, tree bark, and adjacent water systems (Pavlov and Afanaseeva 1997). They verified plutonium contamination at levels equal to the maximum contamination of soils in Belorussia and Ukraine following the Chernobyl accident (Yablokov 1992).[8] Local inhabitants were not informed of the extent of plutonium contamination until 1993 (Pavlov and Afanaseeva 1997). Despite the life threatening nature of these accidents, there has yet to be a comprehensive study of these two sites.

Contamination from Airborne Rocket Debris

Since 1958, the Nyurba region of the Viliui watershed has been the designated area for the drop-off of second stage rockets launched from the Bikanur Cosmodrome in Kazakhstan. The exact number of rocket drops over the Viliui regions is, to this day, a secret. According to the testimony of the local veterinarian who has practiced in the Viliui regions for forty years,

> From 1983 the rockets fall—in October [1983] sixty fishermen saw the [first] rocket and after that they saw many more . . . they fall in four, six, eight pieces. In 1991 the Bikanur representatives came and openly said that only three fell but we have seen more and see the effect to our animals. Our region—in 1995 a cow was born without a skin—then a two-headed, and another. This year another—we have never had this before. There are many more examples of this. . . . (Tobonov 1997)

The shed rocket parts emit highly toxic gases containing heptile (dimethylhydrazine),[9] which contaminates the taiga flora, fauna, and indigenous settlements. The Viliui inhabitants consider this contamination a link to the rise of cancer in their populations since the late 1970s. Local hunters report sightings of entire herds of dead animals and birds found in the taiga where the rockets fall (Crate Field Accounts 1997, 2000).

Official Efforts to Reconcile the Environmental Issues of the Viliui Regions

In the post-Soviet context, the state is accountable for reconciling with past and continuing environmental damage on the Viliui. Its efforts have been mainly twofold: 1) to fund and organize remedial environmental projects in the Viliui Regions, using a percentage of the profits from diamonds; and 2) to increase the environmental programs coordinated by the Sakha Ministry of Ecology.

In 1993, the Sakha government established *Sakhaalmazproinvest* (SAPI) Financial Corporation to receive 2 percent assignments from *Almaz-Rossia-Sakha* (ALROSA), the Russian-Sakha diamond mining conglomerate, and fund remedial socioeconomic and environmental programs in the Viliui's diamond province regions.[10] In 1995, the SAPI Financial Corporation was reorganized into the SAPI Foundation, a not-for-profit organization. This resulted in the Sakha government losing direct control over the 2 percent assignments, and raised concerns about how those funds were being used (Yakovleva and Alabaster 2003:91). Regional representatives conveyed the fact that SAPI was fraught with issues of state-level, regional, and local money laundering, and that SAPI funds were often depleted at the regional level, before even reaching village populations, those most affected by environmental contamination (Romanov 1997). The Sakha Republic's president at that time, Mikhail Nikolaev, made direct references to suspicions of the company's mismanagement, "We await good work from SAPI" (Alekseev 1997). Perhaps in response to the bad press they were receiving, in 1997 SAPI reported a host of environmental programs, such as expeditions throughout the Viliui to study indigenous health, preliminary planning for a monitoring system for drinking water in the Viliui regions, the creation of a series of geographic-ecological maps for the diamond mining areas, the methodological groundwork to develop ecological insurance for the areas, and several cooperative efforts with the Ministry of Ecology conducting research on the Viliui (Andreev 1997). However, these efforts were a clear conflict of interest, since SAPI was a branch of the diamond company.

After several state inspections to investigate the use of SAPI funds revealed resource misuse, in 2000 the Sakha government moved the 2 percent allocation out of SAPI and into the state budget of the Sakha Republic under the government control of the *Tselovoi Fond* (R., Target Fund). In the words of Vasili Alekseev, Minister of Ecology for the Sakha Republic, this was done "... to ensure that the money has a definite address." (2003). But how is the new money being used? Alekseev and his regional representatives all agree that the first and foremost need of Viliui inhabitants is good drinking water. However, none can show that the *Tselovoi Fond* plans to finance water filtration systems in the regions. Presently, the monies are allocated to develop gas, oil, and high voltage electricity development on the Viliui. In the final analysis, the Target Fund is dominated by state control instead of being a dynamic interaction of state, private sector, and civic interests contributing to the proper use of social investments on the Viliui (Yakovleva and Alabaster 2003:96).

The second state effort to reconcile the issues on the Viliui is increased environmental programs. In 1993 the Russian Federation established a federal ecological monitoring system, taking many regional initiatives under its wing. The Sakha Republic's Ministry of Ecology began a program to monitor the Viliui ecosystem in 1996. The goal of the Viliui watershed project was: "to provide objective informational support to assist the state organs, industrial decision-makers, agricultural sector and inhabitants with data regarding the ecological conditions in the region's territories" (Ministry of Ecology, 1997). The ministry, having confirmed the severe environmental state of the Viliui regions, developed regulations to prevent further damage and initiated the Viliui monitoring project. However, with the late 1990s economic downturn, the ministry became financially strapped and underwent a 50 percent layoff, a terrible loss for an organization trying to watchdog a republic twice the size of Alaska. In 2000, Russian president Putin consolidated the Ministries of Environment and of Natural Resources into one. This set the new ministry's priority to be the exploitation of natural resources for Russia's economic renewal.

The Sakha Republic is the only subject within the Russian Federation that has, for the last nine years, had its own Ministry of Ecology. With Putin's changes they have lost their control. Likewise, bureaucrats working in the ministry must accept the reality of coming under Russia's federal structure and taking on Russian laws. There is a lot of contention. When asked about this conflict of interests in the summer of 2003, the Ministry of Ecology's Vasili Alekseev commented, "We can't agree with this—we are a sovereign state of Russia but we don't have our own power—we can only hope that there will be changes and we will get to have our own control again."

Any pressure on the government to make these efforts effective falls on deaf ears, since government bureaucrats tend to downplay the ecological issues on the Viliui based on a lack of "conclusive evidence" (Crate 2001; Marples 1999; Tichotsky 2000). As a result, local inhabitants remain concerned about the effects to their and their progeny's lives. But why haven't concerned Viliui citizens protested these abuses and pressured their government for environmental justice like others have done in post-Soviet Russia? They did. In the early 1990s there was a powerful environmental movement on the Viliui. However, after over a decade of hard work and making much headway, elite diamond interests co-opted the movement. What enabled this citizen activism to emerge and to bring to light the many local environmental and social problems? What were the reasons for this activism's disappearance or descent into apathy? The answers to these questions make up the following section.

The Birth and Demise of the Viliui Committee

In the late 1980s, on the heels of *glasnost* and *perestroika*, inhabitants across the Soviet Union first gained access to information about the environmental offenses of the Soviet period. Empowered by this information, like so many across the Former Soviet Union, in

1989 concerned citizens and representatives of the city's scientific intellectual community founded a public ecological center in the Sakha Republic's capital, Yakutsk, to research and disseminate information about the environmental legacies of their homelands. In the fall of 1989 the center organized a republic-wide conference to discuss ecological problems and to form regional watershed-based organizations to initiate local activism. Many concerned residents of the Viliui regions were in attendance, and there was much discussion of and interest in the complex of environmental issues on the Viliui. One of the watershed organizations formed during the conference, the Viliui Committee, focused on the Viliui watershed. Later that fall the Viliui Committee and Public Ecological Center organized a conference in Mirnyi, the diamond mining center, to meet with representatives of *Almaz-Rossia-Sakha* (ALROSA), the Russian-Sakha diamond mining conglomerate.[11]

Since the Viliui Committee had started its work within the membership of the Public Ecological Center in Yakutsk, it already had substantial support of many government representatives and had received a lot of coverage in the press, "Our press supported us and played a big role in getting the word out," commented Lyubov Yegorova, one of the original founders of the Viliui Committee,

> Soon the whole Republic knew about "The Tragedy of the Viliui," and all the other things they called it. Everyone knew about what was going on. We kept talking about the problems. Then in 1991, with the help of the Committee to Save the World and the Sakha Minister of Ecology, we shot a film about the radiation problems and all the ecological problems. We were working. We gathered a lot of money by showing the ecological problems throughout the Republic. (Yegorova 2003)[12]

During this time, concerned citizens throughout the Viliui regions initiated local chapters of the Viliui Committee and began taking action by organizing village meetings and discussing environmental concerns and contentions. At first, these public meetings were largely soapbox venues—a time to gather the local citizenry and express anger and disdain at the damages done. As the committee matured, regional representatives organized scientific conferences and drafted citizens' petitions to the government.

In 1993 a new guiding member, Pyoter Martinov, experienced in the technology of diamond transport and passionate about citizen advocacy, joined the committee. Martinov traveled with most of the ecological expeditions, researching the nuclear accident sites in the Viliui. He also traveled frequently to Yakutsk to meet with representatives in the state parliament. It was under his leadership and vision that the committee became actively involved in the legal process.

In 1994, the diamond company announced their discovery of "the biggest diamond column in the Viliui regions," located near several indigenous communities in the Nyurba region. While assessing the area, they discovered a second column. Nearby inhabitants openly voiced their opposition to these new mines, claiming that their settlements had already received their share of environmental havoc from previous mining activity. Most did not believe the company's promise to abide by full environmental protection, including impact statements and monitoring, based on the past history. The Sakha Ministry of Ecology promised extensive monitoring of the new diamond area prior to any activity to establish a "before" picture as a baseline to measure contamination levels, a step not taken with the first mine sites forty years earlier (Martinov 1996). The ministry curtailed monitoring due to a lack of funds.

Martinov was a life-long resident of the Nyurba region and focused all of his efforts toward the blockage of these new mining ventures. He took every opportunity to speak openly about his conviction that these new diamond reserves needed to be mined only after the diamond company had adopted environmentally safe technology and had justly appropriated a percentage of the diamond profits to Viliui inhabitants. In 1996 he spearheaded several referendums that impeded the diamond industry's plans to exploit new diamond columns, based on their failure to perform comprehensive environmental impact assessments. But these only temporarily set back the company plans. In 1997 Pyoter Martinov died an untimely death after a several-year struggle with liver cancer. With this loss, the Viliui Committee suffered a severe setback. Martinov was the guiding vision and force behind the committee. His energy inspired others and his organizational skills maintained a distinct pathway for all to follow.

After Martinov's death and the series of failed referendums, most of the original Viliui committee members left the organization. Concurrently, the diamond company started a propaganda campaign aimed to avert the remaining environmental concerns. Between 1997 and 1999, Viliui citizens were told outright that if they pushed their rights to a clean environment too far, that they would risk losing their state salaries, subsidies, and pensions. While conducting research during this span of years, it was evident that this propagandizing worked. I witnessed an active and concerned citizenry turn into a silent and apathetic one over the course of those two years. This, in turn, influenced Viliui Sakhas' symbolic representations of diamonds. From a herald of devastation in the early 1990s, diamonds began to appear more as a symbol of pride, reminiscent of the Soviet period. By the late 1990s, I began seeing subtle images of Sakha diamonds integrated artistically in Sakha cultural practices (figure 5.5).

The regional representatives of the Viliui Committee also changed markedly. While the committee was preparing to celebrate its tenth anniversary in 2000, a complete turnover of membership produced new priorities that were anything but environmental activism. The new personnel, all key figures in regional economic development, transformed the Viliui Committee from an environmental NGO focused on involving the citizenry in environmental activism, to a bureaucratic board of local officials who gather privately to discuss their plans. In short, the active environmental agenda of the original Viliui Committee had been successfully co-opted.

Environmental Victories in Post-Soviet Russia: A Recipe for Success?

How does this case contrast with successful cases redressing environmental problems in other parts of Russia and the circumpolar north?[13] Over the last decade, concerned citizens of Russia have

Figure 5.5.   Diamond symbolism in a Sakha mural at the yhyakh *festival*

accomplished substantial environmental progress, under the fa-
cilitation of international NGOs, to build civil society, considered
the essential first step to successful environmental movements
(Soubotin 2002). There are also cases of success redressing environmental problems within Russia. The key to each successful

movement is the presence of a strong urban base and of international representation. One need only look at the web pages of United States NGO's such as The Initiative for Social Action and Renewal in Eurasia (ISAR), Pacific Environment, Sacred Earth Network (SEN), World Wildlife Fund (WWF), and so forth, to understand how key this international/urban connection is.

In the context of environmental redressing and indigenous peoples (IPs), many victories can be cited through the work of the Russian Association of Indigenous Peoples of the North (RAIPON), an association of Russia's numerically small peoples,[14] founded in 1990. The organization has a central office in Moscow and seeks ways to work with the Russian government. RAIPON's strategy of action in Moscow and other centers across Russia includes getting indigenous representatives into positions of public office and influencing state authorities through the dissemination of information (lobbying) and court appeals. In the regions RAIPON focuses on, local representatives facilitate seminars to educate residents on environmental and legal issues; organize negotiations between RAIPON and managers of regional and local environmental ministries, environmental organizations, and industry; and assist in the organization of civil actions and collective appeals in cases of illegal industrial acts. RAIPON also disseminates information about its activities and court precedents, and about the infringement and protection of indigenous peoples' rights through its "Indigenous World–Living Arctic" publication.

One strong case of environmental redress through RAIPON's efforts is the establishment of the Tkhsanom Specially Protected Natural Territory of Traditional Natural Resource Use (TTNRU),[15] located in the Koryak Autonomous Okrug of Kamchatka in Russia's Far East and encompassing 2,100,000 hectares[16] (Kohler and Wessendorf, 2002:224–245). The key to the 1998 establishment of the territory was local leadership and vision; the knowledge and use of environmental and indigenous legislation to protect the area; the involvement of the Itelmen's Revival Council, the local indigenous RAIPON group, and RAIPON's Moscow representation; and support by international organizations, most notably WWF. However, in the swiftly shifting tides of Russian internal politics and economic reform, a short two years after establishment of the territory, the new governor of the Okrug abolished the territory's status to open the area for industrial development of its natural resources. The key to continued protection of the area is legal coordination between the Tkhsanom communities through their work in the Itelmen's Revival Council, RAIPON, and international pressure to make use of the new federal laws that ensure their rights to the historical lands of their ancestors and to protect the environment of their inhabitancy.

Imagining a Future of Environmental Justice on the Viliui

To this day, diamond mining proceeds on the Viliui with only minimal environmental control. The Ministry of Ecology, charged with protecting and monitoring the Viliui watershed, was usurped by the Ministry of Natural Resources in 2000. Diamond mining is a highly lucrative activity. The Sakha Republic depends on diamonds for 80 percent of its state revenue. Threats by the diamond interests successfully co-opted a growing and successful citizen movement. All these factors have rendered the Viliui regions and its inhabitants environmental scapegoats.

Is there a way for Viliui Sakha out of their environmental predicament? What were the movement's strengths and weaknesses? The Viliui Committee had many of the salient features of contemporary successful environmental movements in Russia, including a strong urban base with support and interest by elected officials, knowledge and use of existing environmental legislation, and a strong local leadership. What went wrong? There are several moments to contemplate. First, a series of failed referendums that served only to stall the mining company's operations. Perhaps if the Viliui Committee had some central representation in Moscow and on the international front, there could have been sufficient pressure to carry through these legal processes. The second crucial moment was the loss of Pyoter Martinov, whose guiding vision and unfailing vigilance was central to the committee's success in the mid-1990s. Lastly, and most significantly, was the co-option of the movement by elite diamond interests involving both the deliberate subduing of its citizens' nascent environmental movement through repeated threats to their economic livelihood should they act in favor of environmental protection, and the appointment of bureaucrats to the empty seats left in the regional chapters of the Viliui Committee when citizen activists left following Pyoter Martinov's death in 1997, a move that rendered the committee politically impotent.

Is there a chance of reviving this vital citizen movement to work toward realizing environmental justice in the Viliui regions, or will it remain a relic of activism gone to apathy and a clear example of co-option by elite diamond interests? Based on the success stories described above, for the Viliui Committee to revive its original vision of environmental protection and justice, it needs more outside contact including representation in Moscow and on the international front. As also detailed above, much of the successful environmental redressing for Russia's IPs is through their coordinated efforts with RAIPON. However, Sakha are not a numerically small people, a factor that precludes this as an option. The strong support by political representatives in Yakutsk that the committee enjoyed during its formative years, like the committee's regional representation, has been replaced with elite diamond interests. This leaves finding support and interest from an international and/or Moscow-based group as the Viliui Sakhas' main hope in reviving their environmental movement. This is a strong possibility given the establishment of many international NGOs with representation in Moscow.

Similarly, there is a growing concern in the international community for the health of our circumpolar environment. The Viliui River is a major tributary of the Lena and thereby contributes to the biological health of the Lena Delta and the Arctic Ocean environment. Once this international attention is achieved, the inhabitants of the Viliui can move forward and take up the fight they began in the early 1990s for a healthy environment for generations to come.

Or can they? What about the other vital components of a successful environmental victory, including local empowerment and some level of self-government? In the post-Soviet context inhabitants of Russia can no longer depend on the center to provide for them. Dependence on the state is a thing of the past, beginning with Gorbachev's mid-1980s privatization and self-accounting policies and culminating with Yeltsin's "shock therapy" tactics of structural adjustment policies (Shaw 1999:83–87). Since the introduction of these policies, inhabitants of Russia have been scrambling to adapt to the overnight change from centralized to decentralized government and from a command to a market economy. In sum, the keys to redressing of environmental issues in post-Soviet Russia include a strong urban base, international contact, local leadership, and a knowledge of and power to enforce existing legislation. These are the same characteristics that predated the redressing of environmental issues in other parts of the circumpolar north (Young and Osherenko 1993). For example, the devolution of power from central governments to indigenous communities that has occurred in Greenland/Denmark with the establishment of Home Rule, and in parts of Canada through comprehensive land claims and political settlements including extensive use of comanagement.

The increasing globalization of the world capitalist economy, with production and finance organized on a transnational basis, has been key to the spread of capital-intensive high-value, world market–oriented extractive industries. It has also been central to the growth of informed and sophisticated indigenous movements in affected areas. The Arctic presents an especially provocative case due to the increased focus on sustainable development of both renewable and natural resources in an age when world demand for those resources increases daily. In defense of their lands and their livelihoods, some arctic indigenous peoples' organizations are striving to ensure a workable participatory approach between indigenous peoples, scientists, and policy makers toward sustainable and equitable futures. The case of diamonds in Canada, the subject of the next chapter, is especially illustrative of these nascent efforts and potentially provides a clear model for realizing sustainable futures for Viliui Sakha and other indigenous inhabitants of Russia confronting economic and environmental dependence on regional mining.

Notes

This chapter is based in part on previously published articles, in *Polar Geography* (Crate 2003c) and in *Cultural Survival* (Crate 2003d), and are included here under permission by the respective publishers.

1. With a 2331-square-kilometer (900-square-mile) surface area and 40,407 million-cubic-meter (52,850 million-cubic-yard) capacity, the reservoir has some local temperature moderating effect when seasonal extremes fluctuate from −60°C to +40°C (−76°F to +104°F) and back again.

2. Including 1355 square kilometers (334,880 acres) of forests and shrubs, 23 square kilometers (5,683 acres) of pasture, and 61 square kilometers (15,000 acres) of swamp.

3. In 1926–1927, Bragatsko-Sadinskii had 325 people, 466 reindeer, 355 cows, and 51 horses.

4. Phenol levels have stabilized (IAE 1993), but the effect of previous contamination remains unresearched and undocumented. Phenol's red sedimentation reduces light infiltration and affects river biota life cycles. The pre-hydrodam river had twenty-six fish species, and now there are six (Crate 1995a:11).

5. Thallium is readily absorbed and toxic to the human metabolic system (IAE 1992). Thallium poisoning results in hair loss, neurological damage, and death. Normal blood thallium levels are under 2 milligrams per liter with concentrations greater than 100 milligrams per liter toxic (Moore, House, and Dixon 1993).

6. A 1993 study found five times the safe levels of thallium in the river water and fourteen times in the shoreline's sand and soils. Thallium, like all metals, tends toward sorption onto organic (detritus) and inorganic (clay, sand, etc.) particles, found throughout the Viliui river bottom. IAE found nine to eight hundred times the allowed levels of thallium and projects that thallium will contaminate the Viliui for centuries (IAE 1993).

7. The diamond pipes continue hundreds of meters into the earth, far below the permafrost layer.

8. Plutonium can enter the human organism via the mouth (ingestion), the nose, and through the skin.

9. The International Agency of Research on Cancer has classified dimethylhydrazine as a possible carcinogen to humans (www.epa.gov/ttn/atw/hlthef/dimethyl.html)

10. Including eight regions: Anabar, Lensk, Mirnyi, Nyurba, Olenek, Suntar, Verkhnyviliuisk, and Viliuisk.

11. This meeting set the initial plan to allocate 2 percent of diamond profits toward Viliui environmental remediation, fully realized with the 1993 establishment of the SAPI fund.

12. Former Sakha president Mikhail Nikolaev also played an advocacy role by writing an article in the Russian newspaper about the atomic explosions on the Viliui.

13. The term "circumpolar north" includes the arctic and subarctic areas (Nuttall 1998:21–22).

14. Groups under fifty thousand are "numerically small." There are forty recognized groups within Russia, totaling three hundred thousand people, with the largest group being the Nenets at thirty-five thousand (Kohler and Wessendorf 2002).

15. TTP is the abbreviated form of *Territorii Traditzionnoe Prirodapolzovanie* or Territory of Traditional Nature Use.

16. Equal to 21,000 square kilometers (5,189,310 acres).

6

Diamond Mining and Indigenous Rights in Comparative Context: The Case of Canadian Diamonds

Contemporary Viliui Sakha subsistence survival is inextricably linked to diamond mining in three central and interdependent ways. First, the main source of household cash is government transfer payments, originating from the Sakha state budget, 80 percent of which is made up of revenues from diamond mining. Second, the myriad of environmental issues on the Viliui, which impact the subsistence ecosystem and human health, are a result of past and ongoing unsound mining practices. And third, diamonds have a dynamic and integral presence in Viliui Sakhas' daily life, lore, and symbolic culture. The dependence on a diamond economy binds Viliui Sakha to a present and future largely out of their control. They have been successful at adapting to changes in post-Soviet subsistence production but not to the forces of globalization and modernity that have disembedded their economy and that threaten their health and ecosystem.

How does their situation compare to other indigenous peoples affected and dependent on mining? We can learn a lot by comparing the Viliui Sakha case with the "best-case scenario" for diamond mining and indigenous peoples in the north, the case of Canadian diamonds. In contrast with the Russian case, Canada's local stakeholders have won benefit and impact agreements, marginal environmental protection, and other concessions from mining activities. By carefully weighing the pluses and minuses of the Canadian case, we should be able to clarify exactly what can and should be fought for not only in the Viliui Sakha (Russian) case but also in the multitude of scenarios involving indigenous peoples and mines worldwide.

There are both commonalities and contrasts between these two cases. Both Viliui Sakha and Arctic Canadian aboriginal groups (and all indigenous inhabitants throughout the circumpolar north, for that matter) are affected by the popular stereotypes of the north, a world area seen as both a resource frontier and a centuries-old homeland for resilient indigenous cultures. Both had similar histories of colonization based on a fur trade. The Canadian and Russian cases contrast due to the presence and recognition of aboriginal title in Canada. Named and written into British common law in the mid-eighteenth century and more fully recognized starting in the mid-twentieth century, the legal developments enforcing land claims and indigenous rights have resulted in indigenous awareness and, in many cases, successful interventions to northern resource development.

Stereotypes and Definitions of the North

When I ask students on the first day of circumpolar north seminar to list descriptors of "the north," most write: snow, cold, ice, barren, white, empty, reindeer, aurora borealis, Eskimos, silence, permafrost, blue, midnight sun.... They are keenly interested to learn that the north is both a crucial global ecosystem important to maintain both arctic and subarctic biodiversity and global ecosystem services, and a thriving homeland to diverse cultures, important in maintaining arctic and subarctic ethnodiversity. The north is a final frontier not just of nonrenewable resources but, perhaps more importantly, of our common survival. Even in our twenty-first-century context of information about and access to all corners of the globe, there remain major misconceptions and stereotypes of the north.

How is the north defined? To an outsider it is the realm of pop culture and mythology. To a physical geographer it is defined as a harsh, forbidding land with extreme winters located within the limit of permafrost. A sociocultural anthropologist may approach a definition based on the breakdown of indigenous and non-indigenous settlement. Evolutionarily the north is considered primitive with potential to develop. Economically, the north is characterized by boom-and-bust resource-based economies and as the future source of nonrenewable resources for temperate world regions (Coates 1995). In all these instances the north is defined in relation to the outside world—considered a resource and military base for the "south." Certain structural characteristics limit the options for white settlement: a harsh climate, a restricted agricultural capacity, and a sparsely settled and unproductive land. Poor, expensive supply lines make manufacturing that is otherwise mobile not feasible. Where resource extraction is ongoing, there are often racial schisms between newcomers and native inhabitants, between laborers and management, and between the urban and rural sectors. Displacement of indigenous populations and annexation of ancestral lands further exacerbate racial tensions and cultivate other social ills including unemployment, alcohol and drug abuse, poor health, and suicide.

Some characterize the north by its culture of opposition, which "originates with nonindigenous struggle against a harsh environment and indigenous inhabitants and which expands to include struggles with southern governments, transients, corporate influences and the south's popular conceptions of northern realities (Coates 1995). Considering the growing world awareness of the north for its crucial role in global environmental processes, it is imperative that former stereotypes be broken and the north be recognized as a keystone[1] ecosystem. Until then, the central struggle of economic and political development of the north will swing back and forth between two visions: a frontier and a homeland (Berger 1977:1; Bone 2003:1). What is the historical basis of these two visions of the north?

A History of Northern Exploration and the Fur Trades of Russia and Canada

The first recorded travel to the north was in 320 BC by Pytheas, a Greek of present-day Marseilles, in search for tin. He brought back new information that greatly expanded the knowledge and understanding of the "world" at that time and contributed toward completing world map constructions (Chevallier 1984). Over a millennium later, in the sixteenth century, the new incentive to find northern sea routes to Japan, China, and the East Indies and thus circumvent the blockages by Spanish and Portuguese, spurred the next travel to the north. It was at this time also that the Hudson's Bay Company was exploring the Canadian north to make land claims and exploit furs, directly paralleling Russia's easterly and northerly imperial expansion to the same ends. Eighteenth-century northern exploration largely focused on the naval pursuits by Britain, France, and Russia via the scientific exploration by the national academies of those countries. The 1725–1740 northern expeditions by Bering landed him successfully in Alaska by way of the strait named after him. Russia moved across coastal Alaska, Canada, and down to San Francisco, compelled by Catherine the Great's insatiable thirst for furs.

The years that followed saw increasing activity in the north to continue with the exploitation of furs for the growth of European and North American economies, the expansion of scientific exploration to include multidisciplinary research, and the quest to find the northern passage. By 1847 the arctic coasts of Alaska and Canada had been explored, and after the 1848 disappearance of Sir John Franklin the forty expeditions sent in search of him and his crew over the next decades resulted in complete mapping of the coasts (not the sea channels nor inlands) of the Canadian Island Archipelago by 1870 (Potter 2004). Following this, Swedish and Russian expeditions, and finally Stefansson's Canadian Arctic Expedition of 1913–1918, explored and found the last major areas of unknown arctic lands (Weber and Roots 1990). Expansion to the north was vital for the economies and resource claims of Europe and the New World.

There is another version of the story of northward expansion—that of the "history-less peoples" inhabiting the northern landscapes (Wolf 1982:194). For more than three centuries the fur trade thrived in Europe and Asia, expanding to North America once the Iberians (Spanish) allowed passage. In Russia, imperial expansion between the fourteenth and twentieth centuries increased the country's territorial domain from 200 to 2 million square kilometers (77 to 772,200 square miles) (Shaw 1999:2–4), and was largely driven by the eastern and northern move to exploit sable pelts across the vast Eurasian plain. In North America, traders sought the beaver, prized for wool hats. In both cases the "whites"' mode of extracting these fur resources was by trading with, as in the Canadian case, or taxing, the norm in Russia, the native inhabitants.

Russia's territorial expansion across Siberia began with the opening of the Urals to the east after the defeat by Yermak of the Siberian Khanate in the mid-1500s. Prior to that time private individuals had crossed the Urals via the Arctic Sea route and traded glass beads for fur. Following Yermak's opening, the Russian State extracted *iasak*, using methods similar to the Spanish conquerors in Peru and Mexico, by coercing natives into submission and exploiting them as producers of imperial wealth. Each male member of a tribe, fifteen years or older, paid *iasak* annually in a fixed payment of furs (Forsyth 1992:41). By 1620 the Russian state had fully annexed western Siberia, adding 1.25 million square kilometers (482,625 square miles) of land to the Russian state holdings. Sable pelts were the source of Russia's economic growth in the sixteenth and seventeenth centuries, the principal commodity of foreign exchange with Renaissance Europe for Muscovite Russia. Wherever imperial Russia extended its territory, it used armed force to extract *iasak* from the native peoples. Regardless of how "humane" the rules were made in Moscow for tribute payments, in the hinterlands collectors abused the natives by demanding more *iasak* to keep for themselves, by overstepping their *iasak* territories, and, in many cases, by enslaving natives (Forsyth 1992).

The European fur trade began in Canada in the early 1600s when Basque fishers began trading beaver pelts with Algonquin Indians along Newfoundland's shores. Over the course of two centuries, the Canadian fur trade extended to the Pacific, extending to the foragers and horticulturalists of the eastern woodlands and subarctic, then to indigenous groups of the Great Lakes and western subarctic and, in late 1800s, to groups of the Pacific Northwest (Wolf 1982:160–161). France and England participated in the Canadian fur trade and after decades of fierce competition, they merged in 1821 to form the Hudson's Bay Company. Both the Russian and Canadian fur trades brought disease and warfare to native inhabitants. Indigenous communities were broken up, driven from their lands, or decimated. Others were subjugated by incoming colonizers who turned regional power over to their native elites.

Beginning in the 1800s, colonial powers began to develop the mineral resources in both countries. This further dislocated indigenous populations. With the exhaustion of sable across Siberia by the early eighteenth century, imperial Russia's efforts now went toward mineral extraction, most notably gold. Exploitation began in the Urals in 1696 to mine high-quality ores for Peter the Great's military arsenal. These efforts soon led to the discovery of precious metals including gold and silver, first in the Ural mountain area then across Eurasia. Extraction of minerals became imperial Russia's newfound economic boom. The forced labor of political exiles fueled that boom (Forsyth 1992:116).

A similar trend occurred in Canada. Shortly after the Canadian north was transferred from Britain to Ottawa's holdings in 1870, the 1896 Klondike Gold Rush transformed the Yukon from a fur-trapping to a resource economy. The sudden influx of newcomers resulted in outsiders occupying Indian lands, killing wildlife for food, and bringing more devastating "new" diseases. This sudden encroachment and huge increase of population brought administrative attention to the Yukon and the government introduced new laws to protect wildlife and the native way of life.

The next change to these Canadian and Russian expanses was the establishment of military outposts. In Russia, Siberian military presence began with the 1892–1905 construction of the Trans-Siberian Railway and its ferrying of military hardware over great distances, allowing large-scale settlement and increased military occupation. Twentieth-century Soviet economic development plans extended the country's military presence to each distant corner of the vast country via industrialization and collectivization. The state forced indigenous populations to forego their lands, resources, and subsistence ways. Mineral exploration and exploitation, mostly to meet military needs, predominated in the Russian north and incoming workers from European Russia settled to mine and make a living, displacing the local indigenous populations from their homelands and subsistence resources. World War II saw an increase in industrial-military activity in Asiatic and northern Russia, moving industrial activities across the Urals to protect them from German invasions and to bolster Soviet borders in the most distant hinterlands. Cold war period military activity focused on developing nuclear capacity, involving extensive nuclear testing, the building of nuclear power plants, and developments of a nuclear arsenal.[2]

The advent of World War II similarly thrust Canada into the geopolitical limelight (as it did most regions of the circumpolar north) as one of several vital strategic regions for the Allied Forces. Following 1945 the Canadian north continued to serve as a buffer between two aggressive superpowers—the United States and the Soviet Union. An indirect result of military development in the Canadian north was the opening of the once isolated area's natural resources to world markets via the construction of roadways and airstrips. Indigenous inhabitants were affected by these developments. Incoming populations and industrial/military enterprises disrupted native subsistence practices, especially along the Alaska Highway, built by the U.S. Army in 1942–1943. Such southern presences encroached on subsistence resources and lands, and dislocated native communities by recruiting locals into the workforce. In the post–World War II context, the resource economy of Canada boomed, and native communities saw accelerated infringement on their lands and resources, in some cases threatening the integrity of their populations (Bone 2003:69). One stark example is the 1931 discovery and exploitation of uranium on Great Bear Lake, which resulted in high cancer rates for Dene, who were employed to carry sacks of the radioactive material on their backs. Some of this uranium reacted in the atomic bombs dropped on Hiroshima and Nagasaki.

The impacts of colonization on indigenous peoples of Russia and Canada had broad geopolitical and economic similarities. The introduction of New World diseases, warfare, European goods, institutions, and values changed the lifestyle, subsistence priorities, and spatial distribution of aboriginal societies. Colonial expansion also worked to erode aboriginal customs and spiritual practices via parallel conversion efforts to bring the "pagan savages" to the light of Christianity and Orthodoxy. In the twentieth century the indigenous peoples of both Russia and Canada were instructed in the lingua franca—Russian or English and French, respectively. These changes, combined with an increasing dependence on resource economies, worked to undermine indigenous subsistence ways, knowledge systems, and a life independent of the state.

The Case of Diamonds in Arctic Canada

The Canadian case is, to date, the best-case-scenario for northern indigenous peoples and diamond mining. When multinationals arrived in the North West Territories (NWT) to stake their claims, they were met by aboriginal communities who were both expected and empowered to negotiate directly with them. Between the 1970s and the mid 1990s native inhabitants of Canada's NWT, involved in both the lengthy hearings on oil and gas development and indigenous rights and the first modern land claims of 1975, went from being inexperienced spectators, slightly naive about the long-term impacts of megadevelopment, to active stakeholders who demonstrated a new political capacity. They obtained some of the best legal and negotiation advice available and drove a hard bargain. Similarly, multinationals were met by a territorial government body that also proved savvy and informed at the negotiation table.

The diamond industry has transformed the economy of the NWT, which in one decade has gone from having the highest unemployment rates in Canada, since the fur trade collapsed in recent decades, to an unemployment rate of 6.1 percent, the lowest in all of Canada. The mining activity has brought much-needed employment and service contracts to the northern areas and its inhabitants. In native villages signs of prosperity include new trucks and snowmobiles in the driveways of some aboriginal families and an increase of new homes being built beside "teepees" where inhabitants continue to dry caribou and white fish.

However, there were many nuances to the negotiation process and subsequent progress to date that tend to cast a different light on the story. Consider, for example, the passage below,

> As darkness falls, we near the treeline at the south end of McKay Lake. My friend murmurs at last, "...Some of the chiefs had the heart taken out of them when this mining started."...There is certainty, I think, in the lifeless, mined-out pipes and the waste-rock piles. Aboriginal title is extinguished practically, if not legally...Who will want this desecrated land? It is no longer the land and the life that the Dene signed their treaties to preserve.... My friend speaks again, "The way they say it in our language... 'the elders' hearts are broken over a white stone.'"...I [am reminded] of the Ekati diamonds I once saw gracing a woman's neck. The model was faceless; only her jaw and lips and neck showed in the photograph.... A cool pale blue, the hue of Arctic water pooled on the melting ice of a sunny day, coloured the diamonds with the slightest gleam. We are hostage to diamonds, I think, like the frozen beauty of that nameless woman. We are bound by the notion that these diamonds—their mystique and beauty and power—will fill the void in our spirit, the places of our imagination, left empty when the land is finally gone.
>
> —Ellen Bielawski, *Rogue Diamonds: The Rush for Northern Riches on Dene Land*

Passages like this motivate us to question the long and the short-term implications of arctic Canadian diamonds from the standpoints of all stakeholders. What are the long-term reverberations of this economic boom? Couldn't this rapid change in Native community life provoke many of the same social pathologies and pollution that afflict communities in the south? What will be the environmental impacts of both the mining operations and the increased consumer-orientation of northern life? In the context of this book's larger themes, what are the prospects for the long-term sustainability of diamond mining in the arctic?

To engage a balanced comparison of the Russian and the Canadian cases with the objective of clarifying what indigenous peoples and their advocates can and should fight for, it is important to first understand how Canadian aboriginal groups and regional governments evolved into competent negotiators (albeit not as competent as their opposition), how their actual negotiations went with the diamond companies, and what the pluses and minuses of these developments are. Much of the success of these aboriginal groups is based on the presence and recognition of aboriginal title in Canada.

The Cultural and Historical Landscape of Canadian Land Claims

The Canadian Arctic, covering more than half the country, is home to only 0.3 percent of the population (Osherenko and Young, 1989: 81). The largest native group is Inuit who have their highest populations in the North West Territories (NWT). Other native groups in the NWT include Dene, a collective name encompassing a number of Athapaskan tribes, and Metis, peoples of mixed aboriginal and other ancestry. Although colonial presence worked to settle native groups, the post–World War II resettlements of the 1950s into poorly insulated box houses made a decisive break from extensive to town-oriented settlement patterns. Living off the land for subsistence was now complicated by finding transportation to and from hunting, trapping, and fishing grounds. As a result, northern Canadian native populations increasingly relied on relief payments to purchase goods in lieu of their former subsistence sources. By the 1970s, the southern interests of Canada began focusing on the resource wealth of their arctic, specifically the oil, minerals, and hydropower. It was at this time that the process of realizing aboriginal title began.

Land claims settlements in Canada are agreements between Canada and aboriginal claimant groups. Founded on the British Royal Proclamation of 1763, and expanded over the decades to follow throughout the course of transferal from British to Canadian sovereignty, aboriginal claims, mostly through Treaties 8 and 11 (1899, 1921 respectively) with Canada, served native groups by allowing them to continue to hunt and trap on Crown lands. Resource developments and the coming of megaprojects in the 1970s instilled new meaning to these claims. Legal battles and a concerted effort to educate residents about the social and environmental impacts of resource development, especially the proposed MacKenzie pipeline, resulted in indigenous awareness and opposition to northern resource development (Berger 1999).

The first land claim in Canada was in response to the 1973 Calder Case of the Nisga'a nation of British Columbia. The process was lengthy and began in 1967, when the Nisga'a Tribal Council first approached Thomas Berger in his law office to ask him to assist them in court. The next several years were spent in debate over whether aboriginal title still existed or was implicitly extinguished by pre-Confederation enactments of the old colony of British Columbia. When the case made its way to the Canadian Supreme Court, after a lengthy process of deliberation, six out of seven justices recognized the continued existence of Native aboriginal title. This led to a major policy shift on the government's willingness to reopen the treaty for aboriginal title. On August 8, 1973, Jean Chretien, then Minister of Indian Affairs, announced that the federal government intended to settle native land claims in all parts of Canada where treaties had not yet been made, thus beginning a process that continues to this day. During this time, Canada established a policy for settlement of aboriginal claims, revised in 1987, to include two claim categories: comprehensive claims, which addressed continuing aboriginal title to land and resources, and specific claims, addressing claims arising from treaty obligations or obligations under the Indian Act. Between 1970 and 2001, Canada dealt with thirty specific claims in the Yukon, the NWT, and Nunavut. Comprehensive claims are based both on Canada's willingness to recognize aboriginal rights and aboriginal groups' willingness to give up original rights in exchange for specific rights defined in a revised agreement.

But awareness is a first step toward action on what needs to be done—to fulfill aboriginal treaties—bilateral, nation-to-nation agreements—before development can proceed. This was Thomas Berger's main point in 1977, when he reported the conclusions of the landmark MacKenzie Valley Pipeline Inquiry. The commission Berger led recommended a ten-year moratorium on major development so that Native claims could be settled and the northern economy diversified beyond major resource extraction.

His judgment parallels Viliui Committee representative Pyoter Martinov's referendum request to require ALROSA to delay opening new mines adjacent to native settlements in order to have the time to develop environmentally clean technology and to complete the process of building local village economies in the post-Soviet context. Today it is clear that ten years was not long enough to settle all the aboriginal claims in the NWT and that Canada still clings to negotiating agreements that require extinguishment. This is important because southern Canadians think that all claims are settled, when in fact none were when the diamond rush began (Bielawski 2003).

The first modern negotiated agreements were the 1975 James Bay and Northern Quebec Agreement (JBNQA) and the 1978 Northern Quebec Agreement. Both resulted when North Quebec Cree and Inuit filed a lawsuit, based on their claimed title, to halt plans for a massive hydroelectric project aimed to dam the great rivers of northern Quebec. The two groups insisted that the state fulfill the legal obligations assumed by Quebec in 1912 prior to proceeding with the massive hydropower development begun in the early 1970s. They lost their case but settled with the provincial and federal governments as the project proceeded, resulting in the James Bay and Northern Quebec Agreement, signed in 1975 and extinguishing any original native claim in exchange for land, resources, and limited self-government powers. Specifically, beneficiaries received hunting rights, a guarantee of participation in environmental protection measures, over $200 million in compensation, and an additional $70 million in the 1990s to ameliorate conditions due to unfulfilled obligations. This watershed agreement became the model in future Native claims settlement in Canada.

The next modern negotiated agreement was the 1984 Inuvialuit Final Agreement for the 2500 Inuvialuit inhabiting the northwest corner of NWT. This settlement, spurred by early 1980s oil and gas development in the region, involved the extinguishment of aboriginal rights in exchange for ownership of 91,000 square kilometers (35,000 square miles) of land, cash compensation totaling approximately $170 million, participation in resource management with preferential hunting rights in the region, and subsurface (mineral) rights to a small portion of the land.

In 1993, Inuit signed the Nunavut Agreement, which provided specific land and resource management rights, ownership of 351,000 square kilometers (135,500 square miles) of land, a small share of resource royalties, and a $1.1 billion cash compensation administered by Nunavut Tungavik Inc. Subsequent to the agreement, in 1999 a new territory, Nunavut, was created, which was identified as a homeland for its majority of twenty thousand Inuit residents, with a public assembly and government administration committed to promotion and development of Inuit culture.

The 1990s saw several prominent modern land claim agreements in Canada, each one extinguishing aboriginal rights in exchange for some combination of land ownership; partial subsurface rights; monetary compensation; resource royalties; temporary tax relief; participation in land, water, and resource use planning and management; and a federal commitment to negotiate self-government. Examples include the 1992 Gwich'in Comprehensive Land Claim Agreement, the 1990 Yukon Umbrella Final Agreement, and the 1993 Sahtu Dene and Metis Agreement. There exist many unresolved claims and many continuing claims.

Diamonds and Developments in the North West Territories

During the early 1990s' diamond rush, international diamond companies including Broken Hill Propriety (BHP), DeBeers, and Kennecott-Diavik staked huge claims on the Barren Lands. To date there are two working mines and one soon to begin operation. The first mine, Ekati, began operation in 1998. Aber Resources, one of the many who staked claims in 1991, discovered pipes in 1994 and established the Diavik Diamond Mine, which began production in early 2003. Both these operating mines are located approximately 300 kilometers (185 miles) north of Yellowknife, the capital of the NWT. A third mine, a DeBeers venture at Snap Lake, received a heavily conditioned approval in 2003 and is due to begin construction shortly.

The twenty years of oil and gas negotiations and land claims settlements preceding the 1991 discovery of NWT diamonds were a crucial part of the development of aboriginal civic involvement in settlements over diamonds. The native groups involved inhabit the Great Slave Geological Area and include Dene groups—the Tli Cho (Dogrib) and Akaitcho; the North Slave Metis; and the Kitikmeot Inuit. The case discussion that follows details the negotiations between Dene, the Government of the North West Territories (GNWT) and BHP. Canada signed Treaty 8 with the Akaitcho First Nations in 1899. The treaty gave the aboriginal people the right to unlimited hunting, fishing, and trapping on their traditional lands. The Crown (later Canada) was interested in making its living from the land's mineral resources, specifically the gold.

From the beginning these two stakeholders had different understandings of what this treaty meant (Bielawski 2003). For Dene it was a proclamation of peaceful coexistence. For Canada it was the extinguishment of aboriginal title to the Crown. These conflicting interpretations are clear in how the treaty has been handled in the last century. Treaty 8 holds that land will be set aside for Dene use and that the Crown will act as fiduciary for the Dene. To act in their best interest means preserving the land that supports them and their right to fish and trap. For the last century Canada has not set aside or protected land from development and has given priority to third-party interests. The legacy for Dene are increased cancer rates from the 1931 Great Bear Lake uranium mining and the wasteland of open pits and shacks left after 1933 Ndilo gold mining activities. Gas and oil development on the Barren Lands has occupied Dene negotiations from the 1970s. The latest player in the Dene's resource extraction drama are diamonds (Bielawski 2003). Recent negotiations to implement Treaty 8 have stalled since the diamond rush began. Canada will continue to honor third-party interests until the Akaitcho Treaty 8 First Nations are in a position to choose land for themselves. Canada's delay in appointing a new Treaty 8 negotiator allowed diamond miners to choose land before Akaitcho Treaty 8 First Nations did. To fully analyze the pluses and minuses of Canadian diamond mining, it is important to understand the complex negotiation processes from the discovery of diamonds at Lac de Gras in 1991 to the official opening of the first (Ekati) mine in 1998 to the present day.

An Historical Overview from Discovery to Exploitation

Charles Fipke had already spent twenty years studying the indicators for and landscapes of diamonds, before his 1991 discovery of the first kimberlite pipes and large-carat diamonds under a small lake adjacent to Lac de Gras in the NWT.[3] With the financial backing of the Australian mining giant, Broken Hill Propriety (BHP), Fipke formed his own exploration company, Dia Met Mineral Ltd (Bielawski 2003:29). Fipke's discovery triggered the NWT "diamond rush," the largest staking rush in North American history.

Before BHP could begin mining diamonds in the arctic they were required to negotiate with the Canadian federal government, the GNWT, and with aboriginal peoples living in the impact area of the mine. Their first step was for an environmental assessment review panel (EARP) to investigate the mine's predicted impacts and produce an environmental impact study (EIS). Two years later, in 1996, the panel produced the report. BHP's EIS sold the diamond mining process as a clean process, requiring only mechanical means to separate out the diamonds. It would have minimal impacts on the environment limited to the draining of several lakes and the mining of rock.

With report in hand, the Department of Indian Affairs and Northern Development (DIAND) and the GNWT held a press conference in Ottawa to announce the federal cabinet's decision on the proposal by BHP Diamonds, Inc. and Dia Met Minerals Ltd. to mine diamonds at Lac de Gras. There was heated controversy about the thoroughness of the four-person EARP's recommendation to proceed. The Northern Environmental Coalition, including representatives from the Canadian Arctic Resources Committee (CARC), Canadian Nature Federation, Ecology North, and World Wildlife Fund Canada, questioned the validity of the panel's work. Although most local and regional representatives wanted the mines for the employment and revenues they would bring, they also wanted the EARP to set clear, comprehensive conditions that would minimize environmental costs and maximize local economic benefits. Critics accused the EARP for disregarding the full impacts of mining on the Barren Lands, including constructing and maintaining accommodations for a thousand employees, the loss of waterfowl and fish habitat when draining lakes, the release of chemicals and minerals into the ecosystem when removing the diamonds, the acid drainage from the tailings piles, the building of roads, the quarrying of gravel, the diverting of water, the hauling of fuel, ad infinitum.

They further voiced their concern over three main issues. First, that BHP's exclusive right to a 4000-square-kilometer (1545-square-mile) claim block was void of aboriginal use considerations and so went against aboriginal land claims and treaty entitlement. Second, that the soundness and longevity of a northern diamond economy had not been addressed, emphasizing that the cartel system of the world diamond market went against Canada's free-trade credentials, and that the stability of the world diamond market was unsure. Lastly, local and regional stakeholders questioned DIAND's federal capacity in the north, based on their vested interest in the diamond industry's success displayed by their preferential performance at the hearings and on the ground. They argued that DIAND should not be responsible for environmental assessments and requested an independent monitoring agency for the BHP project.

These expectations were heightened by the testimony of Alex Maun, an aboriginal resident of Papua New Guinea, who showed how Australia-based BHP had generated severe environmental damage at its Ok Tedi mine. In his testimony Maun stated that BHP had the reputation for not respecting aboriginal rights and for creating language that made it a criminal offense for those affected by the mining operation to press charges against BHP (O'Reilly 1996).

At the end of the day, Honorable Ron Irwin, the minister of DIAND, granted BHP conditional permission to mine based on their ability to show "significant progress on both an environmental agreement and an impact benefit agreement" within sixty days. This short time period favored industrial interests because it allowed the company time to begin site construction before winter and it also coincided with a season when Dene and other groups would be on the land, harvesting and preparing for winter, with little time to dedicate to claims and negotiations. Within that short time frame BHP had to complete socioeconomic agreements with the GNWT on behalf of the public and draw up separate impact and benefit agreements (IBAs) with each of four aboriginal groups: Inuit downriver from the mine, Metis with interests in the diamond fields, the Dogrib Treaty 11 First Nations, and the Akaitcho Treaty 8 First Nations.

Almost three weeks into the sixty-day process, in a national process unrelated to the diamond environmental review, native leaders were invited to meet with the Crown. Among the items on the agenda were changes in extinguishment policy. The chiefs reminded the Crown that Treaty 8 did not extinguish their title or cede it to the Crown and that negotiations had been greatly stalled since the rush to mine diamonds. They voiced their concern for their land, which was under great deal of development pressure since the diamond discoveries.

The following week, First Nations members held a day-long strategy session to contemplate their bids for the IBAs with BHP. Participants recounted the history of the Talston dams that impoverished prime Dene lands, lakes, and resources without one cent of compensation paid. They worried that the diamond developments may result in similar scenarios. Foremost of their concerns was how they could effectively state their needs and have them met. In the past, even when First Nations deliver a clear message, the Crown rarely listened.

On day thirty-two of the sixty-day process, the NWT Water Board held a public hearing on BHP's application for a Class A water license. This was a pivotal moment for two reasons: One, because it was the first public discussion of the mine since the sixty-day deadline was set and two, because the water license represented the strongest leverage local inhabitants had to delay the mine opening. The meeting had translations in most languages with the exception of Dene Sonline, which limited full aboriginal participation, especially by elders. DIAND could not change the conditions of the license but was expected to either accept or reject it.

The hearing began with presentations by six BHP representatives, each speaking in highly technical jargon, difficult for most aboriginal participants to follow. After making a round of introductions, BHP's project manager overviewed the company's assets, described BHP's NWT Diamonds Project, and detailed a list of the company's intended water uses including drinking water at the three camps, water to wash the diamonds, water that would become "waste" as it travels through the waste kimberlite, waste water from treated sewage, and the company's plan to "dewater" (drain) six lakes, five to mine as open pipes and one as a quarry. Next BHP's engineer responsible for the holding dams described the company's plan to use "frozen core dams" that utilize the natural cold of the north. Following was a presentation by BHP's environmental manager who described the company plans to use CO_2 as a buffering agent to neutralize the basic property of crushed kimberlite.

During the break that followed, the meeting's chairman asked the questions on all the local stakeholders' minds: What was the urgency to mine, and Why not wait until there can be protection of the people and land? BHP's fourth presenter, the manager of external affairs, responded with a flurry of reasons. She explained that the company had already invested $200 million in the project, that BHP had willingly gone through the highest level of environmental review, that thousands had applied for mine jobs and they wanted them now, that BHP would be the largest single purchaser of supplies and the largest employer in the north next to the government, and that the project would contribute $2.5 billion in direct revenues via taxes and royalties, $2.5 million to GNWT gross domestic product, and $6.2 billion to the GDP of Canada over the life of the mine. In short, that the longer the company waited to mine, the longer it would take for local, regional, and federal stakeholders to realize the economic benefits.

Following her appeal, the audience inquired about the possibility of having more time to gather sufficient information, for example, on the potential environmental effects to the land-based economy, to which BHP's project manager commented that there really was no time to wait because at present the world diamond market was high and if they would act immediately, there will be maximum investment before the threat of competition. The company needed to cut into DeBeer's control of the global diamond market. Next on the agenda, the hearing opened discussion to the issue of "dewatering" lakes, a process that will permanently lose, in this case, six lakes.[4] BHP defended their strategy due to lack of evidence for any specific use of lakes. Local stakeholders questioned the company's research methods and testified to both their ancestral and ongoing use of these areas and lakes.

On day thirty-five the board announced its decision to extend the hearing until October 21 (thirteen days after the sixty-day deadline) due to concern that elders who spoke did not understand BHP's technical jargon and that BHP didn't understand the elders. To set the tone for the future hearing, a member of the board reminded all that the water board's main objective was to conserve, use properly, and protect the water for people. However, based on past negotiations, the people too often are forgotten. He questioned BHP's employment of the same caliber of social scientists representing sociology, history, anthropology, and culture as it had natural scientists.

With the water board hearing now set in the future, day forty began the process of negotiating the environmental agreement between BHP and Canada. Recommendations were made to monitor the health of the Bathhurst Caribou herd that migrates through the diamond area, to address water quality issues not covered in the water license, to consider the need for long-term monitoring of the mine, and to structure the final agreement so local peoples had more responsibility for monitoring than was presently allowed.

On day forty-one the discussion focused on IBA negotiations between Akaitcho Treaty 8 and BHP. However, the day was largely unproductive due to BHP's use of a predetermined template to start the negotiations and their exclusion of native individuals because of questionable First Nation status. The days that followed continued in similar patterns of disjuncture between multinational and aboriginal interests.

On October 21 the water board hearings resumed with the Department of Fisheries and Oceans (DFO) at the intervener's table. Local stakeholders again expressed their concern that mining activity would alter their lives by threatening their subsistence resources, affecting caribou migrations, and, once the mines were depleted, leaving their land impoverished and unreclaimed. An engineer testified that the company used faulty science to assess the impacts of exposing kimberlite ore, especially acid rock drainage, arguing that there was simply not enough known to be able to assess the short- and long-term consequences. Another report questioned the longevity of the proposed frozen-core dams and the network of mining-wastewater tailings ponds. A third report highlighted BHP's lack of a plan for reclamation once the mines are mined out. The next speaker recommended various research projects to address concerns about draining lakes, including studies on basic fish biology, on how to enhance fish habitat once it is degraded, on how to deal with acid pulses and high levels of aluminum (which concentrates in fish gills and eventually suffocates the fish), and on how to maintain fish habitat in downstream waters that will experience a change in temperature and other "side effects."

The next day DIAND took DFO's place as intervener for the continuing water board hearings. The questions continued on a variety of concerns about the company's plans for monitoring, for assessing cumulative effects, for reclamation and dealing with the "bust" once the diamonds run out, about the piecemeal funding to keep the communities informed, and about the environmental agreement. Someone pointed out that the issues being raised were the same issues raised twenty-five years ago, adding doubt that any progress would be made in the hearing process. The hearings ended with a sense of compromise—BHP wanted a long-term license and the First Nations wanted a short-term license; the final agreement gave the company a seven-year Class A license.

Immediately after the hearings two technical committees for the water board convened to determine the extent of regulation needed and the safe levels of aluminum, copper, ammonia, and cadmium for Barren Lands surface waters. During the same period, Native representatives flew to Ottawa to express the urgent need for Treaty 8 negotiations to proceed so that they can protect their lands from further third-party interests.

The next steps were completing native communities' negotiations with BHP on IBAs and environmental agreements. Meetings were held in the communities, but people needed more time to fathom the implications of the agreements. Noteworthy was the decision to establish an Independent Environmental Monitoring Agency (IEMA). In early November the GNWT and the federal government signed their socioeconomic agreement with BHP, the Treaty 11 Dogrib signed their IBA and the Akaitcho Treaty 8 signed the implementation protocol for the environmental agreement. The Treaty 8 IBA signing was, at that time, stalled until mid-November, when there was consensus in the community. By February 1997 BHP was granted the land and water permits to build and operate the Ekati mine. Operation began in 1998.

The Pluses and Minuses of the Canadian Arctic Diamond Economy

With this case scenario in mind, the task now is to review the pluses and minuses of Canadian diamond activities. This exercise will highlight how indigenous peoples and their governments were, on the one hand, successful in winning environmental protection and impact and benefit agreements but subsequently lost at negotiating safeguards against the boom-and-bust nature of the operations and the long-term cumulative environmental and social impacts of the mines.

Pluses of the Canadian diamond industry are mainly economic. The mines provide employment, for native peoples and northerners, according to the socioeconomic agreement targets between GNWT and the companies. Similarly, those agreements set targets for companies to contract local services and goods to the mines, also stimulating the local economy. Depending on the specific agreements made in each tribe's IBA, there also may be preferential rights for communities or aboriginal organizations for jobs or contracts with the mines. However, IBAs are confidential, so it is not public knowledge if these targets are being met. There are also joint ventures between aboriginal groups and southern services, for example, catering companies in Edmonton.[5] The mining companies pay corporate taxes to GNWT, taxes and royalties to the federal government,[6] and cash payments to aboriginal governments through their IBAs. Although exact figures on the latter are not known, estimates are that about $1 million cash per annum is given to each of the four aboriginal groups involved (O'Reilly 2004). The GNWT also gets revenues by directly taxing the companies, and from the personal and payroll taxes paid by nonresident workers. The economy is also boosted by secondary industry created when GNWT convinced the companies to sell raw diamonds locally to cut and polish.

There are also minuses to the economic changes of the Canadian diamond industry, specifically of a socioeconomic nature. Native village life has undergone unprecedented change with the advent of regional diamond mining. Jobs in the mines are two weeks on and two weeks off. This schedule disrupts the rhythms of native life and often results in either family breakups, a high turnover in native employment, or both. Alcoholism is on the rise in the villages. The growing economic disparity between village households is also disrupting native communities. Out-migration to the center, Yellowknife, to be closer to jobs and better services, taxes village populations and increases housing pressure and costs in the center. The Yellowknife administration is having difficulty retaining employees for its service sector due to higher wages paid elsewhere, especially the mines. The boost in the economy has stimulated a drug market, most notably for crack cocaine. Crime is also increasing. There have been several incidences of diamond theft and the RCMP (Royal Canadian Mounted Police) has added three officers to deal specifically with diamond-related crime.

Another socioeconomic minus is the lack of preparation for the eventual bust of the boom-and-bust diamond economy. The industry presently generates a significant part of NWT gross domestic product (GDP) at 25 percent. However, there is nothing being done to prepare for the industry's inevitable crash. Local dependence on the diamond economy is further reinforced by the secondary cutting and polishing industry. There has been only vague mention of setting up a trust fund to buffer the crash, modeling other countries, but no exact plans to do so.[7] Recent moves toward devolution, which would transfer the management of subsurface resources to local communities, may result in more equal revenue sharing.[8]

There are also economic minuses that affect environmental and social aspects. The federal government is many years behind in its promise to systematically monitor active and exploratory mine areas because of a lack of funds. Although the federal government's exact take from diamonds is not known, we do know that it receives between $40 and $60 million per year for all GNWT resources taken. GNWT has also made it clear that the diamond revenues they receive do not cover costs of environmental and social remediation, training, and so forth. This is highway robbery if we consider the checks and balances of the diamond industry. After the first two to three years of operation, these companies will have paid off their capital costs (for BHP: $800 million; for Diavik: $1.5 billion) and will be (are) making from $300 to $500 million per year in clear profit. The federal and regional governments are bound to the agreements they made, without public disclosure, to a fixed royalty, a very complicated formula with write-offs for exploration, operating costs, and depreciation that is neither clear nor transparent.

Both governments were reluctant to negotiate for more diamond revenues, and opted instead to create a secondary cutting and polishing industry to improve the local economy. This strategy has not worked out well. The nascent NWT operations cannot compete with established cutting and polishing industries in Belgium, Israel, and India due to the substantially higher capital and operating costs in the north. Similarly, the federal government has not been very supportive in setting up secondary industries, in branding the "clean" Canadian diamonds, or in marketing.

There are also minuses associated with the increasing in-migration of southern labor, a phenomenon that further exacerbates environmental and social issues. The GNWT's socio-economic agreement with the companies guarantees a high percentage of jobs for aboriginal residents, but the labor force at the territorial level is close to exhaustion. The two operating diamond

244 / Chapter 6

companies are finding it hard to keep their targets for aboriginal employment. In addition, the federal government recently approved two new mines, one with DeBeers and another just across the Nunavut border at Jericho by Tahera.

The environmental minuses of Canadian diamond mining include a whole series of water-related issues. Diamond mining involves the blasting, moving, and multiple washings of huge quantities of ore, and the draining of lakes that, in the process, destroys both a lake's existing biological community and its links to the larger interdependent ecosystem.[9] Lake draining also stirs up naturally occurring phosphorus and, in combination with the blasting residue, containing fuel oil and fertilizer (called "AMFO"), results in nutrient surges in downstream aquatic systems. Citizens concerned about the nutrient issue have been rebuffed by Diavik representatives, who explain that increased nutrients are actually a plus because they will result in bigger fish. Draining lakes also results in a loss of local biodiversity. Each lake that is drained detracts from the genetic diversity of the surrounding ecosystem, weakening the system's natural resilience. This is exacerbated because northern ecosystems are low in diversity and slow to rebound after disturbance. Once the mines are mined-out, the landscape is transformed and characterized by cavernous holes in the ground and huge tailing piles.

There are terrestrial mammal issues, most notably of caribou, the keystone/bellwether indicator of the ecosystem health in the arctic tundra. The Bathurst Caribou herd is the largest herd in the NWT, averaging 375,000 head. Many variables affect herd size including the density of annoying insects, the impacts of climate change on forage resources, and the disturbances created by diamond mining activity. Counts in the summer of 2003 showed a drop in the population to 185,000, which, being within the natural variability of the herd, could be considered a natural population dip. However, when the herd is in such decline, it is more susceptible to disturbance. There are no permanent protected areas in the land between Yellowknife and the Arctic Coast, which is both where most of the diamonds have been found and the area essential for caribou migrations.

Nine native communities depend on the Bathurst herd for their subsistence. Although the communities do not use the caribou as intensively as they have in the past, they continue to build much of their daily lives and annual practices around the reindeer herd. There is some site-specific monitoring to tell what happens when individual caribou get close to the mining operation, but it has no capacity to monitor fluxes in herd size and health. No such systematic research exists because neither the government nor the mining company was made responsible to carry it out vis-à-vis original contracts of agreements.

There are significant barriers to long-term environmental protection highlighted by the absence of land-use plans in both areas where diamonds are actively mined and those most likely to be developed. Another major minus of the Canadian case is the lack of information about cumulative effects—both socioeconomic and environmental. There was pressure on both the companies and governments to address these effects, but in each case the mines went forward without concrete plans to monitor for cumulative effects.

In response to that void, two independent efforts are working to monitor and assess cumulative effects. First is the Independent Monitoring Agency, established when the BHP Ekati mine was reviewed by an independent panel under EARP. The agency operates under a legally binding agreement because no one trusted the government to do the monitoring and enforcement around the mine. BHP has to fund this monitoring group. Diavik has a similar arrangement but less independent. The Independent Monitoring Agency is responsible for reviewing the design of monitoring programs and environmental management plans, for analyzing the results and the actions of regulators, and for making recommendations to the government and the company.[10] This is not the best arrangement, since the agency has no power. However, it is building accountability. For example, the agency was first to notice evidence of acid generation at the BHP Billiton Ekati Mine from waste kimberlite. The company's research earmarked to watchdog this was not.

The second independent effort is the CARC's "Plan for the Land" program, an effort to assess the present and future impact of the combined and cumulative effects of diamond mining in a relatively untouched and fragile ecosystem. Launched in 2002 in response to CARC's concern with the government's approval of Diavik's faulty mine plan, the Plan for the Land focuses on indicators, thresholds, limits of acceptable change, and modeling what existing and planned developments will do to alter the northern landscape and society. The primary goal of Plan for the Land is to develop predictive modeling techniques to inform decisions made by communities and regional boards about proposed development. CARC clearly states that they are not antidevelopment but are dedicated to providing data to northerners so they can make informed decisions about what development should occur. By 2004 the project had created a compilation map showing existing activities and two projection maps, using a modeling program, with one estimating the impact of current developments and another including the impact of current and planned developments. Running the latter model, 25 percent of the study area is affected. Plan for the Land also intends to add variables to include modeling projected socioeconomic effects. They plan to use indicators generated by their Community-Based Monitoring Pilot Project, launched in 1996, to fill this need.

Charting a Course to Sustainability for Indigenous Peoples and Mines

The case description and tallying exercise suggest that native communities and their advocates can and should fight for a more representative voice at the negotiation table and comprehensive protections for long-term impacts of economic development schemes. For one, local stakeholders, in this case the aboriginal communities, were not given sufficient time or appropriate explanations to fully understand what the company and their governments were negotiating for. The diamond company successfully defended their urgency to mine by explaining how economic benefits were greatest if the operation was allowed to begin immediately. This served to dampen the repeated requests for more time to be able to understand the immediate and cumulative effects of the mining. Similarly, this case demonstrates the gap of understanding for both parties. The company's use of highly technical jargon and the lack of translation to Dene Sonline during most of the negotiations hindered full native participation. Likewise, the company lacked the native vocabulary, specifically, a capacity to understand native relations to the biosphere—the aboriginal holistic approach to the land and to community. Because of this deficiency, the company failed to engage the necessary dialogue and repeatedly rebuffed native testimony throughout the negotiations process.

Secondly this case examination shows the failure of federal and regional governmental bodies to be more aggressive in negotiations, specifically to negotiate for: 1.) sufficient diamond revenues to cover the costs of comprehensive environmental protection, control and monitoring; 2.) economic development initiatives in native communities once the mining is gone; 3.) the complete reclamation of mining areas after activities have ceased; and 4.) research into and programs for the reintroduction of biological diversity to depleted ecosystems.

But even if these areas were covered, there remains the question of the sustainability of the diamond industry in northern communities and ecosystems. Conservation advocates have their perspective, "Diamond mining, or any sort of mining is clearly not sustainable. You dig a hole, you take stuff out of the hole, and take it somewhere else. Eventually, the hole runs out of stuff you were digging up. That is not sustainable" (Wristen 2003). Diamond mining, not unlike other mining for precious mineral and metals, is an activity that involves the removal and processing of millions of tons of substrate to render small amounts of minerals for a lucrative and highly vulnerable consumer market. How sustainable is such a venture as the basis of expanded northern development? With the average life of a diamond mine at fifteen to twenty years and the amplified environmental impact due to a highly sensitive arctic ecosystem, how sustainable will the diamond economy be in a century to come?

In addition, the multinational companies who are staking their claims and mining in the north do not have environmental protection as a priority. Consider the closing statement at the recent De Beers Snap Lake Public Hearings:

Functional (biotic) communities will remain in Snap Lake but not to the same extent as is presently the case. The Lake will not be dead but it will be impaired, and this impairment will remain for decades past abandonment, before recovery occurs. And it is likely that the recovery will not result in exactly the same eco-system as presently exists in Snap Lake. And that, in our view, is the environmental cost of doing business. (Wristen 2003)

Other developments cast further doubt on the long-term sustainability of diamond mining in the north. Even if environmental offenses were minimal, how secure is the global diamond market? DeBeers, who controls the world diamond market, does so via cartels of secrecy and misleading advertising schemes. Secrecy is nothing new in Russia. But no one can say that the world market for diamonds will continue to be dependable. In the meantime, areas that are developing or have begun mining operations are building local economies dependent on those revenues, either directly (mining towns made up mostly of newcomers to work at the mines) or indirectly (native communities who are paid or subsidized by state budgets based on diamonds). In short, long term socioeconomic and environmental sustainability of diamond mining and diamond economies is questionable. Furthermore, some specialists contest Canadian diamonds' reputation as "clean" and "conflict-free," arguing that instead they are dirty and conflict-ridden, akin to the conflict diamonds of more temperate parts of the world. Although there has been no verifiable proof that northern stones are moved into illegal trading by warring factions to finance conflict including supporting rebels, buying arms, and funding attacks, it can still be argued that the stones are not as clean as some think (Smillie 2002). Since development is inevitable, the main question is what sustainable or quasi-sustainable life ways northerners might develop with the income from diamonds during the ten to eighty years before all the diamonds are mined from the Great Slave Area?

Implications for Viliui Sakha

Despite the many minuses of the Canadian diamond economy, the impact and benefit agreements that were signed with aboriginal groups went far beyond anything that the mining industry had ever done, by way of recognizing that social dislocation and other social problems occur when a wage economy is introduced. In comparison with the Viliui Sakha case, Arctic Canadian aboriginal groups are faring well. They have land claims and civic rights that entitle them to function as stakeholders in negotiations with third-party interests. The mining of diamonds on their lands has resulted in employment and direct revenues for their communities. Similarly, they are able to advocate for and participate in environmental protection and monitoring. Viliui Sakha have none of these rights and advantages.

With so much divergence between the cases, it is hard to see how the Canadian model might work to inform the plight of Viliui Sakha. The latter's lack of land claims, civic involvement, and participatory government represent insurmountable barriers. However, the last decade of circumpolar cooperation and pan-arctic exchange of experiences between aboriginal communities is setting the precedents for more equitable and sustainable indigenous futures. The basis of that sustainability is gaining more control over balancing local needs and outside forces through self-government and self-determination. The starting point to these achievements is building local capacity at the community level. If Viliui Sakha can begin dialoguing about what they need to realize sustainable communities, they can nurture their local capacity for self-determination. How Viliui Sakha perceive a sustainable future, the changes that need to come about to realize those perceptions, and the opportunities and hurdles to those changes is the subject of the next chapter.

Notes

1. This recognition will reflect the Arctic's multiple roles as a stabilizer of climate, a filter of the earth's water and air and a sink of industrial pollution. Along with Antarctica, the Arctic is the most susceptible of the earth's regions to global warming.

2. On Novaya Zemlya alone the Soviet government performed 130 underground, atmospheric, and underwater tests between 1955 and

1990. The government increased cold war military presence by establishing nuclear power plants across the country. The Kola Peninsula is home to 18 percent of the world's nuclear reactors. Its surrounding seas were used as a nuclear dumping grounds until 1986, when international pressure forced waste disposal to stop. Russia's northern coast is scattered with rusting nuclear submarines that threaten local and global ecosystems. Industrial activities in the Russian north continue without environmental controls and have decimated much of the arctic pasture lands for reindeer.

3. Fipke had several decades of experience studying mining techniques and indicator minerals for diamonds in South America, Africa, and New Guinea.

4. This is the norm for diamond mining in northern granite areas. Since kimberlite is softer than granite, when the last glaciers receded, they scooped out the kimberlite to form lakes in the Barren Lands.

5. Many native groups have aboriginal corporations, which they set up shortly after settling land claims and modeled after aboriginal corporations in Alaska, in order, in part, to handle the revenues from resource extraction. Inuvialuit corporations, who have had a big success with petroleum revenues, are examples.

6. The federal government still owns the land. After land claims are settled, 10–15 percent of the land goes to natives and 85–90 percent remains under federal control. Diamond royalties go to the federal government which retains the subsurface rights.

7. In Alaska, Alberta, and Norway there are permanent heritage funds established where a portion or all of the government revenues (taxes and royalties) from hydrocarbon development are set aside in a special account. This is then built up over time and invested (in Norway a portion of the funds is invested in socially and environmentally responsible businesses). In some cases, only the interest is used to help fund government operations (Norway), or interest may be given to residents in the form of an annual per capita payment (Alaska). The theory is that once the resources are gone, there is still a large pot of money to work with and provide some stability for the bust (Taylor 2004).

8. The north was a federal jurisdiction controlled from Ottawa, then in 1967 the government made GNWT responsible for health, education, and forest resources. www.gov.nt.ca/MAA/index_devolution.htm

9. All Canadian diamond mines are under lakes except the Tehara project, which is land-based.

10. For more information see www.monitoringagency.net/

7

Investigating Viliui Sakha Sustainability

Viliui Sakhas' post-Soviet cows-and-kin adaptive strategy is inextricably linked to a diamond economy that both supplies the main source of household cash and degrades the health of local ecosystems and communities. Diamonds, by both underpinning and undermining local livelihoods, represent the antithesis of sustainability for the Viliui Sakha. If other circumpolar indigenous experiences are setting a precedent, then one way for Viliui Sakha to move toward more sustainable futures is through building local capacity.

Defining Sustainability on the Local Level

In 2003 my Sakha husband-turned-researcher and I began a research project aimed to initiate that process. Our goal was to define sustainability on a local level, clarify the barriers to those definitions and create models of village-level sustainability.[1] To these ends, we conducted focus groups and semistructured interviews in four Viliui Sakha villages.[2] We chose villages that represented a range of population densities: Elgeeii (3000 pop.), Kutana (1000 pop.), Kuukei and Khoro, the latter both approximating 350 each (refer to figure 4.2). The main effect of this population range is variance of resource access: the smaller the population, the greater the access to land for pasture, hay harvest, wood, and foraging areas.

Defining Sustainability in Focus Groups

In each of the four villages we facilitated two six-member focus groups, one male and one female, made up of two members from three age-groups, youth (age 18–25), middle (26–54) and elder (55+). We separated the groups by gender because our experience in the culture taught us that men and women speak more openly in their respective gender group. We gathered in a common village space, either a local museum or school. Sessions lasted approximately two hours. We began the focus groups by asking participants to free-list their answers to the question, What do you and your community need to ensure a sustainable future?[3] We next tallied each group's ideas and discussed them further (figure 7.1). Following that, we discussed four questions that we had developed before entering the field, based on our research to date and concerning issues relevant to all villages: 1) What jobs could resolve the unemployment problem in their village; 2) How they can work toward bettering the future of village youth; 3) How can they integrate the knowledge and survival strategies of their ancestors and contemporaries to contribute to their models of future sustainability; and 4) How can they bring

Figure 7.1. Focus groups tallying their answers

their ideas (re.: what they say they need for a sustainable future) into reality.[4]

We organized the tallies from the eight focus groups under four broad themes that emerged in all focused discussions, grouping ideas according to their focus and including both general references (main headings) and specific ones (bullets) (table 7.1).[5] We did not include the number of times each idea was voiced since this was a free-listing exercise and not intended to show statistical relevance.

The first three themes concerned the building of local capacities: 1) to develop diversified village economies; 2) to empower the village community; and, 3) to safeguard community health; and the fourth to solicit continued state support, mostly voiced by elders, 4) to introduce subsidies for youth education and to increase subsidies for disadvantaged elders, those without family to care for them. The first two themes coincide with a general awareness that the era of state paternity is over and that decentralization means a relocalization of production and management. The third theme underscores local concerns about how health is affected not only by regional environmental issues but also by the spin-offs of economic decline, which have generated increased alcohol and drug abuse and decreased nutritional intake. The final theme shows a residual cling to paternalism, mostly voiced by elders with occasional votes by middle-aged participants for seed monies to start-up local projects and businesses. In general, these results reflect a common desire for local control over the resource inputs and production outputs of their local communities and livelihoods.

How to Resolve Unemployment

Following the tally exercise, we began discussion of the four questions. The first focused question concerned resolving unemployment. In the post-Soviet context Viliui Sakha households, like their rural counterparts across the Arctic, depend on a mixed cash economy, a combination of traditional subsistence production and cash inputs (Caulfield 2000: 485; Maher 2004). Unemployment and lack of products has replaced the full employment

Table 7.1. Tally of Focus Group Responses into Larger Themes

I. To Develop Diversified Village Economies

Expansion of Wage Employment
- Cottage Industries: food processing, tourism, furniture manufacture, sawmill
- Local Services: cafés, hairdressers, tailors
- Private Businesses and Professional Employment

Increased Non-wage Subsistence Involvement
- Domestic and Wild Food Production

Education/Practical Job Skills
- Job Training for Village Youth

II. To Empower the Village Community

Common Goals/United Mindset
- Work in "Twelben" (neighborhood groups w/in village): village clean-up, family support groups

Cooperative/Collective Food Production
- Localization of Production: grain for feed, garden produce for consumers
- Specialization of Production: increase animal numbers, increase farm machinery

Local Governance
- Native Self-Government and Leadership: order, youth guidance, family and community values

Construction, Public and Private
- Housing Equity for All

III. To Safeguard Community Health

Health Education
Nature Protection
- Drinking Water

Culture: Physical and Spiritual
- Sport and Ethics

Anti-Drug and Alcohol Programs

IV. To Receive Continued State Support
- Youth Education
- Displaced Elders

Subsidies Geared Toward Community Development:
- Start-up Funds for Businesses
- Low- or Zero-Interest Credit

and product availability of the late Soviet period. Most household cash comes from state transfer payments in the form of salaries, pensions, and subsidies, and to a lesser extent from unofficial transactions.

As detailed in Chapter 3, the majority of salaried jobs are state-subsidized white-collar positions in administration, health care, and education. The remainder are blue-collar and highly seasonal, including shoveling coal for one of the many village furnaces or haying for a village cooperative. Half of all households depend on "freelance" or self-employed income, including odd jobs (including anything from cow-care for another household, one-time house or barn building, tractor hauling services for hay, firewood and ice, etc.), home crafts (including reindeer boot manufacture and repair, tailoring, fur hat and coat making, quilt making, etc.), the sale of plant and animal products, and income from hauling hay, wood, or ice by tractor and truck. Most households depend on one or more pension incomes. Although the majority of pension income is from elder kin living in-house or within the immediate village, households also receive pensions for a range of invalid categories, for single parents, for widows, and for orphaned children.

Most households are involved in home food production, which supplements a lack of monetary resources. Over half of all households keep cows and other domestic animals to produce meat, milk, and eggs. Seventy percent grow a substantial portion of their own food and 65 percent forage, hunt, and fish to supplement domestic food production. Today, rural Sakha have increased their dependence on both pre-Soviet and contemporary household-level modes of food production to supplement the gap left by a shift from dependence on the socialist infrastructure for employment and consumer goods to the unemployment, poor distribution, and other economic hardships of post-Soviet times.

When discussing the need to resolve unemployment, participants were certain that job creation would not only bring much-needed cash income to households but also bring a suite of other benefits including 1) an increase in the local tax base that could be used to fund projects, 2) employment for underemployed youth, and 3) a decrease in alcohol abuse.

Participants considered the creation of local jobs the key to solving other local problems, including generating taxes that would fund local projects:

> However many people are working, taxes will come into the government and through that we will have funds for culture and sport. (middle male: To protect my consultants' anonymity, the following quotes are not referenced except by sex and age group.)

Local job creation is seen as paramount to solving both the problem of delinquent village youth and of attracting educated youth back to the village to stay:

> Youth without work may go here and there and drink, but most youth are going for education. They already understand. They know they need to have salary. They won't come back here if there is no work. (male youth)

Lastly, increasing local jobs was considered one pathway to decreasing village alcohol abuse: "If there are work places for all then we won't have the alcohol problem. If you are going to work the next day, why would you get drunk?" (male middle).

Participants were also outspoken that jobs needed to be locally oriented in terms of their creation, the product base they relied on, the demand they served, and their diversification. If inhabitants could develop a local economic base to create jobs rather than bringing in outside enterprise, they could recapture much of the added value of their vocations. Ideas for local economic development to increase employment included businesses to add value to raw products, for example, milk and meat products that the villages already were producing,

> I think we need to build our own food processing plant, then we can make our own butter and products and turn these things around ourselves. We have a lot of animals, and so if we could build a minifactory and process all these products we produce, that could be our first source of jobs and local wealth building. (male middle)

Similarly, many felt that the key to long-lasting employment was the development of businesses that are useful to the village populations and that utilize the natural and social capital that already exists in the village communities. One example was to organize a clothing factory, reminiscent of the *bitovoi* (R., literally "everyday necessities," and the term used to refer to these factories) of the Soviet period, that used locally produced materials to make utilitarian clothing that villagers need and could use daily, "The products we get from other countries are bad. We need to get rid of them. We need to produce our own goods for our people" (male elder).

Finally, many mentioned the need for economic diversification. They felt the first step toward this was to consolidate village-level horse and cattle husbandry efforts into one or several small collectives to pool resources and equipment and form a farming sector that would supply the rest of the salaried community with animal products. Inhabitants also considered specialization important to maximize the resources particular to village conditions, "If we [Khoro, with lots of hay land for animals] could produce all meat and milk and Elgeeii could do vegetables" (female middle).

The discussion of resolving unemployment included general comments about the barriers to realizing ideas expressed. Many commented that despite the quorum for the need to work for themselves and to take the initiative to solve their own problems locally, ideas could not happen due to a lack of personal initiative:

> In Elgeeii, one barrel of water costs 30 rubles—a very high price! It would be cheap to have water "provada" [lines]. We have several kilometers of water lines lying and not being used and we just need to make them. Also in Elgeeii there are 120 uninhabited lots. Neighboring households could use those lots to make more gardens, increase their animals, or just use it for pasture or hay. However, our people need to be active. (male middle)

Part of this discussion was about people's tendency toward apathy and overall lack of initiative to make ends meet:

> It is all dependent on a person and how they go at their life. If they think they are going to be poor and if they wait for the state,

they will never make it. If they have a small salary, then they need to think of other ways to make ends meet. It all depends on the person and how they decide. (female middle)

A second major barrier to resolving unemployment is the lack of start-up capital. Respondents had many ideas about developing the local economy to increase jobs. The real issue, most agreed, was that they needed initial funding. One source of that funding was the government:

The government could start us off and then the private businesses can take it up from there. We could maybe make clothes or produce food and process it. We need specialists to come and teach us and we need start up money. Then the private people would take over with their profit. (female middle)

Others voiced the opinion that start-up funds could come from overdue village-level compensation for the mineral and natural resources that the government exploits locally:

The diamonds, the gas, and the other resources that we have, we receive no percent but we should be living off a lot of that. Sakha know we live over a very rich land with lots of resources under the ground, but other people from other lands come and take those resources and we never see them. China and Japan make the pipe to take our gas, but we live a few kilometers from the gas and don't see a bit of it. (male elder)

This is an important point and one that most certainly needs to be further investigated to gauge how realistic it is given the Sakhas' lack of land claims and other territorial rights that allow such direct benefit agreements in other arctic areas.

Much like the tallied responses, in our focused discussions about resolving unemployment, inhabitants emphasized the need for local economic diversification that would recapture the utility of available human, social, and natural capital. Job creation is viewed as a means to resolving other local issues such as increasing local tax bases, employing youth, and alleviating alcoholism. However, barriers are significant and include a general apathy in populations to work toward these goals and a lack of start-up capital. One possible source of start-up capital is compensation for resource exploitation.

How to Better the Future of Village Youth

The focused discussion about the future of youth centered on the lack of village-level youth employment. The youth unemployment problem is not due to lack of education. The majority of Viliui Sakha youth go on to get a higher education, much as they did during the Soviet period. However, unlike the Soviet period, when rural school graduates were guaranteed a job upon returning from receiving an advanced degree from the university or institute, today employment and opportunity are largely found outside rural Viliui Sakha villages, creating a pull to these places for both high school graduates and youth who desire work by their professional training. Additionally, the parents and relatives of high-school graduates encourage them to leave the village for the regional or capital centers, where they can get a degree and find employment.

Most youth who leave intend to get a higher education and return to their home village to work and raise a family but find no job opportunity upon returning. They often cannot return for years, if at all, due to the lack of village jobs. Youth who stay or decide to return to the village despite the lack of opportunity are jobless and delinquent. Some village youth, and predominantly female, help their parents maintain the family cow herd. Males tend to be unengaged.

Respondents agreed that if they could bring employment up, this would attract youth back to the villages and engage the youth that were already there. They blamed the lack of youth jobs for generating other social problems including delinquency, drug and alcohol abuse, suicide and homicide, theft, vandalism, and other crime. But who was to blame for the lack of youth jobs? Participants blamed the village head, negligent parents, and the education system.

Many respondents felt that their village head was responsible, "The (village) head needs to find work for them by finding what talents the youth have and get them credit to start their own works. Then they will be independent and already on their way with it" (middle male). Others blamed negligent parents for delinquent village youth:

> You go to a household and the very healthy youth are sleeping. Their parents are doing all the work. I see it. The old idea was that we use the strength of our youth to build the future. The youth now don't think about the future. There are many ways to develop our youth but we don't do them and so we don't get close to the youth. They are not with us. If someone's son brings in a few pieces of firewood, their parents will say, "Oh, look, our boy helps us!" So now all think that a strong, healthy twenty-four-year-old boy who brings in one armful of wood is a huge helper. We don't teach our youth to work. We don't use their strength. We need to work with them and teach them. (male elder)

Still others blamed the education system. One male youth emphasized the need to bring more technology to the villages to support and teach the children and youth, "I think the best way (to get village youth more active) is to get the children involved in progress from early on. We need to have a phys-ed complex and we need lots of computers so that the young will progress. We need to bring in the internet and a movie theater."

The "blame" for youth unemployment and alienation is much more complex and multisided. Like other peoples of the Russia's north, many of Sakhas' social problems are founded in a Soviet legacy of disengaging families in the socialization and upbringing of their youth (Pika 1999:151). In Viliui Sakha villages this was achieved by farming children out to boarding schools and devaluing the knowledge and experience of preexisting subsistence-based communities. In the Soviet period youth could return and find work in their village's state farm operation or local administration. Now that crucial link is gone, and youth are either absent or jobless and delinquent.

How to Utilize Elder Knowledge toward Sustainability

Our third focused question concerned how to transfer elder knowledge and survival skills that bolstered ideas of sustainability to the coming generations. Similar to the issues of delinquent youth, loss of local knowledge is a direct effect of a Soviet legacy that devalued the knowledge and experience of community elders. Northern Russia's villagers need to make greater use of the experience and knowledge of nonprofessional teachers—people of older generations (Pika 1999:152).

The processes of Soviet collectivization, agricultural industrialization, and acculturation worked to spatially, temporally, and socially undermine Viliui Sakha local knowledge. Contemporary elders, who know clan-based subsistence (albeit the majority were born after 1917, pre-Soviet practices did not change much until the early 1930s) early collectivization, state farm consolidation, and the break-up of the Soviet Union, straddle between three worlds—the pre-Soviet, the Soviet, and the post-Soviet present.

When interviewing elders about their past, I was surprised that their children and grandchildren showed little interest in their remembered past. On the other hand, such disinterest did coincide with the alienation of Sakha youth from both village life and their ancestral past. What do the youth, the grandchildren, and great-grandchildren of these elders, know about their past? In Viliui Sakha villages youth are not active in learning and carrying on the cultural history of their forebears. Part of the reason for this is the orientation of folklore practice in the last century (see chapter 4 on "Knowing the Land"). In the post-Soviet context, elder knowledge is an invaluable resource for survival, but there are no local, regional, or state efforts to document, interpret, and use that resource (Crate 2002). Instead, knowledge is lost due to the lack of time and resources to document, interpret, and disseminate it and, more importantly, the lack of local valuation for its utility in modern life.

How to revive and make use of the resource of local elder knowledge? Participants, first and foremost, emphasized the need to reinstate the family as child-rearer, a reinstatement of the pre-Soviet practice of the family as the central foundation in the upbringing of children:

In the Party (Soviet) time we were all considered children of the school. Now that has continued and I think it is a mistake.

"Whose child is that?" "Oh that's the school's child." But where
are the parents? No one knows who they are. The school is responsible for raising the children. In my opinion, it is the parents
and the family who are responsible now. Instead children have
no parental input, often because the parents have no work, are
unemployed, they drink and are poor. Their children do not
study well. We have a lot of families like this. The children are
strolling about at all hours of the night and their parents don't
care or watch for them. (male middle)

Second, participants agreed that the teaching and practice of *Sier
Twom* (Sakhas' ancient belief system, based on respect for nature
and fellow humans, and on love and stewardship of birthland)
was the best route to sustainability. Elders commented that most
youth now do not know the old ways. For example, they do not
know many hunting terms and lack knowledge and appreciation
for self-reliance.

Before, Sakha lived off of cow and horse breeding and hunting.
That was their way of survival. Their children learned this all
from an early age. Our children now learn some of this, mostly
the horse and cow raising. But the hunting is lacking. The youth
go into the woods now and they can't hunt. They don't know
the hunting terms, for example *sokh-so* (trap). "What is that?"
you ask and they don't have an idea. Same is you ask about
the different kinds—*kili sokh-so, kelbete sokh-so,* and they have
no idea. Also the *kwobakh aialakha* (arrow trap for rabbits) and
the *cha-kan* (bow trap). Our youth have no idea what they are.
They need to go with us hunting and learn about all this. Before,
youth never hunted out of season. They fished and rabbit- and
duck-hunted, and knew all the seasons. Now youth go fishing
and they take the fish from another's *ilim.* (male elder)

Our focused discussions about reviving local elder knowledge to
bolster village sustainability had much overlap with the previous
discussion on youth. In both cases participants emphasized the
break-down in continuity between generations that makes for an
uncertain future and the concomitant need to reintegrate across
the generations.

How to Bring Ideas of Sustainability into Reality

The final focused question asked how inhabitants thought they could bring their ideas of sustainability into reality. They emphasized three crucial factors: to develop a common mindset, to have strong leadership, and to realize protection and rights. The first two points reflect the communities' orientation to their communist past. The historical context for this in our research villages is the success of the Elgeeii State Farm, directed by Zhuravlev, that won the *Ordena Lenina,* an honor given to only a handful of farms across the vast USSR for unprecedented growth in production (see chapter 2 discussion of Zhuravlev).

With the 1991 fall of the USSR, the local community context changed drastically. With the break-up, local state farm operations disbanded and divvied up farm resources. Local Soviet elite transferred state farm resources, including machinery, animals, land allotments, and other capital reserves, of the resources to themselves, their kin, and their constituents. This reflected the rural village-level equivalent of the national trend toward "crony capitalism," the transfer of a majority of state capital into private hands (Rutland and Kogan 2000:141). The remainder they divided among village households, resulting in an uneven allocation that left many without sufficient resources to generate household-level subsistence. People survived by pooling their resources with kin. The Soviet period incentive and precedence given to working collectively was replaced with a post-Soviet priority to survive either through cronyism or kinship.

Although there is a trend toward personal initiative and entrepreneurship in the contemporary villages, people tend to adhere to a Soviet legacy of collective mindset and centralized administration. The most popular theme in our focus group discussion was the former, the need to cultivate a common mindset:

> I think first of all we need to develop our mindset so we are all thinking the same way and going the same way. We can have meetings and people can talk about the way they want to see Elgeeii go and what work needs to be done. We have highly educated people here and a lot of potential. (male middle)

In order to achieve that mindset, participants emphasized the need for strong leadership, again reminiscent of their Soviet past:

> We need a strong leader, someone who is interested in the people here and helping to live well on the resources here. How they appear and their life needs to be in second place. First place are the people. It was like that in our [the Soviet] time. (male elder)

Participants felt that their village head should be a community organizer who works hard to: 1) create jobs based on the skills and ideas of the village inhabitants including delinquent youth; 2) secure funding from government grants for much-needed construction projects and start-up for local cottage industries; and 3) guide the village in its development of a productive community founded on common goals.

The third factor emphasized by participants as crucial to realizing their ideas of sustainability is to achieve protection and rights. They voiced a desire to gain rights to land, clean drinking water, and comprehensive environmental protection. In the local context, the abuses to and lack of such rights is a result of large-scale diamond development. This reflects a new way of thinking based on international models, especially from their aboriginal counterparts in Canada and the United States (Anderson 2002:108). It is too early to say if such thinking could bring about similar stake-holder arrangements between industrial resource extraction and local communities.

Defining Sustainability in Interviews

Interviews were effective for further probing focus group findings and exploring other areas specific to future village-level sustainability including food security, environmental security, youth issues, and making ideas a reality. Regarding village-level food security, three salient points were made. First, participants disagreed with an idea that has been discussed in the media in recent years: that in the move to modernity, rural Sakha will abandon cow-keeping. Interviewees emphasized that cow-keeping will continue to be the main survival strategy for rural Sakha because it: 1) is Sakhas' ancestral survival mode; 2) is integral to Sakha cultural identity; and 3) is the only way to have fresh products in the villages, where transportation in the post-Soviet context is problematic.

A second food security issue that people discussed was the government's 2001 introduction of subsidies for home milk production. This is part of a larger Republic-wide project to raise the living standard in the villages, enabling cow keepers to receive income by selling their milk to a village milk station. The program is successful at bolstering household cash reserves and renewing interest in cow keeping for young families. However, many participants did voice concern that households with young children are selling all their milk for needed cash and depriving their children of necessary nutrition. The final food security issue discussed was the need to change how their villages kept cows by maximizing the economies of scale through specializing cow-care in collectives, thereby pooling resources (equipment, land, and labor) and providing salaries.

The main village-level environmental security issue was drinking water contamination. Although fully aware that regional diamond mining activities generate a complex of environmental issues, including drinking water contamination, inhabitants were reluctant to criticize it since it is the main source of state salaries, pensions, and other subsidies that form the cash basis of their mixed cash economies (Crate 2003c). Respondents were vocal about other ecological issues including the deforestation of adjacent woodlands from harvesting wood to heat homes, pasture deterioration due to overgrazing in the more populated villages, and the lack of proper disposal for commercial waste and excess manure.

Interview questions were identical across the three age groups except for youth, with whom we also discussed issues relevant to their, and thus their village's, future (figure 7.2). Topics included youth unemployment, youth alienation from villages, youth propensity (or lack thereof) for cow keeping, youth knowledge of and ties to kin, and their valuation of elders' knowledge. Most of the youth interviewed were getting a higher education and said they planned to settle in their birth village if they could

Figure 7.2.   Viliui Sakha youth

find work there. They agreed that the lack of village jobs needed to be resolved so they could return to their home villages to work and help improve the local economy and community. Several youth who were training to become school teachers commented that pensioned elders were monopolizing jobs for newly trained teachers by staying in village teaching jobs past retirement and "double-dipping" by receiving both salaries and pensions. This also impedes the advancement of educational content and methods in village schools, since young professionals trained in the latest advancements cannot enter into teaching positions.

The lack of jobs was not the only reason youth may not be returning to their home villages. Five of the twenty youth said they wanted to live in the city or regional center because villages are backward and unprogressive and they want a better education for their children and better living conditions, like hot and cold running water and paved streets. This discussion fed into exploring youths' vision of their village's future. When asked how they thought their village would be in twenty years, a majority were hopeful that living conditions would improve, with new construction that offered central heat and water, and that this would keep inhabitants there and also attract new families. The other youth respondents said there would either be no change, that their village would be the same in twenty years as it is now, or that there would be both advances and declines.

We asked youth about their interest in keeping cows and a majority said they would keep cows because it was the best way to have fresh, healthy Sakha food and save their monetary resources for other needs. Middle-aged and elder respondents were doubtful that youth would take up cow-care, commenting that their children were active in cow-care until sixth grade, when their interest waned. After that time the trend was to live off their parents' cow-caring until the parents were elderly and physically unable to continue the vocation. Only then would they take over. Perhaps youth will be motivated by the new monetary incentives of government subsidies for milk, mentioned earlier. It will be important to see if youths' stated intent to keep cows will become reality in the next few years when these youth finish their degrees and decide where to settle and how to live.

We also asked youth about their knowledge of ancestral kin. Most knew their ancestry only one or two generations back, a trend that stands in stark contrast to the Sakha tradition of knowing patrilineal kinship lines nine generations. However, this had no bearing on their ties to kin. All youth interviewees felt obligated to help with their, or their kin household's, summer hay cutting, a critical part of rural Sakha subsistence survival. Further, most said they could not imagine village life without kin because helping and being helped by kin is the main mode of village survival. Several others said that village survival without kin is possible but only with a good paying job and friends to fill the need for social support.

Youth interviews also gave us the opportunity to ask about the utility of elder knowledge. All but one of the twenty agreed that elder knowledge plays a vital role in future village sustainability. They argued that via elder knowledge individuals 1) compare their life with the past to gauge progress, to build on former skills and wisdom, and to avoid past mistakes; 2) know local history, including genealogy, and can then pass that history on to future generations; 3) know how Sakha lived before and can thereby maintain cultural practices; and 4) know the place names and sacred areas of the local landscape and can actively maintain them. Youth directly associated elder knowledge with future sustainability in its utility for contemporary subsistence and survival. They cited many examples of this including information pertaining to horse and cattle husbandry; haying techniques; *Sier Twom*; nature protection and stewardship; medicinal plants use and other healing practices; clothing and textile manufacturing; hunting, fishing, and foraging practices; the building of utilitarian wooden structures and objects, including fences, houses, barns, and an array of other outbuildings used for subsistence horse and cattle-husbandry, *sergei*, *chorons*, and other containers; "country food" production (including uses of all animal parts and a wide array of milk foods); weather forecasting; and a love of work and occupation.

At the end of all interviews across the age groups, we asked questions to check responses in the focus group setting, specifically by asking participants what they felt were the most important elements of future sustainability of their village. First, respondents said that a change of people's mindsets toward thinking about how they can make their own lives better, how they can make work for themselves, how they can have the best relations with their neighbors and community members, and how they can work together to tackle common problems—was most important. Second, they said that village-level sustainability depended greatly on all inhabitants being occupied, referring not only to salaried employment, but also to entrepreneurial efforts and engagement in livelihood activities including domestic food and agricultural production; hunting, fishing, and foraging; construction; and crafts. Third, sustainability depended on the ability of their village head to work with the people. They needed a strong leader who spoke well and could guide the people and also get funding for needed projects. Several respondents, and all elders, put the main responsibility for future village sustainability on the government. Youth placed a great emphasis on community building—on the need to learn how to work together and coordinate efforts.

Bringing Findings into a Larger Discussion

Our results suggest that Viliui Sakha define sustainability as the building of local diversified economies, communities, and health via strong local leadership, a shared vision to work toward common goals, the reinstatement of local knowledge, and rights to land and resources. Not surprisingly, our respondents may not be saying much that is different from other indigenous contexts; however, the ethnographic context, including the Soviet and post-Soviet legacy of these peopled villages, and their dependence on a centralized government system until the recent past, renders these findings quite compelling. Inhabitants not only understand the need for local food production and consumption, reversing the Soviet trend of exporting all local production to adjacent urban areas and importing all village-level consumer goods, but also the necessity for other village-level economic activity including food processing, manufacturing of raw materials, the production of animal feed, the forming of small collectives to make cow and horse breeding efforts more efficient, and the development of entrepreneurial business activities including tourism, service professions, and job training.

Additionally, most of the Sakha youth interviewed understood that the future is in their hands and that the key to having a productive and ample standard of living is to acquire some form of education beyond high school and to get a good job. This is a far cry from the apathy apparent in Sakha youth during the late-Soviet/early-post-Soviet periods (Crate 2002). Most do desire to return to their villages to work in their professions, but they face an immediate lack of village jobs. They appreciate and value knowledge of their elders and understand that it holds a central role in sustainable village futures.

However compelling these findings are, considering the novelty of these ideas and desires in the context of the Soviet and post-Soviet legacy, without action they remain for naught. Viliui Sakha face many hurdles to realizing their ideas. In the comparative context of Canadian diamonds, these findings generate new questions. How can Viliui Sakha and other post-Soviet indigenous peoples realize the sustainable future they envision in lieu of possessing land claims, being civically engaged, and participating in a transparent government? Even if they had those entitlements it would not necessarily mean that they could achieve a sustainable existence. The Canadian case, our best scenario for mining and indigenous peoples in the north, still has many unresolved issues for indigenous stakeholders.

The larger question that looms over both the Canadian and the Russian cases is whether indigenous rights and empowerment in and of themselves are enough to bring about sustainability for local communities. We need a better understanding of how the other stakeholders operate, specifically the mining companies and their patrons. We need to take a hard look at the development of and drivers fueling the global mining economy—how and why did it develop, what has been and is its role in the global economy, and is it possible to do it sustainably?

Notes

. This chapter is based in part on a published article in *Arctic* (Crate 2006b) and is included here under permission by the publisher.

1. Investigating the Economic and Environmental Resilience of Viliui Sakha Villages: Building Capacity, Assessing Sustainability, and Gaining Knowledge. NSF OPP-0240845.

2. We had to complete data collection before hay-cutting began in mid-July, when most inhabitants would be unable to participate. We hired a village research assistant in each village to find participants for and organize focus groups and interviews.

3. After explaining the project goals and participants' right to anonymity.

4. Focus groups were consistent in their pattern of participant response across age groups. Elders were most talkative, middle-aged participants relatively, and youth the least. This pattern reflects Sakha respect for elders and could mean that the focus groups method is

problematic in this setting. We dealt with this in two concrete ways. First, we did have some success in evening out the input by giving all participants equal time to speak, which worked well except for male youth, half of whom didn't speak a word during the entire two-hour session despite our solicitations. Second, we followed up the focus groups with interviews to confirm group responses. In this context we were able to directly solicit male youth responses given the one-on-one nature of the interviews.

5. These themes were also repeatedly reinforced during the focused discussions and interviews.

8

Global Mining, Indigenous Peoples, and Sustainability

Capital-intensive mining plays a central role in the twenty-first-century world economy. Along with the economic benefits of mining come many costs. Both the extraction and processing phases deplete the earth's carbon sinks and generate high levels of greenhouse gases, making mining a key contributor to global warming. The mining industry is also a leading contributor of the world's sulfur dioxide emissions. Mining extraction and processing consumes one-tenth of all nonrenewable energy produced annually. Mining activity threatens ecologically fragile regions of the world, including an estimated forty percent of the world's large, untouched forests, home to endangered and threatened species of plants and animals. In their wake these operations leave behind huge waste piles of contaminated tailings and overburdened earth, moved to reach the desired resources. Mining irreversibly alters the lives of local people living in adjacent regions and downstream from operations. Adjacent communities are either resettled or stranded on their homeland to live with poisoned water, altered landscapes, and polluted air from nearby extraction (Starke 2003:118).

To propose how indigenous communities, who find themselves directly or indirectly dependent on mining activities, can realize sustainability, we need to first understand the forces and drivers of the mining industry. The Russian and Canadian cases show that industrial stakeholders are not alike. Russian diamond mining is controlled within national borders while Canadian operations are run by multinational corporations (MNCs). Both national and MNC operations produce for a world market driven

273

by western consumerism. Paradoxically, mining, the very technology that gave humankind one of its greatest advancements into modernity, is the same technology that today is threatening many world indigenous groups—the most highly adaptive and resilient human communities on earth.

This chapter contextualizes the analysis of the Viliui Sakha and the Canadian cases in a global perspective to further tease out how indigenous peoples can move toward more sustainable futures. The chapter begins with a selected review of world mining to track how western societies' dependence on mined resources has interplayed with the earth and its inhabitants since the beginning.

Mining in Historical Perspective

One of the most significant cultural breakthroughs in history involves the reduction of ores to metals, the treatment of metals, and the alloying of one metal with another to produce a new metal with desirable properties. (Flawn 1966:75)

Mining, the digging and processing of metals and minerals from the earth, is humankind's oldest industrial activity (Mines and Communities 2003). The means and methods of mining have, over time, undergone quantum change. Early mining technology was crude, based on surface findings and simple smelting. The earliest smelters date back some six thousand years ago in the Fertile Crescent. Mining technology was slow to advance for the first several thousand years. The 1453 discovery of the process of liquation, liberating silver from copper, revived the ailing mineral fields (Lynch 2002:19). Modern mining involves high technological and capital inputs for the discovery, extraction, and processing of nonrenewable resources for fabrication and energy (Mikesell 1987). Today, a given nation's capacity to mine and consume resources is considered a measure of its development. Both industrial and agrarian nations depend on mineral resources to feed the world's growing population (Flawn 1966:75). Although the technology of mining has changed over time, at least one aspect of the process has not—the generation of waste in the form of tailings. Thanks to tailings that have remained largely unchanged in the landscape to this day, we are able to date much of the archaeological record of mining. At the same time, the persistent nature of these ancient tailings is a foreboding reminder of what we are leaving on the landscape, scaled up thousands-fold, with modern mining operations.

The history of world mineral exploitation parallels much of the history of world colonization and the creation of the third, or underdeveloped world. In most areas where mining assumed a pivotal role, it shifted the key economic focus away from subsistence-based production to the exploitation of metal and minerals for distant markets. This in turn brought about changes in state policies for the areas and in the production of food stuffs and raw materials. In places where mining took precedence, it created a new sociopolitical landscape by "altering the ecological, economic and political conditions of the conquered populations" (Wolf 1982:141). We can see how these shifts from subsistence-based to state-controlled livelihoods occurred in the examples of New World and African mineral exploitation.

Iberians sought precious metals in the New World beginning in the fifteenth century. First gold, then silver became the mainstay of Spanish wealth. Spaniards discovered silver deposits in the western mountains of Mexico. However, the richest find was Potosi, the "silver mountain," in what is now Bolivia. They employed the local native American populations to mine these deposits,[1] but most wages received went toward paying the Indians' tribute to the state. The drafted laborers first had to travel an average of two months with their families to the mines, located three hundred miles away. They then worked for four months in the mines and an additional two months in compulsory service. Their return added another two months for a total of ten months away from their homelands. The long absence made it difficult for most to maintain a subsistence in the homeland. More and more Indians remained in the mining districts and lost their cultural and linguistic connections to their home villages.

The work also had severe health hazards. It was labor-intensive to haul baskets of ore out of the depths on makeshift ladders to the mine's mouth. Some of the hazard was more deadly. Work duties for some involved the extraction of silver ore with mercury, which led to mercury poisoning and silicosis (Wolf 1982). Between 1503 and 1660, thanks to the labor and sacrifice of native peoples, Iberians transferred over 3.2 million kilograms (7 million pounds) of silver from America to Seville. Even so, these amounts were not enough to relieve the debt Spain incurred in its military pursuits around the globe at the time.

In Africa, Arabs began exporting East African slaves, ivory, iron, rhino horn, shell, amber, and skins to India and East Asia starting in 1000 BP. In the eleventh century they created the first major port on the continent, Kilwa, to control the gold trade. The wealthy Arabs and then Shona-speakers who moved in to control the gold trade, augmented the landscape and livelihoods of local East African cattle-keeping tribes (Wolf 1982:42–44). Similar changes occurred in West Africa at the same time, with the gold mines and the local inhabitants enslaved to work them, there supplying a major portion of Old World precious metals (Wolf 1982:38–39). African mineral exports of gold and diamonds from South Africa and copper from the Congo and northern Rhodesia rose sevenfold between 1897 and 1935. During that time two-thirds of all European investment in Africa went into mining (Ponting 1991:216).

The growth of South African mining, an industry run on African labor, meant the move of thousands from subsistence to subservience. In 1874, eight years after diamonds were first discovered, ten thousand Africans worked the mines. Ninety-seven thousand were working the gold mines a short ten years after the 1886 gold strike. By 1910 numbers had increased threefold. Europeans invested to bring the minerals to their homelands but did little to invest in conditions in the colonies that generated their wealth. Working conditions, housing, and local economies remained in impoverished states.

From its beginning, colonization, founded on the extraction of metals and minerals for foreign states, undermined the resilience of local indigenous communities. Similar patterns can be seen in other country contexts of the period. These colonial patterns prevailed around the globe and are the foundational roots of contemporary globalization—the increasing demand for distant resources to fuel consumer markets. Most of world mining history is characterized by labor-intensive operations exploiting pure forms of metals and minerals, like those described above. Technological advances of the last century have altered the means of world mining and also the impacts it renders.

Mining in the Twenty-First Century

The technology of today's mining bears little resemblance to its past. The last century has been revolutionary for the worldwide mining industry due to the development of technology that can extract and process low-grade ores for their valuable components. This advance, in concert with increased consumer demand, makes mining one of the world's six most economically successful sectors and its CEOs some of the highest paid in the world (Mines and Communities 2003).

Mining interests have also changed in the last century. With contemporary global resource struggles pivoting along a north-south axis, economic power, formerly based in governments, is increasingly concentrated in global multi- or transnational corporations (MNCs or TNCs respectively). These corporations are the key agents in the process of globalization (Evans et al. 2002:xii). Ownership and control of world mining is heavily concentrated in a small number of MNCs. Even many smaller mines, concentrating in gold, silver, diamonds, and precious stones, are being systematically replaced by multinationals with advanced extractive technologies (Mikesell 1987:9).

The consumer market for minerals is also different from in the past. Consumers are caught up in the vicious cycle with minerals. The demand for higher standards of living by more and more of the world's population fuels the world demand for those resources, which in turn bolsters the capital investment in more exploration to find new sources to exploit. "Resource expropriation by the industrial world spins in ever-widening circles to locate materials to exploit" (Hyndman 1994:1). Like buzzards circling in for the carrion, mining MNCs work across industrial sectors to maintain a global reach, indifferent to the physical, cultural, and economic boundaries of nation-states.

How do these MNCs operate? There has been a groundswell of interest in the often conflicting corporate cultural dynamics of MNCs (Moreno and Tegen 1998). Here I will speak in general terms about overall economic features of MNC mining. Mining is a capital-intensive, multiple-stage process. It first involves the exploration for resources. Once found, a company next performs feasibility studies. The final step is the exploitation of the resource through the construction and operation of the mine and associated infrastructure. Each stage requires major investments of money, time, labor, and resources. MNC mining operations involve capital outlays averaging in the billions of dollars. The exact level of capital investment in a mine depends on whether it is an open-pit or an underground operation. Open-pit operations tend to be less capital-intensive and focus on lower grade ores, containing only 1 percent of the valued resource.

MNC mining activity gets strong support from the state governments where they operate because they offer states a portion of their profits. In turn state governments create shelters and incentives for these large companies, often driving down environmental and labor standards, that end up disadvantaging local peoples and environments (Evans et al. 2002). The United States, Russia, Australia, Canada, and South Africa are the leaders in world mineral production.

The Local Impacts of Twenty-First-Century Mining

Capital-intensive mining is highly disruptive to local ecosystems and their inhabitants. In heavy competition with their peers for access to capital and resources around the globe, mining companies drive down local and global environmental, social, labor, and fiscal regulations, gaining carte blanche to impede and often negate the viability of communities and environments adjacent to their activities. Impacts are far-reaching and include the loss of productive land and subsistence resources, the degradation of ecosystems, and the disruption of local community-based social systems.

Tailings are a huge environmental casualty of capital-intensive mining. When low grade ores are mined, one hundred parts of associated materials (rock, sand, mineral substrates, etc.) are dug up for every part of valuable mineral or metal produced. Scoops fill trucks with the mass of earth and haul it to a processing plant. Once the valuable component is extracted, a mountain of tailings is left as waste, far from the original mine site (Townsend 2000). This process not only disrupts the landscape of the mined area but also creates a tailings landscape that pollutes the land and waters with leached toxic materials. Other environmental abuses include deforestation, air and water contamination, and the loss of productive lands for mining areas. Mining projects, the ecosystems they operate in, and the human populations they affect vary greatly. It is beyond the scope of this writing to provide such details. Instead, I will make broad generalizations that apply to most operations.

Mines tend to be located in areas away from populated centers—in mountains, deserts, or rainforests. A large part of the capital investment in a mine goes toward infrastructure to provide the operation power and water, highways, railroads, and port facilities. MNCs often import their own workforce. This requires more infrastructure for living quarters, public education, and other community services (Mikesell 1987:3). Combined, all the infrastructure needed for mining displaces local communities. Mining operations also generate local discontent because of the contrast between the relatively low level of local economic improvements and the higher level of benefits privileged to mining employees. Profits of the mining operation are usually vastly disproportionate to the amounts received by regional and state governments. Long-time inhabitants are resettled, physically removed from ancestral lands and placed in a foreign environment, left without sufficient subsistence means.

Many capital-intensive mining operations produce an income, directly or indirectly, for local peoples inhabiting adjacent areas. If local communities are not removed from the mining area, they can be employed as laborers, introducing a cash economy that is both beneficial and disruptive to subsistence. Overall, the economies of mining do not account for the social and ecological relations of local people to their lands and resources, resulting in a compromised quality of life, impoverished health, environmental degradation, and dependence on state assistance. Additionally, most communities are marginalized and left without power to make their predicament known and to seek resolve.

In the last several decades the global recognition of the damage to local human and ecosystem health due to MNC mining activities has been increasing. This development is due to several events beginning in the late 1970s to early 1980s: 1) The explosion of mining activity across the globe, the majority of which is located in greenfields or frontier areas inhabited by relatively self-sufficient indigenous communities; 2) the growth of recognition for indigenous rights, substantiated in 1982 through the United Nations Working Group on Indigenous Populations and draft of the UN Declaration on the Rights of Indigenous Peoples; 3) the institution of impact assessment for MNC activity that integrates affected indigenous communities as stakeholders; and 4) the growth of a broader mining community via: a) widespread use of the internet and other mass communication and b) increased civic involvement precipitated through the work of national and international NGOs, legal agencies, and individual lawyers (Ballard and Banks 2003:288–289). Increased worldwide environmental concern has bolstered local demands for compensation via a share of the mining rents. Mining companies now incorporate some level of local compensation and more actively seek and implement environmentally friendly operating technologies and techniques.

These developments, along with bringing more equitable conditions across stakeholder fronts, have also generated other issues. Many MNC mining operations implement environmental safeguards and improve the socioeconomic conditions for locals in the immediate vicinity of the mine but neglect the ecosystems and communities in outlying areas. MNCs can often pay more in rents and compensation than they do, another factor that contributes to tensions. There is often discrepancy between agreed conditions and how they play out on the ground. These factors have led to conflict, for example the well-documented cases witnessed in the 1990s in the Asia-Pacific regions: the Bouganville Rebellion in Papua New Guinea (Filer 1990; Denoon 2000); disputes over the environmental devastations at the Ok Tedi Mine (Banks and Ballard 1997; Kirsch 2002a, 2002b, 1997); and human rights abuses at mines in Indonesian Papua or Irian Jaya (Abrash 2002). The best possible scenario is when MNC company-community relations are mitigated by an independent audit, by an NGO or otherwise, who can mediate and regulate these conditions, and provide transparency of the company's finances with local communities (Auty and Mikesell 1998:209).

The last decades have also shown increasing attention to the true costs of mining, to include both short- and long-term effects. The "boom and bust" nature of most mining activities leaves local communities in their wake without mining rents or subsistence means. Other long-term effects include: the environmental contamination from lasting residues; the permanent loss of sacred and significant sites; forced resettlements of indigenous communities to make way for mining activities; social dislocation of and inequity to affected women and children; and poor health and safety standards for workers, who suffer accidents and early death due to impoverished health (Mines and Communities 2003).

Affected local peoples are taking an increasingly active role in defending their lands and livelihoods, asserting their right of local self-determination and veto over global corporate interests. Their movements are of both local and global reach, and often operate transnationally. Affected peoples and their advocates protest and lobby against mining company actions and also enact the power of international boycotts and campaigns. There have been results. The international campaign in South Africa against Rio Tinto, formerly the world's largest mining company with a comparable myriad of abuses to the environments and peoples in its sites of operation, is heralded as the first global trade union campaign focusing on a transnational corporation that not only addressed protection of workers' collective bargaining rights but also environmental, indigenous, and human rights abuses (Evans et al. 2002:xvi).

Such activities have in turn increased pressure on the global mining industry to act more environmentally and socially responsibly. In 1998 the nine MNC mining companies belonging to the Mining and Minerals Working Group of the World Business Council for Sustainable Development (WBCSD)[2] launched the Global Mining Initiative to establish the mining industry's commitment to global sustainable development. Their main effort has been the Mining, Minerals, and Sustainable Development (MMSD) project, a two-year initiative involving a wider group of thirty MNC mining companies and their relevant stakeholders to conduct independent global analyses. The project, administered by the International Institute for Environment and Development (IIED) has, to date, been largely condemned on accounts of corporate greenwash (Mines and Communities 2001). The initiative's fine print states that the main objective is not to come to terms with past and ongoing abuses but rather to improve public perception, that is, to use a massive sales pitch to convince influential consumer populations that global mining interests are to be considered in truest alignment with sustainable development trajectories (MMSD 2002). In short, to maintain the status quo via a new, and largely undeserved, public image.

The World Bank's Extractive Industries Review is the other recent effort to reconcile global mining's poor image (EIR 2003). The issues to be addressed include poverty alleviation, transparency, governance, renewable energy, inclusion, sectoral composition, and environmental and social ills (World Bank 2005). The EIR process involved extensive regional workshops with involvement of all levels of stakeholder interest. Much consideration was given on how to build civil societies in affected areas. Despite the potential outcomes for this level of engagement, the recommendations were strongly biased in favor of corporate interests and left out the diversity of views articulated in the meetings, misrepresenting the interests of local and state stakeholders. The group sold the illusion that extractive industries are committed to poverty alleviation and environmental sustainability, but, at the same time, took no action to reform how these operations perform on the ground. In the end, the World Bank rejected the EIR recommendations.

One major problem the World Bank had with the EIR recommendations was the push to grant veto power to local communities when their area is under consideration for extractive industry development. Instead the World Bank (WB) allows only, "a process of free, prior, and informed consultation with affected communities that leads to the affected community's broad acceptance of the project" (World Bank 2004:9). The choice of such language is interpreted by most affected peoples and their advocates as coercion. These and other efforts by corporate interests to appear more socially responsible on the world stage have not worked. Although there has been some progress, it is a misnomer to portray the industry as ready to redress human rights abuses; compensate for past social, economic, and environmental damage; and create local partnerships based on economic growth for all (Mines and Communities: Charter).

The Ok Tedi Case

One of the best known cases of environmental and socioeconomic destruction due to global mining activity is the Ok Tedi mine in Papua New Guinea. Beginning in the late 1980s, the mine has dumped over 80,000 tons of waste into the adjacent river, crippling the watershed ecosystem and threatening local inhabitants' health and subsistence resources for decades to come. A description by Stuart Kirsch, an anthropologist who has worked on the Ok Tedi since 1984, provides a stark account of the changes to the local ecosystem after a little over a decade of mining activity:

> I used to travel by canoe along the rivers, and you'd have a towering wall of green on either side of you as you traveled along the river. You'd see hornbills, flocks of hornbills. And you'd also see kingfishers along the river and herons and egrets. In the forest itself you could find lots of wild animals. And now if you walk along the Ok Tedi River, it's like a ghost forest. All you have are trees with no leaves on them. All the birds have gone away. There are no fish left in the rivers and streams. It's like a winter landscape in the tropics. (LOE, 2000)

Kirsch's scholarly writings detail how this affected ecosystem likewise affects the people living in the villages along the lower Ok Tedi River:

> Mine waste has been deposited onto forest and garden land, into adjacent wetland areas and upstream into the numerous creeks and streams that flow into the Ok Tedi. This is in stark contrast to the alluvium that once fertilized the river's flood plains, turning them into ideal garden land. The mine wastes have had adverse impact wherever then have been deposited, killing plants, trees, and disrupting local ecosystems. The damage extends for forty kilometers or so along the river, with areas of dead trees that extend to two or three kilometers from the main channel.... This land was particularly valuable to villagers because it is located within easy walking or canoe distance and because it offered resources not readily available in the rain forest interior. (Kirsch 1997: 121–122)

The root of this devastation is the state's dual role as both steward of its resources and business partner in their exploitation (Johnston 1994:87). Since its independence from Australian colonial rule in 1975, the Papua New Guinea government has generated substantial revenues from resource rents by inviting MNCs with their capital and technology to extract minerals. In 1990, a few short years after Broken Hill Propriety's (BHP) Ok Tedi Mining Ltd began producing gold and extracting copper, the local press heralded the company as being key to the island's economic growth and development. But there were costs for these short-term economic gains, most salient to our discussion being the affects on local environments and indigenous communities at the mine site and downstream from it.

The company employed local Wopkaiman males to make up a small percentage of the workforce to construct the mine. These locals' entry into wage labor brought with it a series of changes: a move from subsistence areas to squatters' villages; a change of diet from natural game to canned products; increased alcohol consumption leading to estrangement, abuse, and other problems; and an increase of infectious diseases. The introduction of a cash economy eroded a people's formerly resilient and self-sufficient socioeconomic system based on renewable forest and river resources and founded in kin-oriented, not capitalist, modes of production (Hyndman 1994; Townsend 2000).

The downstream effects of BHP's negligence of environmental controls became clear after a series of incidents in 1984 including: a 1-kilometer-long (0.6-mile-long) landslide in the area slated for the mine's permanent tailings dam; a barge spill into the river estuary of 2,700 sixty-liter drums of cyanide, and the release of another 991 cubic meters (35,000 cubic feet) of concentrated cyanide waste directly into the Ok Tedi River (Johnston 1994: 90). Despite the company's pledge to protect the watershed by building a tailings dam, in 1986 the Papua New Guinea (PNG) government agreed to permit unlimited direct discharge into the river. By 1990 copper and other heavy metals were measured to be one hundred to two hundred times higher than before the mine. By 1997, 250 square kilometers (100 square miles) of riverside forest were dead, and adjacent areas soon to be. The Australian Conservation Society announced the Ok Tedi River itself to be "biologically dead" (Townsend 2000:59). Over the course of one short decade, a major watershed area of New Guinea on one of the most environmentally complex and culturally diverse islands in the Pacific, was rendered ecologically impotent, affecting tens of thousands of peoples dependent on that ecosystem for their subsistence and causing multiple reverberations throughout the entire patchwork of island bioregions for decades, if not centuries, to come.

Beginning in the late 1980s the Yonggom and other downstream inhabitants began petitioning their government and the mining company to stop the reckless destruction of their homelands and subsistence resources. Their cries fell on deaf ears. Anthropologist Stuart Kirsch, who became involved in the local peoples' plight after coming to the regions to conduct cultural anthropology research, helped the local inhabitants make their voice heard on an international level. In 1992 they presented their case to the International Water Tribunal in The Hague, bringing Ok Tedi into the international spotlight (Ghazi 2003). Two years later they took their case to Melbourne, Australia, the corporate headquarters of BHP, and filed a $4 billion civil suit against the company (Townsend 2000:60). In 1996 the two sides reached an out-of-court settlement to enclose the tailings and pay compensation for affected areas and peoples (Hyndman 2001:34). Four years later representatives of the downstream communities returned to the Victorian Supreme Court in Melbourne, the home base of BHP, to charge the company with breach for failing to halt contamination of the river (Kirsch 2002b:15).

In 2000, BHP announced its plan to withdraw from the mine, based on the World Bank's recommendation (Kirsch 2002b:15). The PNG government and local inhabitants rebelled, arguing that the closing of the mine would break their state economy, deprive local residents of jobs, and, ironically, stop the funds they needed to address their environmental problems. BHP transferred all its equity in the mine (52 percent) to a new initiative, the Papua New Guinea Sustainable Development Program Company, an organization with the strict objective of spending dividend income on development programs. This move released BHP from their indemnity for all past and future pollution liability. With the mine scheduled to close in 2010, the question now is whether local control and forthcoming revenues can effectively abate the severe damage already done.

The PNG Sustainable Development Program Company's jargon bears a strong resemblance to BHP's:

> The Ok Tedi mine is a major producer of copper concentrate for the world smelting market. Ok Tedi Mining Limited is working with the people of the Western Province to help build a sustainable long-term future from the wealth that the mine has created.
>
> —*The Ok Tedi Statement* (www.oktedi.com)

The salient question is how sustainable is this pattern of corporate irresponsibility for the local environments and peoples affected? BHP essentially created an ecological catastrophe then took their money and ran. It turns out this is a common response by corporate giants who are confronted by affected communities, NGOs, and other concerned groups. Instead of becoming more proactive and citizen friendly, MNCs abandon their projects (Kirsch 2002b:15).

Mining, Indigenous Peoples, and Sustainability

> Mining and its products, especially gold and oil, have often been the *raison d'etre* for imperialism and its many misadventures. Mining companies have historically played a key role, as partners with both colonial and post-colonial governments, in securing a flow of resources from the South to the North, deliberately exploiting their leverage over weak regimes keen for economic development. Mineral wealth has, however, rarely translated into general local prosperity. Rather, large-scale mining development, like that at Ok Tedi, has in many places in all continents ruined traditional means of livelihood and natural environments, and left once-sustainable local economies and societies dependent on foreign corporations and overseas markets. (Evans et al. 2002:xii)

Indigenous communities are increasingly signaling us about our failing global economic system that generates environmental and cultural destruction, much like the canaries miners once carried with them into the depths of the earth to signal fatal exposure to toxic gases. But just as the increasingly globalized world capitalist economy, with production and finance organized on a transnational basis, has been key to the spread of capital-intensive high-value, world market–oriented mining industries, it has also been central to the growth of informed and sophisticated indigenous movements in affected areas. For over a decade affected indigenous communities have spoken out about the injustices being done to their communities and homelands by global mining operations. Anthropological research and advocacy since the late 1980s is one main source of witness to this movement. The Ok Tedi case above highlights some of the severe environmental, socioeconomic and cultural impacts for local indigenous groups adjacent to capital-intensive multinational mining operations and the struggles they face to protect their homeland.

The Russian, Canadian, and PNG cases show how divergent local and national contexts are. The Canadian case is perhaps closest to an ideal of sustainability, but there are many unanswered questions about long-term environmental and socioeconomic effects. The PNG case shows how MNCs have carte blanche to act irresponsibly with no corporate expectation to account for and undo the damage done. Viliui Sakha are left in a powerless position, without land claims, civic involvement, or government transparency with which to push for a more equitable arrangement.

Given these insights from case accounts, we can derive a list of needs for mining to be sustainable for affected indigenous peoples. First, there need to be measures taken to mitigate the effects of external shocks that result when the mining operation introduces a cash economy and a transient labor population. The company needs to minimize and abate environmental damage to the extent that local ecosystems remain functional and intact once the mining operations pull out. Benefit agreements need to allocate part of the company revenues toward investing in replacing the income stream from the depleting mineral asset. One of the most productive legacies a mine can leave in a community is education and training to maintain a local economy once a mine is gone. Mining companies can play a positive role in building social capacity. Since most mineral-exporting countries continue to have a largely rural population, it is especially important that rents be directed toward rural development (Auty 1998:219). Finally, local communities need a degree of empowerment to be the decision makers for their environments and peoples.

Notes

1. They extended the mandatory labor draft, in existence since Inca times, to include work in the mines and required that every village make one seventh of its adult male population available for mine labor.

2. Anglo American, BHP Billiton, Codelco, Newmont, Noranda, Phelps Dodge, Placer Dome, Rio Tinto, WMC Limited.

Epilogue

What does the Viliui Sakha case tell us about human adaptation and resilience in the face of ongoing or unprecedented change? What lessons can we learn from Viliui Sakhas' experience of globalization and modernity? Lastly, how can this ethnography inform what sustainability means for Viliui Sakha and indigenous peoples globally? I begin to address these questions by first reflecting on how the chapters speak to the book's central themes.

Revisiting the Central Themes

Indigenous cultures, by nature, possess a relatively high capacity for adaptation to uncertainty and change due to both a generalist and time-tested knowledge of subsistence survival, and a propensity for innovation in the context of environmental, sociocultural, political, and economic change. The resilience of human or nonhuman systems is a function of a capacity to adapt. Viliui Sakha represent a stellar case of adaptation and resilience in several ways. First, they adapted a southern horse and cattle agropastoralist subsistence to the northern climate to make their home in Siberia. We use terms like "carrying capacity" and "ecosystem recovery" to refer to a biological community's degree of resilience and "adaptive capacity" for a human system's resilience. Both ecosystems and the humans that inhabit them have varying levels of resilience, or capacities to respond and adapt to change (Berkes, Colding, and Folke 2003:13). Some of Viliui Sakhas' adaptations are based on the same principles as the native flora and fauna of the northern ecosystem—to maximize energy accumulation through feeding and storing in the brief and activity-driven temperate period and to minimize energy expenditure through the long winter by way of protective shelter and low activity. Viliui Sakha were successful at adapting by foddering their herds in barns nine months of the year and utilizing the summer to harvest hay and other foodstuffs. In contrast to other biological systems, human-environment interactions are more highly complex, involving multiple feedbacks that generate new effects and outcomes. One way that humans negotiate these more complex relationships is via belief. Viliui Sakhas' adaptation to the subarctic is highly dependent on maintaining the proper relationships with the spiritual world, which grounds them as part of an intricate web of plant, animal, and spirit relationships. Marusa's hanging of the *salama* testifies to the resilience of that sacred belief system to this day.

The complexity of human-environment interactions further increases when different cultures interact and compete for resources and/or exert power over the other to control resources. The outcome of those interactions is often determined by the power and sophistication of each group. Although possessing a high capacity for adaptation and resilience, indigenous cultures are often overwhelmed and exploited by more technologically advanced groups. We can see these power relations in Viliui Sakha history over the centuries of making their home in Siberia. By engaging history in our analysis we have been able to clarify how events over time interplay with Viliui Sakha adaptive choices (Crumley 2001, 1994; Egan and Howell 2001). The account of Viliui Sakha settlement history shows how Viliui Sakha have been both the subduers, of the local hunting-gathering cultures who inhabited the Viliui regions from early times, and the subdued, by Russian and later Soviet forces. Most significantly, in the Soviet period we see a transformation of Viliui Sakhas' mode of production when, upon the discovery of Viliui diamonds, the state consolidated all collectives into state farms, with the explicit objective of supplying meat, milk, and other foodstuffs for the nascent mining centers. With this move, Viliui Sakha lost their collective relationships in which they were part owners of the farm resources and products, and became members of the working class. This was also the historical moment when diamonds "got a life" and began their direct and indirect penetration of Viliui Sakhas' local culture, social relations, and politics. Diamonds soon became a many-sided cultural symbol: the state's highest pride of socialist industrial activity; the republic's boast of lucrative mineral wealth; the Viliui Region's way forward into the highest fulfillment of the (Soviet) Plan; and, to many local inhabitants, a bittersweet omen of a race into modernity that would, in the end, undermine the adaptation and resilience of their people.

In the post-Soviet context, we see again how Viliui Sakha have adapted, this time to the rapid change from a socialist centralized system to a decentralized household-level cows-and-kin production system. Viliui Sakha were able to adjust their production mode because of their resilient adaptive capacity. They moved quickly to reorganize themselves into household and inter-household level production units based on kin relations—household-level arrangements based on the pooling of resources, labor, land, and technology. Members of household and extended kin arrangements have a responsibility to each other that was absent in other social arrangements in the villages in Soviet times. In many ways, post-Soviet production exceeded that of the late Soviet period because inhabitants had once again gained ownership of their means and modes of production. The post-Soviet cows-and-kin adaptation, based on household and inter-household production, is parallel with the adaptive responses of other peoples of the world. Robert Netting's analyses of smallholder-householder systems provides many examples of that common ground (Netting 1993). Research in the circumpolar north that analyzes how groups have adapted to recent environmental and socioeconomic changes, similarly emphasizes the centrality of household-level production (Caulfield 1997; Nuttall 1992, 2000; Ziker 1998).

The success of cows-and-kin, Viliui Sakhas' post-Soviet adaptive strategy, is founded on having and knowing land. Local inhabitants pool land resources with kin to realize the amounts of hay fodder they need to over winter their herds. Accessing enough land for sufficient fodder is and will continue to be problematic for most Viliui Sakha. Households have to continually negotiate issues of: 1) transportation to and from outlying areas to harvest and haul hay; 2) changing climate patterns that can render hay plots either too wet or too dry for production; and 3) labor needs to cut, stack, and haul hay. The latter is increasingly difficult with the alienation of youth, who should be moving into adult hay harvesting responsibilities for their household and extended kin but are instead tending to be less involved in the activity. In part this alienation is due to the effects of globalization and modernity—as post-Soviet youth are increasingly privy to and influenced by the mass media and other forms of input from the outside world, they orient their goals to a global perspective beyond their small village. This, combined with the longer-term disruption of local knowledge bases, which began in the early Soviet period with collectivization and continued through the state farm period, has rendered local knowledge of little importance in the contemporary context. For decades other circumpolar countries have paid attention to the part that indigenous knowledge plays in native survival (Wenzel 1999). Although such efforts continue to be severely lacking across post-Soviet Russia, perhaps this analysis, showing the inherent and practical value of elders' knowledge, could be instrumental in encouraging local documentation efforts. With much elder knowledge informing the cows-and-kin strategy, there should be enough motivation for "insiders," the local Viliui Sakha inhabitants, to formulate useful and objective questions, to record elders' experiences, and to use the knowledge in their daily lives and in the education of their youth. Similarly, these same redeeming qualities of the knowledge gives "outsiders," anthropologists, advocates, and others the cue to pay attention to the practical value of those narratives and the imperative need to document them.

How do these forces interplay with Viliui Sakhas' experience of globalization and modernity? Local capacities for adaptation and resilience often have no propensity for the pace of change ushered in by globalization. In the indigenous context, the forces of globalization are frequently translated on the local level as the exploitation of nonrenewable resources for distant markets. Since the industrial revolution, the global competition for resources is intensified in response to increasing consumer demand for products and the ability to transport them over long distances. Economic globalization favors specialists of portable professions who can move freely to maximize gains. Indigenous cultures, who survive via a generalist knowledge of local ecosystems, very much rooted to place, cannot compete (Young 1998:5). Likewise, local communities like Viliui Sakha often find themselves in the globalization process via a cash economy based on nonrenewable resource extraction. This in turn can transform the local mode of production from subsistence-based to working class and, in turn undermine the survival strategies of locally adapted and resilient cultures (Hyndman 1994).

Hand-in-hand with globalization, modernity offers both advantages and disadvantages for local groups. For Viliui Sakha modernity means education and literacy, health care, and a higher standard of living. It brings access to mass media and consumer products. The combination of an accessible "window to the world" since the end of the cold war, and the revaluation of pre-Soviet subsistence strategies, the temporality of the village setting is mixed—time both races forward and stands still. In the meantime, relevant issues, like who will take on the cows-and-kin legacy when the present-day stewards are unable and how to balance modern ways with time-tested subsistence modes frame the questions of modernity in Viliui Sakha villages.

The environmental history of the Viliui shows one concrete example of how globalization and modernity have played out locally. Viliui Sakha are caught in a conflicting relationship with diamonds. On the one hand, diamonds supply the much-needed cash for households' mixed cash economies. On the other hand, diamonds continue to threaten the foundations of Viliui Sakha subsistence production mode—the health of the local ecosystem and human populations. Despite a vital citizen effort to find compensation for and amelioration of the environmental injustices on the Viliui, elite diamond interests successfully co-opted the movement.

The understanding of how unjust the Viliui Sakha situation is next led us to comparing their plight with other similar cases. The circumpolar north has many examples of civic empowerment including, for our interests, "the best-case scenario" of diamonds and indigenous peoples of the north, the case of diamonds in Canada's Northwest Territories. Circumpolar countries are home to very relevant indigenous success stories of self-determination[1] and self-government—the Alaska Native Settlement Claims Act (1971), Greenland Home Rule (1979), and the Nunavut territory (1999). Key to these successes are land and resource rights, civic and political savvy, and native leadership. Although Viliui Sakha lack these essential qualities, by comparing their case with the Canadian diamonds experience we get a glimpse of what is needed for mining to become more environmentally just on the Viliui. The Canadian comparison also helps to clarify issues for local stakeholders on a more global scale by showing that, even in the "best-case scenario" there remain many unknowns that threaten the adaptation and resilience of local peoples. Most notably these include the long-term effects on both the environment and the socioeconomic fabric of village communities.

The bridge between adaptation and resilience on the one hand and globalization and modernity on the other is the balancing act of sustainability. Viliui Sakha define sustainability as, first and foremost, the building of both their village economy and local community. They talk about reinstating some level of pre-Soviet communal relationships and human-environment interactions, to reconnect people to their past and present, in order to provide a context for building sustainable communities into the future. Their ideas are creative and exciting, giving hope to the contemporary village contexts. However, they face many hurdles in realizing their ideas of sustainability. Above all, their diamond dependence, which encroaches on lands and subsistence means, displaces communities to develop resource bases, and degrades local environments through ecologically unsound practices.

Negotiating a diversity of factors to survive via a resilient adaptive capacity is a strategy familiar to Viliui Sakha and other indigenous cultures globally. However, the challenge takes on new meanings when the consumer demands for resources of the globalized world economy increasingly threaten tenacious human-environment systems. The case of the world mining industry highlights how powerfully and blatantly multinational corporations can undermine indigenous life ways and bear no responsibility for doing so. In such a climate of corporate irresponsibility, where can we begin to define and work toward sustainability? For that matter, what exactly do we mean by sustainability?

Toward an Ethnography of Sustainability

This ethnography explores how Viliui Sakha, one group of northern Russia's indigenous peoples, have been and continue to be challenged to balance a resilient adaptive capacity with the forces of globalization and modernity. This ongoing balancing act, the "work of sustainability" compares and contrasts to circumpolar and global indigenous struggles. The task before us is to take what we know, from both our local and global understandings of indigenous sustainability, and translate it into something theoretically and practically meaningful. We need to begin by understanding the history of precedence for sustainability and sustainable development and the ongoing dilemma of defining those directives.

Today, most inhabitants of the developed world are no longer challenged by daily survival but by the long-term maintaining of both our planet and a global human civilization (Hammond 1998:7). In the late twentieth century, due to the increasing scrutiny over the compatibility of economic development and environmental protection, the concept of sustainability and sustainable development became the keystones of the global dialogue about the human future. The concept of and priority for "sustainable development" first became popular in 1987 when the Brundtland Commission defined the need for, "development which meets the needs of the present without compromising the ability of future generations to meet their needs" (WCED 1987). Critiques of early efforts, spurred by the Brundtland Report, toward development that was sustainable, focus on their attempt to manage systems globally by an undefined "we" who knows what is best for the world as a whole (Escobar 1995:192–193). In the almost two decades since its inception, the concept has gone through numerous rewordings to be more inclusive and holistic and to enhance cultural and environmental priorities, illustrated by the following examples:

> Sustainable development seeks human well-being through an equitable and democratic utilization of society's resources, while preserving cultural distinctiveness and the natural environment for future generations.
>
> —Canada's definition, created while chair of the Arctic Council (Graham 1997:101)

> Sustainable development must integrate environmental stewardship, economic development and the well-being of all people ... not just for today but for countless generations to come. This is the challenge facing governments, non-governmental organizations, private enterprises, communities and individuals.
>
> —World Summit

> Sustainable development is the growth of population, industry, and agriculture in a way that will allow the present generation to meet its own needs without damaging those of future generations.
>
> —United Nations

> The overall challenge of sustainability is to avoid crossing irreversible thresholds that damage the life systems of Earth while creating long-term economic, political and moral arrangements that secure the well-being of present and future generations. (Orr 2004:59)

Despite these refinements, the concepts of sustainability and sustainable development have most often become an empty cliché of governments and policy makers (Jull 2003: 21). An example of this, relevant to our discussion, is the history of sustainable development in Russia. When Russia became an independent state in 1991, the worldwide priority of sustainable development was already codified in numerous international environmental conventions and documents (e.g., Club of Rome, Limits to Growth, 1972; IUCN, World Conservation Strategy, 1980; United Nations, World Charter for Nature, 1982; WCED, Our Common Future, 1987). The Russian government adopted sustainable development as a framework for economic and environmental decision-making, incorporating it as a priority stance in official documents and government administration. However, from this early introduction the concept was lost in translation. The Russian term, *ustoichivoe razvitie*, translates back to English as "stable development," and is more akin to economic rather than sustainable development. By the end of the 1990s the Russian government had officially dropped their sustainable development ideals in light of material gains (Henry 2002).[2]

The earth's continuing environmental decline is proof of humankind's inability to successfully implement the concepts of sustainability. Since the 1992 establishment of the concepts of sustainability as global priorities in Agenda 21, the earth's population has increased from 5 to 6 billion and we have witnessed unprecedented loss of world forests and biodiversity (McCabe 2003a:91). In part the failure to realize global sustainability is due to insurmountable barriers, most prominently, loss of ecosystem viability (WRI 2003:5). Free and automatic ecosystem services, such as the maintenance of clean air and water, and the natural regeneration of fertility in soils, are under dire threat due to the consumptive resource demands of increasing world populations, environmental degradation, deforestation, and climate change (Lovins and Link 2001:1–2).

In the same breath, there are actions that can be taken on our part to alleviate these trends. However, they remain largely untaken. Humans have a record of adapting behaviorally by developing technology and other innovative techniques, witnessed in our technological diversity of subsistence practices, including hunter-gathering, horticulture, pastoralism, agrarianism, and commercial-industrial systems. Human adaptive capacity is exemplified in technologies that mitigate the balance between rates of depletion and recovery, such as fallowing in agricultural systems (Redman 1999:122). However, archaeological evidence reveals numerous accounts of human maladaptation—civilizations falling due to the human failure to adapt to change (Redman 1999:122). In short, humans can act as agents for and as agents against sustainability.

In part, our failure affirms the faults of the dominant Western top-down economic worldview, which manages ecosystems based on generalized prescriptions rather than on specific contexts. Researchers have recently been developing alternative approaches that defy conventional deductive reasoning by arguing that sustainability and sustainable development are not static prescriptions but flexible discourses and meeting points for different ideas on how to achieve human betterment (Dryzek 1997:123–125). If sustainability is a discourse about finding a balance between human and environmental systems so that the integrity of each remains intact, then it is intuitive that the conditions for such a balance will vary according to the specific local characteristics of ecosystem dynamics, cultural ways, and the interactions between the two. Furthermore, these interactions need to be dynamic and adaptable, "a livelihood is sustainable when it can cope with and recover from stresses and shocks, maintain or enhance its capabilities and assets, while not undermining the natural resource base" (Scoones 1998:5).

Socioecological systems research defines sustainability in direct terms of resilience. "A resilient social-ecological system, which can buffer a great deal of change or disturbance, is synonymous with ecological, economic, and social sustainability" (Berkes, Colding, and Folke 2003:15). Maintaining sustainability means working within the resilience "limits" of a system to enhance diversity and variability and to facilitate a system's capacity for self-organization, learning and adaptation (Gunderson and Holling 2002). In the last decade social scientists have developed working models for the varying degrees of human resilience, efforts considered under the rubric of "sustainability science," a problem-driven science with both its end goal of creating knowledge for sustainable development decision-making and its emphasis on the coproduction of knowledge to ensure its utility and longevity to local users (Clark and Dickson 2003:8059).

Resilience, founded on adaptive capability, is a defining characteristic of sustainability and forms a logical partnership with development when directed toward maintaining maximum opportunity for adaptation (Gunderson and Holling 2002:76). In other words, truly sustainable development would both enlarge the range of local people's choices to make development more democratic and participatory and would incorporate an in-depth knowledge of local ecosystems and culture(s). If the general parameters for sustainable development are maintaining resilience of social and ecological systems, then how can we successfully model and implement policy for sustainability in the context of the homogenizing forces of globalization? Similarly, how do we decide the age-old development dilemma, in this case, sustainability for whom and by whose parameters? Additionally, with adaptation to change as one key to sustainability, and with globalization bringing increasing change to local contexts, to what degree can communities maintain their social integrity in the name of adapting?

Researchers, communities, and governments could make it their priority to develop locally determined definitions of sustainability that are culture-and-environment-specific, can be locally conceived and maintained, and that are "shaped by particular historical and political-economic contexts" (Fratkin and Mearns 2003:119). Anthropological research contributes to an empirical basis for such locally generated understandings of sustainability and sustainable development with its emphasis on the needs and perspectives of local communities.

Sustainability Research in Anthropology

Anthropology is a natural discipline to pursue sustainability research because it accounts for the variance in ecosystems and the values, expectations, and changing needs of communities. Anthropological research considers diverse contexts and local needs that require an equally diverse set of solutions. Anthropologists have long engaged the concept of sustainability in their work. In many of the subfields of anthropology, take for example cultural and political ecology, sustainability is often priority criteria for analysis (Netting 1993:135–145; Hyndman 2001:177–181; Robbins 2004:13). Anthropologists have also contributed to understandings about small-scale societies in which conservation is rare but sustainable use and management is common (Smith and Wishnie 2000:493). Anthropology recognizes that globalization affects local systems. In the subfield of development anthropology, the sustainable development concept is anthropology-friendly because it extends measures of development beyond economic criteria to consider environmental protection and social equity and has potential to provide a framework (model) to assess alternative development scenarios.

Recent anthropological scholarship in sustainability, although varying in their views of the concept, do reach consensus that social systems are central to sustainable ends (Stone 2003:95). Local sustainability is founded on three variables: persistence, innovation, and responses. It follows that locally determined definitions must acknowledge each local population's move toward change and modernization by ascertaining what cultural features are key to a community's sustainability and therefore need to persist and what can be discarded in exchange for innovation (Stone 2003:96). In addition to analyzing a local culture's need to persist in some practices and discard others for innovation, sustainability also encompasses adaptations to the larger context, beyond the locale, or a culture's responses to stresses and shocks that do not undermine a community's natural resource base.[3]

The case of local fisheries management in the Brazilian Amazon shows how local communities have innovated by replacing their conventional management system with community management based on accords that protect their fisheries from encroaching commercial fisheries (de Castro and McGrath 2003:132). Contemporary research also reveals the capacity for cultural innovations to achieve more sustainable livelihoods. North Tanzanian Maasai communities changed from pastoralist to agropastoralist subsistence strategies in response to the stresses of increasing human population, fluctuating livestock populations, reduced pastureland, and a mixed cash economy (McCabe 2003b:100). In this case, innovation is also a means to persistence of Maasai pastoral identity, which could not have been retained without diversification to agriculture to respond to stress factors threatening it (McCabe 2003b:106)—sustainability via innovation and persistence. Clearly the emphasis on local definitions of what is sustainable is producing results. The challenge now is to develop flexible criteria that incorporate sensitivity to local socio-ecological variance.

Sustainability and Indigenous Peoples

There are and will continue to be a variety of definitions of and applications for sustainability and sustainable development. This study focuses on sustainability that informs twenty-first-century indigenous survival. The Brundtland Report, which brought world attention to the concept of sustainable development, contained a detailed section on indigenous peoples that, among other things, clearly accused formal development projects of destroying the only cultures that were able to adapt in their environments (Jull 2003:22). It emphasized the need to recognize traditional rights and to protect the local institutions that manage resource use. Despite the report's official prescriptions, such understanding is "an astonishing idea to many governments" (Jull 2003).

In the last two decades, the cultural survival of the world's indigenous populations has received much attention, which, in its turn, has generated new understandings of what is meant by sustainability and sustainable development. Albeit the political, economic, environmental, and sociocultural terrain of this focus is diverse, there are also overarching commonalities.

In the wake of Western commercial/industrial expansion and population pressure, indigenous peoples are among the global inhabitants who are increasingly experiencing encroachment on their lives and lands. Their lands are often despoiled by adjacent environmental contamination and degradation. Yet indigenous peoples depend on these local ecosystems for subsistence and market resources, knowledge systems, settlement area, and a spiritual base. They have practical and ancestral mastery of their local natural environments, including an intimate understanding of climate, annual cycles, weather patterns, spatial distribution of resources, adaptive strategies, faunal migrations, and practical uses of animal, vegetative, and other renewable resources. This expertise is often termed "indigenous knowledge" and defined as "knowledge and values that have been acquired through experience and observation, from the land or from spiritual teachings and handed down from one generation to another" (Abele 1997:iii).

Indigenous discourses of sustainable management, founded on the complex relationships between land, nature, animals, subsistence practices, and the cyclical and spiritual realms, challenge Western scientific approaches that focus on the environmental management of discrete resources.

> "The wisdom of the elders" and the skills they teach remain important: courage, tenacity, patience, focus. Such skills are precisely the characteristics needed to navigate the modern world.
>
> —Sheila Watt-Cloutier, Chair, Inuit Circumpolar Conference
> (Nuttall 2005:xxxvii)

Indigenous knowledge is increasingly considered a highly valuable and often superior framework to build environmental management schemes. Consider Principle 22 of the Rio declaration:

> Indigenous peoples' communities and other local communities, have a vital role in environmental management and development because of their knowledge and traditional practices. States should recognize and duly support their identity, culture, and interests and enable their effective participation in the achievement of sustainable development. (United Nations 1993)

However, development projects often allow these peoples only two choices: to return to an ancient and "primitive" life way or to assimilate into a Western mode.

In the last decade native groups have made a claim to their resources, knowledge, and rights with a measure of success (Berkes 1999; Dahl, Hicks, and Jull 2000). These successes have also brought to light that sustainability for indigenous peoples does not end with improving the quality of their lives without compromising the future quality of life for their descendants. Indigenous sustainability also entails social and economic equity, cultural survival, and political devolution.

Indigenous Sustainability in the Arctic Context

Since World War II circumpolar governments increasingly have been drawn into territorial national northlands for access to resources; to construct transportation corridors and facilities for education, health care, and administration; and for purposes of national defense. Concomitantly, arctic indigenous peoples have been compelled and empowered to defend their homelands and cultures (Jull 2003:23). The Arctic thus is a proving ground for localizing indigenous sustainability (AHDR 2004; Caulfield 1997; Habeck 2003; Nuttall 1998; Sejersen 2002; Sirina 2005; Wilson 1999).

Self-government (political devolution) and self-determination (the ability and right to live a particular way of life, to use language, to practice cultural or religious ways, and to determine economic development) are the central foci of indigenous sustainable development in the Arctic. The establishment of the Alaska Native Claims Settlement Act (1971), Greenland Home Rule (1979), and the first indigenous territory of Nunavut, (1999) are prime examples of these efforts. These successes prove that indigenous peoples can gain rights to land and resources and serve as examples of indigenous sustainability in other Arctic and global contexts.

Many good examples of implementing local sustainability are found in the Arctic, most especially, comanagement, a mode of resource management that draws on both indigenous knowledge and Western science (Caulfield 2000:486). Arctic communities use indigenous knowledge to guide the management of, and long-term planning for, subsistence resources (Nuttall 1998:23). Arctic comanagement is sustainable because it is tailored to local contexts and actors—a case in point is the Little Red River Cree Nation, who in collaboration with social scientists assessed their situation to develop a system of adaptive community-based management that is responsive to the values, expectations, and changing needs of community members (Natcher and Hickey 2002:353–354).

Other projects in the circumpolar north analyze contemporary indigenous practices to gauge long-term economic, ecological, and cultural sustainability (e.g., Anderson and Poppel 2002).

Many focus on empowering local resource users and integrating indigenous knowledge. One of them, the Sustainability of Arctic Communities Project, has as one of its objectives to define sustainability in local cultural contexts. Project researchers analyzed local indigenous literature to decipher five elements of sustainability common to the project's four communities that focus on building locally based economies, community infrastructures, and healthy lifestyles (Kofinas and Braund 1996).

Circumpolar cooperation has facilitated the localization of sustainability in the Arctic. The Arctic 8 share common problems and have found ways to translate those shared concerns into ideas of sustainability. The greatest challenge for the Arctic Council, the governance body of circumpolar cooperation, is to link new developments in international Arctic cooperation within the overarching global framework of sustainable development. Recommendations to these ends include subsistence preference, comanagement, and the development of environmentally appropriate technologies and practices (Nuttall 1998:44).

Comparative analysis between northern Russia's environmental and socioeconomic plight and that of other circumpolar cases has been ongoing for at least a decade (Chance and Andreeva 1995).[4] A survey of the progress in self-government and the degree of autonomy and self-determination among indigenous peoples of the Arctic reveals that the indigenous peoples of Russia are severely behind. In contrast with circumpolar counterparts, Russia's indigenous peoples lack land claims and resource rights, and the political experience necessary to secure them. Many also lack strong leadership with vision and aspiration to cultivate the mindset of self-determination and self-government. This contrast is largely a result of history, most profoundly the effects of collectivization and Sovietization, as Bruce Grant termed it so succinctly, the last century of *perestroika*s (1995:xiii).

In part the explanation of the difference between northern Russia's indigenous peoples' plight and other circumpolar areas is linked to the country's economic legacy. Russia bears a double curse. For one it is resource cursed, or one of several resource-abundant developing countries that have consistently underperformed resource-deficient developing countries in the

last decades (Auty 2001:3). In the resource curse model, a resource dependent state will not control its most important sectors
of the economy (diamonds, oil, and gas in the Sakha Republic).
However, these sectors dominate the state economy and thereby
hinder the development of other sectors, a phenomenon referred
to as resource-led development. At the same time, the dependence on one commodity leaves the economy highly vulnerable
to global markets and economic disorders. Russia's resource curse
is directly tied to its second disabling factor, the Siberian curse.
Here we are referring to the post-Soviet reality of a seventy-year
centrally planned Soviet economy that was not planned on freedom of the market but rather on Engel's "Freedom of Space."
The confining elements include: 1) the persistence of nonmarket
distribution, across the Siberian territory, of labor and capital; 2)
the strategic location of Siberian industries, first to allow Gulag
prisoners to conquer and industrialize Siberia's vast territory and
later to entice new workers via high wages and other amenities
to Siberia to fulfill the communist plan; and 3) the poor transportation and communication links that serve to stifle efforts for
the development of market or for interregional trade (Hill and
Gaddy 2003:1–3).

Indigenous Sustainability in the Russian North

Russia's indigenous peoples, like their counterparts worldwide,
desire control over their lives, economies, and local resources,
and hope for their children's sustainable future and for that of
the coming generations. Post-Soviet Russia's indigenous communities struggle daily with the reality of failing political, economic, ecological, and social systems. This is further complicated
by both 1) the Soviet legacy that undermined local ecological
knowledge, kinship settlement patterns, land and resource rights,
and healthy natural ecosystems, and 2) the contemporary effects
of globalization and modernity. In addition, northern Russia is
known as a place where the government largely ignores the interests and needs of local indigenous populations when devis-
ing natural resource management strategies, the effects of which

further exacerbate a loss of exclusive rights in historically based economic spheres (Langlais 1999:65).

The ongoing challenge of post-Soviet survival is adapting to rapid socioeconomic change. Approaches to resolve in the last decade among inhabitants of the twenty-six post-Soviet countries have been diverse. Case studies verify the need to "understand the perspective of ordinary people in the region, to look at the survival strategies and how people are coping in their new situations, the people who were supposed to be the empowered citizens of post-communist societies, but who have more often come to perceive themselves as victims" (Hann 1997).

The existing efforts to investigate indigenous sustainability in the Russian north (Klokov and Jernsletten 2002; Pika 1999; Krupnik 1993) have no aspect of working within local communities specifically to define sustainability. Local investigation is a crucial step and directly linked to the preserving of a given culture's social, human, and natural capital that redeem it a sustainable system and to discard unsustainable modes to make way for innovation. Working with communities, discussing what they need for sustainable futures, should reveal which aspects of contemporary life work (should persist) and which do not (should be discarded). Additionally, the process should clarify what hurdles exist to achieving local definitions.

For northern Russia's indigenous peoples local contexts and conditions are shaped by a colonial legacy, beginning in the seventeenth century by the Russian imperial government (Forsyth 1992).[5] In the process, indigenous self-determination was compromised by the introduction of new diseases, the demands of fur tribute payment, and the coveting and encroachment of native lands (Forsyth 1992; Wolf 1982:158–194). However it was the Soviet period that brought the most profound changes. Collectivization preempted a dependence on indigenous subsistence production, communal resource distribution, and clan-based land tenure and settlement patterns. Sovietization undermined indigenous culture, language, and spirituality. The socialist system created dependence on a central state that provided guaranteed employment, free education and health care, extensive social services, and access to consumer goods.

After three generations had adapted to the Soviet system, it ended in 1991. Over a decade later, most indigenous peoples are relying on some form of pre-Soviet subsistence for day-to-day survival. Research analyzing post-Soviet indigenous survival shows that native inhabitants of Russia have adapted to the conditions of the transition by reinstating some level of pre-Soviet subsistence strategies (Crate 2003a, 2003b; Crate and Nuttall 2004; Fondahl 1998; Golovnev and Osherenko 1999; Humphrey 1998; Kerttula 2000; Ziker 2002). For most it is a struggle, since local resources are not evenly distributed and cases of elite confiscation abound. Our sustainable communities research shows that Viliui Sakha are not lacking for creative ideas on how to build sustainable futures for their communities and future generations. The challenge is realizing those ideas. Post-Soviet indigenous peoples have similar needs as their global counterparts but they also face many barriers. They lack the land and resource rights to instate local management and use, the politically experienced leaders needed to bring about native self-government, and the common mindset of self-determination to bring about change.

The past century of Sovietization and dependence on the state has left an indelible mark. Take, for example, the issue of local leadership. In the Soviet period each village had a head of administration whose job it was to run the village for the central government. Toward the end of the Soviet period many of these leaders assumed a less than honest work ethic, and the general tendency was to allocate most of the available local resources from the state farm and other village coffers when the Soviet Union fell. Call them mafia or not, village leaders in the early post-Soviet context are characterized as self-interested and corrupt, misallocating much-needed state funding, intended for local social services and taking advantage of village human resources to their own advance (Crate 2003b). In the contemporary context of a growing understanding and appreciations for the basic tenants of democracy, inhabitants increasingly call their village heads on their abuses and demand fairer strategies. In this context, we could argue that inhabitants' desire for a strong leader to guide them in common goals and the realization of local sustainable economies as the formative stages of native self-government.

Even if locals gain access to subsistence resources, in many cases there has been a significant loss of pre-Soviet subsistence knowledge coupled by a dependence on Western mass media and consumer lifestyles that complicates a return to the land.

Geography plays both a negative and positive role in post-Soviet indigenous survival. Collectivization transformed indigenous survival and settlement patterns from subsistence-based and extensive across the landscape to production-based and consolidated around a central state farm operation. Private ownership was replaced first with collective then state ownership. Farm operations supplied foodstuffs for adjacent industrial complexes that generated a variety of environmental casualties to local ecosystems. Landscapes remain decidedly Soviet, characterized by centralized settlements, and environmental degradation persists. Inhabitants are unemployed and lack access to consumer goods, health care, and other social services. Geographic isolation, although never allowing for complete immunity to Soviet influence, did serve to facilitate a partial retention of kinship bases, spirituality, and indigenous ecological knowledge, all key elements of post-Soviet survival.

Contemporary cases studies of post-Soviet indigenous peoples conclude with a futuristic chapter portraying indigenous peoples as resilient survivors who, based on the retention of pre-Soviet survival mechanisms including dependence on kin-clan social systems, communal land tenure, and sharing, reemerge as the victors in the post-Soviet context. In Caroline Humphrey's final chapter, "Rural Culture and Visions of the Future," she describes Buriat pastoralists as survivors of the transition, not because of their adherence to Soviet blueprints but through their collective enterprises fueled by a sustainability that combines a locally retained pre-Soviet reliance on clan-based economies with ideas from globalized management-speak (1998:482). John Ziker's final chapter, "The Future Is in Their Hands," explains how the hunting and fishing Dolgan and Nganasan of the Taimyr Peninsula have revived their reliance on family-clan groupings, obliged sharing, and cooperation through informal and nonmarket relations to make up for the void left after the pullout of Soviet social and economic infrastructure (2002:151). Andrei Golovnev and Gail Osherenko's concluding chapter, "Cultural Survival in the Twenty-First Century," details the resilient characteristics of Nenets culture including extensive traditional knowledge systems, self- and mutual-reliance on reindeer that provide most of their food, materials, and transport, and a nonconsumer ethic that defers a need for material possessions, as key to survival through the transition (1999:140–143).

Similarly, research analyzing the post-Soviet adaptive strategies of Viliui Sakha agropastoralists finds the reemergence of pre-Soviet life ways as central, including household and inter-household kin-based food production, a retrieval of clan-based horse and cattle breeding methods and a revival of indigenous resource management (Crate 2003a). Although the cases conclude with a message of hope for the future based on resilient indigenous life ways, many of these same communities continue to struggle with issues of unemployment, a lack of cash resources, rampant alcoholism and drug abuse, poor schools and medical care, a native youth largely interested in modernity and Western culture, and pervasive environmental contamination of local subsistence resources. Clearly there is a need for analysis of the larger issues pertaining to environmental and social equity, indigenous rights, and local governance.

Even though there remain many hurdles for Russia's indigenous peoples in building sustainable communities, there are optimists. Some researchers working with Russia's indigenous peoples argue that although "the aboriginal self-determination movement and the democratic legal space in contemporary Russia has not yet matured to the point when historical claims to territory might be transferred into property rights, material compensation and ultimately self-determination arrangements, it is an inevitable trajectory, as precedents and native rights movements cross international boundaries" (Thompson 2003:22). Hope comes from continued collaboration with circumpolar researchers and communities that facilitates the influx of ideas and models of success from other arctic regions.

Organizations concerned with environmental redressing and cultural survival for Russia's indigenous peoples do exist. These groups, many of which are indigenous, are versed in citizen activism including issues of environmental justice, through their contact and collaboration with adjacent northern countries (NRC 2001). They have developed declarations that accuse the Russian government of discrimination and even genocide based on the contemporary conditions, under which they are forced to live (Kohler and Wessendorf 2002).

As discussed in chapter 5, there have been marginal indigenous victories through the work of RAIPON. Much of RAIPON's success is due to international collaborations, most prominently via its permanent membership of the Arctic Council[6] and special status in the United Nations Economic and Social Council (ECOSOC). It has also improved its political and executive structure primarily through funding from international projects (Kohler and Wessendorf 2002:26). RAIPON is nonetheless limited in its scope and Russia's indigenous peoples' plight worsens as President Putin focuses his country's economic policies on natural resource exploitation (Peterson 2001). The sacrificed health of native rural populations is regarded as one price to pay for economic advance.

Additional hope for facilitating local ideas and desires for sustainability in Russia's communities comes in the potential outcomes of intergovernmental action between Russia and its circumpolar neighbors via the Arctic Council.[7] Russia assumed the two-year chairmanship of the council in November 2004. This gave the country an unprecedented opportunity to build on Gorbachev's legacy and emerge as a leader in circumpolar cooperation,[8] by moving that agenda to new levels and dealing constructively with the increased pressures, challenges, and opportunities related to globalization, economic development, and environmental change in the north.

One example is Russia's lead in formulating the Arctic Council's Sustainable Development Action Plan (SDAP) under the auspices of the Sustainable Development Working Group (SDWG). The plan presents real opportunities for decisive implementation of concrete sustainable development initiatives that will greatly improve the living conditions and economies of people throughout the Arctic. The preliminary work to develop an Arctic Sustainable Development Strategy (ASDS), clarifying four groups of issues, highlights the distinct local issues that need to be addressed across northern areas, including: 1) managing human uses of the Arctic's living resources, 2) controlling the impacts of industrial activities in the Arctic, 3) enhancing community viability in the Arctic, and 4) protecting the Arctic from exogenous pressures (Young 1998).[9]

Expectations are high that the Arctic Council will act seriously on the policy recommendations resulting from the Arctic Climate Impact Assessment (ACIA), including filling the large gaps in knowledge about the impacts of climate change in the Russian north, especially within the context of rapid social, cultural, and economic change (Crate and Nuttall 2004). Other significant initiatives with important development policy implications, such as an assessment of potential impacts of oil and gas activities in the Arctic (a report that will build on and expand the AMAP assessment completed in 1997), will be developed during Russia's chairmanship. The Arctic Council also gives Russia the opportunity to make a substantial contribution to the forthcoming Fourth International Polar Year (IPY4) in 2007/08, and Russia's leadership will be crucial in determining how this contribution can be defined and implemented.

Key to all these opportunities is the active and critical involvement of international and circumpolar indigenous groups, research initiatives, and governmental bodies to facilitate the flow of ideas, experiences, and examples of indigenous movements to cross international boundaries (Crate and Nuttall 2004). With such active international collaboration and Russia's chair of the Arctic Council, there is great potential that sustainability will become more and more of a reality for Russia's indigenous peoples. Central to these efforts is the implementation of sustainability criteria that are flexible and adaptable to given local contexts.

The Dialogue of Sustainability

The ultimate goal of this ethnography is to participate in the dialogue of global sustainability. Contemporary efforts for indigenous sustainability are not limited to documenting and maintaining the status quo of resilient cultures. The power in contemporary efforts toward sustainability is in the dialogue it generates and substantiates between indigenous and industrial societies. For indigenous peoples, sustainability goes beyond mainstream sustainability parameters of protecting resources for future generations' use to include the ownership and stewarding of those resources via self-government, land tenure and rights, comanagement, and self-determination. For industrial societies, sustainability goes beyond developing the proper technology to accommodate an increase in consumption for more and more people to include a relearning of small-scale community engagement, environmental stewardship, social equity, and local knowledge.

The twenty-first-century practices of Western societies, characterized by increasing consumption of nonrenewable resources, are unsustainable. Perhaps if we, of Western society, renew our essential sociocultural and human-environment relationships, we can creatively avoid continuing on what appears to be a road to destruction. One way to achieve this is to recognize the intrinsic value of partnering between indigenous peoples and Western-science populations and to initiate such partnerships to build a sustainable global future. We have much to learn and gain from each other and the time is ripe for active dialogue. This book is written to provide one of many resources for that dialogue.

Notes

1. Self-determination is having the ability and right to live a particular way of life, to use your own language, to practice a particular culture or religion, and to determine your own future course of economic development.

2. The Russian interpretation of sustainable development is linked to spiritual and cultural needs, suggesting that 1) official Russian interpretations of sustainable development could be inclusive of indigenous views of human-environment interactions, and 2) that such an expansion of the largely economic-based paradigm of sustainable development could inform the international discourse (Oldfield and Shaw 2002:396).

3. This discussion dovetails with the concept of sustainable livelihoods:

> A livelihood comprises the capabilities, assets (including both material and social resources) and activities required for a means of living. A livelihood is sustainable when it can cope with and recover from stresses and shocks, maintain or enhance its capabilities and assets, while not undermining the natural resource base. (Scoones, 1998:5)

4. Recommendations include collaboration in joint projects, the involvement of indigenous representatives in local development projects, the resolution of environmental problems through social change, the internalization of "externalities" to reflect the true cost of development, the conversion of environmental impact assessment processes to encompass holistic approaches, and the reorganization of the political economy to reflect more egalitarian forms of social development.

5. There were earlier cases, like the attempt in 1383 by the monk Stefan Khrap, to convert the Komi (Forsyth 1992:5).

6. Since the late 1980s, the eight circumpolar countries—Norway, Sweden, Finland, Iceland, Denmark/Greenland, Russia, Canada, and the United States—have entered into cooperation on many levels to address their common problems, including issues related to globalization and the increasing pressure on northern resources; environmental impacts on the sensitive arctic ecosystem and global change; indigenous rights to lands, resources, and a healthy environment; and building locally sustainable economies (Nuttall and Callaghan 2000). The Arctic Council is an intergovernmental forum tasked to facilitate circumpolar cooperation. Six organizations, representing pan-arctic indigenous peoples, are permanent members on the council. Issues dealing with the lives and livelihoods of arctic residents are high on the Arctic Council's agenda, in contrast to the overt emphasis on the environment and wildlife conservation in the early days of arctic cooperation in the 1990s. The Arctic Human Development Report (AHDR) has been identified as one effort offering possibilities for further cooperation. Together with Arctic Climate Impact Assessment (ACIA), the AHDR is illustrative of the kinds of Arctic Council projects that are establishing baselines for the knowledge needed for the purposes of defining more specific projects in social and economic development.

7. Other initiatives to assist Russia include: Resolution No. 564 of the Government of the Russian Federation (27 July, 2001) that establishes a Federal Target Program on the Economic and Social Development of the Small Indigenous Peoples of the North up to the Year 2011; the European Commission's Second Northern Dimension Action Plan

(SNDAP), which emphasizes the need to pay particular attention to Russia, and the future of the Russian north; the Arctic Council Action Plan to Eliminate Pollution in the Arctic (ACAP), established as a follow-up to the Arctic Monitoring and Assessment Programme (AMAP) to address identified sources of pollution, and which is sponsoring several projects directed toward Russia; and research priorities from results of the Arctic Climate Impact Assessment (ACIA).

8. Although cooperation between the Arctic 8 had been evolving since the mid-twentieth century, many credit Mikhail Gorbachev's 1987 Murmansk speech, when he declared the north a "Zone of Peace," to have been the critical moment that brought circumpolar cooperation into full force.

9. The preliminary work to develop an Arctic Sustainable Development Strategy (ASDS), clarifying four groups of issues, highlights the distinct regional issues that need to be addressed across northern areas, including: 1) managing human uses of the Arctic's living resources, 2) controlling the impacts of industrial activities in the Arctic, 3) enhancing community viability in the Arctic, and 4) protecting the Arctic from exogenous pressures (Young 1998).

Glossary

Note: Russian words are indicated with "R."; all other words are Sakha.

aaghar balaghan reading house
Aan Alakhchyn the deity of spring and fertility
abaahy evil spirits
achchyk jyl starvation year
agha uuha patrilineal clan
aiyy gods
Aiyyhyt the goddess of childbirth
alaas a round field bordered by woods, usually with a lake in the
    center
aladye R., pancakes
algys sung prayer
allaraa lower
Allaraa Doidu the lower world
ampaar outbuilding
artel' R., collective work brigade

baachchy fur-lined vests and pants, both with removable linings
Baianai spirit keeper of the taiga, forest, all wild animals, and of
    the hunt
balaghan winter house
balbaakh manure

baliksit fisher
bania R., bathhouse
bipak fermented cow's milk
bitovoi R., literally "everyday necessities," and the term used to refer to village or town industries that manufactured needed clothing and other goods.
BKh abbreviation of *Bahanai Khazaitsvo* or peasant farming cooperatives
bohuuke ice cream
bugul a small, waist-high haystack
buluus a deep storage area nearing the permafrost where foodstuffs remain frozen
bykvar' R., language primer

chabychakh shallow, wide, birch containers that Sakha could skim cream off of daily
cha-kan bow trap
choron wooden chalices

dal corral
dargha an open area
dekulakization R., the liquidation of wealthy land and/or resource holders
desiatina R., a unit of area approximately equal to 2 3/4 acres
dokladi R., papers
dungur shaman drum
dyrahaangka aspic

ebe grandmother
ehe grandfather
Eiekhsit the cow deity
ejiiy older sister, used also for older cousins and aunts

funt R., a weight measure, one *funt* equals 1 pound sterling

glasnost R., opening
gramota R., certificates of achievement

GUP R., abbreviation of *Gosudarstvennye Unitarnye Predpriiatiye* or state-subsidized agricultural enterprises

iasak R., fur tribute
ichchi spirits
ilim standing net
inorodnoia glava R., administrative center
inorodtsy R., "people of another stock"
intelligentsia R., intellectuals
iye uuha matrilineal clan

Jaajay Baraan Khotun the earth spirit
Juhugey god of horses
Jyl Oghuha Bull of Winter

keghe cuckoo
kehii a house gift
kelii a hand mill made from a vertically hollowed-out log in which materials are pounded with a club
ketekh private
khahaa stable
khaiakh made in the same manner as butter but with added soured cream
khallaan upper (or sky)
khamyyakh shallow wooden spoon
khara oiuun black shaman
khontyora main offices
khoton cow barn
khoton urde an old *khoton* of which only roof and corner posts are still standing
kniaz R., prince
kniazhna (R., princess)
komsomols R., the youth party affiliate of the Communist Party
komuluok an open fire pit in the center of the room
kopeika R., kopek, a Russian money form, 100 kopek equals one ruble
korenizatsiia R., nativization

kulak R., of the wealthy class

kultovoi R., a license permitting taking of wild animals for immediate use when working in the woods and fields

kuluhun kune literally "sweat day" and referring to a day of work

kuoregei meadowlark

kurchuk whipped cream, sometimes with berries added for flavor

kurum brideprice

kuyuur a long wooden pole with a basket shape catch at the end

kwobakh aialakha arrow trap for rabbits

KX R., abbreviation of *kollektivni khazaistvo* or collective farm

kyhynny jiye winter house

kymys fermented mare's milk

Lik-Bez R., liquidation of illiteracy programs

malyi predpriiaimatel' R., small proprietor

MMK R., abbreviation of *Molochnyi-Miasnoi Kombinat* or the Meat and Milk Complex

mooytoruk a hoop of several dozen squirrel tails looped several times around the neck

MTC R., abbreviation of *Mashinno-Traktornaia Stantsiia* or Machine and Tractor Station

mungkha large sweep net

Narkomnat R., People's Commissariat of Nationalities

nasleg R., district or county

norma R., quota

n'urguhunnar snow drops

obshchina R., communal kin-based grouping

ohuokhai Sakhas' circle dance fueled by improvisatory master singing

oibon a water hole cut in lake or river ice

oiuun shaman

Olonkho Sakhas' epic poem

Ordena Lenina R., Lenin Medal

orto middle
Orto Doidu the middle world
Osobaia Okhraniaemaia Territoriia R., Area of Special Preserve
  Status
oton cowberries

pai R., shares
perestroika R., restructuring
pochyetnaya doska R., respected worker board
pud R., one *pud* is equal to 16 kilograms (35 pounds)
pushnaia baza R., fur stores

Raisovet R., the District Soviet

saar-yagas a huge ceremonial birch bark container
Sakha Omuk Sakha People
salama a sacrificial gift to honor the sky deity-protectors and that
  serves as their pathway from the sky into the *khoton*
samostrel R., self-firing crossbow
saylyyk summer home
sayynny jiye summer house
sblizhenie R., rapprochement
Selpo R., abbreviation for "village distribution center"
sergei horse-hitching post
sibiinne uiata pig house
Sier Twom Sakhas' ancient belief system, based on respect for nature and fellow humans, and on love and stewardship of birthland
sirgha a wooden trailer, holding approximately 2 tons
sir tungetige division of land
sliianie R., merging
sobo crucian carp, the predominant lake fish
sokh-so trap
sorat yogurt
stogovoz R., a large skid for a haystack
suugey crème fraîche
SX R., abbreviation of *Sovkhos* or State Farm
sylgyhyts horse watchers

sylgylyyr yrgha a big open pasture where mares are gathered to milk

sylyhar burbot or *Lota lota*

taar fermented milk mash

taar ampaar a specialized building for milk products

taar kaahi fermented milk mash gruel

talaakh willow

tammakh literally "water drop," a forked branch packed solid with snow and hung by the *komuluok* with the melt water dripping into a birch-bark pan below

tammakhtar droplets

tetricheskiie knigi R., church records

toion elite clan head

TOO R., abbreviation of *Tovarishchestvo s ogranichennoi otvetstvennost'iu* meaning Limited Liability Company

TTP R., abbrev. for *Territorii Traditzionnoe Prirodapolzovanie* or Territory of Traditional Nature Use

tupte horse dung burned to ward off insects

uhaat wooden barrel

ulus region

Uluu Tunakh Saghana time of summer milk abundance

uraha an open, airy, birch bark teepee, resembling the year-round dwelling of local Tungus

uraha turda place where an *uraha* stands

urung as white or milk foods

Urung Ayii Toion Great Lord Master and highest god of Sakhas' sky pantheon

urung oiuun white shaman

ustoichivoe razvitie R., how "sustainable development" is translated into Russian, but translates back to English as "stable development"

volost'i R., district

wohakh first, colostrum-rich milk

wot ichchite spirit of the fire

yejegei curds
yhyakh Sakhas' annual summer *kymys* festival
Yraas Olokh Clean Life
ytyk sacred
Ytyk Dabaty sacred ceremony in which a herd of horses is chased
    away

zaiavleniye R., declaration

References

Abele, F. 1997. Traditional Ecological Knowledge in Practice. *Arctic* 50(4): iii–iv.

Abrash, A. 2002. Development Aggression: Observations on Human Rights Conditions in the PT Freeport Contract of Work Areas with Recommendations. Report for the Robert F. Kennedy Memorial Center for Human Rights, Washington, DC.

AHDR. 2004. *Arctic Human Development Report*. Akureyri, Iceland: Stefansson Arctic Institute.

Alekseev, N. A. 1975. *Traditzionnie Religioznie Verovanie Yakutov v XIX–nachalye XX v* [Traditional Religious Belief of the Yakut from the 19th to the Beginning of the 20th Century]. Novosibirsk: Nauka.

———, et al., eds. 1995. *Predaniie, Legendi I Mifi Sakha* [Traditions, Legends, and Myths of the Sakha]. Novosibirk: Nauka.

Alekseev, V. G. 1997. Personal interview. Yakutsk.

———. 2003. Personal interview. Yakutsk.

Anderson, D. G. 2000. *Identity and Ecology in Arctic Siberia: The Number One Reindeer Brigade*. Oxford: Oxford University Press.

———. 2002. Entitlements, Identity, and Time: Addressing Aboriginal Rights and Nature Protection in Siberia's New Resource Colonies. In *People and the Land*, ed. E. Kasten, 99–123. Berlin: Dietrich Reimer Verlag.

Andreev, B. N. 1974. *Ptitsy Viliuiskovo Basseina* [Birds of the Viliui Basin]. Yakutsk: Yakutskoe Knizhnoe Izdatel'stvo.

———. 1987. *Ptitsy Viliuiskovo Basseina* [Birds of the Viliui Basin]. Yakutsk: Yakutskoe Knizhnoe Izdatel'stvo.

Andreev, V. 1997. Personal correspondence. Yakutsk.

Argunova-Low, T. 2004. Diamonds: Contested Symbol in the Republic of Sakha (Yakutia). In *Properties of Culture-Culture as Property: Pathways to Reform in Post-Soviet Siberia*, ed. E. Kasten, 257–265. Berlin: Dietrich Reimer Verlag.

Auty, R., ed. 2001. *Resource Abundance and Economic Development*. Oxford: Oxford University Press.

Auty R., and R. Mikesell. 1998. *Sustainable Development in Mineral Economies*. Oxford: Clarendon.

Ballard, C., and G. Banks. 2003. Resource Wars: The Anthropology of Mining. *Annual Review of Anthropology* 32:287–313.

Balzer, M. M., and U. Vinokurova. 1996. Nationalism, Interethnic Relations, and Federalism: The Case of the Sakha Republic. *Europe-Asia Studies* 48(1): 101–120.

Banks, G., and C. Ballard, eds. 1997. *The Ok Tedi Settlement: Issues, Outcomes, and Implications*. Canberra: Australian National University.

Barnosky, A. D., et al. 2004. Assessing the Causes of the Late Pleistocene Extinctions on the Continents. *Science* 306(5693): 70–75.

Basharin, G. P. 1956. *Istorrii Agrarnikh Otnoshenii v Iakutii* [The Agrarian History of Yakutia]. Moscow: Akademiia Nauk.

———. 1989. *Istoriia Zemledeliia v Yakutiia 17c.–1917* [History of Agriculture in Yakutia: Seventeenth Century through 1917]. Vol. 1. Yakutsk: Yakutskoe Knizhnoe Izdatel'stvo.

———. 1990. *Istoriia Zemledeliia v Yakutiia 17c.–1917* [History of Agriculture in Yakutia: Seventeenth Century through 1917]. Vol. 2. Yakutsk: Yakutskoe Knizhnoe Izdatel'stvo.

Bassin, M. 1991. Inventing Siberia: Visions of the Russian East in the Early Nineteenth Century. *American Historical Review* 96(3): 763–794.

Berkes, F. 1999. *Sacred Ecology: Traditional Ecological Knowledge and Resource Management*. Philadelphia: Taylor and Francis.

Berkes, F., J. Colding, and C. Folke. 2003. Introduction. In *Navigating Social-Ecological Systems*, ed. F. Berkes, J. Colding, and C. Folke, 1–29. Cambridge: Cambridge University Press.

Berger, T. 1977. *Northern Frontier, Northern Homeland*. Ottawa: Supply and Services Canada.

———. 1999. *A Long and Terrible Shadow*. Seattle: University of Washington Press.

Beteille, A. 1998. The Idea of Indigenous People. *Current Anthropology* 39(2): 187–192.

Bielawski, E. 2003. *Rogue Diamonds: The Rush for Northern Riches on Dene Land*. Vancouver and New York: Douglas & McIntyre.

Bone, R. M. 2003. *The Geography of the Canadian North: Issues and Challenges*. 2nd ed. Oxford and New York: Oxford University Press.

Borgerhoff Mulder, M., and T. M. Caro. 1985. The Use of Quantitative Observational Techniques in Anthropology. *Current Anthropology* 26(3): 323–335.

Borisov, A. A. 1996. The Ulus Organization of the Yakut in the 17th Century. Ph.D. diss., Yakutsk State University.

Brown, M. 2003. *Who Owns Native Culture?* Cambridge, MA: Harvard University Press.

Bryson, R. A., and F. K. Hare, eds. 1974. *World Survey of Climatology*. Vol. 11. New York: Elsevier.

Buckley, C. J. 1995. Back to the Collective: Production and Consumption on a Siberian Collective Farm. In *Rediscovering Russia in Asia: Siberia and the Russian Far East*, S. Kotkin and D. Wolff, eds., 224–229. Armonk: M. E. Sharpe.

Buckley, M. 1989. *Women and Ideology in the Soviet Union*. Ann Arbor: University of Michigan Press.

Burtzev, I. S. 1993. *Iadernoe Zagriaznenie Respublika Sakha: Problema Iadernaia Bezopasnost'i* [Nuclear Contamination of the Sakha Republic: The Problem of Nuclear Safety]. Yakutsk: Poligraf.

Burtzev, I. S., and E. N. Kolodoznikova. 1997. Sovromennaia Radiatsionnaia Obstanovka na Ob'ektakh Avariinykh Podzemnykh Iadernykh Vzryvov [The Contemporary Radiation Conditions at the Objects of Catastrophic Underground Atomic Explosions]. In *Bol' i Tragediia Sedovo Viliuia* [The Suffering and Tragedy of Grey (Ancient) Viliui], ed. N. P. Pavlov and V. M. Afanaseeva, 38–41. Yakutsk: SAPI-Torg-Knigi.

Caulfield, R. 1997. *Greenlanders, Whales, and Whaling: Sustainability and Self-Determination in the Arctic*. Hanover, NH: University of New England Press.

———. 2000. Political Economy of Renewable Resources in the Arctic. In *The Arctic: Environment, People, Policy*, ed. M. Nuttall and T. Callaghan, 485–513. Amsterdam: Harwood Academic Publishers.

Chance, N. A., and E. N. Andreeva, 1995. Sustainability, Equity, and Natural Resource Development in Northwest Siberia and Arctic Alaska. *Human Ecology* 23:217–240.

Chayanov, A. V. 1986 [1925]. *The Theory of Peasant Economy*, ed. D. Thorner, B. Kerblay, and R. E. F. Smith. Madison: University of Wisconsin Press.

Chevallier, R. 1984. Greco-Roman Conception of the North from Pytheas to Tacitus. *Arctic* 37(4): 341–346.

Clark, W. C., and N. M. Dickson. 2003. Sustainability Science: The Emerging Research Program. *PNAS* 100(14): 8059–8061.

Coates, K. 1995. The Rediscovery of the North: Towards a Conceptual Framework for the Study of Northern/Remote Regions. *The Northern Review* no. 12/13 (Summer 1994/Winter 1995):15–43.

Collier, J., and S. Yanagiasko, eds. 1987. *Gender and Kinship: Essays toward a Unified Analysis.* Stanford, CA: Stanford University Press.

Conquest, R. 1986. *The Harvest of Sorrow: Soviet Collectivization and the Terror-Famine.* New York: Oxford University Press.

Constantinov, I. V. 1975. *Yakutia and Her Neighbors in Ancient Times.* Yakutsk.

Coughenour, et al. 1985. Energy Extraction and Use in a Nomadic Pastoral Ecosystem. *Science* 230(4726).

Crate, S. Field Accounts. 1994. 1995. 1996. 1997. 1999. 2000.

———. 1995a. *Kwek Teen* [Green Spirit]. Yakutsk: Bichik.

———. 1995b. Environmental Problems in Sakha, Siberia. *Surviving Together* 13(4): 17–19.

———. 1997. Silent Spring in Siberia: The Plight of the Sakha. *Cultural Survival Quarterly* 20(4): 14–16.

———. 2001. *Cows, Kin, and Capitalism: The Cultural Ecology of Viliui Sakha in the Post-Socialist Era.* Ph.D. diss., University of North Carolina, Chapel Hill.

———. 2002. Viliui Sakha Oral History: The Key to Contemporary Household Survival. *Arctic Anthropology* 39(1).

———. 2003a. Viliui Sakha Post-Soviet Adaptation: A Subarctic Test of Netting's Smallholder Theory. *Human Ecology* 31(4).

———. 2003b. The Great Divide: Contested Issues of Post-Soviet Viliui Sakha Land Use. *Europe-Asia Studies* 55(6): 869–888.

———. 2003c. Co-option in Siberia: The Case of Diamonds and the Vilyuy Sakha. *Polar Geography* 26(4) (2002): 289–307.

———. 2003d. The Legacy of the Viliui Reindeer Herding Complex. *Cultural Survival Quarterly* 27(1): 25–27.

———. 2004. Gendered Nature of Viliui Sakha Post-Soviet Adaptation. In *Post-Soviet Women Encountering Transition*, 127–145. Baltimore, MD: Johns Hopkins University Press.

———. 2006a. *Ohuokhai*: Sakhas' Unique Integration of Social Meaning and Movement. *Journal of American Folklore* 199 (472): 161–183.

———. 2006b. Investigating Local Definitions of Sustainability in the Arctic. Insights from Post-Soviet Sakha Villages. *Arctic* 59(3): 115–131.

Crate, S., and M. Nuttall. 2004. Russia in the Circumpolar North. *Polar Geography* 27(2) (April–June 2003): 85–96.

Cruikshank, J., and T. Argunova. 2000. Reinscribing Meaning: Memory and Indigenous Identity in Sakha Republic (Yakutia). *Arctic Anthropology* 37(1): 96–119.

Crumley, C., ed. 1994. Historical Ecology: Cultural Knowledge and Changing Landscapes. Santa Fe: School of American Research Press.

———. 2001. *New Directions in Anthropology and the Environment: Intersections.* Walnut Creek, CA: Alta Mira Press.

CSA (Central State Archive): 1- Fund 343-I, Op. 1, delo 124.

CSA: 2- Fund 226-i, Op. 8, delo 45 (1877); Op. 14, delo 52-427 (1884–1895); Op. 15, delo 8-631 (1896–1908). "Elgeeiiski Predtechiskoy Tserkvi: Tetricheskiye knigi" [Diaries of the Elgeeii Church].

CSA: 3- Fund 109, Op. 1, delo 13, pp. 17–19. "Zemsji Zasedatel 3 uchastik Viluiskovo okrug: Perepiski o mezhdvorimi podvodak ob otkriti stanzii Suntar-Elgeeii nach. 1906-okonchil 1914" [Land Assessor of the Third Sector of the Viliui Okrug: Notes on discussions about opening the Suntar-Elgeeii station beginning in 1906–ending 1914].

CSA: 4- Fund 343-I, Op. 1, delo 480, 505. "Iakutsk Oblast Statisticheskai Komitet—Suntarski Inorodoy Upravi—Viliuiski Okrug" [Yakutsk Oblast Statistical Committee-Suntar Area—Viliuisk Okrug].

CSA: 5- Fund 66, Op. 1, delo 51. "Inventory of Dry Goods and Supplies, Viliui District Kholbos."

CSA: 6- Fund 1179, Op. 1, delo 19. "Announcements and Notes from I Bordong Land Committee, 1930."

CSA: 7- Fund 151, Op. 1, delo 9. "List of Poor and Middle Class of I Bordong, June 29, 1929."

CSA: 8- Fund 267, Op. 1, delo 11. "Po Iakutizatsii i Korenizatsii Apparata" [About Yakutization and Nativization of the Staff] March 15–December 30, 1931.

Dahl, J., J. Hicks, and P. Jull. 2000. *Nunuvat: Inuit Regain Control of Their Lands and Their Lives.* IWGIA Document No. 102, Copenhagen.

de Castro, F., and D. G. McGrath. 2003. Moving Toward Sustainability in the Local Management of Floodplain Lake Fisheries in the Brazilian Amazon. *Human Organization* 62(2): 123–133.

Denoon, D. 2000. *Getting under the Skin: The Bouganville Copper Agreement and the Creation of the Panguna Mine.* Carlton South: Melbourne University Press.

Diamond, J. 1999. *Guns, Germs, and Steel.* New York: Norton.

Dryzek, J. S. 1997. *The Politics of the Earth: Environmental Discourses.* Oxford: Oxford University Press.

Dugarov, D. S. 1991. *Istoricheski Korni Belovo Shamanstva* [The Historical Roots of White Shamanism]. Moscow: Nauk.

Duval, D., T. Green, and R. Louthean. 1996. *The Mining Revolution.* London: Rosendale Press.

Dylis, N. V. 1961. *Listvennitsa Vostochnoi Sibiri i Dalnego Vostoka* [The Larch of Eastern Siberia and the Far East]. Moscow: Academy of Sciences of the USSR.

Egan, D., and E. Howell, eds. 2001. *The Historical Ecology Handbook.* Washington, DC: Island Press.

Elliot, J. 2002. *An Introduction to Sustainable Development.* London: Routledge.

Engels, F. 1985 [1902]. *The Origin of the Family, Private Property, and the State.* Middlesex, UK: Penguin Books.

Ergis, G. U. 1974. *Ocherki pa Yakutskomy Folklory* [Essays on Yakut Folklore]. Moscow: Science Publishers.

———. 1960. *Istoricheski Predaniye I Rasskazi Yakutov* [Historical Legends and Tales of the Yakut]. Vol. 1. Moscow: Akademiia Nauk.

Escobar, A. 1995. *Encountering Development.* Princeton, NJ: Princeton University Press.

Espiritu, A. A. 2002. The Local Perspective: Interviews with Sakha in the Viliui River Region. *Central Eurasian Studies Review* 1(1): 15–17.

Evans, G., J. Goodman, and N. Lansbury. 2002. *Moving Mountains: Communities Confront Mining and Globalisation.* London and New York: Zed Books.

Evans-Pritchard, E. E. 1940. *The Nuer.* Oxford: Clarendon Press.

"Expedition News." 1895. Vol. 4, p. 35. Irkutsk. Cited in A. I. Gogolev, *The Problem of Sakha Ethnogenesis*, 6. Yakutsk: Sakhapoligrafizdat, 1993.

EIR (Extractive Industries Review). 2003. What Is the EIR? www.eireview.org (accessed May 24, 2006).

Faubion, J. 1996. Kinship Is Dead: Long Live Kinship. *Comparative Studies in Society and History* 38:67–91.

Fedorova, Y. N. 1998. *Nasileniye Yakutii: Proshloye I Nastoyasheye* [The Population of Yakutiya: Before and Now]. Novosibirsk: Nauka.

Filer, C. 1990. The Bouganville Rebellion, the Mining Industry, and the Process of Social Disintegration in Papua New Guinea. *Canberra Anthropology* 13:1–39.

Fitzpatrick, S. 1999. *Everyday Stalinism.* New York: Oxford University Press.

Flawn, P. T. 1966. *Mineral Resources: Geology, Engineering, Economics, Politics, Law.* Chicago: Rand McNally.

Fogerty, J. 2001. Oral History: A Guide to Its Creation and Use. In *The Historical Ecology Handbook*, ed. D. Egan and E. Howell, 101–120. Washington, DC: Island Press.

Fondahl, G. 1998. *Gaining Ground?* Boston: Allyn & Bacon.

———, et al. 2001. Native 'Land Claims,' Russian Style. *The Canadian Geographer* 45(4): 545–561.

Forsyth, J. 1992. *A History of the Peoples of Siberia.* Cambridge: Cambridge University Press.

———. 1989. "The Indigenous Peoples of Siberia in the 20th Century." In *The Development of Siberia*, ed. A. Wood and R. A. French, 72–95. London: MacMillan.

Fox, R. 1983. *Kinship and Marriage.* Cambridge: Cambridge University Press.

Fratkin, E., and R. Mearns. 2003. Sustainability and Pastoral Livelihoods: Lessons from East African Maasai and Mongolia. *Human Organization* 62(2): 112–122.

Fyodorov, V. 2000. Personal interview. Yakutsk.

Garutt, V. E. 1946. Opyt Plasticheskoy Rekonstruktsii Vneshnego oblika Sherstistogo Mamonta [An Attempt at a Reconstruction of the External Appearance of the Wooly Mammoth]. *VLGU* [Herald of Leningrad State University] no. 3:138–140.

Ghazi, P. 2003. Unearthing Controversy at the Ok Tedi Mine. WRI Features: newsroom.wri.org/wrifeatures_text.cfm?ContentID=1895.

Giddens, A. 1990. *The Consequences of Modernity.* Stanford, CA: Stanford University Press.

Glassie, H. 1975. *All Silver and No Brass.* Bloomington: Indiana University Press.

Gogolev, A. I. 1983. *Istoricheskaia Etnografiia Iakutov* [Historical Ethnography of the Sakha]. Yakutsk: Sakhapoligrafizdat.

———. 1986. *Istoricheskaia Etnografiia Iakutov: Voprosy Proikhozhdeniia Iakutov* [Historical Ethnography of the Sakha: The Question of Sakha Origins]. Yakutsk: Sakhapoligrafizdat.

———. 1993. *Iakuty: Problemy Etnogeneza i Formirovaniia Kul'tury* [The Yakut: Problems of Ethnogenesis and Cultural Formation]. Yakutsk: Sakhapoligrafizdat.

———. 1994. *Mifologicheskii mir Iakutov: Bozhestva I Dukhi-Pokroviteli* [The Mythological World of the Yakut: Gods and Spirit-Protectors]. Yakutsk: Tsentr Kultury I Iskusstva.

Golovnev, A., and G. Osherenko. 1999. *Siberian Survival: The Nenets and Their Story.* Ithaca, NY: Cornell University Press.

Goody, J. 1990. *The Oriental, the Ancient, and the Primitive: Systems of Marriage and the Family in the Pre-Industrial Societies of Asia*. New York: Cambridge University Press.

GosKomStat: 1- Sakha Republic, 1998. "Vosrastno-Polovoi Sostav Naseleniye po Ulusam Respublika Sakha" [Age and Gender of the Populations by Ulus in the Sakha Republic].

Graham, B. 1997. *Canada and the Circumpolar World: Meeting the Challenges of Co-operation into the Twenty-first Century*. Report of the House of Commons Standing Committee on Foreign Affairs and International Trade.

Grant, B. 1995. *In the Soviet House of Culture: A Century of Perestroikas*. Princeton, NJ: Princeton University Press.

Gray, P. A. 2001. The Obshchina in Chukotka: Land, Property, and Local Autonomy. Working Paper #29. Halle: Max Planck Institute for Social Anthropology Papers.

Gunderson, L. H., and C. S. Holling. 2002. *Panarchy: Understanding Transformations in Human and Natural Systems*. Washington, DC: Island Press.

Habeck, J. 2003. Sustainable Development of the Pechora Region in a Changing Environment and Society. Rovaniemi: University of Lapland. www.ulapland.fi/home/arktinen/spice/spice.htm (accessed May 24, 2006).

Hammond, A. 1998. *Which World? Scenarios for the 21st Century*. Washington, DC: Island Press.

Hann, C. 1997. Foreword. In *Surviving Post-Socialism: Local Strategies and Regional Responses in Eastern Europe and the Former Soviet Union*, ed. S. Bridger and F. Pine. London: Routledge.

———. 2001. Not the Horse We Wanted! The Demise of Cooperative Property in Tazlar. Working Paper #26. Halle: Max Planck Institute for Social Anthropology Papers.

Heinrich, W. 1979. *Vegetation of the Earth*. 2nd ed. New York: Springer-Verlag.

Henry, L. 2002. Thinking Internationally, Acting Locally: The Norm of Sustainable Development and the Russian Environmental Movement. Paper presented for the 2002 AAASS Conference, Pittsburgh, PA.

Hill, F., and C. Gaddy. 2003. *The Siberian Curse: How Communist Planners Left Russia Out in the Cold*. Washington, DC: Brookings Institution Press.

Hindus, M. 1931. *Red Bread*. New York: J. Cape & H. Smith.

Hoffecker, J. F., W. R. Powers, and T. Goebel. 1993. The Colonization of Beringia and the Peopling of the New World. *Science* 259(5091): 46–53.

Humphrey, C. 1998. *Marx Went Away–But Karl Stayed Behind*. Ann Arbor: University of Michigan Press.

Hutchinson, G. 1957. *A Treatise on Limnology*. New York: Wiley.

Hyndman, D. 1994. *Ancestral Rain Forests and the Mountain of Gold: Indigenous Peoples and Mining in New Guinea*. Boulder, CO: Westview Press.

———. 2001. Academic Responsibilities and Representation of the Ok Tedi Crisis in Postcolonial Papua New Guinea. *The Contemporary Pacific* 13(1): 33–54.

IAE (Institute of Applied Ecology). 1992. *Ekologiia Basseina Reki Viliui: Promyshlennoe Zagriaznenie* [The Ecology of the Viliui River: Industrial Pollution]. Yakutsk: Siberian Russian Academy of Sciences.

———. 1993. *Ekologiia Reki Viliui: Sostaianie Prirodnoi Sredy i Zdorovie Naseleniia* [The Ecology of the Viliui River: The Status of the Natural Environment and the Health of the Inhabitants]. Yakutsk: Siberian Russian Academy of Sciences.

Iak-Epar. 1900. "Iakutskiia Eparkhialniia Vedomosti" [Yakutsk Diocese Gazette] #14, June 16, 1900.

Iakovlev, A. 1999, September. Specialist consultation. Suntar.

Ides, I., and A. Brandt. 1967. *Zapiski o Russkom Posoltsve v Kitai 1692–1695* [Notes of the Russian Consulate in China, 1692–1695]. Moscow.

Ignataev, N. 1992, May 10. Personal interview, Viliuisk.

ILLA (Institute of Language and Literature Archive). 1- Fund 4, Op. 1, delo 12. "Opisaniye Yakutskovo Isiakha Gemlinim [Gmelin's Descriptions of Isiakh]."

Ivanov, G. 1995. *Khangalastan Khaannaakhtar* [Legends of the Khangalas People]. Yakutsk: Poligrafist.

Jochelson, W. 1933. The Yakut. *Anthropological Papers of the American Museum of Natural History* 33(2). New York.

Johnson, A., and O. R. Johnson. 1988. Time Allocation among the Machiguenga of Shimaa. In *Cross-Cultural Studies in Time Allocation*, vol. 1, *Human Relations Area Files*, ed. A. Johnson. UCLA, Los Angeles.

Johnston, B. R., ed. 1994. *Who Pays the Price? The Sociocultural Context of Environmental Crisis*. Washington, DC: Island Press.

Jull, P. 2003. The Politics of Sustainable Development: Reconciliation in Indigenous Hinterlands. In *Indigenous Peoples: Resource Management and Global Rights*, ed. S. Jentoft, et al. Delft: Eburon Academic Publishers.

Kerttula, A. 2000. *Antler on the Sea: The Yup'ik and the Chukchi of the Russian Far East*. Ithaca, NY: Cornell University Press.

Kharitinov, N. I. 1996. *Elgeeii Sevodnia* [Elgeeii Today]. Mirnyi.

Kharkiv, A. D., N. N. Zinchuk, and V. M. Zuyev. 1997. *Istoriia Almaza* [The History of Diamonds]. Moscow: Nedra.

Kirsch, S. 1997. Is Ok Tedi a Precedent? Implications of the Lawsuit. In *The Ok Tedi Settlement: Issues, Outcomes, and Implications*, ed. G. Banks and C. Ballard. National Center for Development Studies: Canberra.

———. 2002a. Anthropology and Advocacy: A Case Study of the Campaign against the Ok Tedi Mine. *Critical Anthropology* 22:175–200.

———. 2002b. Litigating the Ok Tedi (Again). *Cultural Survival Quarterly* Fall: 15–19.

Klokov, K. B., and J. L. Jernsletten. 2002. *Sustainable Reindeer Husbandry*. University of Tromso.

Kofinas, G. and S. Braund. 1996. Defining Community Sustainability: A Report from Community Involvement Phase 1 of the NSF Community Sustainability Project. www.taiga.net/sustain/lib/reports/sustainability.html (accessed May 24, 2006).

Kohler, T., and K. Wessendorf, eds. 2002. *Towards a New Millenium: Ten Years of the Indigenous Movement in Russia*. Copenhagen: IWGIA.

Kondakova, P. I. 1997. Personal interview. Mirnyi.

Korotov, G. P. 1967. *Elgeeii Sovkhos* [Elgeeii State Farm]. Yakutsk: Yakutknigoizdat.

Kovacs, K. 1996. The Transition in Hungarian Agriculture: 1990–1993. In *After Socialism: Land Reform and Social Change in Eastern Europe*, ed. R. Abraham. Providence, RI: Berghahn Books.

Krupnik, I. 1993. *Arctic Adaptations*. Hanover: University Press of New England.

Ksenofontov, G. V. 1975. *Elliada*. Moscow.

———. 1992 [1937]. *Uraangkhai Sakhalaar* [Points in Ancient History of the Sakha]. 2nd ed. Vol. 2. Yakutsk: Natsinal'noye Izdatel'stvo.

Kulakovski, A. E. 1979. *Nauchni Trude* [Scientific Works]. Yakutsk: Yakutskoe Knizhnoe Izdatel'stvo.

Kuper, A. 2003. The Return of the Native. *Current Anthropology* 44(3): 389–402.

Langlais, R. 1999. Envisioning a Sustainable Arctic: Nunavut in Contrast to the Russian North. In *Dependency, Autonomy, and Sustainability in the Arctic*, ed. H. Petersen and B. Poppel, 65–78. Aldershot, UK: Ashgate.

Larsen, J. A. 1980. *The Boreal Ecosystem*. New York: Academic Press.

Little, M. A., and P. W. Leslie, eds. 1999. *Turkana Herders of the Dry Savanna: Ecology and Biobehavioral Response of Nomads to an Uncertain Environment*. New York: Oxford University Press.

LOE (*Living on Earth*). 2000. *Living on Earth* interview with Stuart Kirsch, March 10, 2000. www.loe.org/shows/shows.htm?programID=00-P13-00010#feature6 (accessed May 24, 2006).

Lomanov, I. K., ed. 1996. *Resursi Osnovnikh Vidov Okhotnichnikh Zhivotnikh I Okhotnichni Ugodya Rossii* [The Main Hunting Resources and Their Ranges in Russia]. Moscow: TsNIL.

Lovins, H., and W. Link. 2001. *Insurmountable Opportunities? Steps and Barriers to Implementing Sustainable Development.* Comments to the UN Regional Roundtable for Europe and North America, Vail, Colorado. Rocky Mountain Institute and Global Academy.

Lynch, M. 2002. *Mining in World History.* London: Reaktion.

Maak, R. K. 1994. *Viliuiski Okrug* [The Viliui Okrug]. 2nd ed. Moscow: Yana.

Maher, S. 2004. Traplines and Tar Sands: An Ethnographic Analysis of Intersecting Economies in a Subarctic Indigenous Community. *Scott Polar Research Institute.* www.spri.cam.ac.uk/research/projects/traplinestarsands/ (accessed May 24, 2006).

Maksimov, P. S. 1992. *Viliui: Znak Bedi* [Viliui: The Symbol of Poverty]. Yakutsk: Yakutsk Book Publishers.

Marcus, G. 1998. *Ethnography through Thick and Thin.* Princeton, NJ: Princeton University Press.

Marples, R. 1999. Environmental and Health Problems in the Sakha Republic. *Eurasian Geography and Economics* 40(1): 62–77.

Martinov, P. N. 1996. Personal interview. Nyurba.

McCabe, J. T. 2003a. Toward an Anthropological Understanding of Sustainability: A Preface. *Human Organization* 62(2): 91.

———. 2003b. Sustainability and Livelihood Diversification among the Maasai of Northern Tanzania. *Human Organization* 62(2): 100–111.

McGovern, T. 1980. Cows, Harp Seals, and Churchbells: Adaptation and Extinction in Norse Greenland. *Human Ecology* 8(3): 245–275.

Mikesell, R. F. 1987. *The World Mining Industry: Investment Strategy and Public Policy.* Boston: Allen & Unwin.

Miller, F. 1990. *Folklore for Stalin.* Armonk: M.E. Sharpe.

Mines and Communities. Charter. www.minesandcommunities.org/Charter/Charter.htm (accessed May 24, 2006).

———. 2001. The London Declaration. www.minesandcommunities.org/Charter/londondec.htm (accessed May 24, 2006).

———. 2003. Annual report. www.minesandcommunities.org/Charter/annualreport2003.htm (accessed May 24, 2006).

MMSD (Mining, Minerals and Sustainable Development project). 2002. *Breaking New Ground: Mining, Minerals, and Sustainable Development.* London: Earthscan.

Ministry of Ecology. 1997. *Tekhniko-Ekonomicheskoe Obosnovanie Sistemy Ekologicheskovo Monitoringa Viliuiskovo Regiona* [The Technical and Economic Appropriation for the System of Ecological Monitoring for the Viliuisk Regions]. Unpublished governmental document. Yakutsk: Ministry of Ecology.

Moore, D., I. House, and A. Dixon. 1993. Thallium Poisoning. *British Medical Journal* 306(6891): 1527.

Moreno, A.-M., and A. Tegen. 1998. *World Mining Directory.* Surrey, UK: Metal Bull. Books; Stockholm: Raw Mater. Group.

Morgan, L. H. 2000 [1870]. *Ancient Society.* New Brunswick, NJ: Transaction Publishers.

Natcher, D., and C. Hickey. 2002. Putting the Community Back into Community-Based Resource Management: A Criteria and Indicators Approach to Sustainability. *Human Organization* 61(4): 350–363.

Needham, R., ed. 1971. *Rethinking Kinship and Marriage.* London: Tavistock.

Netting, R. McC. 1968. *Hill Farmers of Nigeria: Cultural Ecology of the Kofyar of the Jos Plateau.* Seattle: University of Washington Press.

———. 1981. *Balancing on an Alp: Ecological Change and Continuity in a Swiss Mountain Community.* Cambridge: Cambridge University Press.

———. 1993 *Smallholders, Householders: Farm Families and the Ecology of Intensive, Sustainable Agriculture.* Stanford, CA: Stanford University Press.

Nikolaev, I. (Ukhkhan). 1992. *Sakha Almaaha—Sakha Kharaghin Uuta* [Sakhas' Diamonds—Sakhas' Tears]. *Sakhaada* newspaper, April 22, 1992:9.

Nikolaev, S. I. 1970. *Iakuty: Nauchnyi Otchet* [The Yakut (Sakha): Scientific Accounts]. Yakutsk: Russian Academy of Science, Siberian Department. Fund 5, Op. 1, delo 501.

Nikolov, N., and H. Helmisaari. 1992. Silvics of the Circumpolar Boreal Forest Tree Species. In *A Systems Analysis of the Global Boreal Forest*, ed. Shugart, H. H., R. Leemans, and G. B. Bonan. Cambridge: Cambridge University Press.

Nogovitzin, D. D. 1985. *Vodnye Resursy Iakutii i Ikh Ispol'sovanie* [The Water Resources of Yakutia and Their Use]. Yakutsk: Siberian Russian Academy of Sciences.

NRC (National Research Council). 2001. The Role of Environmental NGOs: Russian Challenges, American Lessons: Proceedings of a Workshop. Washington, DC: National Academy Press.

Nuttall, M. 1992. *Arctic Homeland: Kinship, Community, and Development in Northwest Greenland.* Toronto: University of Toronto Press.

———. 1998. *Protecting the Arctic.* Amsterdam: Harwood Academic Press.

———. 2000. Indigenous Peoples, Self-Determination, and the Arctic Environment. In *The Arctic: Environment, People, Policy,* ed. M. Nuttal and T. V. Callaghan, 377–409. Amsterdam: Harwood Academic Publishers.

———, ed. 2005. *Encyclopedia of the Arctic.* Vol. 1. New York: Routledge.

Nuttall, M., and T. V. Callaghan, eds. 2000. *The Arctic: Environment, People, Policy.* New York: Taylor and Francis.

Okladnikov, A. P. 1955. *Iakutiia do prisyedeniia k russkomy gosudarstvy* [Yakutia Before Its Incorporation into the Russian State]. Moscow.

———. 1970. *Yakutia.* Montreal: McGill-Queens.

———. 1976. *Istoriia I kul'tura Buriatii: sbornik statei* [History and Culture of Buriatia: Collection of Papers]. Ulan-Ude: Buriatskoe knish. izd-vo.

Oldfield, J. D., and D. J. Shaw. 2002. Revisiting Sustainable Development: Russian Cultural and Scientific Traditions and the Concept of Sustainable Development. *Area* 34(4): 391–400.

OMRI (Open Media Research Institute). 1997 (February 12). *Russian Regional Report.* archives.tol.cz/Publications/RRR/Index.html.

O'Reilly, K. 1996. Diamond Mining and the Demise of Environmental Assessment in the North. *Northern Perspectives* 24(1–4). www.carc.org/pubs/v24no1-4/mining.htm (accessed May 24, 2006).

———. 2004. Personal interview, Yellowknife, NWT.

Orr, D. 2004. *The Last Refuge: Patriotism, Politics, and the Environment in an Age of Terror.* Washington, DC: Island Press.

Osherenko, G. 2001. Indigenous Rights in Russia: Is Title to Land Essential for Cultural Survival? *The Georgetown International Environmental Law Review* 13(3): 695–734.

Osherenko, G., and O. Young. 1989. *The Age of the Arctic.* Cambridge: Cambridge University Press. Pakhomov, I. O. 1999. *Economics in the Context of Market Economic.* Yakutsk.

Pakhomov, I. O. 1999. *Upravlenie zemel'nymi otnosheniiami v Iakutii* [Administration of Land Relations in Yakutia]. Yakutsk: Sakhapoligrafizdat.

Pavlov, N. P. 1999. *Direktor* [Director]. Yakutsk: Kunduk.

Pavlov, N. P., and V. M. Afanaseeva, eds. 1997. *Bol' i Tragediia Sedovo Viliuia* [The Suffering and Tragedy of Grey (Ancient) Viliui]. Yakutsk: SAPI-Torg-Knigi.

Pekarski, E. K. 1958 [1899]. Slovar Iakutskovo Iazika [Dictionary of the Sakha Language]. Vol. 1. 2nd ed. Yakutsk: Russian Academy of Science.

Peterson, D. J. 1993. *Troubled Lands: The Legacy of Soviet Environmental Destruction*. Boulder, CO: Westview Press.

———. 2001. The Reorganization of Russia's Environmental Bureaucracy: Implications and Prospects. *Post-Soviet Geography and Economics* 42(1): 65–76.

Petrov, V.T., ed. 1991. *Nurbakaan Ujuordara* [Nurbachaan Ancestors: Old Tales and Legends]. Yakutsk: Akademiia Nauk.

Petrova, V. A. 1997. Personal interview. Nyurba.

Pika, A. I. 1999. *Neotraditionalism in the Russian North: Indigenous Peoples and the Legacy of Perestroika*. Seattle: University of Washington Press.

Pitassio, A., and V. Zaslavsky, eds. 1985. *Soviet Peasants by Lev Timofeev*. New York: Telo Press.

Ponting, C. 1991. *A Green History of the World*. London: Sinclair-Stevenson.

Potter, R. A. 2004. The Fate of Franklin. www.ric.edu/rpotter/ SJFranklin.html (accessed May 24, 2006).

Povinelli, E. 1993. *Labor's Lot*. Chicago: University of Chicago Press.

Prokhorov, A. M., ed. 1980. *Sovyetski Encyclopedicheski Slovar* [Soviet Encyclopedia Dictionary]. Moscow: Soviet Encyclopedia.

Raeff, M. 1956. *Siberia and the Reforms of 1822*. Seattle: University of Washington Press.

Rappaport, R. A. 1967. *Pigs for the Ancestors: Ritual in the Ecology of a New Guinea People*. New Haven, CT: Yale University Press.

Redclift, M. 1987. *Sustainable Development: Exploring the Contradictions*. London and New York: Methuen.

Redclift, M., and G. Woodgate. 1994. Sociology and Environment: Discordant Discourse? In *Social Theory and the Global Environment*, ed. M. Redclift and T. Benton, 51–66. London and New York: Routledge.

Redman, C. L. 1999. *Human Impact on Ancient Environments*. Tucson: University of Arizona Press.

Robbins, P. 2004. *Political Ecology*. Oxford: Blackwell.

Romanov, A. 1997. Personal interview. Nyurba.

Romanova, E. N. 1987. *Yakutski Praznik Isiakh: Traditsii i sovremenost* [The Yakut Holiday Isiakh: Traditions and Modernity]. Ph.D. diss., N. N. Mikhailo-Maklaya Ethnographic Institute, St. Petersburg.

Rutland, P., and N. Kogan. 2000. The Russian Mafia: Between Hype and Reality. In *Contemporary Russian Politics*, ed. A. Brown, 139–147. Oxford: Oxford University Press.

Ruttan, L. M., and M. Borgerhoff Mulder. 1999. Are East African Pastoralists Truly Conservationists? *Current Anthropology* 40(5): 621–652.

Sahlins, M. 1972. *Stone Age Economics*. New York: Aldine de Gruyter.

Schneider, D. 1984. *A Critique of the Study of Kinship*. Ann Arbor: University of Michigan Press.

Schweitzer, P. P., ed. 2000. *Dividends of Kinship: Meaning and Uses of Social Relatedness*. London: Routledge.

Scoones, I. 1998. *Sustainable Rural Livelihoods: A Framework for Analysis*. Sussex, UK: Institute of Development Studies, Working Paper 72.

Sejersen, F. 2002. Local Knowledge, Sustainability, and Visionscapes in Greenland. Eskimologis Skrifter No. 17. Copenhagen: University of Copenhagen.

Seroshevski, V. L. 1993 [1896]. *Yakuti*. Moscow: ROSSPEN.

Seton-Watson, H. 1986. Russian Nationalism in Historical Perspective. In *The Last Empire: Nationality and the Soviet Future*, ed. Robert Conquest, 14–29. Stanford, CA: Hoover Institute Press.

Shadrin, A. P., ed. 1984. *Antropogennoe Vozdeistvie na Vodnye Resursy Iakutii* [Anthropogenic Influences on the Water Resources of Yakutia]. Yakutsk: Siberian Russian Academy of Sciences.

Shaw, D. 1999. *Russia in the Modern World: A New Geography*. Oxford: Blackwell Publishing.

Shnirelman, V. 1999. Introduction: North Eurasia. In *The Cambridge Encyclopedia of Hunters and Gatherers*, ed. R. Blee and R. Dalys, 119–173. Cambridge: Cambridge University Press.

Shugart, H. H., R. Leemans, and G. B. Bonan, eds. 1992. *A Systems Analysis of the Global Boreal Forest*. Cambridge: Cambridge University Press.

Sirina, A. A. 2005. Clan Communities among the Northern Indigenous Peoples of the Sakha (Yakutia) Republic: A Step to Self-Determination? In *Rebuilding Identities: Pathways to Reform in Post-Soviet Siberia*, ed. E. Kasten, 197–216. Berlin: Dietrich Reimer Verlag.

Sivtsev, D. K. 1996 [1947]. *Sakha Fol'klora: Khomyyrynn'yk* [Sakha Folklore Collection]. Novosibirsk: Nauka.

Sleptsov, P. A. 1972. *Sakhalyy-Nuuchchalyy Tyljyt* [Sakha-Russian Dictionary]. Moscow: Soviet Encyclopedia Publishers.

———. 1989. *Sakha Family Traditions and Rituals*. Yakutsk: Yakutsk Scientific Center.

Slezkine, Y. 1991. The Fall of Soviet Ethnography, 1928–38. *Current Anthropology* 32(4): 476–484.

———. 1994. *Arctic Mirrors*. Ithaca, NY: Cornell University Press.

Smillie, Ian. 2002. *Fire and Ice: Benefits, Protection, and Regulation in the Canadian Diamond Industry*. Ottawa: Partnership Africa Canada.

Smith, E. A., and M. Wishnie. 2000. Conservation and Subsistence in Small-Scale Societies. *Annual Review of Anthropology* 29:493–524.

Smith, G. 1990. Nationalities Policy from Lenin to Gorbachev. In *The Nationalities Question in the Soviet Union*, ed. Graham Smith, 1–20. London: Longman.

Sokolov, S. Y. 1977. *Areali Derev'yev i Kustarnikov SSSR* [Trees and Shrubs of the USSR]. Leningrad: Nauka.

Solzhenitsyn, A. 1974. *Letter to the Soviet Leaders*. Translated from the Russian by Hilary Sternberg. New York: Harper & Row.

Soubotin, X. 2002. Building Civil Society through Environmental Advocacy. Paper presented for *Russia's Environment: Problems and Prospects* conference, October 24–26, Miami University, Oxford, Ohio.

Stone, M. P. 2003. Is Sustainability for Development Anthropologists? *Human Organization* 62(2): 93–99.

SRA (Suntar Regional Archive): 2- Fund 43, Op. 1, delo 63. "Annual Bookkeepers' Records, Molotov KX."

SRA: 3- Fund 75, Op. 8, delo 382. "Report on the Consolidation of KXs, Suntar Regional Committee, 1951."

SRA: 4- Fund 1, Op. 1, delo 94. "Material on the Assigning of Administrative Centers, 1951."

SRA: 5- Fund 9, Op. 1, delo 42. "Material of the January 1st, Report, Suntar Region, 1952."

SRA: 6- Fund 1, Op. 1, delo 94. "About the Liquidation of Nasleg Administrative Centers and Consolidations within Suntar Region, 1951–1952."

SRA: 7- Fund 33, Op. 1, delo 1. "Orders and Instructions Concerning Formation of State Farms."

SRA: 8- Fund 33, Op. 1, delo 47. "Annual Account of Elgeeii State Farm's Production for the 1957 Year."

SRA: 9- Fund 33, Op. 1, delo 44. "Confirmation of Plans for the Organization of Workers and Service People. 1957."

SRA: 10- Fund 75, Op. 14, delo 67. "Material about Production Activities of the Elgeeii State Farm, 1957."

SRA: 11- Fund 33, Op. 1, delo 15. "Orders of the State Farm Director about Major Activities, 1960."

SRA: 12- Fund 75, Op. 15, delo 151, 97, 63. "Accounting and Projects of Elgeeii State Farm, 1959, 1960, 1961."

SRA: 13- Fund 75, Op. 18, delo 16. "Announcements, Appeals, and Information of the Suntar Regional Committee, 1969." Pp. 63–65.

SRA: 14- Fund 75, Op. 18, delo 8. "Information and Notes of the Suntar Regional Committee, 1968."

SRA: 15- Fund 33, Op. 1, delo 482. "Orders of the State Farm Director, Order #11: Assignment of a Director for Gasification of the State Farm."

SRA: 16- Fund 33, Op. 1, delo 483. "Decree of the Break-up of the Elgeeii State Farm into Collective Ventures."

SRA: 17- From Introductory Words to the Opis or 'List' of Documents Concerning the History of the Elgeeii State Farm.

Starke, L., ed. 2003. *State of the World: A Worldwatch Institute Report.* New York: Norton.

Stevenson, M. 1996. Indigenous Knowledge in Environmental Assessment. *Arctic* 49(3): 278–291.

Stuart, A. 1991. Mammalian Extinctions in the Late Pleistocene of Northern Eurasia and North America. *Biological Reviews* 66: 453–562.

Suny, R. G. 1993. *The Revenge of the Past.* Stanford, CA: Stanford University Press.

Suslov, S. P. 1961. *Physical Geography of Asiatic Russia.* San Francisco: Freeman.

Taylor, A., et al. 2004. *When the Government Is the Landlord.* The Pembina Institute. www.pembina.org/publications_item.asp?id=171 (accessed May 24, 2006).

Thompson, N. 2003. The Native Settler: Contesting Local Identities of Russia's Resource Frontier. Conference paper for Young Researcher's Conference, Miami University.

Tichotsky, J. 2000. *Russia's Diamond Colony: The Republic of Sakha.* Amsterdam: Harwood Academic Publishers.

Tishkov, V. A., ed. 1994. *Narody Rossii* [Peoples of Russia]. Moscow: Nauchnoye Izdatel'stvo.

Tobonov, A. 1997. Personal interview. Nyurba.

Tokarev, S. A. 1958. *Etnografiia narodov SSSR: istoricheskie osnovy byta i kul'tury* [The Ethnography of the Peoples of the USSR: History, Way of Life, and Culture]. Moscow: Moscow University Publishers.

Tokarev, S. A., and I. S. Gurvich. 1964. The Yakuts. In *The Peoples of Siberia,* ed. M. G. Levin and L. P. Potapov, 241–304. Chicago: University of Chicago Press.

Townsend, P. K. 2000. *Environmental Anthropology: From Pigs to Policies.* Prospect Heights, IL: Waveland Press.

Troshanski, V. F. 1902. *Evolutziia Chorni Veri u Iakutof* [The Evolution of the Yakut Black Belief]. Kazan: Kazan Universitet.

Tsepliaev, V. P. 1965. *The Forests of the U.S.S.R.* Jerusalem: Israel Program for Scientific Programs.

Tugolukov, V. A. 1985. *Tungusy Srednei i Zapadnoi Sibiri* [Tungus of Middle and Western Siberia]. Moscow: Nauka.

United Nations. 1993. Earth Summit Agenda 21: The United Nations Programme of Action from Rio. New York: United Nations Department of Public Information.

Ushnitzkai, P. 1993. *"Mir" truupka kuolaghaiygar kyersuhuuge kelbitter ohuokaidara* [Ohuokhai Singers Meeting in the Mir Pipe]. *Keskil* newspaper, December 12, 1993: 2.

Vasilievich, G. M. 1969. *Evenki* [The Evenk]. Leningrad: Nauka.

Verdery, K. 2002. Fuzzy Property: Rights, Power, and Identity in Transylvania's Decollectivization. In *Postsocialism: Ideals, Ideologies, and Practices in Eurasia*, ed. C. Hann, C. Humphrey, and K. Verdery, 53–81. London: Routledge.

Vinokurova, U. A., et al. 2002. *Kyn Juhugai Ayii* [Sun-Horse God Protector]. Yakutsk: Bichik.

Viola, L. 2000. *The Role of the OGPU in Dekulakization, Mass Deportations, and Special Resettlement in 1930*. Pittsburgh, PA: University of Pittsburgh Press.

Watson, D. 1997. Indigenous Peoples and the Global Economy. *Current History* 96(613): 389–391.

WCED (World Commission on Environment and Development). 1987. *Our Common Future*. Oxford and New York: Oxford University Press.

Weber, J. R., and E. F. Roots. 1990. Discoveries and Explorations of the Circumpolar Lands and Seas from Antiquity to the Twentieth Century. *Canada's Missing Dimension: Science and History in the Canadian Arctic Islands*, Vol. 2, ed. C. R. Harington, 744–767. Ottawa: Canadian Museum of Nature.

Wegren, S. K. 1998. *Agriculture and the State in Soviet and Post-Soviet Russia*. Pittsburgh, PA: University of Pittsburgh Press.

Wenzel, G. 1999. Traditional Ecological Knowledge and Inuit: Reflections of TEK Research Ethics. *Arctic* 52(2): 113–124.

Wilk, R. R. 1999. *Household Ecology: Economic Change and Domestic Life among the Kekchi Maya in Belize*. Dekalb: Northern Illinois University Press.

Wilson, E. 1999. *Conflict or Compromise? Traditional Natural Resource Use and Oil Exploration in Northeastern Sakhalin/Noglikskii District*. Slavic Research Center: Hokkaido University. src-h.slav.hokudai.ac.jp/sakhalin/eng/71/wilson3.html (accessed May 25, 2006).

Wolf, E. 1982. *Europe and the People without History*. Berkeley: University of California Press.

World Bank. 2004. Striking a Better Balance: The Extractive Industries Review. iris36.worldbank.org/domdoc/PRD/Other/PRDDCon tainer.nsf/All+Documents/85256D240074B56385256FF6006820D2/$ File/execsummaryenglish.pdf (accessed May 24, 2006).

———. 2005. World Bank Group Board Agrees Way Forward on Extractive Industries Review. iris36.worldbank.org/domdoc/PRD/ Other/PRDDContainer.nsf/WB_ViewAttachments?ReadForm&ID= 85256D240074B563852570D50055E086& (accessed May 24, 2006).

WRI (World Resources Institute). 2003 *World Resources 2002–2004: Decisions for the Earth*. Washington, DC: WRI.

Wristen, K. 2003. Diamonds and Sustainable Development? Canadian Arctic Resources Committee (CARC) www.carc.org/mining_sustain/ diamonds_arent.php (accessed May 24, 2006).

Yablokov, A. V. 1992. The Recent Environmental Situation in Russia. *Environmental Policy Review* 6(2): 1–12.

Yakovleva, N., and T. Alabaster. 2003. Tri-sector Partnerships for Community Development in Mining: A Case Study of the SAPI Foundation and Target Fund in the Republic of Sakha (Yakutia). *Resources Policy* 29:83–98.

Yegorova, L. 2003. Personal Interview, Yakutsk. Young, O. 1998. Creating an Arctic Sustainable Development Strategy. www.svs.is/OranYoung .htm (accessed May 24, 2006).

Young, O., and G. Osherenko. 1993. *Polar Politics: Creating International Environmental Regimes*. Ithaca, NY: Cornell University Press.

Zhuravlev, S. M. 1967. Along the New Path. In Korotov, G. P. *Elgeeii Sovkhos* [Elgeeii State Farm], 3–21. Yakutsk: Yakutknigoizdat.

Ziker, J. P. 1998. Kinship and Exchange among the Dolgan and Nganasan of Northern Siberia. In *Research in Economic Anthropology*, vol. 19, ed. Barry Isaac, 191–238. Greenwich, CT: JAI Press.

———. 2001. Land Use and Social Change among the Dolgan and Nganasan of Northern Siberia. In *Parks, Property, Power: Managing Hunting Practice and Identity within State Policy Regimes*, ed. D. G. Anderson and K. Ikeya, 47–66. Senri Ethnological Studies No. 59. Osaka: National Museum of Ethnology.

———. 2002. *Peoples of the Tundra: Northern Siberians in the Post-Communist Transition*. Prospect Heights: Waveland Press.

Zikov, I. E. 1978. Major Moments in Sakha Ethnic History According to the Archeological Record. *The North Star* 5:128–132.

Zverov, D. S. 1995. *Aman Us* [Dedications to My Father]. Smolensk: Smolensk Polygraph.

Index

Note: Page numbers in italic type refer to figures or tables.

production under, 67;
specialization under, 75; in
Viliui regions, 66–72; World
War II and, 70
colonization: and indigenous
peoples, 227–28; mining and,
275–77; Russian, 55–60
comanagement, 303
competitions, socialist, 75
containers, for milk and milk
products, 22, 45
cow cultures, 111
cows: aboriginal, 157–58; in belief
system, 24; breeding of, Soviet
program for, 69; care of,
111–21; feeding/watering, 24,
116–17; hay for, 26–27; horses
versus, 24; importance of,
110–11, 264–65; *khoton* for,
117–19; life of, 93; manure
management for, 114–16; milk
of, 24–26; seasonal activities
for, 114–21; sheltering of, 25;
slaughter of, 119–20; time
allocation for, *112*; in villages,
93–94, 111; yards for, *94*, 94;
year-round activities for,
112–14. *See also* cows-and-kin;
horse and cattle husbandry
cows-and-kin, 110–41; as
adaptive, 96; advantages/
disadvantages of, 139–41; case
studies of, 128–35; cows' role
in, 110–21; household
operation and, 136–39;
inter-household dependencies,
122–24, *123*; kin role in, 124–27;
patterns of, 127–28; system of,
121–22; theoretical context of,
135–39
crafts, 22

Cruikshank, Julie, 189
culture, Sakha: medieval central
Asian culture and, 46;
Scythian-Siberian culture and,
46, *47*; southern Siberian
culture and, 46; steppe culture
and, 46
cutting and polishing industries,
243
Cyrillic alphabet, 63, 64

Dahurian larch, 13
Danilov, Aleksey, 57
DeBeers, 233, 244, 247–48
demography,
early-twentieth-century, *59*
Dene, 230, 234–41
Department of Fisheries and
Oceans (DFO), 240
Department of Indian Affairs and
Northern Development
(DIAND), 235–36, 238, 240
development anthropology, 300
Dia Met Mineral, 235
diamond industry:
anti-environmentalism of,
211–12; in Canada, 221–22,
228–49; ecological threat of,
191–93; economic impact of,
191–92, 194, 215; establishment
of, 73–74, 195–99; significance
of, 74, 221; Soviet
industrialization and, 195–99;
sustainability of, 247–48;
symbolism of, 192–93, *193*, 212,
213; workers in, 197, 199
Diavik, 243–46
diet: diamond industry effect on,
74; fish, 27–29; forage, 27–30;
meat, 27; milk and milk
products, 24–26; wild plants, 29

komuluok (open fire pit), 19, 21
Kraton-3 (nuclear explosion), 205
Kristall (nuclear explosion), 205
kulaks, persecution of, 67
kuluhun kune (sweat day), 67, *69*
Kurykan, 49
Kutana, 165
Kuukei, 176–82, *178*
kuyuur (fishing basket), 28–29
kymys (fermented mare's milk), 22
kymys festivals, 48

lakes, 9–11, *10*, 26–27, 52–53, 244
land: ancestral right to, 164; *BKh*s and, 155–64; elders' stories about, 167–87; having, 145–66; households and, 148–54, 163–64; hydroelectric dam effect on, 201; post-Soviet division of, 145–48; redistribution of, 166; Soviet policies on, 145
Langas, F. I., 32
language, 45–46, 63–64
Latin alphabet, 63, 64
leadership, and sustainability, 264, 307
Lena region, 44, 46
Lenin, Vladimir, 60, 63
literacy, 63–66
Little Red River Cree Nation, 303
local knowledge. *See* indigenous knowledge

Maasai, 300
MacKenzie Valley Pipeline Inquiry, 231
mammoths, 5–6
manure management, 114–16, *115*

marriage: customs of, 32–33; gift giving and, 33; polygamy, 32–33
Martinov, Pyoter, 211–12, 215, 232
"Mat' Viliui" (Mother of the Viliui), 74
Maun, Alex, 236
meat: consumption of, 27; storage of, 25, 94–95
Metis, 230, 234
Midwest, American, 111
milk: characteristics of Sakha, 24–25; containers for, 22; storage and use of, 25–26; subsidies for home production of, 265. *See also taar* (fermented milk mash)
mineralized brine water, 204
minerals, 7, 194, 226
Mining and Minerals Working Group of the World Business Council for Sustainable Development (WBCSD), 282
mining industry: and colonization, 275–77; and environment, 279–80; global impact of, 277; harms from, 273, 281; in historical perspective, 274–77; local impacts of, 278–86; MNCs and, 277–86; sustainability of, 288; in twenty-first century, 277–86. *See also* diamond industry
Mining, Minerals, and Sustainable Development (MMSD) project, 282
Mirnyi Diamond Mine, *205*
modernity: costs of, 63; definition of, xxiii; indigenous peoples and, 293; Soviet introduction of, 63

About the Author

Susan Crate is a writer and scholar who has conducted research across Siberia since 1988 and worked with Viliui Sakha communities of western Sakha, northeast Siberia, Russia, since 1991. She is assistant professor of human ecology at George Mason University and conducts research in the areas of cultural and political ecology, environmental policy, sustainable rural development, and climate change with people from Siberia, Russia, and the circumpolar North. She lives with her husband, Pronya Yegorov, daughter, Kathryn Yegorov-Crate, and cat, Kisa-Kisa, in Fairfax, Virginia.